Sustainable Development Goals Series

The **Sustainable Development Goals Series** is Springer Nature's inaugural cross-imprint book series that addresses and supports the United Nations' seventeen Sustainable Development Goals. The series fosters comprehensive research focused on these global targets and endeavours to address some of society's greatest grand challenges. The SDGs are inherently multidisciplinary, and they bring people working across different fields together and working towards a common goal. In this spirit, the Sustainable Development Goals series is the first at Springer Nature to publish books under both the Springer and Palgrave Macmillan imprints, bringing the strengths of our imprints together.

The Sustainable Development Goals Series is organized into eighteen subseries: one subseries based around each of the seventeen respective Sustainable Development Goals, and an eighteenth subseries, "Connecting the Goals", which serves as a home for volumes addressing multiple goals or studying the SDGs as a whole. Each subseries is guided by an expert Subseries Advisor with years or decades of experience studying and addressing core components of their respective Goal.

The SDG Series has a remit as broad as the SDGs themselves, and contributions are welcome from scientists, academics, policymakers, and researchers working in fields related to any of the seventeen goals. If you are interested in contributing a monograph or curated volume to the series, please contact the Publishers: Zachary Romano [Springer; zachary.romano@springer.com] and Rachael Ballard [Palgrave Macmillan; rachael.ballard@palgrave.com].

Ayodotun Stephen Ibidunni ·
Oyedele Martins Ogundana ·
Maxwell Ayodele Olokundun
Editors

Innovation, Entrepreneurship and the Informal Economy in Sub–Saharan Africa

A Sustainable Development Agenda

palgrave
macmillan

Editors
Ayodotun Stephen Ibidunni
Department of Business Administration
Chrisland University
Abeokuta, Nigeria

International Centre for Policy Research
and Industry Linkages (ICePRIL)
Shaveh Consulting
Abeokuta, Nigeria

Centre for Economic Policy
and Development Research (CEPDeR)
Covenant University
Ota, Nigeria

Maxwell Ayodele Olokundun
Department of Business Administration
London Metropolitan University
London, UK

Oyedele Martins Ogundana
Accounting and Finance Department
Nottingham Trent University
Nottingham, UK

ISSN 2523-3084 ISSN 2523-3092 (electronic)
Sustainable Development Goals Series
ISBN 978-3-031-46292-4 ISBN 978-3-031-46293-1 (eBook)
https://doi.org/10.1007/978-3-031-46293-1

Cover illustration: Harry Marx Alamy Stock Photo

This Palgrave Macmillan imprint is published by the registered company Springer Nature Switzerland AG
The registered company address is: Gewerbestrasse 11, 6330 Cham, Switzerland

Paper in this product is recyclable.

In praise of God for the wisdom and help to accomplish this book project.

We also dedicate this book project to our respective wives—Oyebisi Mary Ibidunni, Damilola Ogundana, and Omolara Olokundun; and all our children—Oreofe, Aanu, Ara, Ayomide, and Olaoluwa. Thank you for your continuous love, patience, and support of our career aspirations.

Foreword

I am highly delighted to write this Foreword to this timely collection by Ayodotun Stephen Ibidunni, Oyedele Martins Ogundana, and Maxwell Ayodele Olokundun for their book titled "Innovation, Entrepreneurship and the Informal Economy in Sub-Saharan Africa: A Sustainable Development Agenda". The book is very topical and germane to the needs of the African continent given that Africa has vast human and natural resources, which is ironically regarded as one of the poorest continents. While a large volume of discussions and publications on Africa's sustainability potentials occupy several public domains, the present book makes a unique contribution through a pool of topics that emphasizes institutionalization, motivational factors, and harnessing the innovative potentials of Africa's informal sector entrepreneurs and their supportive role in achieving sustainability.

The book is sectionalized into critical areas including Sub-Saharan Africa (SSA)'s Informal Entrepreneurship Ecosystem, Innovations in Entrepreneurship Practices in SSA, and Economic Impact of Entrepreneurship in SSA. Each of these areas has topics that address the multidisciplinary nature of transforming Africa's resources and opportunities through innovation and entrepreneurship.

My experience as Professor of Economics, with numerous publications that focused on African economies, reveals to me that SSA is at a point where much emphasis should be on the role of entrepreneurship and innovation across all levels of its economy. The recent myriads of events, including the pandemic, intra/inter-border crisis, and major economic policy shifts across global economies have formed a compendium of shocks that have affected African economies. These unfolding events point to the need for SSA to be more focused on exploiting its resources through the efforts of entrepreneurial actors and innovative capabilities across sectors of the economy.

The entrepreneurship ecosystems in SSA need to be approached from a multi-stakeholders' approach to fulfil their sustainability potential. A stakeholder's approach implies a synergistic effort of entrepreneurial and innovation actors, theorists, and policymakers interdependently addressing the gaps that surround the entrepreneurship ecosystem while strengthening the existing breakthroughs accomplished. As highlighted in the book, the present situation in which firms in the informal economy of SSA operate by a self-reliance mechanism poses a challenge to the growth of the sector and overall economic performance. This assertion draws from the huge reliance of the African economies on the informal sector as a major contributor to job creation, contributor to gross domestic product (GDP), and a transformer of economic resources to valuable goods.

Therefore, I congratulate the book editors (Ayodotun Stephen Ibidunni, Oyedele Martins Ogundana, and Maxwell Ayodele Olokundun) for the good job they have done in putting this book together. Undoubtedly, their wealth of experience has showcased itself through the successful completion of this project and the valuable insights they are projecting to support the growth of sustainability theory and practice in SSA. I am assured that readers will find the content of the book fascinating and useful.

Prof. Evans S. Osabuohien
Professor of Economics at
Covenant University, Chair
and Lead Economics, DePECOS
Institutions and Development
Research Centre (DIaDeRC)
Ota, Nigeria

Preface

Welcome to this book, a comprehensive exploration of the intricate web of connections that lie at the heart of innovation and entrepreneurship within the informal economy of Sub-Saharan Africa (SSA). In the following pages, we embark on a journey to unveil the concealed relationships, motivations, and aspirations that define the entrepreneurial landscape of this dynamic region.

Sub-Saharan Africa, with its diverse cultures, challenges, and opportunities, serves as the backdrop for our exploration. The canvas we paint upon is one of burgeoning population growth, a shifting landscape of traditional employment, and a complex interplay of limited resources. As the voices of individuals across the continent rise in determination to secure their livelihoods, the informal sector swells, driven by a quest for economic sustenance. Yet, this sector often operates with minimal legislative support and access to vital resources, such as training and capacity-building.

The threads that interweave within this tapestry form a compelling narrative. Our goal is clear—to expand the boundaries of knowledge surrounding innovation and entrepreneurship models. Through this expansion, we aspire to lay the foundation for sustainable development, forging a more resilient economic landscape for the African continent.

While existing research has contributed significantly to our understanding of entrepreneurship and innovation in Africa, there remains a substantial knowledge gap. This void encompasses the subtle motivations that steer Africa's informal sector innovation, leaving these intricacies largely unexplored. While studies have dissected gender dynamics among African entrepreneurs and probed the influence of institutional factors, the true essence of Africa's informal sector innovation remains enigmatic.

Our book project stands as a bridge across this gap. Within these chapters, we shed light on the institutional underpinnings, motivational catalysts, and untapped innovative potential that reside within Africa's informal sector. These elements hold the key to nurturing a more sustainable African region. As existing literature underscores the pivotal role of institutions, both formal and informal, in shaping entrepreneurial and innovative outcomes, we delve deeper. We seek to uncover the nuanced interactions and interventions that propel entrepreneurship and innovation within SSA's informal economy.

At its core, this book is a contribution—a piece of the ongoing dialogue surrounding innovation, entrepreneurship, and sustainable development. Our mission is to unearth patterns that fuse entrepreneurship theories, offer novel perspectives on the harmony between entrepreneurship and innovation management, and illuminate the roles of varying institutional interventions. These collective insights aim to chart a course towards sustainable development within the evolving informal sector of Africa.

Spanning a wide array of subjects, the chapters within this book present a multidisciplinary and culturally diverse panorama of entrepreneurship theories and practices across Africa. With the researcher, academic, policymaker, entrepreneur, and student in mind, our endeavour is to provide a deeper understanding of the symbiotic relationship between innovation and entrepreneurship. Together, we navigate the labyrinth of the informal economy, paving the way for a more resilient and vibrant Africa.

Join us on this intellectual journey, as we unravel the intricate tapestry of innovation and entrepreneurship in Sub-Saharan Africa's informal economy.

Abeokuta, Nigeria — Ayodotun Stephen Ibidunni
Nottingham, UK — Oyedele Martins Ogundana
London, UK — Maxwell Ayodele Olokundun

Acknowledgement

The editors acknowledge the contributions of all the 36 authors who shared their works to actualizing this book project. We are equally grateful to all the anonymous reviewers for their critical, yet helpful comments on each submission made to the book project. Together, we have contributed to the debate in the field of innovation, entrepreneurship, and sustainable development by domesticating entrepreneurship theories on the complementarity of entrepreneurship activities and innovation management for achieving sustainable development in Africa's growing informal sector.

Contents

1 **Introduction: Innovation and Entrepreneurial Capacities as Facilitators of Sustainable Development in Sub-Saharan Africa's Informal Economy** 1
Ayodotun Stephen Ibidunni, Oyedele Martins Ogundana, and Maxwell Ayodele Olokundun

Part I Sub-Saharan Africa's Informal Entrepreneurship Ecosystem

2 **Jump on the Bandwagon: Finding Our Place in the Entrepreneurial Ecosystem Discourse** 19
Oladele Seun, Oluwatimileyin Helen Adigun, and Olaosebikan Johnson Olusola

3 **Small and Medium Enterprises Sustainability Strategies Beyond the Periods of Environmental Shocks: Evidence From a Developing Economy** 67
Babatunde Daniel Agbi and Ayodotun Stephen Ibidunni

4 **Motivating Entrepreneurial Activities to Achieve Sustainable Development in Sub-Saharan Africa** 93
Chioma Onoshakpor and Oyedele Martins Ogundana

5 **Informality in Africa in Relation to Sustainable Development Goals 8 and 9: Framework for Innovation and Sustainable Industrialization** 121
Muhammed Olawale Hakeem Amuda

Part II Innovations in Entrepreneurship Practices in Sub-Saharan Africa

6 **Towards an Integrative Model of Innovative Entrepreneurship Education for Institutional Sustainability** 143
Mercy Ejovwokeoghene Ogbari, George Uzoma K. Chima, Favour Oluwabukola Olarewaju, Maxwell Ayodele Olokundun, and Daniel E. Ufua

7 **Entrepreneurial Ecosystem and the Role of Telecom Multinationals in Achieving SDG 9 in Developing Economies** 171
Ugbede Umoru, Justin Udie, and Victor Udeozor

8 **Transportation and Economic Development: Advancing Technological Innovation and Sustainability in the Transportation Sector of a Developing Nation** 197
Toyin Samuel Olowogbon, Segun B. Fakayode, and Adebisi Oloruntoba Luke

9 **Drivers of Eco-Innovation Among Manufacturing Firms in Nigeria** 217
Olufemi Adebola Popoola and Grace Oluwatofunmi Popoola

10 **Open Innovation Across the Innovation Value Chain: An African Perspective** 249
Lerato E. Mdaka and Mpumelelo Jr. Longweni

11 **Empirical Analysis of the Impact of Institutions on Innovative Entrepreneurship in Sub-Saharan African Countries** 279
Muftau Olaiya Olarinde and Shehu Auta

Part III Economic Impact of Entrepreneurship in Sub-Saharan Africa

12 **Microfinance as a Vehicle for Zero Poverty and Gender Equality in Nigeria** 309
Damian Kalu Ude

13 **Financial Inclusion and Poverty Reduction in Sub-Saharan Africa Region** 333
Achugamonu Bede Uzoma, Francis Abolade Akintola, Owolabi Folashade, and Isibor Areghan

14 **Adaptiveness of MSMEs During Times of Environmental Disruption: Exploratory Study of Capabilities-Based Insights from Nigeria** 353
Ayodotun Stephen Ibidunni, Ayeni Adejuwon Ayobami Adebanji William, and Bisayo Otokiti

15 **Entrepreneurship and Economic Development: A Leadership Framework** 377
Abdullah Promise Opute, Bridget N. Irene, Caroline Jawad, and Patricia C. Agupusi

16 **Conclusion: Informal Economy as a Springboard for Innovation and Entrepreneurship Development in Sub-Saharan Africa** 405
Ayodotun Stephen Ibidunni, Oyedele Martins Ogundana, and Maxwell Ayodele Olokundun

Index 417

Notes on Contributors

Oluwatimileyin Helen Adigun is a Ph.D. student in Business Administration at Bowen University in Iwo, Osun State. She is also a member of professional bodies such as the Chartered Management Institute (CMI). Her broad research interests are sustainability, entrepreneurship, small businesses, and sustainable entrepreneurship in local and international contexts. Her current work explores sustainable entrepreneurial opportunity recognition and its exploitation in the Nigerian Context. The research explores recent studies in sustainable entrepreneurship, raising questions about Nigeria's position on sustainability incorporation. She has published in journals like the Journal of Entrepreneurship in Emerging Economies.

Dr. Babatunde Daniel Agbi is a Faculty member and Acting Head of the Department of Business Administration at KolaDaisi University, Ibadan, Nigeria. His research interest includes Marketing Management, Strategic Management and Entrepreneurship Development in emerging economies. His research works have been published in reputable international journals including Forum for Social Economics, Harvard Deusto Business Research and Journal of the Knowledge Economy among others. Dr. Agbi was the pioneer Director of the Centre for Entrepreneurship Development Studies, at Chrisland University, Abeokuta, Nigeria.

Patricia C. Agupusi Ph.D. is Assistant Professor School of Social Science and Policy Studies at Worcester Polytechnic Institute Massachusetts US. Her research interests include state capacity, entrepreneurship, and the political economy of development. She obtained her Ph.D. in International Development with a specialization in political economy from the University of East Anglia, UK.

Francis Abolade Akintola is Associate Professor of Finance at Babcock University Illishan Remo, Ogun State. He obtained his B.Sc. (Finance) and M.Sc. (Finance) from the University of Lagos, Nigeria. He also obtained his Ph.D. from Babcock University where he teaches, Strategic Financial Management, and Business Finance among other subjects. He is a fellow of the Institute of Chartered Accountants of Nigeria and Chartered Institute of Bankers of Nigeria. He is an Examiner with several professional bodies in Nigeria. Dr. Akintola has almost 30 years of professional and academic experience with several high-impact journal publications to his credit.

Prof. Muhammed Olawale Hakeem Amuda holds the faculty chair of Welding Process Analysis and Surface Modification at the University of Lagos. He was the pioneer head of the University's Innovation Unit, building the structure for the innovation ecosystem leading to the first set of about 20 institutional patents in the University. He is the Team Lead of several research groups in the University with a grant portfolio of about seven hundred thousand USD covering innovation ecosystem, affordable medical devices, and improving water security in selected African cities. He is a Council Member, the African Network of Scientific and Technological Institutions.

Dr. Isibor Areghan is a lecturer and researcher in the Department of Banking and Finance, Covenant University whose research interest is Development Finance. He has published more than fifty articles in several high-impact local and international journals including the Journal of Central Banking Theory and Practice. He has also attended several local conferences. He has also served as a member of the editorial board and guest editor for several international and local journals. He is a member of the American Finance Association and the Academy of Management of Nigeria.

Shehu Auta is a postgraduate student Department of Economics, Usmanu Danfodiyo University Sokoto. He has completed his programme and presently serving as a Tutor.

Dr. George Uzoma K. Chima is the President/Chairman of Council of the Chartered Institute of Administration of Nigeria and Professor of Entrepreneurship and Business Administration with over 11 years of experience. With his B.Sc. in California University FCE and Ph.D. in Universidad Empresarial de Costa Rica for Business Management, his outstanding contributions and publications in business and academia are prominent. Additionally, as the CEO of Legacy Associated Consults Ltd Apapa, Lagos State, Nigeria and Huge Investment Ltd, his experience as a Fellow Institute of Professional Financial Managers UK, Management Consultants Nigeria, and Directors Nigeria has spanned global recognition till date.

Prof. Segun B. Fakayode is Professor of Agricultural Economics at the University of Oye-Ekiti, Nigeria. He is currently a senior faculty and Director of the Institute for Food Security and Commercial Agriculture at the same University. He has over 25 years of professional experience. He has published in both local and international academic outlets to his credit. His research interests include Resource and Environmental Economics, Development Economics, and Market Access.

Owolabi Folashade has over fifteen years of industry and academic experience. She is a Lecturer at Covenant University where she teaches cost, management, and financial accounting. She has published several academic papers in reputable journals. She is a graduate of Mathematics from the University of Ilorin and holds a master's degree in Business Administration from the same University. Folashade obtained a B.Sc. Degree in Applied Accounting from Oxford Brookes University, United Kingdom, and a Master of Science and Ph.D. degree in Accounting from

Covenant University, Ota. She is a member of the ICAN and an affiliate of the Association of Chartered Certified Accountants.

Ayodotun Stephen Ibidunni is Senior Lecturer and Head of the Business Administration Department at Chrisland University, Nigeria. His research interests are Strategic Management, Operations Management, and Entrepreneurship in developing economies. He is the pioneer Director of the International Centre for Policy Research and Industry Linkages (ICePRIL). He has published over 100 peer-reviewed articles in high-impact international journals, including the Journal of African Business, Managerial and Decision Economics, Journal of Workplace Learning, among others. Dr. Ibidunni serves on the editorial board and as guest editor of many international journals.

Bridget N. Irene is a senior lecturer at the Leicester Castle Business School, De Montfort University. Her scholarly interests range widely, encompassing entrepreneurship and focusing on the culturally instantiated facets of the debate on gender entrepreneurship, entrepreneurial competencies, family businesses, entrepreneurship education, and the informal economy. Her Ph.D. research contributes to the already established discourse on gendering entrepreneurship and provides explicit feminist perspectives highlighting the inadvertent reinforcement of women's subordination to men in the context of entrepreneurial endeavours.

Dr. Caroline Jawad Senior Fellow of the HEA, is the D.B.A. Programme Manager at the Institute of Management and Health, University of Wales Trinity Saint David, UK.

Dr. Mpumelelo Jr. Longweni (OrcID 0000-0001-9670-3648) is Lecturer of Management Sciences in the Faculty of Management and Economic Sciences at the North-West University, Potchefstroom, South Africa. He teaches operations management and problem-solving for managers courses and conducts research in managerial competencies.

Dr. Adebisi Oloruntoba Luke holds a master's and Ph.D. Degrees in Agricultural Economics from the University of Ilorin, Ilorin, Nigeria.

His research interest includes Development Economics, Rural Development, and Impact evaluation. He has over 10 years of professional experience in his research interest. He is Senior Scientific Officer at the Agricultural and Rural Management Training Institute, Ilorin, Nigeria. He has published over a dozen journal articles in both local and international outlets. In addition, he has successfully conducted various studies in Nigeria on impact evaluation.

Lerato E. Mdaka (OrcID 0000-0002-9761-1291) is Lecturer of Management Sciences in the Faculty of Management and Economic Sciences at the North-West University, Potchefstroom, South Africa. She teaches strategic management and entrepreneurship courses at undergraduate and postgraduate levels and conducts research in the area of innovation and entrepreneurship.

Dr. Mercy Ejovwokeoghene Ogbari is an associate professor and Head of Business Administration, the Department of Business Management at Covenant University, Ota Nigeria. She holds a B.Sc. in Coop Econs & Mgt from UNIZIK, M.Sc. and Ph.D. in Business & Entrepreneurship at Covenant University. She has made great landmarks in the field of business, entrepreneurship, entrepreneurship education, student start-ups, Strategy, technological progress, and organizational sustainability, particularly for small and medium enterprises (SMEs). Over the years, she has collaborated with highly skilled experts in similar fields and her research prowess has gained coverage nationally and internationally.

Oyedele Martins Ogundana holds the position of Senior Lecturer in Accounting and Finance at Nottingham Trent University. His academic pursuits encompass a diverse range of research interests, notably in areas like Women Entrepreneurship, Venture Growth, Micro-entrepreneurship, Family businesses, International Entrepreneurship, and International Business. Oyedele Ogundana has achieved noteworthy accomplishments in academia, having his work featured in esteemed journals including the Journal of Business Research, the Journal of Small Business Management, the International Review of Entrepreneurship, and the International Journal of Entrepreneurship and Small Business, among others. His dedication to research has also been acknowledged through the acquisition of several small research grants. Notably, his research has garnered various awards, including the prestigious best paper award for women's entrepreneurship at the 2022 ICSB World Congress held in Washington DC, USA. Oyedele Ogundana's expertise has led to his regular invitations as a guest speaker, with notable appearances including invitations from institutions like the US Department of State.

Favour Oluwabukola Olarewaju obtained her M.Sc. and B.Sc. in Economics from Covenant University, Ota, Nigeria in 2020 and 2016 respectively, emerging as a first-class graduate. Her research interests include labour economics, development economics, and international economics. Over the years, she has acquired almost 3 years of research experience as a Research Assistant in Top Research Companies—Centre for Economic Policy and Development Research (CEPDeR), Baum Tenpers Research Institute, BusinessDay Media, including her Alma Mater. She is currently a Doctoral candidate at the Economics Department of the University of Memphis, Tennessee USA.

Muftau Olaiya Olarinde is Associate Professor of Economics and current Postgraduate Coordinator of the Department of Economics, Usmanu Danfodiyo University, Sokoto. His research interests are Development Economics, Institutions, Welfare and Conflict studies. Muftau has published over 35 peer-reviewed articles in high-impact international journals, including the Journal of Economics Development. He serves on the editorial board and as editor of many international journals. Muftau has won many research grants including the TETFund National Research Fund and CORN West Africa/ USIP project, and as Co-researcher in MacArthur Foundation research grants.

Maxwell Ayodele Olokundun is a researcher and a member of the faculty in the Department of Business Management at Covenant University. He holds a master's degree in Culture, Creativity and Entrepreneurship from the University of Leeds, United Kingdom, and a Ph.D. with a specialisation in Business and Entrepreneurship. His published works on entrepreneurship, entrepreneurship education, social entrepreneurship, and student startups have been widely cited. Recent awards include top 10 global authors in entrepreneurship research on Elsevier SciVal by scholarly output, 2017–2020, a leading author in entrepreneurship research on Elsevier SciVal by number of publications in Nigeria, 2013–2019, 2018 exceptional researcher award Covenant University.

Dr. Toyin Samuel Olowogbon is an Agricultural Economist with the Centre for Sustainable Agricultural Empowerment, Nigeria. He is also a Research Fellow with the Centre for Economic Policy and Development Research (CEPDeR), Covenant University, Ota, Ogun State, Nigeria. Olowogbon, Toyin holds a master's and Ph.D. in Agricultural Economics from the University of Ilorin, Nigeria. He is a Development Economist passionate about engaging development studies as a tool for evidence-based policymaking and advocacy. Olowogbon has over 15 years of experience developing and testing digital interventions using experimental methodologies. He has published widely in his areas of research interest.

Olaosebikan Johnson Olusola, Ph.D. is Associate Professor at Bowen University, Iwo, Osun State, Nigeria with research interests in Entrepreneurship and Skills Reengineering. A product of the University of Ibadan to his Ph.D. which was in Skills Reengineering and Employees Productivity. He is a seasoned academic, well published and visible on recognizable academic platforms, links like Google Scholar, ResearchGate, and LinkedIn among many others. He is a passionate academic about promoting entrepreneurship studies as a means of improving our nation, addressing some of the challenges in goods and services production, efficient utilization of our abundant human and material resources and better living standards for the citizens.

Chioma Onoshakpor is a lecturer in management and entrepreneurship, an experienced entrepreneur, and an accomplished non-profit female advocate leader with ten (10) years of experience in helping female entrepreneurs scale their businesses in Africa. She runs the Boss Babes NG platform, advocating for women's growth through business financing. As a lecturer at the Aberdeen Business School of Robert Gordon University, she teaches both entrepreneurship and core management modules. Her core research interest is in the field of entrepreneurship, with a specific interest in the areas of gender, access to finance, and entrepreneurial motivation.

Dr. Abdullah Promise Opute is a freelance academic and management consultant. Currently, he is a Lecturer and postgraduate research supervisor at the Management School, University of Wales Trinity Saint David, UK. Dr. Opute is an Academic consultant at several African and European universities. His research has been published in top international journals, including the Journal of Business and Industrial Marketing, International Journal of Entrepreneurship and Small Business, Journal of Entrepreneurship and Innovation in Emerging Economies, International Journal of Management Education, Team Performance Management, and so on. He researches inter-functional Integration, Relationship Management, Cross-Cultural Management, Consumer Behaviour, Entrepreneurship and SMEs, Strategic Marketing, Strategic Management Accounting, etc.

Bisayo Otokiti, Ph.D. is a lecturer in the Department of Business and Entrepreneurship, Kwara State University, Malete, Ilorin, Kwara State. With over 10 years of experience in teaching, research and development. She is presently an Assistant Director at the Centre for Technical, Vocational and Entrepreneurship Training at Kwara State University and the Editorial coordinator for the International Journal of Entrepreneurship Innovation and Management. Over the years she has mentored over 10000 students directly and 50000 indirectly.

Olufemi Adebola Popoola is a research fellow at the Innovation and Technology Policy Department (ITPD), Nigerian Institute of Social and Economic Research (NISER), Ibadan, Nigeria. He is quantitatively inclined and proficient in the use of analytical software. His interests are in the areas of development economics, impact evaluation, technology and innovation Studies. He has a number of publications in learned journals and attended international conferences.

Grace Oluwatofunmi Popoola holds a Ph.D. in Agricultural Economics and is a lecturer in the Department of Agricultural Economics, Bowen University Iwo, Nigeria. Her research interests are in the areas of development economics, food security and climate change, and resource and environmental economics. She has a number of publications in learned journals and attended international conferences.

Dr. Oladele Seun has a background in business administration and practical experience as an entrepreneur. His research focuses mainly on understanding entrepreneurial ecosystems in emerging economies. His recent publications revolve around exploring structures, challenges, and interactions in emerging entrepreneurial ecosystems. He has research publications in peer-reviewed journals, a monograph, and book chapters covering aspects of innovation, entrepreneurship, marketing, and management.

Dr. Damian Kalu Ude is a senior lecturer in the Department of Economics, Michael Okpara University of Agriculture, Umudike, Nigeria. His research interests are Macroeconomics, Econometrics, Finance and Public Sector Economics, and Entrepreneurship in developing economies. He is a member of the Econometric Society and a research fellow at the Centre for Economic Policy and Development Research (CEPDeR), Covenant University, Ota, Nigeria. His recently published work on Youth Employment Challenge and Rural Transformation in Africa, E. S. Osabuohien (eds) in the Palgrave Handbook of Agricultural and Rural Development in Africa, has been widely cited.

Dr. Victor Udeozor is a senior lecturer in Entrepreneurship and Strategy. He has been a lecturer at Nottingham Trent University since 2014 and has a wealth of experience in teaching and pastoral care for students. He is passionate about youth development, community development and nation-building. He combines creativity and innovation with a can-do attitude to initiatives that can be executed and measured for success. His research interest is in Sustainable Startups, Entrepreneurship and Sustainable Energy.

Dr. Justin Udie is a Senior Consultant in Climate Adaptation, Net Zero, Carbon Management and Strategy with Akins Global. He has taught Global Business issues at, Demontfort University and was Senior Lecturer in Sustainability and Business Strategy at Nottingham Trent University. He holds a Bachelor of Science (B.Sc.) in Genetics and Biotechnology; a Bachelor of Art (B.A.) in Global Business Management;

a Master of Science (M.Sc.) in Oil and Gas Management and a doctorate (Ph.D.) in Climate Impact Assessment from De Montfort University, Leicester. His research interest is in climate change impacts, Sustainable Startups, and Carbon Management potentials for SMEs.

Daniel E. Ufua with over 50 academic research publications has addressed entrepreneurial challenges with a focus on micro and small businesses alongside other seasoned colleagues. His M.B.A. and Ph.D. in Management and System Sciences from the University of Hull in England Metropolitan Area have added to his practical exposure within and beyond Nigeria.

Dr. Ugbede Umoru is Senior Lecturer in International Business, Management and Strategy at Nottingham Business School and London School of Economics. His research interest includes MNEs' international expansion; Firm's Performance & Strategy; International Entrepreneurship; Transnationalism; and Institutionalism. Ugbede is a Fellow of the Higher Education Academy (FHEA) UK, a member Chartered Management Institute (CMI), and a member of several research and corporate groups including the Centre for International Business Strategy and Decisions (CIBSD); China-Africa research group; Academy of International Business (AIB); European Academy of Management (EURAM); and the British Academy of Management (BAM).

Achugamonu Bede Uzoma is a Lecturer, Finance and Investment Analyst and Researcher at Covenant University, Ota. He obtained his Ph.D. in Finance and M.Sc Finance at Covenant University, Ota, and University of Lagos respectively. He obtained a B. Sc (Accounting) from Ambrose Alli University, Ekpoma, Edo State. He is a Fellow of ICAN, a member of the Chartered Institute for Securities and Investment, United Kingdom, and an Associate member, Chartered Institute of Bankers of Nigeria respectively. He has more than 40 high-impact journal publications. He teaches Strategic Financial Management, Auditing, Banking Law, Ethics & Corporate Governance among other courses.

Ayeni Adejuwon Ayobami Adebanji William has degrees in B.Sc. (Accounting), M.Sc, and Ph.D. in Business Administration (Informal Entrepreneurship) from Covenant University, Nigeria. A member of the

Nigerian Institute of Management and Institute of Debt Recovery Practitioners of Nigeria with over eight years in Academia and currently serving at Landmark University. He has served on many committees within and outside the University functions. A prolific writer with evidence of Scopus publications in the informal economy, human resource, strategic, and educational management amongst others while being a reviewer for high-impact outlets.

List of Figures

Fig. 6.1	The experiential learning cycle and basic learning styles (Kolb, 1984)	158
Fig. 6.2	The Integrative Model of Innovative Entrepreneurship Education—IMIEE. Authors' Compilation (2021)	161
Fig. 7.1	MNEs, Entrepreneurial ecosystem and achieving SDGs	175
Fig. 7.2	Data structure	183
Fig. 7.3	A model showing the Nigerian technology entrepreneurial ecosystem and MNEs influence in achieving SDG 9	184
Fig. 8.1	Effect of transport invention and innovation on the economy (*Source* Adapted from Meersman and Nazemzadeh [2019])	200
Fig. 8.2	Marital status of respondents	207
Fig. 10.1	Conceptual graph of the idea generation phase of the innovation value chain using open innovation (*Source* Mohalajeng and Kroon [2016])	256
Fig. 10.2	Conceptual graphic of the idea conversion phase of the innovation value chain (*Source* Mohalajeng [2016])	260
Fig. 10.3	The idea diffusion phase in the innovation value chain (*Source* Mohalajeng [2016])	264

Fig. 10.4 Summary of the marketing mix (*Source* Anon [2022a]) 268
Fig. 10.5 Funding streams in the innovation value chain (*Source* Adapted from Smith [2015]) 269
Fig. 10.6 Open innovation across the innovation value chain with support mechanisms (*Source* Mohalajeng [2016]) 275
Fig. 12.1 Savings per capita and GDP growth rate in Nigeria (*Data source* The World Bank, World Development Indicators [2020]) 319
Fig. 12.2 Microfinance credit and poverty headcount in Nigeria (*Data source* The World Bank, World Development Indicators [2020]) 320
Fig. 12.3 Microfinance credit and poverty headcount in Nigeria (*Data source* The World Bank, World Development Indicators [2020]) 322
Fig. 12.4 Growth of microfinance credit in Nigeria (*Data source* The World Bank, World Development Indicators [2020]) 323
Fig. 12.5 Percentage of poverty headcount and access to microfinance credit in Nigeria (*Data source* The World Bank, World Development Indicators [2020]) 324
Fig. 13.1 Line graph showing number of deposits in commercial banks per 1000 adults 348
Fig. 14.1 Analysed response on effects of COVID-19 on MSMEs 364
Fig. 14.2 Analysed response on operational strategies of MSMEs during Corona Virus Disease Pandemic 366
Fig. 14.3 Analysed response on future business operations and probable strategy contexts during corona virus disease pandemic 367
Fig. 14.4 Analysed response on implication of Corona virus disease pandemic on developing economies 370
Fig. 15.1 A leadership framework for steering economic growth impacting entrepreneurship 396

List of Tables

Table 2.1	Selected definitions of the entrepreneurial ecosystem	25
Table 2.2	Summary of selected empirical literature	32
Table 3.1	Respondents' Background Information	79
Table 4.1	Characteristics of interview participants	102
Table 4.2a	Sample quotes, second-order codes and over-arching themes	103
Table 4.2b	Sample quotes, second-order codes, and over-arching themes	105
Table 5.1	Degree of informality in business enterprises adapted from Onwe (2013)	128
Table 5.2	Structure of employment in five African countries: Distribution of formal and informal sectors (Heintz &Valodia, 2008)	129
Table 5.3	Distribution of men's and women's total employment by economic sector (Heintz & Valodia, 2008)	131
Table 5.4	Most significant activities in non-agricultural informal sector (Heintz & Valodia, 2008)	132
Table 7.1	Description of research of interviewees	178
Table 8.1	Socio-economics of respondents	206
Table 8.2	Outcome variables for both groups at baseline	208

Table 8.3	Average program effect on average weekly income (Naira)	209
Table 8.4	Average program effect on average weekly savings (Naira)	209
Table 8.5	Average program effect on average weekly labor productivity (Naira/hours)	210
Table 8.6	Average program effect on average weekly health expenditure (Naira)	210
Table 8.7	Average program effect on average weekly fuel cost	211
Table 8.8	Constraints to efficient utilization of smart transportation ($N = 100$-O-riders only)	211
Table 9.1	Description of variables	226
Table 9.2	Region of establishment	228
Table 9.3	Firm characteristics	230
Table 9.4	Education of top manager	231
Table 9.5	Adoption of eco-innovation	232
Table 9.6	Categories of eco-innovation	232
Table 9.7	Distribution of drivers of eco-innovation	233
Table 9.8	Factors influencing firm's decision to adopt product eco-innovation	235
Table 9.9	Factors influencing firm's decision to adopt process eco-innovation	238
Table 11.1	Institutions and innovative entrepreneurship	296
Table 12.1	Impact of microfinance on poverty eradication in Nigeria	318
Table 12.2	Probability of gender equality with respect to microfinance in Nigeria	318
Table 12.3	Factors constraining access to microfinance services by women and poor entrepreneurs in Nigeria	321
Table 13.1	Definition of variables	341
Table 13.2	Long-run and Short-run dynamics of FI and poverty for overall sample	342
Table 13.3	Long-run and Short-run dynamics of FI and poverty for large saving countries	342
Table 13.4	Long-run and Short-run dynamics of FI and poverty for small saving countries	343
Table 13.5	Identification number for each of the countries	347
Table 13.6	Number of deposits in commercial banks per 1000 adults (2007–2017)	348

Table 14.1 Background information of interviewees 363
Table 15.1 Ranking of Entrepreneurial Activity Types in Africa (GEM, 2017) Percentage of Population aged 18–64 years 382
Table 15.2 Opportunity- and Necessity-drive TEA rates amongst the adult population of South Africa. Percentage of population aged 18–64 years 383
Table 15.3 Prevalence Rates (%) of Adult Population Entrepreneurial Activity in South Africa, 2001–2017. Percentage of Population aged 18–64 years 384
Table 15.4 GEM economies by geographical region & economic development level 2017 390

1

Introduction: Innovation and Entrepreneurial Capacities as Facilitators of Sustainable Development in Sub-Saharan Africa's Informal Economy

Ayodotun Stephen Ibidunni, Oyedele Martins Ogundana, and Maxwell Ayodele Olokundun

1.1 Introduction

This book project focused on demystifying the interconnectedness between the factors and actors involved with innovation and entrepreneurship development in Sub-Saharan Africa's (SSA) informal economy for more effective, result-oriented outcomes amidst the rising population in Africa and the lowering opportunities for white collar jobs

A. S. Ibidunni (✉)
Department of Business Administration, Chrisland University, Abeokuta, Nigeria
e-mail: aibidunni@chrislanduniversity.edu.ng

International Centre for Policy Research and Industry Linkages (ICePRIL), Shaveh Consulting, Abeokuta, Nigeria

Centre for Economic Policy and Development Research (CEPDeR), Covenant University, Ota, Nigeria

A. S. Ibidunni et al. (eds.), *Innovation, Entrepreneurship and the Informal Economy in Sub–Saharan Africa*, Sustainable Development Goals Series,
https://doi.org/10.1007/978-3-031-46293-1_1

and the continent's limited access to resources. In addition, the resolution of many persons living on the continent to secure their livelihood also projects the number of participants in the informal sector with very minute legislative support and access to firm capability-building resources (Gurtoo, 2009; Ibidunni et al., 2021). These complex relationships, therefore, result in the critical need for an expansion in the knowledge area of innovation and entrepreneurship models (practices and theories) that embed a sustainable development agenda and achieve a more robust economy for the continent.

Existing research, including previous special calls for papers (Ingenbleek, 2019; Madichie et al., 2017), has attempted to contribute to entrepreneurship and innovation research in Africa, especially Sub-Saharan Africa. Studies have investigated gender relativity among African entrepreneurs (Akinboade, 2005; Damilola et al., 2020; Ogundana et al., 2022). Also, the literature has made a submission regarding the role of institutional factors that influence entrepreneurship (Aparicio et al., 2016; Otache, 2017; Urbano et al., 2019) and a generic sense of entrepreneurship in Africa's informal sector (Ibidunni et al., 2017; Jevwegaga et al., 2018), without necessarily exposing the underlying motivations that define uniqueness in Africa's innovation and entrepreneurship ecosystem and particularly in the informal sector. Indeed, there remains a vast knowledge gap concerning institutionalization, motivational factors, and harnessing the innovative potentials of Africa's informal sector entrepreneurs and their supporting role in achieving a more sustainable African region (Acheampong et al., 2014; Ogundana, 2022). Extant literature asserts the role of institutions (North, 1990), that is, formalized procedures and organizations that govern interactions and behaviors

O. M. Ogundana
Department of Accounting and Finance, Nottingham Trent University, Nottingham, UK
e-mail: Oyedele.ogundana@ntu.ac.uk

M. A. Olokundun
Department of Business Administration, London Metropolitan University, London, UK

among social agents (Fuentelsaz et al., 2019) or informal interactions among social and economic actors (Waylen, 2014), on entrepreneurial and innovation outcome in SSA. Indeed, assertions exist that formal and informal institutional factors dominate the interconnectedness and success of entrepreneurship activities and innovativeness at the firm and regional levels (Aidis et al., 2008; Guzmán & Javier Santos, 2001). In other words, while entrepreneurship and innovation are complementary (Singh & Gaur, 2018), this interaction is facilitated by different types and levels of institutional interventions (Donbesuur et al., 2020). Nonetheless, the theoretical explanation of formal and informal institutions in motivating entrepreneurship and innovation activities in the informal economy, especially in the SSA, remains a scantily explained area. Therefore, this book project seeks to contribute to the ongoing debate in the field of innovation, entrepreneurship, and sustainable development by identifying patterns of domesticating entrepreneurship theories, harnessing papers that project novel insights about the complementarity of entrepreneurship activities and innovation management can occur, and coupled with the roles of different types and levels of institutional interventions in achieving sustainable development in Africa' growing informal sector.

Chapters in this book cover a wide array of topics that discuss a multidisciplinary and multicultural perspective on entrepreneurship theory and practices in Africa. This book project will benefit researchers, academics, policymakers, entrepreneurs in large firms and SMEs, and students interested in understanding the interconnected roles of innovation and entrepreneurship in improving Africa's informal economy and achieving sustainable development across the region's informal markets.

1.2 Sub-Saharan Africa's Informal Entrepreneurship Ecosystem

The informal sector in Sub-Saharan Africa (SSA) consists of micro, small, and medium enterprises (MSMEs) that operate within the resource-constrained and institutionally void economic setting (Ibidunni et al., 2021). Thus, firm survival and sustainability in the SSA lie in the ability of the firms to dwell on internal capabilities and innovate with accessible limited resources (Igwe et al., 2020). However, while the existing literature has made significant contributions to the economic outcomes of firms in SSA's informal economy (Hinson et al., 2022; Madichie et al., 2021), the implications derivable from various interactions of the elements within the entrepreneurial ecosystem of SSA have not received elaborate explanations to the present. Therefore, the topics within section one of this book examine the economic and social motivations that capture different forms and levels of impact of the entrepreneurial ecosystem on entrepreneurship and innovation in SSA.

The study by Oladele, Adigun, and Laosebikan titled "Jump on the Bandwagon: Finding Our Place in the Entrepreneurial Ecosystem Discourse." Their study identified and discussed salient gaps in the study of EE globally that require attention, narrowing the same to Africa, specifically Nigeria, and propose overarching research questions to guide Nigerian researchers in the study of EE. The study provides compelling arguments on why Nigerian literature needs to pay attention to this area of research, especially with the recent surge in entrepreneurial activities in selected regions in the Nation. The paper also identifies some key research questions based on the identified gaps in concepts, theories, empirical works, frameworks, methodology, geography, industry, and level of analysis that can help researchers start studying EEs in Nigeria. Finally, the study concludes that the time is right for Nigerian scholars to jump on the bandwagon.

Similarly, Agbi and Ibidunni drew data from a developing economy, namely Nigeria, to investigate the "Small and Medium Enterprises (SMEs) Sustainability Strategies Beyond the Periods of Environmental Shocks." Their study adopted the qualitative research design to demonstrate how the disruption influenced SMEs' survival, adaptation and future thinking strategies and their implications for Small and Medium Enterprises in South-Western Nigeria. Interviews were conducted using open-ended questions emailed to forty-three Owners and Owner-managers of SMEs across South-Western states in Nigeria. The study results indicate a negative impact of the economic and health shocks on Small and Medium Enterprises (SMEs) sales, income, and profitability in Nigeria. Considering the sudden nature of the pandemic, operators of SMEs developed various novel coping strategies to minimize the impact and survive during and after the pandemic. However, the study has implications for policymakers toward supporting SMEs' growth and future adaptation, especially in developing countries like Nigeria.

The title "Motivating Entrepreneurial Activities to Achieve Sustainable Development in Sub-Saharan Africa" was investigated by Onoshakpor and Ogundana. They explained that entrepreneurial activities are crucial for sustainable development in any developing economy. Nevertheless, the percentage of the population involved in business start-ups still needs to be improved in Africa compared to other continents, including the developed world. Thus, Onoshakpor and Ogundana explored the factors motivating entrepreneurial activities among women and men in Nigeria's developing economy. To do this, they conducted ten in-depth interviews, which were transcribed and thematically analyzed using QSR NVivo. The findings revealed that women and men are motivated by different factors. This finding implies that female entrepreneurs should be treated as a homogenous group separate from their male counterparts. Doing this will enable policymakers to design more effective entrepreneurial policies that encourage entrepreneurial activities that stimulate sustainable development, especially in Sub-Saharan Africa.

Umoru, Udie, and Udeozor, in their study titled "Entrepreneurial Ecosystem and the Role of Telecom Multinationals in Achieving SDG 9 in Developing Economies" observed that entrepreneurship is vital to the sustenance of the local economy of any country. Particularly in developing economies where there is a need for an entrepreneurial ecosystem consisting of a network of government, Multinational Enterprises (MNEs), start-ups, and other institutional bodies tasked to contribute to entrepreneurial innovation and shape the creation of new businesses. Nevertheless, how the contributions of MNEs in the ecosystem help achieve the UN sustainable development goals (SDGs) have been largely understudied. They contribute to the growing body of literature through a qualitative case analysis of four telecom MNEs. Their study shows a novel model that demonstrates that telecom MNEs contribute by "building technology infrastructure" and "information communication technology centres" to support start-ups in Nigeria.

Moreover, the study's analysis revealed the role of government as an exogenous factor mediating how MNEs contribute to SDGs. These findings contribute to the broader discussion regarding the contributions of MNEs to the entrepreneurial ecosystem in developing economies.

1.3 Innovations in Entrepreneurship Practices in Sub-Saharan Africa

The complementarity of innovation and entrepreneurship research in SSA is an emerging area of theoretical investigation and, in practice, is nascent (Olokundun et al., 2022). Unlike the developed economies where investigations that pertain to innovation and entrepreneurship are widely explained (Jiang et al., 2023; López-Muñoz et al., 2023), SSA as a developing region has scarcely received any precise theoretical investigations into the various stages of innovation and entrepreneurship development (Saka-Helmhout, A. et al., 2020). Hence, it is not clear at the moment what exact stage or type of innovation is happening within the SSA region. With this gap in existence, the innovation in entrepreneurship practices section of this book contains a collection of chapters that demystify the varying relationships, impacts, and implications derivable from a well-knitted understanding of the interactions between innovation and innovation entrepreneurship in SSA. These relationships are derived from complementary efforts of actors, factors, cultures, and systems that define different outcomes. The study by Ogbari, Chima, Olarewaju, Olokundun, and Ufua titled "Towards an Integrative Model of Innovative Entrepreneurship Education for Institutional Sustainability" demonstrated the role of educational institutions as facilitators of innovation and entrepreneurship in SSA. This paper advocates and posits the Integrative Model of Innovative Entrepreneurship Education (IMIEE). This is achievable by exploring entrepreneurship by educating students and aspiring entrepreneurs to become innovative rather than imitative and non-disruptive. However, given the current overly theoretical nature of teaching schemes across higher institutions today, the curriculum needs to be completely overhauled to incorporate a more innovative approach of practical and hands-on experiences that fosters innovative entrepreneurial practice. Therefore, an integrative model for innovative entrepreneurship education becomes imperative for insight and guidance for pedagogy and practice in a way that drives institutional sustainability. Thus, this theoretical paper contributes to the existing literature by analyzing various empirical works and previous models, such as the Design Thinking Approach, DISRUPT, the experiential model, and National Innovation Systems (NIS). Some shortcomings in previous models inform the need to posit an integrative model that synthesizes vital elements.

Amuda studied "Informality in Africa in Relation to Sustainable Development Goals 8 and 9: Framework for Innovation and Sustainable Industrialization." This paper deconstructs the concept of informality in industrialization and manufacturing on the African continent, which has impacted inclusive and sustainable economic growth concerning United Nations' Sustainable Development Goals (SDGs) 8 and 9. Characteristic features of informality on the African continent are highlighted based on the International Labour Organization's classification of an informal economy. Informality behavior in some selected African countries' economies is elucidated in relation to sectorial spread and gender distribution. Factors driving the growth of the informal sector, such as gender disequilibrium (notably, the feminization of poverty), low economic growth and rapid urbanization, globalization and redundancies, institutional and legal barriers, conflicts and social crisis, and the adoption of capital-intensive manufacturing processes are highlighted. Frameworks to innovate the informal sector to drive Industrialization on the African continent are equally presented. Some of these frameworks include standardization of products and protocols of informal sectors, skill upscaling and training, and building an ecosystem of skill mismatch to cascade the informal sector to formal status via the pooling of resources.

Olowogbon, Fakayode, and Adebisi adopted the quasi-experimental approach to estimate the impact of the O-pay technological innovation in transportation services on development outcomes in Kwara State, Nigeria. Their study is titled "Transportation and Economic Development: Advancing Technological Innovation and Sustainability in the Transportation Sector of a Developing Nation." The study showed that the average weekly income increased by 137% for participating O-riders to (N30, 220(84 USD) from N22, 050 (61 USD) at baseline) attributed to the intervention. The average weekly savings of O-riders increased by 355% (N4, 875($14) to N17, 309($48) at baseline). We found an increase in average weekly labor productivity at 160% (625.06 Naira/hour ($1.7) from N 389.6/hour ($1.1) at baseline). In addition, the intervention led to a reduction in resource wastage; for example, the weekly fuel cost was reduced by 21% (N1254 ($3.48) out of N6020 ($16.7) when compared with the non-O-pay participants. Although, evidence in the short term revealed that smart transportation has the potential to address significant development issues, including poverty, unemployment, financial exclusion, resource wastage, poor health, and well-being, among others. Evidence showed a need to plan and invest in the sustainability of technological innovations rather than focusing on innovating alone to harness its full benefits.

The study titled "Drivers of Eco-Innovation Among Manufacturing Firms in Nigeria" was carried out by Popoola and Popoola. The study examined the drivers of adopting eco-innovation by firms in Nigeria's manufacturing sector. Firm-level data from the World Bank Enterprise Survey (ES) and the Innovation Follow-up Survey (IFS) module for 2014/2015 were employed. The logit regression model determined the factors influencing a firm's decision to adopt eco-innovation. Evidently, product and process eco-innovation exists among manufacturing firms, and these eco-innovations are mainly new to the local market. Demand-pull factors and regulations were significant factors that significantly influenced the firm's decision to adopt both product and process eco-innovation. In addition, organizational innovation and technology-push factors influenced the firm's decision to adopt process innovation. Through collaboration with relevant agencies such as the Manufacturers Association of Nigeria (MAN) and SMEDAN, policymakers organize awareness campaigns on eco-friendly products and health issues for firms, as this will significantly drive the adoption of both product and process eco-innovations. Moreover, organizational innovation needs to be a necessity for firms. These would significantly influence a firm's decision to adopt process eco-innovation. Therefore, policies that encourage partnerships and interactions of firms with other actors, most significantly, private companies and individuals, and other stakeholders in the innovation system be developed to encourage the adoption of process eco-innovation.

Similarly, Mdaka and Longweni elaborated on "Open Innovation Across the Innovation Value Chain: An African Perspective." The authors argue that although the successes and benefits of Open Innovation are widely spoken about in literature across the globe, there needs to be more understanding of the role open innovation plays across the innovation value chain, particularly in African contexts. This theoretical paper interrogated existing innovation and entrepreneurship literature to provide a conceptual model depicting the role of open innovation across the innovation value chain from an African perspective. Investigating the various academic and industry texts regarding open innovation and the innovation value chain lead to an in-depth understanding of what is needed to bridge the gap from invention or idea to market. An open innovation value chain model, which includes three distinct support mechanisms, is proposed. The derived model helps government stakeholders, industry, and entrepreneurs across Africa to make better decisions about what is needed to foster total early-stage entrepreneurial activity.

Olarinde and Auta studied the "Empirical Analysis of the Impact of Institutions on Innovative Entrepreneurship in Sub-Saharan African Countries." The study employs the two-stage least square technique to analyze panel data from 20 Sub-Saharan African countries from 2001 to 2018. Using the year-fixed and robust standard error options, which control for the time constant at the country level and correct for the threat of multi-collinearities, respectively, the result provided evidence in support of a strong link between institutions and entrepreneurial activities in the Sub-Saharan African countries. The results suggest that policy reforms to achieve entrepreneurship growth and economic development must implement institutional reforms allowing innovative entrepreneurial activity to flourish.

1.4 Economic Impact of Entrepreneurship in Sub-Saharan Africa

Entrepreneurship performs an economic role in developing and growing nations in SSA. The ongoing discourse surrounding the economic impact of entrepreneurship in SSA revolves around entrepreneurship as a measure of firm outcomes (Ogundana et al., 2022), employment opportunities derivable from entrepreneurial engagements (Ibidunni, 2022; Ibidunni et al., 2020), and the financing of entrepreneurial activities (Herrington & Coduras, 2019). While the existing studies have drawn meaningful implications for the economic impact of entrepreneurship research, these studies have primarily limited discussions of economic effects as exogenous manifestations of entrepreneurship and entrepreneurial engagement. In other words, the existing literature around SSA lacks a view that incorporates entrepreneurship as an economic engagement capable of driving a sustainable economy in SSA. The latter view of entrepreneurship and economic co-integration is an endogenous perspective of the economic effects of entrepreneurship and entrepreneurial engagement. Consequently, the chapters in this book's third section draw insights from topics that argue about entrepreneurship as an economic driver of sustainable economies in the SSA region.

Ude examined "Microfinance as a Vehicle for Zero Poverty and Gender Equality in Nigeria." The study asserts that robust economic growth and development cannot be achieved without implementing well-focused policies and programs to reduce poverty and promote gender equality by empowering the people by increasing their access to credit facilities. The latent capacity of people experiencing poverty and women would be significantly enhanced through the provision of microfinance services to enable them to engage in economic activities and to be more self-reliant, increase employment opportunities, enhance household income, and create wealth. Thus, the study sought to investigate how microfinance could be applied as a vehicle for zero poverty and gender equality in Nigeria. The study employed a basic growth–poverty model and descriptive statistics using data from 1980 to 2020. Results show that microfinance is a veritable tool for achieving zero poverty in Nigeria. Results also suggest that gender equality would be significantly addressed with the judicious application of microfinance to women in Nigeria. The study concludes that microfinance services are means of broadening economic participation to include marginal groups that have been left out previously, which makes microfinance institutions effective by their ability to enhance poverty eradication and gender equality. The study recommends that microfinance institutions be adequately capitalized, appropriately regulated, and supervised to address the need for financing at the micro levels of the economy if our objective of sustainable zero poverty and gender equality is to be achieved now and in the future.

According to Achugamonu, Akintola, Owolabi, and Isibor in their study titled "Financial Inclusion and Poverty Reduction in Sub-Saharan Africa Region," there is a consensus among development finance experts and theorists that are granting the poor and vulnerable persons in society access to cheap funds will help them create wealth for themselves, achieve financial security as well as reduce poverty. This study aims to examine the extent to which financial inclusion drives of the government have helped in poverty reduction. The study used the Granger Error Correction Method (ECM) to analyze the decomposed data obtained from the World Bank for 27 Sub-Saharan African (SSA) countries from 2007 to 2017. In addition, the different General Methods of Moments (GMM) were used to resolve the endogeneity and persistence problems associated with panel data. The result shows a long-run correlation between inclusive finance and poverty for the overall and small savings countries. However, the coefficient of the ECM showed evidence of a negative relationship which implies that an increase in per capita income or reduction in the poverty rate will not engender financial inclusion of individuals in the selected countries. Therefore, it recommends that the governments of the affected countries consider other factors like financial literacy, reduction in the cost of funds, deployment of digital financial technology, and increase in payment channels as strategies for driving an inclusive financial system.

Meanwhile, Ibidunni, Ayeni, and Otokiti investigated the "Adaptiveness of MSMEs During Times of Environmental Disruption: Exploratory Study of Capabilities-Based Insights from Nigeria." Their study hinged on the argument that whereas the strategic management literature has widely established firms' responsiveness to human-made and natural disruptions, there needs to be more empirical evidence in the literature about the adaptiveness of firms during periods of unexpected disruptions caused by health-related outbreaks. Therefore, the study adopted a qualitative method to investigate strategies relevant to ensuring the adaptiveness of MSMEs during and after the COVID-19 pandemic. In particular, semi-structured interviewing was conducted to collect data from the respondents. This study revealed that during environmental disruptions, MSMEs in Nigeria are fast adopting digital methods and the possibilities of adjusting their firms' operations and supply chain modalities to virtual possibilities while sustaining the firm's existence.

Opute, Irene, Jawad, and Agupusi, asserted that scholars have increasingly lauded the importance of entrepreneurship activity to economic development. However, unlike in the Western context, where that critical importance has been vigorously documented, survivalist-natured entrepreneurship is reported to be a common trend in the SSA context, where high unemployment and poverty levels remain significant challenges. Reviewed literature also points to a high business discontinuation rate in SSA compared to other continents. Leveraging the fit viewpoint of leadership, their work titled "Entrepreneurship and Economic Development: A Leadership Framework" forwards a dual leadership framework that combines entrepreneurs' and government aspects to contribute not only to knowledge development in this area but also to pinpoint core leadership initiatives for refocusing entrepreneurship activity to impact economic development in the SSA setting. In line with these dual contribution targets, recommendations are offered, as well as core directions for advancing research flagged.

1.5 Conclusion

In summary, this book on Innovation, Entrepreneurship and the Informal Economy in Sub-Saharan Africa: A Sustainable Development Agenda is a timely intervention that documents clear insights regarding the informal entrepreneurship ecosystem, innovation in entrepreneurship practices, and the economic impact of entrepreneurship in sub-Saharan Africa. We strongly believe this book will benefit different entrepreneurship stakeholders, including policymakers, researchers, entrepreneurs, students, and the general public. This introductory chapter offered a succinct summary of the entrepreneurship ecosystem, practices, and impact that will be discussed further in the book. The section that centres on the ecosystem offers insight into the current entrepreneurial climate in Sub-Saharan Africa; and the roles different stakeholders can adopt to sustain entrepreneurial activities. Section 1.2 provides practical innovations in entrepreneurship practices that can support entrepreneurial activities' survival in the context where enterprise demise is on the rise. The third section offers insight into the socioeconomic impact of entrepreneurship in the developing world. Finally, this book offers perhaps a "complete package" from a Sub-Saharan African perspective. It further strengthens the call for a more contextual understanding of entrepreneurship from the developing world. Indeed, this book passes on the baton for more research efforts from that context.

References

Acheampong, G., Braimah, M., Quaye, D. M., & Buame, S. K. (2014). Impact of demographic factors on technological orientations of BOP entrepreneurs in Ghana. *International Journal of Innovation and Technology Management, 11*(6), 1450037. https://doi.org/10.1142/S0219877014500370

Aidis, R., Estrin, S., & Mickiewicz, T. (2008). Institutions and entrepreneurship development in Russia: A comparative perspective. *Journal of Business Venturing, 23*(6), 656–672.

Akinboade, O. A. (2005). A review of women, poverty and informal trade issues in East and Southern Africa. *International Social Science Journal, 57*(184), 255–275. https://doi.org/10.1111/j.1468-2451.2005.549.x

Aparicio, S., Urbano, D., & Audretsch, D. (2016). Institutional factors, opportunity entrepreneurship and economic growth: Panel data evidence. *Technological Forecasting and Social Change, 102*, 45–61.

Damilola, O., Deborah, I., Oyedele, O. & Kehinde, A. A. (2020). Global pandemic and business performance: Impacts and responses. *International Journal of Research in Business and Social Science (2147–4478)*, *9*(6), 01–11.

Donbesuur, F., Ampong, G. O. A., Owusu-Yirenkyi, D., & Chu, I. (2020). Technological innovation, organizational innovation and international performance of SMEs: The moderating role of domestic institutional environment. *Technological Forecasting and Social Change, 161*, 120252.

Fuentelsaz, L., González, C., & Maicas, J. P. (2019). Formal institutions and opportunity entrepreneurship. The contingent role of informal institutions. *BRQ Business Research Quarterly*, *22*(1), 5–24.

Gurtoo, A. (2009). Policy support for informal sector entrepreneurship: Micro-enterprises in India. *Journal of Developmental Entrepreneurship, 14*(02), 181–194.

Guzmán, J., & Javier Santos, F. (2001). The booster function and the entrepreneurial quality: An application to the province of Seville. *Entrepreneurship & Regional Development, 13*(3), 211–228.

Herrington, M., & Coduras, A. (2019). The national entrepreneurship framework conditions in sub-Saharan Africa: A comparative study of GEM data/National Expert Surveys for South Africa, Angola, Mozambique, and Madagascar. *Journal of Global Entrepreneurship Research, 60*, 9. https://doi.org/10.1186/s40497-019-0183-1

Hinson, R. E., Madichie, N., Adeola, O., Bawole, J., Adisa, I., & Asamoah, K. (2022). *New Public Management in Africa*. Palgrave Macmillan.

Ibidunni, A. S., Mozie, C. and Ayeni, A. W. (2020). Entrepreneurial characteristics among university students: Insights for understanding entrepreneurial intentions among youths in an emerging economy. *Education+Training*, *63*(1), 71–84. DOI https://doi.org/10.1108/ET-09-2019-0204

Ibidunni, A. S., Ogundana, O. M., & Okonkwo, A. (2021). Entrepreneurial competencies and the performance of informal SMEs: The contingent role of business environment. *Journal of African Business*. https://doi.org/10.1080/15228916.2021.1874784

Ibidunni, A. S., Olokundun, M. A., Oke, A. O., & Nwaomonoh, I. C. (2017). Enhancing the performance of agro-based SMEs: The role of entrepreneurship competencies. *Covenant Journal of Entrepreneurship, 1*(1), 44–51.

Ibidunni, A. S. (2022). Editorial: Sustainable business models for the growth of indigenous businesses in africa. *World Review of Entrepreneurship, Management, and Sustainable Development, 18*(5/6), 491–499. https://doi.org/10.1504/WREMSD.2022.126160

Igwe, P. A., Odunukan, K., Rahman, M., Rugara, D. G., & Ochinanwata, C. (2020). How entrepreneurship ecosystem influences the development of frugal innovation and informal entrepreneurship? *Thunderbird International Business Review*. https://doi.org/10.1002/tie.22157

Ingenbleek, P. T. (2019). The endogenous african business: Why and how it is different, why it is emerging now and why it matters. *Journal of African Business, 20*(2), 195–205. https://doi.org/10.1080/15228916.2019.1583979

Jevwegaga, H., Ade-adeniji, O., Ibidunni, A. S., Olokundun, M. A., Borishade, T. T., Falola, H. O., Obaoye, D., & Ogunniyi, A. (2018). Role of SMEs' entrepreneurial activities and industrial clustering on SMEs' performance. *Academy of Entrepreneurship Journal*, *24*(1), 1–7. 1528–2686–24–1–127

Jiang, X., Wang, X., Ren, J., & Xie, Z. (2023). Digital economy, agglomeration, and entrepreneurship in Chinese cities. *Managerial and Decision Economics, 44*(1), 359–370. https://doi.org/10.1002/mde.3686

López-Muñoz, J. F., Novejarque-Civera, J., & Pisá-Bó, M. (2023). Innovative entrepreneurial behavior in high-income European countries. *International Journal of Entrepreneurial Behavior & Research*. https://doi.org/10.1108/IJEBR-06-2022-0546

Madichie, N. O., Gbadamosi, A., & Rwelamila, P. (2021). Entrepreneurship and the informal sector: Challenges and opportunities for African business development. *Journal of African Business, 22*(4), 441–447.

Madichie, N. O., Mpofu, K., & Kolo, J. (2017). Entrepreneurship development in Africa: Insights from Nigeria's and Zimbabwe's telecoms. In *Entrepreneurship in Africa* (pp. 172–208). Brill.

North, D. C. (1990). A transaction cost theory of politics. *Journal of Theoretical Politics, 2*(4), 355–367.

Ogundana, O. (2022). Obstacles facing women-owned enterprises: A case for Sub-Sahara African women. *World Review of Entrepreneurship, Management, and Sustainable Development, 18*(5–6), 529–544.

Ogundana, O., Simba, A., Dana, L. P., & Liguori, E. (2022). A growth model for understanding female-owned enterprises. *Journal of the International Council for Small Business*, 1–10. https://doi.org/10.1080/26437015.2022.2100296

Olokundun, M., Ogbari, M., Falola, H., & Ibidunni, A. S. (2022). Leveraging 5G network for digital innovation in small and medium enterprises: A conceptual review. *Journal of Innovation and Entrepreneurship, 11*, 41. https://doi.org/10.1186/s13731-021-00181-5

Otache, I. (2017). Agripreneurship development: A strategy for revamping Nigeria's economy from recession. *African Journal of Economic and Management Studies, 8*(4), 474–483. https://doi.org/10.1108/AJEMS-05-2017-0091

Saka-Helmhout, A., Chappin, M., & Vermeulen, P. (2020). Multiple paths to firm innovation in sub-saharan africa: How informal institutions matter. *Organization Studies, 41*(11), 1551–1575.

Singh, S. K., & Gaur, S. S. (2018). Entrepreneurship and innovation management in emerging economies. *Management Decision, 56*(1), 2–5. https://doi.org/10.1108/MD-11-2017-1131

Urbano, D., Aparicio, S., & Audretsch, D. (2019). Twenty-five years of research on institutions, entrepreneurship, and economic growth: What has been learned? *Small Business Economics, 53*, 21–49.

Waylen, G. (2014). Informal institutions, institutional change, and gender equality. *Political Research Quarterly, 67*(1), 212–223.

Part I

Sub-Saharan Africa's Informal Entrepreneurship Ecosystem

2

Jump on the Bandwagon: Finding Our Place in the Entrepreneurial Ecosystem Discourse

Oladele Seun, Oluwatimileyin Helen Adigun, and Olaosebikan Johnson Olusola

2.1 Introduction

> The future of civilization as we know it depends, at least somewhat, on the spread of entrepreneurship. (Isenberg, 2011: 13)

Life cycle and social prisms propose developmental stages leading to independence and social usefulness. This paradigm is supported by a Yoruba adage that loosely implies that "although one mother delivers a child, a community nurtures the child." The imperatives give credence to the fact that a child is corrected, safeguarded, and celebrated by the

O. Seun (✉) · O. H. Adigun · O. J. Olusola
College of Management and Social Sciences, Business Administration Programme, Bowen University, Iwo, Nigeria
e-mail: seun.oladele2015@gmail.com

O. J. Olusola
e-mail: johnson.olaosebikan@bowen.edu.ng

A. S. Ibidunni et al. (eds.), *Innovation, Entrepreneurship and the Informal Economy in Sub–Saharan Africa*, Sustainable Development Goals Series,
https://doi.org/10.1007/978-3-031-46293-1_2

community and not necessarily the biological parents only. As with a child, this is also the expectation from every startup business. A startup's ability to scale up operations in a region reflects the nature of the environment. It takes the community to provide the right environment for the flow and growth of entrepreneurial firms and, more importantly, the deliberate efforts of all the necessary actors in the community to interact to create a thriving environment. Indeed, unlike the notion that "it takes a city to raise a startup," it is the interaction among the elements in the city that raises the startup, and the fate of an enterprise is contingent on its interaction with the environment in which it operates. This is the heart of the entrepreneurial ecosystem notion, where all key actors and factors are significant to the quality of performance of firms in a region.

The environment that either enables or constrains the creation and growth of firms in a region is described as the entrepreneurial ecosystem (EE). EE describes the interconnectedness of actors, factors, and institutions that facilitate the growth of entrepreneurship in a region (Wadee & Padayachee, 2017). The EE concept was developed in the 2000s (Grigore & Dragan, 2020), gained momentum in 2014 (Maroufkhani et al., 2018; Mukiza et al., 2020), and dominated entrepreneurship literature in 2016 (Grigore & Dragan, 2020). The academic gaze in entrepreneurship research is currently on EE both in developed and emerging economies (Acs et al., 2017; Roundy, 2017; Stam & Van de Ven, 2021). There is a wide consensus about EE being a *sine qua non* for productive entrepreneurship (Stam, 2015), leading to economic growth and development amongst academic, policy, and business literature (Audretsch & Belitski, 2017; Spigel, 2017).

Regions such as Silicon Valley and Tel Aviv have been recognized to have thriving EEs, producing a high level of entrepreneurial activity (in terms of creation and growth of enterprises) in the regions. For example, the USA has the highest number of scaleup firms (scaleup are firms that achieve consistently rapid growth of as much as 20% in revenue and employment for three years) and Unicorns in the world (Unicorns are privately held startups valued at $1billion and more). Following their remarkable success, other regions are also attempting to map their EEs, with considerable success realized in the United Kingdom, Chile, Ireland, and Iceland (Isenberg, 2011). However, replicating the EE recipe from regions like Silicon Valley and Tel Aviv may prove counterproductive in another community (Arruda et al., 2013). However, they can serve as benchmarks for developing ecosystems in light of the regional/national dynamics.

Depending on the regions, the factors that make up the ecosystem vary in their configuration, with some regions stronger in one element than the other. For instance, Calgary's ecosystem strives on the strength of its oil and gas market, and Waterloo strives on the presence of finance and support organizations. Edinburgh's ecosystem is strongly undergirded by her academic and research institutions and strong support organizations (Spigel, 2015). Imperatively, the mere existence of these ecosystem elements is not sufficient. Rather the interaction that takes place between the elements is what makes an ecosystem (Stam, 2015; Stam & Van de Ven, 2021). Research into EE configuration is growing significantly; however, many grounds are yet to be covered. As it stands, theoretical, empirical, and conceptual perspectives have not been sufficiently explored.

In emerging economies like Nigeria, there are many more grounds to be covered. We find a significant gap in the literature on emerging economies such as Nigeria, which is the primary motivation for this study. This study reviews articles to highlight some of the gaps identified in the literature and see how Nigerian scholars can fit into the ongoing EE discourse. We first provide an overview of current conceptual clarifications and the current frameworks used to assess EEs in other regions. We identify gaps to spur Nigerian entrepreneurial researchers' interest into action based on an extensive literature review.

2.2 Conceptualizing Entrepreneurial Ecosystems

The EE construct is quite appealing yet problematic. On one hand, all stakeholders, including scholars, universities, governments, and industries, insist on defining EE based on their preferred criteria. Also, no single definition of EE currently seems to fit all contexts. The EE construct primarily stemmed from the field of biology and, over time, has had significant contributions from other fields such as Geography, Economics, Sociology, Psychology, and Public Administration (Theodoraki et al., 2017). However, the three main disciplines underlying EE frameworks are economy (agglomeration, cluster, supportive economic policies), geography (geographical characteristics, cultural effects, configurations of the ecosystem), and sociology (interactions among ecosystem players) (Theodoraki & Messeghem, 2017). Understanding the EE construct requires a basic understanding of the workings of the natural ecosystem. The natural ecosystem comprises *Biocoenosis* and the *Biotope*. *Biocoenosis* (biotic) relates to living things that evolve through their interaction (a relationship involving different organisms that together form a closely knitted community), and *biotope* (abiotic factors) are the conditions of the environments such as the soil, temperature, water, climates) that provides habitation for the integrated community of organisms.

The interaction between the actors (*biocoenosis)* and the environment (*biotope*) is what makes up the natural ecosystem. "In the most natural sense, an ecosystem ("ecological system") is a biotic community, its physical environment, and all the interactions possible in a complex of living and non-living components" (Acs et al., 2017: 2). The question of why apply the ecosystem concept to entrepreneurship seems to have been addressed by Acs et al. (2017). The authors pointed out that the ecosystem concept is about performance which is exactly what economics is about (that is, understanding systems that explain differential outputs and outcomes). They believed that entrepreneurship is one such output that can either be enabled or constrained by its context (ecosystem).

Based on the workings of the natural ecosystem, Kuckertz (2019) argued that some scholars had related EEs to rainforests indicating they comprise living (e.g., actors) and non-living (e.g., institutions) components that interact in complex ways. However, Stam (2015) cautions that the interpretation and application of ecosystem in biology should not be taken literally within the EE context. His emphasis was that since EE was more of a social interaction between interdependent actors within a community, this is closely related to the approach of "systems" in entrepreneurship.

The definitions of EE are highly (though overlapping) varied among authors, which is common in a field of study that is still emerging. The nature and complexity of the concept have made researchers like Stam (2015) and Kuckertz (2019) advise that the concept be applied with caution. According to Stam (2015: 1765), a set of interdependent actors and factors is coordinated in such a way that they enable productive entrepreneurship. Nicotra et al. (2017: 19) expanded on this definition, describing the EE as "a set of interdependent actors and factors coordinated in a way that favours the accumulation of various forms of capital to enable productive entrepreneurship." Mason and Brown (2014: 4) defined EE as "a set of interconnected entrepreneurial actors (both potential and existing), entrepreneurial organizations (e.g., firms, venture capitalists, business angels, banks), institutions (universities, public sector agencies, financial bodies) and entrepreneurial processes (e.g. the business birth rate, numbers of high-growth firms, levels of 'blockbuster entrepreneurship,' number of serial entrepreneurs, degree of sell-out mentality within firms and levels of entrepreneurial ambition) which formally and informally coalesce to connect, mediate and govern the performance within the local entrepreneurial environment." EEs have also been described as inter-related forces promoting and supporting regional entrepreneurship (Roundy & Fayard, 2020).

From the various definitions, certain features appear to overlap. First is the concept of interdependence, interaction, and the complexity of the interaction among different elements (Cavallo et al., 2018). Wadee and Padayachee (2017) described EE as an interaction of elements (factors), individuals (actors), organizations, or institutions. Roundy (2016) regarded them as "the sets of actors, institutions, social structures, and cultural values", while Theodoraki et al. (2017) related EEs as the interaction of actors, physical infrastructure, and culture. While the definition of Roundy placed emphasis on social structures, Theodoraki et al. (2017) focused more on physical infrastructure.

Second is the presence of multiple actors/factors (Roundy, 2016). According to Shwetzer et al. (2019), EEs are multi-level systems involving multi-actors and exhibit heterogeneous and complex tendencies explaining why Theodoraki and Messeghem (2017) regarded it as a "conceptual umbrella." This made Spigel et al. (2020) conclude that EE is easy to promote but hard to implement. While the literature on EE converges on the point that the entrepreneur is the heart of the ecosystem (Mukiza et al., 2020) who saddles the responsibility of creating, navigating, and managing interaction in the ecosystem (Stam, 2015), the presence and importance of multiple actors have been well documented. Feld (2012) reinforced this notion by relating that although the EE must be led by entrepreneurs, the roles of other actors such as investors, mentors, and government, among others, are equally important even though they play the role of feeders and not leaders.

The third is the notion that entrepreneurship is affected by the external environment, and lastly is, the emphasis that EE occurs within a local boundary (Isenberg, 2010; Szerb et al., 2018). EE has been recognized as a spatial concept (Grigore & Dragan, 2020), with spatiotemporal duality linked to local cultural impact, evolution, and proximity (Theodoraki & Messeghem, 2017). In other words, EE occurs within local/regional boundaries (Isenberg, 2011). The implication of this is that a "one size fits all" approach is not probable (Grigore & Dragan, 2020; Isenberg, 2011). Finally, EEs emerge or occur at different levels. EEs can emerge at regional levels, city levels, and national levels. However, given globalization, some argue that EE participants that are not necessarily situated within the same/close geographical location may be brought together (Mukiza et al., 2020), citing the example of crowdsourcing and crowdfunding (Maroufkhani et al., 2018) (Table 2.1).

In an attempt to synthesize the definitions of EE, this research considers the ecosystem in the entrepreneurship discourse

> as a significant interaction among varying albeit interdependent players comprising individuals, private and public support organisations, and institutions such as Universities and NGOs facilitating the flow of various forms of tangible and intangible capital through formal and informal exchanges, leading to the establishment of new firms, and development of existing firms within a local territory.

The subsequent section discusses the current gaps in literature spanning theoretical, conceptual, empirical, geographical, industry, contexts, and methodological gaps. We draw on literature from advanced and emerging

Table 2.1 Selected definitions of the entrepreneurial ecosystem

S/n	Authors	Definition
1.	(Moore, 1993)	A loosely interconnected network of companies and other entities that co-evolve capabilities around a shared set of technologies, knowledge, or skills, and work cooperatively and competitively to develop new products and services
2.	Van de Ven (1993: 218)	Networks of actors involved in developing each function, and how these functions and networks of actors interacted over time to facilitate and constrain innovation development
3.	Cohen (2006: 2–3)	Entrepreneurial ecosystems represent a diverse set of inter-dependent actors within a geographic region that influence the formation and eventual trajectory of the entire group of actors and potentially the economy as a whole"; "Entrepreneurial ecosystems evolve through a set of interdependent components which interact to generate new venture creation over time
4.	Isenberg (2010: 43)	The entrepreneurship ecosystem consists of a set of individual elements – such as leadership, culture, capital markets, and open-minded customers – that combine in complex ways
5.	Mason and Brown (2014: 4)	A set of interconnected entrepreneurial actors (both potential and existing), entrepreneurial organizations (e.g., firms, venture capitalists, business angels, banks), institutions (universities, public sector agencies, financial bodies), and entrepreneurial processes (e.g., the business birth rate, numbers of high-growth firms, levels of 'blockbuster entrepreneurship,' number of serial entrepreneurs, degree of sell-out mentality within firms and levels of entrepreneurial ambition) which formally and informally coalesce to connect, mediate and govern the performance within the local entrepreneurial environment
6.	Acs et al. (2014: 479)	A dynamic, institutionally embedded interaction between entrepreneurial attitudes, abilities, and aspirations, by individuals which drives the allocation of resources through the creation and operation of new ventures
7.	Stam (2015: 1765)	A set of interdependent actors and factors coordinated so that they enable productive entrepreneurship

(continued)

Table 2.1 (continued)

S/n	Authors	Definition
8.	Mack and Mayer (2016: 3)	Entrepreneurial ecosystems consist of interacting components, which foster new firm formation and associated regional entrepreneurial activities
9.	Spigel (2017: 50)	A combination of social, political, economic, and cultural elements within a region that support the development and growth of innovative startups and encourage nascent entrepreneurs and other actors to take the risks of starting, funding, and otherwise assisting high-risk ventures
10.	Roundy and Bayer (2019)	Systems of inter-related forces that promote and sustain regional entrepreneurship
11.	Corrente et al. (2018: 4)	...the capacity of a territory to create a system of actors and infrastructures supporting the creation and development of innovative business projects, beyond the mere construction of a network structure between companies. It refers to a comprehensive system of heterogeneous elements

Source Modified from Theodoraki and Messeghem (2017)

economies to gain insight into what is currently obtainable in the world and where literature on economies in Sub-Saharan Africa stands relative to advanced economies. We raise some salient questions to help local entrepreneurship scholars in Africa shape their studies.

2.3 Conceptual Arguments on Entrepreneurial Ecosystem

The EE construct is quite appealing yet problematic. In the entrepreneurship discourse, scholars hurry to apply the concept before providing answers to cogent conceptual, theoretical, and empirical issues (Stam & Van de Ven, 2021). During the review of the literature, we found articles that reinforced the need for more conceptual clarification of the EE construct. For example, Isenberg (2016) wrote on "Applying the ecosystem metaphor to entrepreneurship: Uses and abuses"; Nuemeyer and Corbett's (2017) work was on "Entrepreneurial ecosystems: weak metaphor or genuine concept?" Similarly, Cavallo et al. (2018) wrote on "Entrepreneurial ecosystem research: Present debates and future directions," while Muldoon et al.'s (2018) work was titled "Entrepreneurial ecosystem: do you trust or distrust?" published an article titled "Let's take the entrepreneurial ecosystem metaphor seriously!" and Spigel et al. (2020) wrote "A manifesto for researching entrepreneurial ecosystems."

These studies make it glaring that the concept of EE is not very well understood or, in many cases, is misconstrued and applied wrongly. According to Stam and Van de Ven (2021), *prima facie*, the EE constructs sound tautological for two reasons. First, the definition- "entrepreneurial ecosystems are systems that produce successful entrepreneurship, and where there is a lot of successful entrepreneurship, there is apparently a good entrepreneurial ecosystem." Secondly, a long list of EE elements has not spelt out cause and effect nor linked to specific place-based histories. As such, there is no clear evidence of the interdependent effects of EE elements on the level of entrepreneurial activity in regions. This has raised concerns about the phenomenon just becoming another buzzword. The boundaries of

EE are not well established because the concept evolves (Grigore & Dragan, 2020; Stam & Van de Ven, 2021), and the members are not fully identified (Grigore & Dragan, 2020). For example, the work of Grigore and Dragan (2020) introduced political entrepreneurship to EE; Guerrero et al. (2020) examined the entrepreneurship process (potential, nascent, and established entrepreneurship) within EE. Fuller-love and Akiode (2020) introduced transnational entrepreneurship within the EE discourse. Similarly, Duan et al. (2021) introduced immigrant entrepreneurship within the EE context.

Furthermore, EE has heterogeneous tendencies (Al-Baimani et al., 2021; Guerrero et al., 2020; Mukiza et al., 2020; Raposo et al., 2021; Roundy & Bayer, 2018; Roundy & Fayard, 2018; Stam & Van de Ven, 2021); and a proclivity to be peculiar in configurations depending on the region (Isenberg, 2011). These unresolved issues, among others, further complicate conceptualization. Spigel et al. (2020) also expressed certain concerns regarding the study of EEs. Their manifesto drew the attention of researchers to women, older entrepreneurs, the disabled, indigenous, and the minority who have been largely ignored in the EE discourse.

RQ: How can the EE construct be well deconstructed given its evolving and heterogeneous tendencies?
RQ: How can the EE construct be conceptualized to capture the role of women, older entrepreneurs, disabled, indigenous, and minority within the EE?
RQ: How can individual entrepreneurial activities result in a macroscopic phenomenon?
RQ: How can EEs be created, coordinated, and governed in a region?

2.4 Theoretical Gaps in the Study of Entrepreneurial Ecosystem

The EE phenomenon is, albeit a growing area of research interest, it is largely underdeveloped and undertheorized (Spigel, 2017). Mukiza et al. (2020) reviewed 51 articles on EE and found that 39 of those articles had no specific underlying theory. In EE research, what is currently obtainable are frameworks and articles gravitating towards the development of theories that are yet to be substantially validated empirically. Vedula and Kim (2019) summarized methods applied in EE research as far back as 1993, and 60 articles were listed. Half (30) of those articles were theoretical. Some of the common theories that have been applied have been borrowed from other fields, including system theory, dynamic capabilities, institutional theory, social network theory, social capital theory, stakeholder theory, and field theory (Mukiza et al., 2020).

EE specific theories such as the Boulder Hypothesis (Feld, 2012) are still in their development phase requiring empirical validations across regions. The triple helix model has also been applied in some EE studies with much criticism as it implies a top-down approach to developing an innovation ecosystem- an approach that has been seen to not be very effective in many regions (Isenberg, 2011). For example, Iceland, Chile, and Singapore adopted the top-down approach and did not get the expected result. This is interesting because Cao and Shi (2020) reported that the triple helix model was successful in Mexico. On the other hand, Israel has been agnostic for more than four decades in terms of policy stance, and this explains the successful cultivation of their broad-based entrepreneurship (building the highway system) (Ibid.). Roundy (2018), Roundy and Bayer (2018), Roundy and Fayard (2019), Roundy et al. (2018) are notable examples of works dedicated to the development of EE specific theories.

Wurth et al. (2021), acknowledging the wide gap in EE theory, presented certain issues, including "how institutional and evolutionary approaches can be synthesized especially across varying temporal and spatial scales at which EEs evolve. Another issue relates to integrating social network theory with other theories related to relationships, such as the agency theory, proximity, or uneven social power and authority. They also raised the question of bridging the gap between EE structures, dynamic capabilities, and actors' resources. While these gaps are not exhaustive, they present a path toward achieving and developing EE specific theories.

RQ: What theories best explain the nature of EEs in regions?

2.5 Empirical Gaps in the Study of Entrepreneurial Ecosystem

There is a long list of eco-factors believed to shape an ecosystem for productive entrepreneurship but without empirical evidence (Nicotra et al., 2017). Vedula and Kim (2019) compiled and presented literature on regional EE from 1993 to 2018 and found only six articles to be empirically based. Similarly, a dearth of empirical literature was also reported in the systematic review of Cao and Shi (2020) and Mukiza et al. (2020). These studies have found that publications that gravitated towards developing theories, reviews, and case study approaches, including multiple case studies, dominated EE literature (Maroufkhani et al., 2018). Therefore, one particular direction of research is assessing entrepreneurial ecosystem factors using empirical research designs and surveys per se (Maroufkhani et al., 2018). The lack of empirical evidence cuts across developed, and emerging economies as the EE construct is a relatively new area of study. For example, the causal relations between eco-factors and eco-outputs (productive entrepreneurship) have not been sufficiently investigated empirically (Nicotra et al., 2017; Stam, 2015). However, scholars are increasingly examining empirical dimensions in advanced countries (Cao & Shi, 2020; Leendertse et al., 2020).

In the same way, different studies have approached the study of EEs from different perspectives using different frameworks, so the findings also varied significantly. While some regions have shown strengths in some factors, other regions have shown strengths in other factors (see Table 2.2). For example, Wulandari (2021) emphasized culture, finance, policies, and leadership, human capital, markets, supports, and institutions as the essential components of entrepreneurial ecosystems. But, in the study of Arabi and Abdalla (2020) on "The role of the ecosystem for entrepreneurship development in Sudan," nine elements were identified, including finance, government policy, human capital, markets, culture, innovation, regulatory framework, support services, infrastructure and research and development (R&D). In comparison, the work of Corrente et al. (2018), using stochastic multicriteria acceptability analysis, gave preference to cultural and social norms, government programs, and internal market dynamics as the most important factors that accounted for the difference in entrepreneurial ecosystem performance of regions. However, applying a panel data analysis, Mukiza and Kansheba (2020) reported that finance, government support programmes, market, knowledge, and culture were weak determinants of productive entrepreneurship within entrepreneurial ecosystems in Africa without the mediating role of innovation.

Pathak and Mukherjee (2020) introduced the dimension of social entrepreneurship in entrepreneurial ecosystems. This was in line with the concern of Polbitsyn (2020) regarding the need for entrepreneurs and local authorities to increase active participation in improving living standards in rural communities. However, the underlying framework for their research was that of Stam (2015), similar to the work of Iacobucci and Perugini (2021) and Xu and Dobson (2019). In Duan et al. (2021) study, the dimension of immigrant entrepreneurship was also introduced to the context of entrepreneurial ecosystems. The study made a significant contribution by drawing attention to the joint effects that immigrant entrepreneurs enjoy from both effects of host and home country entrepreneurial ecosystems.

Grigore and Dragan (2020), just like Raposo et al. (2021) and Tolstykh et al. (2021), keyed into the idea that the entrepreneur is at the heart of a functioning entrepreneurial ecosystem. They noted that "*the place matters to an entrepreneur just as the entrepreneur matters to a place.*" The study presented an interesting synthesis of theoretical frameworks that have emerged in the study of entrepreneurial ecosystems over time from Cohen (2006) to WEF. Their study further added a custom factor based on specificity concerning the region being studied. The factor added political entrepreneurs as integral actors in the entrepreneurial ecosystem. The study challenged the classical frameworks for having a limitation of not capturing the context of transitioning economies. They argued that the presence of a political entrepreneur in an ecosystem is a virus with capacity of disrupting sustainability agendas. This argument constitutes a significant contribution to knowledge and subsequent studies can begin to test for the presence of the political entrepreneur in ecosystems and their impact.

However, literature in emerging economies is constricted to the development of EE, mapping of EEs, and how to build EEs. In emerging

Table 2.2 Summary of selected empirical literature

S/n	Authors	Country/ Location	Variables	Framework	Methods	Major Findings	Gaps
1.	Iacobucci and Perugini (2021)	*Italy*	Framework, systemic, and human conditions, economic resilience,	Stam (2015)	Regression	The degree of coherence and diversity in the entrepreneurial ecosystem elements determine their level of impact. With time, the different elements of the entrepreneurial ecosystem on resistance and recovery from crisis vary	Limited to two regions in Italy
2.	Raposo et al. (2021)	*General*	Cooperation with universities, research institutes, customers, suppliers, sustainability	Oslo manual framework	Binary and logistic distribution	The greater the simultaneous agglomeration and participation of actors in an ecosystem, the greater the effect of the entrepreneurial ecosystem on sustainability	Neglected regional levels
3.	Meero et al. (2020)	*Bahrain*	Risk-taking attitude, effective motivations, innovation, creativity, persistence, and flexibility	Not mentioned	Exploratory	The challenges and failures in Bahrain's entrepreneurial ecosystems are related to technology, market, customer, and finance	No inferences can be drawn

S/n	Authors	Country/Location	Variables	Framework	Methods	Major Findings	Gaps
4.	Stam and Ven (2021)	*Netherlands*	Quality of entrepreneurial ecosystems	Systems approach	Qualitative	Interdependence and coevolution, upward and downward causation was present in entrepreneurial ecosystem interactions	The study was not predictive
5.	Rashid and Ratten (2021)	*Pakistan*	Sensing, seizing, and transforming abilities	Dynamic capabilities	Qualitative research methods	Three main themes for small businesses to emerge were carte blanche business models (seizing), effectual business functions (transforming), and emergent humanitarian crisis (sensing)	The study could not show that the businesses displayed dynamic capabilities
6.	Tolstykh et al. (2021)	*Russia and Poland*	Density, fluidity, diversity, connectivity, and entrepreneurial environment	Isenberg (2011)	Qualitative research method	A mature, sustainable entrepreneurial ecosystem contributes to the local community's development and the entire country	Limited data

(continued)

Table 2.2 (continued)

S/n	Authors	Country/ Location	Variables	Framework	Methods	Major Findings	Gaps
7.	Duan et al. (2021)	*General*	Human capital, accessible market, social culture, funding and finance, government and institutions, infrastructure, and business support	Dual embeddedness theory, simultaneous embeddedness notions; transnationalism theory	Qualitative	All six entrepreneurial ecosystem elements in the home country, including human capital, accessible market, social culture, funding and finance, government and institutions, infrastructure, and business support, be empirically incorporated when studying immigrant entrepreneurs	Lacks empirical backings

S/n	Authors	Country/ Location	Variables	Framework	Methods	Major Findings	Gaps
8.	Pobee (2021)	*Malawi*	GEI 14 pillars index	Theory of planned behaviour for studying attitude and self-efficacy theory for abilities	Quantitative analysis	Findings show that the entrepreneurial ecosystem of Malawi fell significantly below (12.2/100) acceptable threshold (based on the global entrepreneurship index). This means the entrepreneurial ecosystem in Malawi is weak. Entrepreneurial sub-indices studied, including attitude, ability, and aspiration (AA&A), did not significantly contribute to the economy's GDP per capita	Relied solely on secondary data
9.	Wulandari (2021)	*General*	Entrepreneurial capabilities, entrepreneurial ecosystem, growth of entrepreneurship	Not mentioned	Analytical hier-archy process and simple additive weighing	Entrepreneurial capabilities and the entrepreneurial ecosystem influence the growth of entrepreneurship	Lacked theoretical underpinning

(continued)

Table 2.2 (continued)

S/n	Authors	Country/ Location	Variables	Framework	Methods	Major Findings	Gaps
10.	Mukiza and Kansheba (2020)	*35 African countries*	Eco-factors, innovation, productive entrepreneurship	Not mentioned	Panel regression	"The findings reveal mixed (positive and negative) and weak, insignificant direct influence of eco-factors such as finance, government support and programmes, knowledge, market, and culture on productive entrepreneurship. However, their influence is more pronounced when innovations mediate the relationship"	It relied majorly on secondary data. Secondary data sources are often limited in entrepreneurial ecosystem studies

S/n	Authors	Country/ Location	Variables	Framework	Methods	Major Findings	Gaps
11.	Subrahmanya (2020)	*Bangalore, India*	Market maturity, mentorship, education, and research institutes	Triple helix	Delphi Technique (logistic regression)	"The prevailing entrepreneurial ecosystem for tech startups in Bangalore is significantly different (lower) relative to an ideal ecosystem feasible in the Indian economic environment, as prescribed by the Delphi experts, both at the aggregate level and at the individual component level. Bangalore ecosystem is primarily lacking in terms of one of the Triple Helices, namely, the role of education and research institutions, and two of the five indispensable components, namely, market maturity and mentorship"	The study did not link the prevailing ecosystem condition to the level of entrepreneurial activity. Limited sample size

(continued)

Table 2.2 (continued)

S/n	Authors	Country/ Location	Variables	Framework	Methods	Major Findings	Gaps
12.	Scheidgen (2020)	*Berlin*	Formal exchanges, informal exchanges, knowledge, mentors, and finance	Structuration theory	Qualitative	"Entrepreneurial ecosystems can have different degrees of integration, and that this characteristic strongly impacts how entrepreneurs can acquire resources from the entrepreneurial ecosystem and thus how specific entrepreneurial ecosystems promote different types of entrepreneurs. Heterogeneous structures, therefore, do not only exist between entrepreneurial ecosystems but also within entrepreneurial ecosystems"	The study findings cannot be generalized
13.	Polbitsyn (2020)	*Russia*	Entrepreneurial ecosystem, economic development	Not mentioned	Descriptive and T-tests	For rural territories to grow, there is a need for a special rural entrepreneurial ecosystem	Small sample size

S/n	Authors	Country/ Location	Variables	Framework	Methods	Major Findings	Gaps
14.	Arabi and Abdalla (2020)	*Sudan*	Finance, policy, talent, markets, culture, innovation, regulatory framework, support, infrastructure, and R&D	Institutional theory	Multiple regres-sion	The relationship between entrepreneurial ecosystem and entrepreneurship development was significant in finance, government policy, human capital, infrastructure, research and development, and innovation and regulatory framework but not culture, markets, and support services	Issues with generalization (focused on manufacturing firms)
15.	Grigore and Dragan (2020)	*Bucharest and Cluj-Napoca*	Finance, policy, supports, market, culture, political entrepreneur, regional growth	Mason and Brown	Thematic analysis	The presence of a political entrepreneur in an ecosystem is a virus with the capacity of disrupting sustainability agendas	Lacks in-depth analysis

(continued)

Table 2.2 (continued)

S/n	Authors	Country/ Location	Variables	Framework	Methods	Major Findings	Gaps
16.	Cao and Shi (2020)	*General*	Distinctive features of entrepreneurial ecosystems in advanced and emerging economies	Not mentioned	Systematic review	Ecosystems vary in terms of governance, structure, and resources. Specifically, they identified that structural gaps, resource scarcities, and institutional voids are principal reasons why advanced economy's entrepreneurial ecosystem model cannot be directly applied to emerging economies	No inferences can be drawn

S/n	Authors	Country/Location	Variables	Framework	Methods	Major Findings	Gaps
17.	Mukiza et al. (2020)	*General*	Infrastructure, culture, policy, supports, institutions, and entrepreneurial activity	Not mentioned	Thematic analysis	The article placed the entrepreneur at the centre of the ecosystem specifying the contributions of infrastructure, culture, policies and regulation, business support services, institutions (educational, R&D, and financial) to support the entrepreneur and entrepreneurial activity within the ecosystem	Inferences cannot be drawn
18.	Fredin and Lidén (2020)	*General*	Entrepreneurial ecosystems	Complex adaptative system	Qualitative	The study proposed that studying the components of entrepreneurial ecosystems independently will not allow for a proper understanding of the behaviour of the entrepreneurial ecosystems	No inferences can be drawn

(continued)

Table 2.2 (continued)

S/n	Authors	Country/ Location	Variables	Framework	Methods	Major Findings	Gaps
19.	Leendertse et al. (2020)	*273 European regions*	Stam framework	Systems approach	Regression	"…analyses show that physical infrastructure, finance, formal institutions, and talent take a central position in the interdependence web, providing the first indication of these elements as fundamental conditions of the entrepreneurial ecosystem"	Relied on secondary data. Some of the eco-factors could not be properly measured
20.	Roundy (2018)	*Ohio*	Regional narratives, the functionality of entrepreneurial ecosystems	Not mentioned	Longitudinal study	The study found that without success stories, entrepreneurial ecosystems are bound to underperform	Subject to empirical validations

S/n	Authors	Country/ Location	Variables	Framework	Methods	Major Findings	Gaps
21.	Xu and Dobson (2019)	*Sub-Saharan Africa/ Guild-ford's digital gaming industry*	Culture, markets, policy, finance, supports, talent,	Isenberg (2011) and Stam (2015)	Review	Remoteness, smallness, and lack of resources were some of the critical challenges. However, through a collaborative effort, peripheral areas can leverage digital technology and build a vibrant ecosystem tackling finance, talent, infrastructure, socio-cultural environment, market, and policy issues	The conceptual framework developed requires further empirical inputs for generalizability
22.	Xie et al. (2019)	*China*	Entrepreneurial ecosystem performance, internal ecosystem factors, external ecosystem factors	Not mentioned	Structural equation modelling	"The political environment is the most crucial factor impacting the entrepreneurial ecosystem performance of Internet cultural industries"	Findings were based on the perception of the entrepreneurs

(continued)

Table 2.2 (continued)

S/n	Authors	Country/ Location	Variables	Framework	Methods	Major Findings	Gaps
23.	Roundy et al. (2018)	*General*	The complexity of entrepreneurial ecosystems	Complex adaptive system	Qualitative	The intentionality of entrepreneurs, entrepreneurial activities coherence, and resource injection are three related factors that would influence the emergence of an entrepreneurial ecosystem as complex adaptive systems	Subject to empirical validations

S/n	Authors	Country/ Location	Variables	Framework	Methods	Major Findings	Gaps
24.	Theodoraki and Messeghem (2017)	*France*	Entrepreneurial ecosystem, business incubator systems, entrepreneurial support systems	Complex network theory, institutional theory	Exploratory (case study)	Entrepreneurial ecosystem is a multi-level construct comprising entrepreneurial ecosystem (macro-level), entrepreneurial support ecosystem (Meso level), and business incubator ecosystem (micro-level). Understanding the interplay among sub-ecosystems is key to understanding the entrepreneurial ecosystem's success	The study needs to be extended to business incubators. The cultural aspect of the entrepreneurial ecosystem was also not incorporated
25.	Nicotra et al. (2017)	*General*	Eco-factors, Eco-outputs, productive entrepreneurship	Not mentioned	Qualitative	Financial, knowledge, institutional, and social capital were forms of capital that affect eco-outputs (productive entrepreneurship)	Not empirically validated

Source Authors' Compilation (2021)

economies, a handful of studies have attempted to provide a foundation for the study and theorizing of ecosystems in Sub-Saharan Africa (Manya, 2020; Oluwatobi et al., 2019; Sheriff & Muffatto, 2015). However, these studies have not adequately captured the dynamic elements of these ecosystems within the emerging economic framework or configurations of the observed countries. For example, Oluwatobi et al. (2019) reviewed higher institutions in Nigeria, stating that universities have the potential to be innovation centres. Sheriff and Muffatto (2015) conducted a polygonal study on Egypt, Botswana, Ghana, and Uganda, pointing out that entrepreneurs were present in all the regions, but ecosystem dynamics varied, which explained the differences in the growth of entrepreneurship in the regions.

Due to a dearth of empirical literature, most early attempts in Nigerian studies would be to build EEs, identify the elements of EEs, understand the interactions among the actors, and identify the key challenges to building and growing EEs. This is a long ride away from empirical studies obtainable in the Global North regions, for example, Silicon Valley, but it is surely a step in the right direction.

RQ: What are the causal effects of the EE elements on the level of entrepreneurial activity in the Sub-Saharan region of Africa?

RQ: What is the nature of the interaction among EE elements in the Sub-Saharan region of Africa?

2.6 The Framework Gaps in the Study of Entrepreneurial Ecosystems

There is quite a list of frameworks in literature proposing several components that make up the EE ranging from six elements, including human capital, policy, supports, markets, finance, and culture (Isenberg, 2011); to eight elements, including access to markets, human capital, support system, education and training, funding and finance, regulatory framework and infrastructure, major universities as a catalyst, cultural supports by Foster et al. (2013) to fourteen elements by Acs et al. (2014). Spigel (2017) also grouped all the components commonly mentioned until 2015 into three, including cultural (e.g., supportive culture), material (e.g., Policies, infrastructure), and social (e.g., networks, mentors). For Stam (2015), ten elements make up the EE grouped into framework conditions (formal institutions, culture, physical infrastructure, and demand) and systemic conditions (networks, supports or intermediary services, leadership, finance, talents, and knowledge). These ten elements are the eco-factors that result in productive entrepreneurship (eco-output), which generates economic value (eco-impacts). Stam (2015) argues that framework conditions such as formal institutions determine the (in)effectiveness of the systemic conditions, affecting the outputs and subsequently the outputs. The framework of Isenberg (2011) and Stam (2015) have been applied in many studies.

Currently, the prominent framework existing in Nigeria was developed by the Fate Foundation (2016), including policy and regulation, business support, access to resources, capacity building, access to finance, access to markets, research, and development. The framework drew significantly from the work of Isenberg (2011) and Aspen Network (2013), using a flat structure to describe the elements of the ecosystem. These elements, as prescribed by the Fate Foundation, have also not been empirically tested, and there is a need for more study in that area. Hence the questions:

RQ1: What are the core elements of the Nigerian entrepreneurial ecosystem?

RQ2: Who are the key actors/players in the Nigerian entrepreneurial ecosystem?

2.7 Geographical/Country Focus of Studies on Entrepreneurial Ecosystem

In terms of geographic scope, there have been more studies in developed economies than in emerging economies (Neumeyer & Corbett, 2017; Roundy et al., 2017). Maroufkhani et al. (2018) revealed that 37% of reviewed articles did not specify a particular country, while 21% of the reviewed papers focused on the United States of America, with the UK trailing behind. The result was further reinforced by Cao and Shi (2020), who found the USA and UK to have the highest publications on EE. Given that track record, they iterated that more studies are expected to be carried out in those regions.

Manya (2020) noted that despite EE being a global phenomenon (Acs et al., 2014), much of the academic gaze has been on Silicon Valley, Tel Aviv, Waterloo, Singapore, Dutch, and Australia, which possess entrepreneurial conditions that are usually not present in developing economies like Nigeria (Manya, 2020). The findings from these regions and the models applied cannot be directly applied to emerging countries like Nigeria. Cao and Shi (2020) noted that structural gaps, resource scarcities, and institutional voids are principal reasons why advanced economy's EE model cannot be directly applied to emerging economies. Isenberg (2011) also noted that applying such knowledge of EE in a region such as Silicon Valley to all ecosystems can be disastrous. Countries in Sub-Saharan Africa like Nigeria have not gotten much attention in the EE discourse. Lafuente et al. (2018) attributed the paucity of African literature to the scarcity of local entrepreneurship researchers, the under-researched nature of the subject area, and the lack of entrepreneurs to study. While the first two reasons may be largely true, Nigeria, for example, does not lack entrepreneurs to study. Rather, the lack of cooperation between academia and the industry has threatened the richness of EE study. Additionally, data is largely unavailable.

Although the issue of data unavailability is a major issue in EE studies generally all over the world (Leendertse et al., 2020), this is more profound in Nigeria. As such, many scholars have to rely on primary data, notably interviews and survey questionnaires. However, recently, organizations like PwC, Co-creation hubs, StartupBlink, Bank of Industry, Fate Foundation, Aspen, and Endeavor are showing a remarkable interest in the study of EE and are willing to collaborate with researchers through funding and support. The outstanding performance of Lagos, Nigeria, in appearing in the global startup ecosystem is a "green light," presenting local researchers with the opportunity to delve into the EE discourse.

RQ: *What is the state of entrepreneurial ecosystem study in Sub-Saharan Africa?*

RQ: *What factors affect the study of the entrepreneurial ecosystem in Sub-Saharan Africa?*

2.8 Methodological Gaps in the Study of Entrepreneurial Ecosystem

In terms of methodology, there are more qualitative studies than quantitative studies (Spigel et al., 2020). The systematic review of Mukiza et al. (2020) showed that most EE studies had been mainly literature reviews and conceptual papers relative to quantitative studies. They found that only 8 of those studies were quantitative, and two employed mixed methods out of 51 articles reviewed. The review of Maroufkhani et al. (2018) also supported a striking gap in quantitative modelling and survey-based research design. They found that most of the studies (12 out of 19) towards applying, developing, or reporting case studies in the investigations. Cao and Shi (2020) similarly reported that most empirical studies on EE have been qualitative by using case studies. Most of the case studies have been limited to Western economies such as Silicon Valley and the UK (Maroufkhani et al., 2018), while very few multiple case studies have been applied. They listed 19 key empirical research on emerging economies, and only six were quantitative, while two were mixed methods.

In attempts to improve empirical studies in EE, Spigel et al. (2020), in a manifesto, recommended some new methodologies that can be applied to studying different aspects of EE. For assessing the diversity of EEs in a region, they recommended qualitative comparative analysis (QCA). QCA is a case-based methodological approach that permits analysing multiple cases involving complex interactions. Leendertse et al. (2020) added that this methodology could improve the current understanding of the workings of the EE by explaining the "why" of changes in some cases and not in others. The methodology involves a detailed use or development of theory of change, identification of cases of interest, development of a set of factors, scoring the factors (crisp or fuzzy set), analysing the dataset, and interpreting the findings or revising the change theory. The recent publication titled "Institutional factors affecting entrepreneurship" by Sendra-Pons et al. (2022) is a notable example.

Another methodology recommended that has not been explored much is the bottleneck methodology as applied by the EU. This methodology is considered suitable for understanding the relationship among EE elements and revealing EE attributes that require development. It is suitable for understanding the strengths and weaknesses of ecosystems. The work of Torres and Godinho (2021) on "Levels of necessity of entrepreneurial ecosystems elements" is a notable example. Aspen Network (2013) also put together a firm-level survey instrument for primary data collection. The questionnaire contains 45 questions to get a researcher started on a region's EE survey. They recommended that the survey instrument be adapted to local conditions by removing items that do not apply or adding items peculiar to their local conditions. Furthermore, they suggested that to produce better results, the survey instrument should be administered annually to track the evolution or changes in the ecosystem.

RQ: What methodological options best suit the study of EE in the Nigerian context, given data availability?

2.9 Industry Focus on Studies of Entrepreneurial Ecosystem

In terms of industry scope, industries such as biotechnology, high technology (Sohns & Wojcik, 2020), and education (Al-Baimani et al., 2021; Tsukanova et al., 2017; Wadee & Padayachee, 2017) have been favoured in EE literature (Maroufkhani et al., 2018). In the systematic review of Mukiza et al. (2020) covering 14 years (2006–2019), They reported 12 articles on research and development and education, six on technology, and 33 of those articles did not have a specific sector focus. This was also confirmed in the review of Maroufkhani et al. (2018), noting that education was given more attention by EE scholars. They added that biotechnology, solar services, biomedical, and high technology industries have gained significant attention.

The gap in industry focus calls for more research on other industries, such as e-commerce and agriculture, among others. The focus of Nurcahyo et al. (2018) on the Indian fashion industry; Pathak and Mukherjee (2020) on community-based crafts in India; and Mckague and Wong (2017) on agriculture in rural economies presents opportunities that EE can be studied beyond technology and education. It can be observed that the articles that have focused on other industries were mostly in India. The country is seen to be exploring the options of having a vibrant ecosystem that can spur entrepreneurial growth across industries. Nigeria can also plug into this especially given our resource endowment and potential capabilities.

2.10 Level of Analysis/Context Gaps in the Studies on Entrepreneurial Ecosystem

Quite many studies on EE have focused on the macro-level, while few have channelled their attention to unveiling the meso and micro-perspectives of EEs (Neumeyer & Corbett, 2017; Pobee, 2021; Roundy et al., 2017). In terms of contexts, there are more studies at the national level than in local or regional contexts. Iacobucci and Perugini (2021) noted a lack of empirical evidence on the measures of EE at a local level. According to the authors, the best way to analyse and understand EEs is to study them locally, as the interaction between EE metrics shows large variation. There is a wide consensus that urban and rural EE vary significantly (Polbitsyn, 2020).

Xu and Dobson (2019) worked on the challenges of building entrepreneurial ecosystems in peripheral places. They point out that peripheral areas vary significantly from urban cities in terms of skilled labour and labour diversity endowment, infrastructural endowments, and institutional endowments—elements that are critical to building a striving ecosystem. Xu and Dobson (2019) argued that for rural territories to grow, there is a need for a special rural EE to be created (an aspect that the study argues has received little attention). The study used a traditional literature review approach to identify gaps, patterns and themes in the prevailing research landscape. They stressed that in building entrepreneurial ecosystems in regions, academics and policy makers cannot ignore peripheral places (rural or marginal regions) while focusing on urban cities. They realized that though in the Sub-Saharan part of Africa there is a high level of entrepreneurial activity, their contribution to GDP is not commensurate to the level of activity. This brings to the fore the prevalence of necessity or subsistence entrepreneurship in contrast to opportunity-driven entrepreneurship in those regions.

RQ: How can EEs be developed in rural areas in pursuit of enhancing opportunity-driven entrepreneurship?

We feature a special area of research as presented by (Roundy, 2017). His work focused on describing the nature of EEs that can emerge in small-town economies (advanced and emerging). Roundy stressed that though small towns are "small," they immensely contribute to economic development. However, small cities differ in areas such as resource endowment (human capital, diffusion technology), size, population, infrastructure, and underdeveloped markets from the typical booming urban centres. *Does this serve as a deterrent or lead to innovative entrepreneurial ecosystems?* Also, small cities in developed economies can be said to differ from small cities in underdeveloped or developing economies in their proportion and access to the elements that make up an ecosystem. These variations may have significant effects on the workings of the ecosystem. For example, access to fund sources, large markets, predictable legal and regulatory processes, infrastructure, human capital, and professional services are critical components that drive entrepreneurial success. Some conditions that spinoffs in developing economies as opposed to developed economies do not have in good measure. Ciesinski and Kissick (2016) pointed out that emerging economies are confronted with a lack of or poor access to these resources to kick start, grow, and sustain their venture.

RQ: The question, can thriving entrepreneurial ecosystems stem from small towns, and how especially in developing economies, still lingers?

2.11 Missing links: Where is Nigeria in the Study of Entrepreneurial Ecosystems in Nigeria?

> The irony is that although there are few deliberate entrepreneurship ecosystem approaches, we collectively know a lot about how to impact individual domains of the entrepreneurship ecosystem. We know how to educate entrepreneurs; we know the types and amounts of capital and capital markets that are effective, and their delivery mechanisms; we know how to impact the culture of entrepreneurship; we know a lot about the regulatory frameworks and governance structures; we know how to get large companies to interact with small innovative suppliers and how to actually create new markets of opportunity (...) we know how to create special economic zones, business plan contests. But no one, or precious few, has put them all together, primarily because no one has elucidated the ecosystem strategy. (Isenberg, 2011: 12)

Isenberg's stand largely holds (not exclusively) in Nigerian literature. Extant literature in Nigeria is saturated with fragmentation. Studying the elements of EE in isolation, as observed in the literature, cannot produce the expected outcome of understanding the environmental conditions of a business landscape and how it shapes entrepreneurial activity (Rashid & Ratten, 2021). Isenberg (2011) argued that many governments fail in creating effective entrepreneurship-related policies because of overemphasizing the importance of one or two of the elements of the EE without regard for the dynamic interaction among all the elements. The interaction is much more complex and dynamic, involving exchanges and the flow of information and resources among various actors within the ecosystem. The social structure emphasizes that it is the presence of the elements and the interaction that occurs that makes an ecosystem functional or dysfunctional.

So much has been done on the nature of the Nigerian business environment and the performance of SMEs (Dogara, 2015; Eruemegbe, 2015; Franca, 2014; Obasan, 2014; Obisi & Gbadamosi, 2016; Ogunro, 2014). Scholars have also focused on aspects of innovation (Oladele & Oladele, 2016; Oladele et al., 2017; Raimi & Yusuf, 2020). There are studies on entrepreneurial culture and studies on clusters (Adu et al., 2014; Ekesiobi & Dimnwobi, 2021; Ekesiobi et al., 2018; Oyeyinka, 2017). Some studies have looked at the entrepreneur as a principal factor shaping the outcome of an enterprise. However, Raposo et al. (2021) highlighted that these aforementioned areas hardly constitute novelty in literature. Ekesiobi and Dimnwobi (2021) revealed that a very significant gap in the literature exists on EEs in the Nigerian context.

Currently, very few attempts (if any) have focused on linking these factors together, understanding their systemic nature and interaction, and their evolution in Nigeria. However, there are few studies on Africa that have mentioned Nigeria in passing (Sheriff & Muffatto, 2015). Other studies that focused on Nigeria concentrated on the university ecosystem (Jegede & Nieuwenhuizen, 2021; Oluwatobi et al., 2019). Fate Foundation (2016) represents one of the earliest attempts toward mapping Nigeria's entrepreneurial ecosystem. Aspen Network of Development Entrepreneurs [ANDE] (2017) also provided a snapshot of the Lagos entrepreneurial ecosystem. However, these publications are not journaled publications but are what is currently obtainable.

2.12 Why Study Entrepreneurial Ecosystems in Nigeria?

The Nigerian business landscape has enjoyed considerable growth in recent years with the launching of numerous startups and the performance of scaleups across major cities like Lagos, Abuja, Kano, Port Harcourt, and Aba (Startup Universal). Their improved economic activity draws concern about the uneven concentration of high-growth firms in a few cities across the Nation. For example, in the report by Companies to inspire Africa, Nigeria topped the chart of African countries with the highest concentration of high-growth firms, recording 59 (17%) high-growth startups out of 343 companies from 42 African countries featured in the report (London Stock Exchange Group, 2019). The same report in 2019 also showed Nigeria again topping the chart with a total of 97 (27%) high-growth companies out of 360 companies from 32 countries featured in the report. Most of these companies were launched and are still headquartered in Lagos state (London Stock Exchange Group, 2019).

Currently, Lagos state is considered the commercial hub of Nigeria and the "Silicon Valley" of Africa. In 2017 alone, the state attracted an investment of $ 2 billion, making it the most valuable startup hub in Africa. For the first time, Lagos in 2020 made it to the top 100 cities in the world. Lagos has birthed many startups, especially in the technology industry, cutting across financial services (Paga, Flutterwave, and Paystack), entertainment (Boomplay), and agriculture (Farmcrowdy); healthcare (MDaas Global), and consumer services (Jumia and Konga) among others (StartupBlink). This also follows the report of the Bank of Industry (2018) that the success of ICT in Nigeria has contributed 12.2% to GDP (Manya, 2020). Although compared to advanced economies, this is far behind, and the results so far point to some level of progress in the level of entrepreneurial activity. If there was a time to take the study of the entrepreneurial ecosystem in Nigeria seriously, it is now!

2.13 Implications for Theory and Practice

Viewing the dynamic business environment from the lens of an ecosystem provides a more holistic approach to understanding the nature, interaction, and quality of the entrepreneurial ecosystem that can foster productive entrepreneurship in a region. This is especially important as no two entrepreneurial ecosystems are the same, and it has been stressed that all societies should "cultivate their own." This study would be a major shift away from the numerous fragmented studies that have viewed various aspects of the ecosystem in isolation without taking into consideration the interactions among the diverse actors that shape the ecosystem. Each ecosystem has its configuration. As such, mapping and understanding the strengths and weaknesses of the links, interactions, and exchanges within the ecosystem are essential to improving the performance of the ecosystem. Hence, this study draws the attention of researchers to largely unexplored areas, and by so doing, hopefully, more studies will shine a light on the various aspects of the Nigerian EE to increase our understanding of the ecosystem.

Based on empirical reports from the literature, the expected outcome of a functional ecosystem is productive entrepreneurship that results in economic growth and development, especially in employment, innovation, poverty alleviation, exports, and foreign direct investment. Currently, and as supported in the literature (Isenberg, 2011; Lafuente et al., 2018), most policy stances meant to "support" entrepreneurial growth are antithetical to growth because, so far, the government does not have the compass pointing them to the "True North" (that is at least 1/100,000 high potential venture of any sector) and so they currently navigate by landmarks (Isenberg, 2011). Thus, by unveiling these links and gaps within the EE in Nigeria, the government and significant players in the policy space can tailor policy efforts towards strengthening those areas and truly support the growth of entrepreneurship in the region and Nigeria as a whole.

2.14 Conclusion

We provide compelling reasons why the study of EE in the Nigerian context is important, timely, and attractive. The study identified some gaps in the study of EE globally and also narrowed it down to peculiar gaps in African and Nigerian literature. We also raised salient questions that can get local researchers started in their attempts to study EE in their regions. The study concludes that significant gaps exist in theory, empirical evidence, frameworks, methodologies applied to study EEs, geographical focus, industry focus, and the level of analysis. Fundamentally, a holistic and systemic understanding of EEs in Nigeria is bleak and fragmented. Invariably, relative to what is obtainable in the Western countries, for example, Silicon Valley, the understanding of the Nigerian EE is low. The study also concludes that for the Nigerian economy to benefit from the expected output of a vibrant EE, the starting point is mapping and understanding the dynamics of the ecosystem to identify links, exchanges, and structural gaps in order to focus policy efforts on the right places.

References

Acs, Z. J., Estrin, S., Mickiewicz, T., & Szerb, L. (2014). *The continued search for the solow residual: The role of national entrepreneurial ecosystem.*

Acs, Z. J., Stam, E., Audretsch, D. B., & Connor, A. O. (2017). The lineages of the entrepreneurial ecosystem approach. *Small Business Economics, 49*(1), 1–10.

Adu, J. T., Shokunbi, M. O., & Cole, B. M. (2014). Building sustainable business clusters towards global competitiveness: Case study of furniture making along Owode- Ajegunle axis of Lagos State. *Journal of Poverty, Investment and Development, 5*, 46–51.

Al-Baimani, N., Clifton, N., Jones, E., & Pugh, R. (2021). Applying the ecosystem model in a new context? The case of business incubation in Oman. *Growth and Change*, 1–24. https://doi.org/10.1111/grow.12471

Arabi, N. G. A., & Abdalla, A. M. A. (2020). The role of ecosystem for entrepreneurship development in Sudan. *World Journal of Entrepreneurship,*

Management and Sustainable Development, 16(4), 307–326. https://doi.org/10.1108/WJEMSD-09-2019-0075

Arruda, C., Nogueira, V. S., & Costa, V. (2013). The Brazilian entrepreneurial ecosystem of startups: An analysis of entrepreneurship determinants in Brazil as seen from the OECD pillars. *Journal of Entrepreneurship and Innovation Management, 2*(3), 17–57.

Aspen Network of Development Entrepreneurs. (2013). *Entrepreneurial ecosystem diagnostic toolkit.*

Aspen Network of Development Entrepreneurs. (2017). *Lagos entrepreneurial ecosystem snapshot.*

Audretsch, D. B., & Belitski, M. (2017). Entrepreneurial ecosystems in cities: Establishing the framework conditions. *Journal of Technology Transfer, 42*(5), 1030–1051. https://doi.org/10.1007/s10961-016-9473-8

Bank of Industry. (2018). *Industrial clusters and economic development in Nigeria* (No. 4).

Cao, Z., & Shi, X. (2020). A systematic literature review of entrepreneurial ecosystems in advanced and emerging economies. *Small Business Economics*, 1–36. https://doi.org/10.1007/s11187-020-00326-y

Cavallo, A., Ghezzi, A., & Balocco, R. (2018). Entrepreneurial ecosystem research: Present debates and future directions. *International Entrepreneurship and Management Journal*, 1–24. https://doi.org/10.1007/s11365-018-0526-3

Ciesinski, S., & Kissick, R. (2016). *A Note on Entrepreneurial Ecosystems in Developing Economies* (pp. 1–28).

Cohen, B. (2006). Sustainable valley entrepreneurial ecosystem. *Business Strategy and the Environment, 15*, 1–14.

Corrente, S., Greco, S., Nicotra, M., Romano, M., & Schillaci, C. E. (2018). Evaluating and comparing entrepreneurial ecosystems using SMAA and SMAA-S. *The Journal of Technology Transfer*, 1–35. https://doi.org/10.1007/s10961-018-9684-2

Dogara, G. N. (2015). The impact of the Nigerian business environment on company performance: A case of 20 most capitalised companies in Nigeria. *International Journal of Business and Management, 3*(4), 36–48.

Duan, C., Sandhu, K., & Kotey, B. (2021). Understanding immigrant entrepreneurship: a home-country entrepreneurial ecosystem perspective. *New England Journal of Entrepreneurship*, 2574–8904. https://doi.org/10.1108/NEJE-05-2020-0013

Ekesiobi, C., & Dimnwobi, S. K. (2021). Economic assessment of the Igbo entrepreneurship model for entrepreneurial development in

Nigeria: Evidence from clusters in Anambra state. *International Journal of Entrepreneurial Behavior & Research, 27*(2), 416–433. https://doi.org/10.1108/IJEBR-11-2019-0640

Ekesiobi, C., Kalu, U. D., & Nwokolo, C. (2018). Industrial clusters and industrialization in Nigeria: A micro- assessment of the Nnewi automotive component industrial cluster, Anambra State. *The Nigerian Journal of Economic and Social Studies, 60*(3), 131–162.

Eruemegbe, G. O. (2015). Impact of business environment on organization performance in Nigeria—A case study of Union Bank of Nigeria. *European Scientific Journal*, *Special Ed* (pp. 478–494).

Fate Foundation. (2016). *Mapping study of Nigeria's entrepreneurship ecosystem* (Issue 2).

Feld, B. (2012). *Startup communities: Building an entrepreneurial ecosystem in your city*. John Wiley & Sons, Inc.

Foster, G., Shimizu, C., Ciesinski, S., Davila, A., Hassan, S., Jia, N., & Morris, R. (2013). *Entrepreneurial ecosystems around the globe and company growth dynamics.*

Franca, C. (2014). Business environment and survival of the tourism industry. *Journal of Business and Management, 16*(10), 78–83.

Fredin, S., & Lidén, A. (2020). Entrepreneurial ecosystems: Towards a systemic approach to entrepreneurship? *Geografisk Tidsskrift-Danish Journal of Geography, 120*(2), 87-97. https://doi.org/10.1080/00167223.2020.1769491

Fuller-love, N., & Akiode, M. (2020). Transnational entrepreneurs dynamics in entrepreneurial ecosystems: A critical review. *Journal of Entrepreneurship and Innovation in Emerging Economies, 6*(1), 41–66. https://doi.org/10.1177/2393957519881921

Grigore, A., & Dragan, I. (2020). Towards sustainable entrepreneurial ecosystems in a transitional economy: An analysis of two Romanian city-regions through the lens of entrepreneurs. *Sustainability, 12*(6061), 1–21.

Guerrero, M., Liñán, F., & Cáceres-Carrasco, F. R. (2020). The influence of ecosystems on the entrepreneurship process: A comparison across developed and developing economies. *Small Business Economics*, *August*. https://doi.org/10.1007/s11187-020-00392-2

Iacobucci, D., & Perugini, F. (2021). Entrepreneurial ecosystems and economic resilience at local level. *Entrepreneurship & Regional Development, 33*(9-10), 689-716. https://doi.org/10.1080/08985626.2021.1888318

Isenberg, D. J. (2010). The big idea: How to start an entrepreneurial revolution. *Harvard Business Review*, *88*(6).

Isenberg, D. J. (2011). The entrepreneurship ecosystem strategy as a new paradigm for economic policy: Principles for cultivating entrepreneurships. *The Babson Entrepreneurship Ecosystem Project, 1*(781), 1–13.

Isenberg, D. J. (2016). Applying the ecosystem metaphor to entrepreneurship: Uses and abuses. *The Antitrust Bulletin, 61*(4), 564–573. https://doi.org/10.1177/0003603X16676162

Jegede, O., & Nieuwenhuizen, C. (2021). Assessing the entrepreneurial ecosystem of science, technology, engineering and mathematics (STEM) researchers in Nigeria. *International Journal of Entrepreneurship, 25*(1), 1–20.

Kuckertz, A. (2019). Let's take the entrepreneurial ecosystem metaphor seriously! *Journal of Business Venturing Insights, 11*(February), e00124. https://doi.org/10.1016/j.jbvi.2019.e00124

Lafuente, E., Szerb, L., & Acs, Z. J. (2018). The entrepreneurship paradox: More entrepreneurs are not always good for the economy—The role of the entrepreneurial ecosystem on economic performance in Africa. *Economic Systems*, 1–46. https://doi.org/10.2139/ssrn.3307617

Leendertse, J., Schrijvers, M. T., & Stam, E. (2020). *Measure twice, cut once. Entrepreneurial ecosystem metrics* (20.56).

London Stock Exchange Group. (2019). *Companies to inspire Africa.*

Mack, E., & Mayer, H. (2016). The evolutionary dynamics of entrepreneurial ecosystems. *Urban Studies, 53*(10), 2118–2133. https://doi.org/10.1177/0042098015586547

Manya, V. O. (2020). *Dynamics of a startup ecosystem in Africa: A case study of Yabacon in Nigeria.* International Institute of Social Studies.

Maroufkhani, P., Wagner, R., & Wan Ismail, W. K. (2018). Entrepreneurial ecosystems: A systematic review. *Journal of Enterprising Communities, 12*(4), 545–564. https://doi.org/10.1108/JEC-03-2017-0025

Mason, C., & Brown, R. (2014). Entrepreneurial ecosystems and growth oriented entrepreneurship. *OECD LEED Programme and the Dutch Ministry of Economic Affairs* (pp. 1–38).

Mckague, K., & Wong, J. (2017). Social franchising as rural entrepreneurial ecosystem development: The case of Krishi Utsho in Bangladesh. *The International Journal of Entrepreneurship and Innovation, 18*(1), 47–56. https://doi.org/10.1177/1465750316686240

Meero, A., Rahiman, H. U., & Rahman, A. A. (2020). The prospects of Bahrain's entrepreneurial ecosystem: an exploratory approach. *Problems and Perspectives in Management, 18*(4), 402–413. https://doi.org/10.21511/ppm.18(4).2020.32

Moore, J. F. (1993). Predators and prey: A new ecology of competition. *Harvard Business Review*, 75–86.

Mukiza, J., & Kansheba, P. (2020). Small business and entrepreneurship in Africa: The nexus of entrepreneurial ecosystems and productive entrepreneurship. *Small Enterprise Research, 27*(2), 110–124. https://doi.org/10.1080/13215906.2020.1761869

Mukiza, J., Kansheba, P., & Wald, A. E. (2020). Entrepreneurial ecosystems: A systematic literature review and research agenda. *Journal of Small Business and Enterprise Development, 27*(6), 943–964. https://doi.org/10.1108/JSBED-11-2019-0364

Muldoon, J., Bauman, A., & Lucy, C. (2018). Entrepreneurial ecosystem: Do you trust or distrust? *Journal of Enterprising Communities: People and Places in the Global Economy, 12*(2), 158–177. https://doi.org/10.1108/JEC-07-2017-0050

Neumeyer, X., & Corbett, A. C. (2017). Entrepreneurial ecosystems: Weak metaphor or genuine concept? In *The great debates in entrepreneurship* (pp. 35–45). Emerald Group Publishing Limited. https://doi.org/10.1108/S1048-473620170000027005

Nicotra, M., Romano, M., Del, M., & Schillaci, C. E. (2017). The causal relation between entrepreneurial ecosystem and productive entrepreneurship: A measurement framework. *The Journal of Technology Transfer*. https://doi.org/10.1007/s10961-017-9628-2

Nuemeyer, X., & Corbett, A. C. (2017). Entrepreneurial ecosystems: Weak metaphor or genuine concept? In *The Great Debates in Entrepreneurship* (Vol. 27, pp. 35–45). Emerald Group Publishing Limited. https://doi.org/10.1108/S1048-473620170000027005

Nurcahyo, R., Akbar, M. I., & Gabriel, D. S. (2018). Characteristics of startup company and its strategy: Analysis of Indonesia fashion startup companies. *International Journal of Engineering and Technology(UAE), 7*(2), 44–47. https://doi.org/10.14419/ijet.v7i2.34.13908

Obasan, K. A. (2014). The Impact of Business Environment on the Survival of Small Scale Businesses in Nigeria. *International Journal of Management Business Research, 4*(3), 165–170.

Obisi, C., & Gbadamosi, A. A. O. (2016). Nigerian business environment daunting: Challenges and suggested solutions. *International Journal of Scientific Research in Education, 9*(3), 144–150.

Ogunro, V. O. (2014). Nigeria's business environment: Issues challenges and prospects. *International Journal of Academic Research in Business and Social Sciences, 4*(4), 132–138. https://doi.org/10.6007/IJARBSS/v4-i4/770

Oladele, S., & Oladele, F. (2016). New product and emerging business growth in Kwara State. *World Journal of Entrepreneurship, Management and Sustainable Development, 12*(3), 207–227. https://doi.org/10.1108/WJEMSD-09-2015-0038

Oladele, S., Oladele, F., & Laosebikan, J. (2017). Product improvements engagements and emerging business growth. *International Journal of Entrepreneurship, Innovation and Management*, *2*(2&3).

Oluwatobi, S., Oshokoya, D., Uwoghiren, E., Oyebode, A., & Nsofor, C. (2019). Entrepreneurial ecosystem matrix (EEM): A proposed framework for Nigerian universities to become factories for startup companies. *International Journal of Civil Engineering and Technology, 10*(1), 607–622.

Oyeyinka, O. (2017). *Industrial clusters, institutions, and poverty in Nigeria: The Otigba information and communications technology cluster*. Springer International Publishing. https://doi.org/10.1007/978-3-319-41151-4_1

Pathak, S., & Mukherjee, S. (2020). Entrepreneurial ecosystem and social entrepreneurship: Case studies of community-based craft from Kutch, India. *Journal of Enterprising Communities: People and Places in the Global Economy*, 1–25. https://doi.org/10.1108/JEC-06-2020-0112

Pobee, F. (2021). An analysis of the entrepreneurial ecosystem of Malawi: The global entrepreneurship index (GEI) approach. *Journal of Development and Communication Studies, 8*(1), 224–238.

Polbitsyn, S. (2020). The impact of entrepreneurial ecosystem emergence on rural economic development. *The 14th International Days of Statistics and Economics*, 836–844.

Raimi, L., & Yusuf, H. (2020). A critical discourse of EI and CA in emerging economies: The place of Nigeria within the global innovation ecosystems. *Journal of Entrepreneurship and innovation in Emerging Economies, 0*(0), 1–20. https://doi.org/10.1177/2393957520903625

Raposo, M., Fernandes, C. I., & Veiga, P. M. (2021). We dreamed a dream that entrepreneurial ecosystems can promote sustainability. *Management of Environmental Quality: An International Journal*, 1477–7835. https://doi.org/10.1108/MEQ-01-2021-0010

Rashid, S., & Ratten, V. (2021). Entrepreneurial ecosystems during COVID-19: The survival of small businesses using dynamic capabilities. *World Journal of Entrepreneurship, Management and Sustainable Development, 2042–5961.* https://doi.org/10.1108/WJEMSD-09-2020-0110

Roundy, P. T. (2016). Start-up community narratives: The discursive construction of entrepreneurial ecosystems. *The Journal of Entrepreneurship, 25*(2), 232–248. https://doi.org/10.1177/0971355716650373

Roundy, P. T. (2017). "Small town" Entrepreneurial Ecosystems: Implications for developed and emerging economies. *Journal of Entrepreneurship in Emerging Economies, 9*(3), 238–262. https://doi.org/10.1108/JEEE-09-2016-0040

Roundy, P. T. (2018). Rust belt or revitalization: Competing narratives in entrepreneurial ecosystems. *Management Research Review, 42*(1), 102–121. https://doi.org/10.1108/MRR-01-2018-0019

Roundy, P. T., & Bayer, M. A. (2018). Entrepreneurial ecosystem narratives and the micro-foundations of regional entrepreneurship. *The International Journal of Entrepreneurship and Innovation*, 1–15. https://doi.org/10.1177/1465750318808426

Roundy, P. T., & Bayer, M. A. (2019). To bridge or buffer? A resource dependence theory of nascent entrepreneurial ecosystems. *Journal of Entrepreneurship in Emerging Economies*, 1–42.

Roundy, P. T., Bradshaw, M., & Brockman, B. K. (2018). The emergence of entrepreneurial ecosystems: A complex adaptive systems approach. *Journal of Business Research, 86*, 1–10. https://doi.org/10.1016/j.jbusres.2018.01.032

Roundy, P. T., Brockman, B. K., & Bradshaw, M. (2017). The resilience of entrepreneurial ecosystems. *Journal of Business Venturing Insights, 8*(11), 99–104. https://doi.org/10.1016/j.jbvi.2017.08.002

Roundy, P. T., & Fayard, D. (2018). Ecosystems: The micro-foundations of regional entrepreneurship. *The Journal of Entrepreneurship, 28*(1), 94–120. https://doi.org/10.1177/0971355718810296

Roundy, P. T., & Fayard, D. (2019). Dynamic capabilities and entrepreneurial ecosystems: The micro-foundations of regional entrepreneurship. *The Journal of Entrepreneurship, 28*(1), 94–120.

Roundy, P. T., & Fayard, D. (2020). Place-based advantages in entrepreneurship: How entrepreneurial ecosystem coordination reduces transaction costs. *Journal of Behavioral and Applied Management*. https://doi.org/10.21818/001c.14184

Scheidgen, K. (2020). Degrees of integration: How a fragmented entrepreneurial ecosystem promotes different types of entrepreneurs. *Entrepreneurship & Regional Development, 33*(1–2), 54–79. https://doi.org/10.1080/08985626.2020.1734263

Sendra-Pons, P., Comeig, I., & Mas-Tur, A. (2022). Institutional factors affecting entrepreneurship: A QCA analysis. *European Research on Management and Business Economics, 28*(3), 100187. https://doi.org/10.1016/j.iedeen.2021.100187

Sheriff, M., & Muffatto, M. (2015). The present state of entrepreneurship ecosystems in selected countries in Africa. *African Journal of Economic and Management Studies, 6*(1), 17–54. https://doi.org/10.1108/AJEMS-10-2012-0064

Shwetzer, C., Maritz, A., & Nguyen, Q. (2019). Entrepreneurial ecosystems: A holistic and dynamic approach. *Journal of Industry-University Collaboration, 1*(2), 79–95. https://doi.org/10.1108/jiuc-03-2019-0007

Sohns, F., & Wojcik, D. (2020). The impact of Brexit on London's entrepreneurial ecosystem: The case of the FinTech industry. *EPA: Economy and Space, 0*(0), 1–21. https://doi.org/10.1177/0308518X20925820

Spigel, B. (2015). *Edinburgh's entrepreneurial and support ecosystem.* The University of Edinburgh.

Spigel, B. (2017). The relational organization of entrepreneurial ecosystems. *Entrepreneurship: Theory and Practice, 41*(1), 49–72. https://doi.org/10.1111/etap.12167

Spigel, B., Kitagawa, F., & Mason, C. (2020). A manifesto for researching entrepreneurial ecosystems. *Local Economy, 35*(5), 482–495. https://doi.org/10.1177/0269094220959052

Stam, E. (2015). Entrepreneurial ecosystems and regional policy: A sympathetic critique. *European Planning Studies, 23*(9), 1795–1769. https://doi.org/10.1080/09654313.2015.1061484

Stam, E., & Van de Ven, A. (2021). Entrepreneurial ecosystem elements. *Small Business Economics, 56*(2), 809–832. https://doi.org/10.1007/s11187-019-00270-6

Subrahmanya, M. H. B. (2020). Entrepreneurial ecosystem for tech startups in Bangalore: An exploration of structure and gap. *Journal of Small Business and Enterprise Development, 27*(7), 1167–1185. https://doi.org/10.1108/JSBED-07-2019-0233

Szerb, L., Lafuente, E., Horváth, K., & Páger, B. (2018). The relevance of quantity and quality entrepreneurship for regional performance: The moderating role of the entrepreneurial ecosystem. *Regional Studies, 0*(0), 1–13. https://doi.org/10.1080/00343404.2018.1510481

Theodoraki, C., & Messeghem, K. (2017). Exploring the entrepreneurial ecosystem in the field of entrepreneurial support: A multi-level approach. *International Journal of Entrepreneurship and Small Business, 31*(1), 47–66.

Theodoraki, C., Messeghem, K., & Rice, M. P. (2017). A social capital approach to the development of sustainable entrepreneurial ecosystems: An explorative study. *Small Business Economics, 51*(1), 153–170. https://doi.org/10.1007/s11187-017-9924-0

Tolstykh, T., Gamidullaeva, L., Shmeleva, N., Wozniak, M., & Vasin, S. (2021). An assessment of regional sustainability via the maturity level of entrepreneurial ecosystems. *Journal of Open Innovation: Technology, Market and Complexity, 7*(5), 1–23.

Torres, P., & Godinho, P. (2021). Levels of necessity of entrepreneurial ecosystems elements. *Small Business Economics, May*. https://doi.org/10.1007/s11187-021-00515-3

Tsukanova, T., Morris, M. H., & Shirokova, G. (2017). Student entrepreneurship and the university ecosystem: A multi-country empirical exploration. *European Journal of International Management, 11*(1), 65. https://doi.org/10.1504/ejim.2017.10001679

Van de Ven, A. H. (1993). The development of an infrastructure for entrepreneurship. *Journal of Business Venturing, 8*, 211–230.

Vedula, S., & Kim, P. H. (2019). Gimme shelter or fade away: The impact of regional entrepreneurial ecosystem quality on venture survival. *Industrial and Corporate Change, 28*(4), 827–854. https://doi.org/10.1093/icc/dtz032

Wadee, A. A., & Padayachee, A. (2017). Higher education: Development of an entrepreneurial ecosystem, or ... are we the weakest link? *Science, Technology & Society, 22*(2), 1–26. https://doi.org/10.1177/0971721817702290

Wulandari, S. (2021). Designing an assessment model for entrepreneurial growth using a hybrid method. *Advances in Engineering Research, 201*, 421–427.

Wurth, B., Stam, E., & Spigel, B. (2021). Toward an entrepreneurial ecosystem research program. *Entrepreneurship Theory and Practice, 00*, 1–50. https://doi.org/10.1177/1042258721998948

Xie, X., Xie, X., & Martínez-climent, C. (2019). Identifying the factors determining the entrepreneurial ecosystem of internet cultural industries in emerging economies. *International Entrepreneurship and Management Journal, 1–20*. https://doi.org/10.1007/s11365-019-00562-z

Xu, Z., & Dobson, S. (2019). Challenges of building entrepreneurial ecosystems in peripheral places. *Journal of Entrepreneurship and Public Policy, 8*(3), 408–430. https://doi.org/10.1108/JEPP-03-2019-0023

3

Small and Medium Enterprises Sustainability Strategies Beyond the Periods of Environmental Shocks: Evidence From a Developing Economy

Babatunde Daniel Agbi
and Ayodotun Stephen Ibidunni

3.1 Introduction

The global economy has witnessed pandemonium since the outbreak of COVID-19 in Wuhan City, Hubei Province of China, in December 2019. COVID-19 is a novel coronavirus that has spread to every

B. D. Agbi
Department of Business Administration, KolaDaisi University, Ibadan, Nigeria
e-mail: babatunde.agbi@koladaisiuniversity.edu.ng

A. S. Ibidunni (✉)
Department of Business Administration, Chrisland University, Abeokuta, Nigeria
e-mail: aibidunni@chrislanduniversity.edu.ng

International Centre for Policy Research and Industry Linkages (ICePRIL), Shaveh Consulting, Abeokuta, Nigeria

Centre for Economic Policy and Development Research (CEPDeR), Covenant University, Ota, Nigeria

A. S. Ibidunni et al. (eds.), *Innovation, Entrepreneurship and the Informal Economy in Sub–Saharan Africa*, Sustainable Development Goals Series,
https://doi.org/10.1007/978-3-031-46293-1_3

continent except Antarctica and has posed humanity's most significant challenge since World War II. World Health Organization (WHO) describes Coronavirus disease 2019 (COVID-19) as "an infectious disease that causes severe acute respiratory syndrome coronavirus 2 (SARS-COV-2)" (WHO, 2020). The virus was first reported amid an outbreak of respiratory illness in Wuhan City, Hubei Province, China, on the 1st of December 2019 (Zhu et al., 2019). COVID-19 is more than a health issue because its impact is far-reaching with devastating social and economic consequences. As of the 8th of October, 2020, there were 36,164,596 cases confirmed, 25,242,930 recoveries 1,055,815 deaths worldwide. Indeed, COVID-19 is a novel challenge. Major economic and political power hubs worldwide, including Washington, New York, London, New Delhi, Beijing, Singapore, Rome, and Lagos, were deserted as people were compelled to stay indoors by choice or government. Big businesses worldwide, such as Banks and manufacturing industries, are engaged in skeletal activities, while small businesses like shops, restaurants, food vendors, and artisans have all closed shops. Many industries in the catering and tourism sector took a severe hit (Bajko et al., 2022); Healthcare and related industries had to cope with significant pressure due to changes in people's lives (Ghanemi et al., 2021); Transportation has to keep the momentum in moving people from one point to the other under intense pressure (Turo, & Kubik, 2021). Daily, jobs and income are being lost with the attendant challenge to SMEs. The International Labour Organization (ILO) estimates that 195 million jobs could be lost while developing countries could lose at least US$220 billion in income.

In Nigeria, the Federal government acknowledged the presence of the COVID-19 virus, and there were reported cases in over 32 of the 36 states, including the Federal Capital Territory (FCT). Nigeria Centre for Diseases Control (NCDC), a federal government agency, reported 255,415 confirmed cases nationwide, with 249,601 recoveries and 3,142 deaths as of 31st of March 2022. Meanwhile, of the confirmed cases, about 50% are in the southwestern part of Nigeria, with Lagos state recording 39% of that total sum, making it an epicenter of the crisis in Nigeria. To control the spread of the deadly virus Lagos, Ogun, and

Osun states declared total lockdown in their respective states, halting business activities.

Given the rapid spread of the COVID-19 pandemic, the research community has responded quickly to the new virus with publications primarily centered on causes, prevention, and control. However, considering the significant impact of the pandemic on all sectors of the world economy, including that of Nigeria, it is safe to suggest that the sector most affected are the small and medium enterprises (SMEs). This significant impact is connected with SMEs' unique structure, such as small size, weak ownership structure, inadequate capital, and little or no technology infrastructure.

Locally, we are unaware of any research focusing on the impact of the COVID-19 pandemic on business concerns and coping strategies in a post-pandemic environment, especially in South-West Nigeria.

Therefore, this work aims to investigate to what degree the COVID-19 pandemic will impact Nigeria's business environment during and after the COVID-19 pandemic. Specifically, the paper will:

i. Examine the effect of COVID-19 on Small and Medium Enterprises (SMEs) performance concerning sales, income, and profitability.
ii. To highlight coping strategies SMEs adopted during and after the COVID-19 pandemic.
iii. Identify specific policy measures the government can take to support SMEs post-COVID-19 lockdown.

The scope of the study is Lagos, Ogun, and Osun states in South-Western Nigeria. The three states were selected because they were subjected to total lockdown for over 21 days as against other states such as Oyo, Ondo, and Ekiti, which were on partial lockdown and had some measure of economic activities still going on. SMEs were preferred for this study because they represent a critical mass in the economy's private sector and are considered the bedrock of any sustainable economic development. South-Western zone of Nigeria was the focus of the study because it is the region with a high preponderance of SMEs in the country (SMEDAN, 2019) and collectively harbors 70% of reported cases as of the end of March 2022. The study will adopt the conceptual approach by reviewing relevant literature and drawing an inference concerning the study's objective. The study will conclude by making recommendations that, if implemented, can ameliorate the challenges of post-COVID-19.

3.2 Literature Review

COVID-19

Coronaviruses belong to the Orthocoronavirinae sub-family in the Nidovirales order. Corona represents crown-like spikes on the virus's outer surface; thus, it was named a coronavirus. Coronaviruses are minute in size (65-125 nm in diameter) and contain a single-stranded RNA as a nucleic material (Perlman, 2020). WHO announced that the official name of the 2019 novel coronavirus is coronavirus disease (COVID-19), the year of the outbreak.

The exact origin, location, and natural reservoir of the 2019-nCoV still need to be determined. However, it is believed that the virus is zoonotic, and bats may be the culprits because of sequence identity to the bat-CoV (Perlman, 2020; Zhu et al., 2019). WHO believes COVID-19 may cause symptoms such as pneumonia, fever, breathing difficulty, and lung infection. It is spread primarily through droplets of saliva or discharge from the nose when an infected person coughs or sneezes www.who.int. Most people infected with COVID-19 are also considered asymptomatic, while others will experience mild to moderate respiratory illness. However, older persons from age 65 and especially those with underlying medical challenges like cardiovascular diseases, diabetes, chronic respiratory diseases, and cancer, are more likely to develop a severe illness with fatal consequences in some cases (Li et al., 2020; WHO).

The first laboratory-confirmed case of 2019-nCoV infection was on the 1st of December 2019 in Wuhan, China. The outbreak was said to have occurred in a local market, the Huanan Seafood Market (wet market), with at least 41 cases reported (Huang et al., 2020). It was also reported that live animals such as bats, frogs, snakes, birds, marmots, and rabbits are frequently sold at the Huanan Seafood Market (Wang et al., 2020).

Although there is no known cure for COVID-19-affected persons, a regime of vaccines is now available, which includes Pfizer BioTech, Johnson & Johnson, Moderna, Oxford AstraZeneca, and Sputnik V vaccines. Meanwhile, some affected persons are being treated with a combination of therapies, tested negative, and discharged to go home. However, to prevent and slow transmission, WHO and the Nigeria Centre for Disease Control (NCDC) advocated regularly washing hands with detergent, using alcohol-based sanitizers, maintaining social and physical distancing, and full public awareness about the virus (WHO, ncdc.gov.ng).

In the meantime, the virus has created a total disruption of the world economic order, with almost all countries, including Nigeria, imposing a total lockdown of 21 days in some selected states. A lockdown of any country certainly will come with severe political, economic, and social consequences both in the short and long run. Therefore, this study focuses on the consequences of the lockdown occasioned by the virus on businesses, especially SMEs.

3.3 Small and Medium Enterprises (SMEs)

There is no universal definition for Small and Medium Enterprises since they are often given different descriptions in different countries and economies. These differences are often a result of government policies and programs. Fatai (2012) argued that different authors, institutions, government agencies, and policies have suggested different ways to define SMEs over the years. For example, Henschel (2009) reported that an SME in the United Kingdom (UK) is a company that employs less than 250 workers. In the United States of America, the figure is less than 500 employees. In South Africa, small businesses are categorized into four, namely, micro-enterprises, very small enterprises, small enterprises, and medium enterprises (Smith & Watkins, 2012).

In Nigeria, different government agencies such Central Bank of Nigeria (CBN) Nigerian Council for Industry (NCI) have defined SMEs in different ways using criteria such as asset base or sales turnover. This study will adopt the Small, Medium, Enterprises, Development Agency of Nigeria (SMEDAN) definition. The agency defines SMEs as any enterprise with at least ten employees and a maximum of 199 with assets not less than N5 million and not exceeding N500 million (SMEDAN, 2013).

The SME sector consists mainly of two categories. These are those involved in subsistence level (self-employed) earning income to sustain themselves and family and those involved in growth-related concerns that can scale their businesses. These categories exist in almost all sectors of the Nigerian economy.

Prior to the outbreak of COVID-19, SMEs in Nigeria suffered from various challenges that were identified by the Institute of Development of Administrators of Nigeria (IDAN, 2007), including,

First, SMEs need more funding as they often rely on personal savings and support from family and friends. Financial institutions such as banks are still very reluctant to lend to support SMEs. Although the Central Bank of Nigeria is encouraging a change of attitude on the part of the banks, more than support from banks is needed to help grow the SMEs.

Second, high attrition rate among SMEs due to poor entrepreneurial and technical skills. Essential managerial skills like planning, organizing, leading, coordinating, and controlling need to be improved, resulting in business failure or stunted growth.

Third, poor and inadequate infrastructural facilities such as electricity, roads, water, railway system, etcetera still need to be improved for the growth of SMEs. Electricity is a critical factor in business success generally, and SMEs, mainly, are still epileptic. Cost implications of independent power sources, such as purchasing and maintaining generator sets, could be more cost-effective.

Fourth, weak institutions and multiple taxations also present adverse effects on SMEs. A slow judicial system often weakens the early dispensation of justice, with cases dragging on for years in the Nigerian court system. Equally, multiple and ambiguous taxation system that different level of government levy on SMEs is harming the sector. Although the Federal Government is encouraging ease of doing business in the country, it is yet to be embraced by several states.

Beyond the health challenge posed by the COVID-19 pandemic, the virus significantly impacts international and local economies, especially SMEs (Bajko et al., 2022). There is the fear of unforeseen consequences of COVID-19 on businesses such that significant economies of the world and top Economists are predicting recession (GDA, 2020). Indeed COVID-19 pandemic is tremendously affecting SMEs' profitability and long-term viability (Emejulu et al., 2020; Hadi & Supardi, 2020).

For instance, Lagos, Ogun, and Osun states in South-West Nigeria experienced more than 21 days of total lockdown resulting in the total shutdown of businesses in compliance with a government directive. As a result, the SMEs took a hit with attendant consequences on sales volume, income, and profitability. Indeed, SMEs in states that have experienced lockdown measures are confronted with the harsh reality that could lead to business failure, low productivity, and loss of revenue resulting in a negative profit. Therefore, artisans such as cobblers and masons, who are daily income earners, may face existential challenges due to the lockdown COVID-19 pandemic can threaten the survival of SMEs in Nigeria (Eze et al., 2021).

Another consequence of the lockdown will be staff rationalization and staff reduction leading to unemployment for a productive workforce (Czainska et al., 2021; Rashid & Ratten, 2021; Williams et al., 2017).

Although the government has promised palliatives such as cash transfers, food, and food condiments for the vulnerable in society, more accurate information and data are needed to ensure the program's success. Coupled with this is a weak political decision driven by political and uneconomic considerations.

3.4 COVID-19 and Business Performance of SMEs

The study adopts sales, income, and profitability as the desired variable for use as proxies for business performance. A crisis such as COVID-19 poses a significant threat to the continued functioning of SMEs' performance (Eze et al., 2021). The lockdown in Lagos, Ogun, and Osun states prohibits the movement of people and materials with an attendant direct negative impact on the capacity of business organizations (SMEs) to make sales, earn income, and profit. Whether Nigerian businesses had any strategy to deal with unforeseen crises such as the COVID-19 pandemic is still being determined. Moreover, businesses have yet to be known to predict with certainty the consequences a particular crisis carries with it (Munoz et al., 2019). However, preparation is essential to manage a crisis well, and only a few, if any, SMEs would have prepared for a pandemic such as COVID-19. Studies have shown that SMEs often suffer from crises such as COVID-19 because they are vulnerable to cash-flow interruption as a result of loss of sales and income, lack of funds for recovery, inability to access government financial support, and severe infrastructure problems (Agbi & Rahim, 2021; Runyan, 2006).

Our review of literature such as (Bishop, 2019; Boin, 2009; Cowling et al., 2012; Doern, 2016; Herbane, 2010; Korber & McNaughton, 2018; Kuckertz et al., 2020; Smallbone et al., 2012; Runyan, 2006) suggest that for entrepreneurs, dealing with uncertainty, failure is a normal part of business; and (Ucbasaran et al.,2013), suggest this is even more so when an unforeseen crisis like the COVID-19 pandemic causes the uncertainty.

3.5 Research Propositions

To achieve the objectives set for this study (as earlier highlighted), three research questions were proposed and explored through qualitative studies. In answering the research question (RQ_1) on the effect of COVID-19 on SMEs' performance during the lockdown concerning sales, income, and profitability, our literature review indicates the consequences of pandemics such as COVID-19 on SMEs include a reduction in sales, income, and profitability. This is expected because SME operators cannot go out and affect productive activities, and neither consumers nor users go out to make patronages. Therefore, income and profit are not attainable if sales are not made.

Meanwhile, scholars and economic experts such as Czainska et al. (2021), Adam and Alarifi (2021), Nyikos et al. (2021) have predicted gloom for national economies, especially SMEs. "Thousands of SMEs will die under the weight of formal and informal loans, and bills (rent, electricity, wages, and interest) that continue to accumulate under lockdowns, as well as low demand for their goods and services" (Soludo, 2020). There is also the fear that the owners of SMEs will probably consume their business capital during the lockdowns with no clear helpline afterward (Adam & Alarifi, 2021). Moreover, SMEs are precariously on edge due to the COVID-19 lockdown, as loss of sales, income, and profitability will lead to cost-cutting measures, including staff retrenchment.

RQ_1: What challenges did the COVID-19 pandemic pose to the performance of SMEs, via-a-vis sales, income, and profitability?

In answering RQ_2, the study believes that given the enormous pressure COVID-19 has placed on SMEs and the need to ensure their survival, they will need to adopt some coping strategies. Studies in crisis management in SMEs suggest steps to ameliorate the potential negative impact on sales, income, and employment practices (Doern et al., 2019; Ibidunni et al., 2020). Small and Medium Enterprises have a high capacity for adaptability and flexibility Smallbone et al. (2012), and we expect them to demonstrate this during and after the COVID-19 pandemic. In managing the COVID-19 crisis, SMEs can also adopt a strategy similar to the concept of bricolage, which is a process of improvisation to meet a desired goal. So rather than adopting stringent processes to address the challenges presented by COVID-19, it seems more appropriate for innovative SMEs to embrace iterative and flexible approaches such as effectual logic (Obi et al., 2018; Sarasvathy, 2001). Andreas

(2020) reported the findings from research on the 2012 Emilia earthquakes in Italy to illustrate the point: it is only adaptive and resilient SMEs who created change and opportunities with the resources available at the time, are those that survive which is an effectual principle (Martinelli et al., 2018).

Furthermore, SMEs should adopt relational capabilities that are based on deliberate bricolage, which William et al. (2017), Ibidunni et al. (2017a, 2017b), and Gilbert-Saad et al. (2018) believe will enable leveraging internal and external resources such as goodwill partners, cooperative support, and access to social capital through financial brokers. Changing customers' needs in response to COVID-19 is another possibility. A possible response to such a situation is for SMEs to apply their bricolage response mechanism to solve new challenges while seeking new business opportunities.

Meanwhile, it is not unlikely that the post-COVID-19 lockdown will trigger new initiatives and ways of doing business. Nevertheless, how far this will go depends on the innovation entrepreneurs bring into their organizations.

RQ*$_2$*: *What coping strategies did SME operators adopt to adapt to the effects of COVID-19?*

In answering RQ$_3$, the study believes that it will be inappropriate for the government to rely on SME initiatives and strategies in dealing with the economic and social damage caused by COVID-19. Instead, the government can step in by way of new legislation that will guarantee financial support, removing policies that have inhibited the growth and development of SMEs. Specifically, the government should reduce loan interest rates while improving loan availability. Incidences of high-interest rates and difficulties in accessing loans by SMEs have been significant challenges pre-COVID-19 crisis. This recommendation is supported by calls from developed countries, such as the United States, United Kingdom, France, Germany, and China, to secure financial resources for SMEs to prevent collapse. Also, it serves to strengthen their capacities to deal with the situation. Among the measures suggested by some United States officials is that sustainable development goals (SDGs) should link to economic support to SMEs and entrepreneurs (Kaufman, 2020).

Wyns (2020) believes that if governments succeed in providing relief and support to SMEs under pressure in a way that supports the long-term economic objectives of the countries, COVID-19 could be a blessing in disguise.

Similarly, banks and financial institutions should be encouraged to design their lending policies for SMEs to positively impact and prevent the collapse of such a strategic sector of the economy.

***RQ*3**: *What policy directions are necessary for government and institutions for the SMEs sector post-COVID-19?*

3.6 Methodology

The present study used a qualitative research design to demonstrate the implications of the COVID-19 pandemic on the Nigerian business environment. Small and medium enterprise operators, including owner-managers and managers, form the unit of analysis for this study. According to Morse (2000), a qualitative study with a sample size of eight to twelve respondents is sufficient to generate patterns of responses that can provide sufficient insight into the subject under investigation. Consequently, this study gathered responses from forty-three Owners/managers and managers of small and medium enterprises in Nigeria. The study demystified three critical areas of the research question that pertain to the research objective. These questions include, what challenges did the COVID-19 pandemic pose to the performance of SMEs, via-a-vis sales, income, and profitability? What coping strategies did SME operators adopt to adapt to the effects of COVID-19? Finally, what policy directions are necessary for the government and institutions for the SME sector post-COVID-19? The adoption of qualitative research design helped this research to focus on in-depth inquiry and patterns of respondents' responses about the extent of implications of COVID-19 on SMEs in Nigeria. The questions that guided this study were self-developed based on the researchers' conceptualization of the novel issues surrounding the possible effects COVID-19 on SMEs' business performance and their coping strategies for alleviating these challenges.

Interview Protocol

The interview was conducted using open-ended questions emailed to respondents for this study, and the interview period lasted for 2 Months, starting from July–September 2020. Table 3.1 shows the background information of the interviewees for this research.

Table 3.1 shows that the research covers a significantly sizeable geographic spread across the South-West region of Nigeria. The geographic spread of respondents revealed that 7 respondents were from Ogun State, 9 were from Oyo State, 3 were from Osun State, 20 were from Lagos State, and 4 were from Ekiti State. Hence, the information provided gave insightful directions about the issues relating to the impact of COVID-19 on Nigeria's SME sector. According to gender, the data in the table shows that 35 respondents are male, while 8 respondents are female. The respondents' sectoral spread shows that many respondents operate in the service industry, cutting across generic service areas to education, retail/trade, hospitality, and entertainment. In terms of firm age, there were variations in the responses gathered. The firms included in the sample were of firm sizes ranging from less than 5 employees to more than 40 employees; the age bracket of the firms was from less than 3 years to over 21 years.

3.7 Results and Discussion

This study developed three themes regarding the research questions raised to investigate the implications of the COVID-19 pandemic on the Nigerian Business Environment. The respondents for this study included operators of Small and Medium Enterprises (SMEs).

Theme One: Challenges posed by the COVID-19 pandemic on the performance of SMEs, via-a-vis sales, income, and profitability

Table 3.1 Respondents' Background Information

Respondents	Gender	Industry	Firm Size	Firm Age
Respondent 1	Male	Retail/Trading	Less than 5	10 years
Respondent 2	Male	Services	More than 41	Over 21 years
Respondent 3	Male	Education	05-Oct	Over 21 years
Respondent 4	Female	Hospitality and entertainment	31–40	10 years
Respondent 5	Male	Services	Nov-20	15 years
Respondent 6	Male	Hospitality and entertainment	05-Oct	16–20 years
Respondent 7	Male	Hospitality and entertainment	Nov-20	4–10 years
Respondent 8	Female	Education		
Respondent 9	Male	Retail/Trading	21–30	4–10 years
Respondent 10	Male	Education	Less than 5	4–10 years
Respondent 11	Male	Others	05-Oct	4–10 years
Respondent 12	Male	Others	Nov-20	11–15 years
Respondent 13	Male	Oil & gas	Nov-20	11–15 years
Respondent 14	Female	Oil & gas	31–40	11–15 years
Respondent 15	Male	Manufacturing	Less than 5	Over 21 years
Respondent 16	Male	Oil & gas	Nov-20	Over 21 years
Respondent 17	Male	Manufacturing	05-Oct	11–15 years
Respondent 18	Male	Hospitality and entertainment	05-Oct	4–10 years
Respondent 19	Female	Services	More than 41	16–20 years
Respondent 20	Female	Education	Nov-20	4–10 years
Respondent 21	Male	Others		Over 21 years
Respondent 22	Male	Hospitality and entertainment	Nov-20	4–10 years
Respondent 23	Male	Services	More than 41	Over 21 years
Respondent 24	Male	Oil & gas	Nov-20	11–15 years
Respondent 25	Male	Others	Nov-20	16–20 years
Respondent 26	Female	Retail/Trading	Less than 5	Less than 3 years
Respondent 27	Female	Services	05-Oct	4–10 years
Respondent 28	Male	Services	05-Oct	16–20 years
Respondent 29	Female	Others	Nov-20	16–20 years

(continued)

Table 3.1 (continued)

Respondents	Gender	Industry	Firm Size	Firm Age
Respondent 30	Male	Services	05-Oct	4–10 years
Respondent 31	Male	Services	05-Oct	16–20 years
Respondent 32	Male	Others	Nov-20	Over 21 years
Respondent 33	Male	Services	05-Oct	16–20 years
Respondent 34	Male	Education	More than 41	Over 21 years
Respondent 35	Male	Education	05-Oct	4–10 years
Respondent 36	Male	Hospitality and entertainment	21 – 30	4–10 years
Respondent 37	Male	Services	05-Oct	Less than 3 years
Respondent 38	Male	Services	05-Oct	11–15 years
Respondent 39	Male	Services	Less than 5	Over 21 years
Respondent 40	Male	Manufacturing	31–40	Over 21 years
Respondent 41	Male	Services	Less than 5	4–10 years
Respondent 42	Male	Manufacturing	05-Oct	16–20 years
Respondent 43	Male	Services	Less than 5	Less than 3 years

In order to explore this theme, respondents were asked to briefly describe the challenges faced by their firm during the COVID-19 pandemic, especially concerning the impact of the pandemic on business sales, income level, and profitability.

The responses were as expected regarding the challenges of the COVID-19 pandemic on business sales. There was a general view about the negative impacts of COVID-19 on the sales level of the SME operators interviewed. The insights from this study did not only demonstrate the slowing down effect of the pandemic on SMEs. It also showed the intensity of the pandemic on some of the respondents' businesses. For example, *Respondent 18*, which provides hospitality and entertainment services, established that the lockdown resulting from the pandemic caused a "full shutdown and loss of 100% revenue for two months. Maintenance expenses mostly come from a need for more use of items. Reopen expenses were also significantly high with no clear indication of when normalcy will return." Quiet surprisingly, under conditions where we expected that remote service delivery might be an option, some businesses differed based on their experiences. For example, "a. Customers were restrained from coming out; therefore, the level of patronage dropped steeply, the online option did little or nothing to sustain the same level of patronage we had pre-Covid-19. b. Our projections for the year are badly affected by the pandemic. c. Since our contract staff is remunerated on commission, low patronage has stripped them of that, and three key staff already left the company" *(Respondent 30, Services firm)*.

Also, the respondents shared their views about the income level of their SMEs during the COVID-19 pandemic. The responses were similar to our expectations about the negative impact of the pandemic on business income. For example, according to Respondent 4, "Did not earn any revenue in April 2020, and it may just 25% revenue. Even now, we are on 60% pre-Covid revenue." However, a few other SME operators took advantage of the period to re-engineer their business operations to maintain the inflow of business income slightly. For example, *Respondent 26*, which operates a retail and trading business, opined, "This business is volume-based; when we lost the strength of voluminous sales, we had to resort to retailing mainly." Also, one respondent noted a diversification in their line of business "Income level was on ground zero, except our proactive response to the production of branded face masks" *(Respondent 39)*.

Finally, in the theme of identifying the challenges of the COVID-19 pandemic on SMEs related to the impact of the pandemic on business profitability. Generally, the respondent's view was that their businesses did not record any profits. One of the measures the government took to support Nigerians was a reduction in Premium Motor Spirit (PMS) price. However, for *Respondent 14*, this action taken by the government had a negative toll on that business. The respondent opined, "Recently, the frequent fluctuations of prices of PMS by the government, all in the name of this global pandemic, has done much damage to the profitability of the oil and gas business. We hope for stability."

Environmental disruptions caused by pandemics are noted to have immense effects on the performance of businesses (Day et al., 2004). More critical is that SMEs are perceived to be the most vulnerable to the resultant effects of pandemics, mainly because they generally are limited in their capital base and access to resources that could support them in stabilizing, even if they survive disruptive times (Hans, 2018). This assertion is as accurate to emerging economies as to their developed counterparts (Ayeni et al., 2017; Robin et al., 2020). Consequently, the need arises for SME operators to rethink their competencies in terms of resilience toward unforeseen environmental shocks.

Theme Two: Coping strategies adopted by SMEs operators to adapt to the effects of COVID-19

Theme two pertained to identifying the coping strategies the SME operators used to mitigate the risks of the COVID-19 pandemic. Respondents were asked to describe their businesses' coping strategies to adapt to the effects of the COVID-19 pandemic. Some business operators' response/coping strategy to the pandemic was to emphasize online and digital technology adoption. For example, respondents replied by saying "online marketing" *(Respondent 1)*. Another respondent declared, "we have been able to deploy technology to work 100% from home via the internet" *(Respondent 24)*.

Nevertheless, other respondents adopted strategies that focused on more effective customer service. For example, "by flying all the arsenals to ensure we give our customers the best services through good customer relations. Hence, Making sure we deliver 100% through our dispensing units to maintain our existing customers and gain more from the market share" *(Respondent 14)*.

Some of the operators adopted a diversification strategy to sustain their business continuity. According to *Respondent 26*, "We initially did not do small volume retailing, but we introduced it and increased our product variety. We also added grocery shopping service to retain our clients." However, other operators resorted to outright downsizing. *For example, respondent 18* revealed that "Keep cost tight, scale down head count, accept the new way of living, been seen as a responsible organization that takes safety seriously." Another exciting narrative from the responses was the adoption of philanthropic approaches to meeting customers' requirements. For example, a respondent affirmed that "Sending bulk SMS to the consuming public and reminding them of our existence and the love we have for them. We communicate NCDC rules and regulations to them at least for the safety of our lives" *(Respondent 22).*

The order of responses gathered from the semi-structured interview revealed that SME operators, especially those operating within the context of this study, tend to develop new approaches and strategies that ensure their business survival and resilience beyond environmental disruptions. The character or type of strategy adopted by the SME operators is determined by the dynamics presented by their environment. Similarly, studies such as Ayeni et al. (2018), Ibidunni et al. (2017a, 2017b, 2018) have reported that SME operators in developing economies like Nigeria depend to a large extent on their businesses to survive. Hence these business operators engage diverse forms of innovations and skillfulness in maneuvering harsh economic and social conditions to ensure the survival and continuity of their businesses.

Theme Three: Policy directions necessary for government and institutions for the SMEs sector post-COVID-19

Theme three focused on interrogating issues that relate to policy directions that the government and institutions should implement in supporting SMEs' growth post-COVID-19. This study identified the extent to which government support assisted SME operators during the COVID-19 pandemic. First, respondents were asked whether they received any form of support from the government. The response revealed that only two respondents were affirmative about the government supporting their businesses. *Respondent 12* confirmed receiving government support "Through Nirsal MFB." Also, *Respondent 29* revealed that the "Government reduced our Agric loan interest to 5%." These two respondents also confirmed that the support received from the government was sufficient to help their businesses stabilize during the period of the pandemic. However, a more significant number of respondents confirmed that they did not receive any form of support from the government. Hence, their responses suggest they will likely adopt other sustenance measures for their businesses that rely less on government interventions.

The results from this study are consistent with many existing studies that have proven that the SME sector needs more government support and policy neglect (Khayri et al., 2011). Furthermore, according to the literature, the failure of the government to act as an effective facilitator of a working business environment in the region under study has failed in many firms with massive global competitiveness potential (Uche & Familusi, 2018). Consequently, this study further amplifies the need for adequate support for the growth of the SME sector, especially during the present global economic shock arising from the COVID-19 pandemic.

In addition, the respondents' insights about policy directions necessary for the government or its agencies to implement for the survival of the SME sector post-COVID-19 showed diverse views. Several themes emerged from the replies provided by the SME operators. For example, there was an issue raised about the "Provision of a loan with single digit interest" *(Respondent 1)* and "More access to recovery loans and better transparency" *(Respondent 4)*. Also, communication was identified as a pertinent area of concern, as revealed in "Improvement of communication" *(Respondent 3)*. Views were also expressed about the need to place more emphasis on selected sectors and ensure capacity building "1. Agriculture be given priority; 2. Continuous Training of farmers; 3. Fund be made available for the real farmers and not through association to avoid massive fraudulent heads" *(Respondent 11)*. Another critical issue raised pertained to infrastructure "Provision of infrastructures that would reduce the cost of doing business such as good roads and electricity" *(Respondent 15)*. Also, a respondent highlighted the need for favorable tax policies to be designed "The government should reduce taxes for the current year. Make loans more easily accessible to businesses at a single-digit interest rate. There should be bail-out packages for businesses that are badly hit due to Covid after due diligence by the government" *(Respondent 24)*.

3.8 Implications of the Study

This study has implications directed to theory and policymakers toward supporting the growth of SMEs in developing countries, especially during epidemics and pandemics. Theoretically, the understanding of MSMEs' adaptability and resilience, especially from the developing economies' perspective, has yet to be extensively discussed. Countries in the global south still require significant theoretical underpinnings and explanations about issues related to adopting dynamic competencies that support them in maneuvering periods of environmental turbulence, particularly during unforeseen global pandemics. Consequently, this study contributes to understanding coping strategies that support SMEs' survival during environmental turbulence.

The findings from this study also bring to the fore the critical role of policy formulation and implementation toward advancing the SME sector of developing economies. The general perception reported in this study highlights significant neglect of the SME sector by the government and its institutional organs. The need to drive policy, especially in communication, funding supports, single-digit interest loans, favorable tax policies, and ensuring of business friend environment and infrastructure that support ease of doing business, have been pointed out as critical issues of concern. Policymakers must follow a more conscientious and purpose-oriented approach toward ensuring a sustainable SME sector in the developing economy.

3.9 Conclusion and Further Studies

This study has significantly contributed to the strategic management literature by exploring the coping strategies that support SMEs' survival during adverse environmental disruptions. The findings from this study highlight the importance of SME operators' competencies, especially concerning adopting digital technologies and resilience capabilities to ensure business survival during and after periods of pandemics. Specifically, SMEs looking to recover from the pandemic should invest in affordable digital tools. Similarly, SMEs should embrace creativity and innovation in their service delivery to enhance resilience and sustainability. The study also concludes that government support for SMEs in developing economies, with particular emphasis on the context of this study, should be given priority. Finally, despite the contributions made by this study, further studies should compare the disruptive effects of pandemics from a cross-country perspective of developing nations to offer strong recommendations about dynamic capabilities that are critical to SMEs' resilience.

References

Adam, N. A., & Alarifi, G. (2021). Innovation practices for survival of small and medium enterprises (SMEs) in the COVID-19 times: The role of external support. *Journal of Innovation and Entrepreneurship., 10*(15), 56–65.

Agbi, B. D., & Rahim, A. G. (2021). Creativity and innovation: An imperative for entrepreneurial development in Nigeria, *Nigerian Academy of Management Journal,16* (1),24–36. https://www.namj.tamn-ng.org/index.php/home/article/view/130/123

Andreas, S. (2020). *The impact of COVID-19 on education: Insights from education at a glance 2020*. OECD Publishing.

Ayeni, A. W., Iyiola, O. O., Ogunnaike, O. O., & Ibidunni, A. S. (2017). Negativity of globalization: The Ebola Virus Disease and its health impact on Nigerians. *African Journal of Business Management, 11*(3), 47–56.

Ayeni, A., Ogunnaike, O. O., Iyiola, O. O., Ezenwoke, O. A., & Ibidunni, S. (2018). Data article on institutional framework and business survivals of informal entrepreneurs in electronics market, South-west, Nigeria. *Data in Brief, 19*, 1297–1304.

Bajko, N., Fulop, Z., & Percsi, K. N. (2022). Changes in the innovation- and marketing-habits of family SMEs in the foodstuffs industry, caused by the coronavirus pandemic in Hungary. *Sustainability, 14*, 2914. https://doi.org/10.3390/su14052914

Bishop, P. (2019). Knowledge diversity and entrepreneurship following an economic crisis: An empirical study of regional resilience in Great Britain. *Entrepreneurship & Regional Development, 31*, 496–515.

Blogs—The Huffington Post. Retrieved from https://advance.lexis.com/api/document?collection

Boin, A. (2009). The new world of crises and crisis management: Implications for policymaking and research. *Review of Policy Research, 26*, 367–377.

Cowling, M., Liu, W., & Ledger, A. (2012). Small business financing in the UK before and during the current financial crisis. *International Small Business Journal, 30*, 778–800.

Czainska, K., Sus, A., & Thalassinos, E. I. (2021). Sustainable survival: Resource management strategy in micro and small enterprises in the rubber products market in Poland during the COVID-19 pandemic. *Resources, 10*, 85.

Day, B., Ishman, M., Burnice Mckay, R., & Chung, E. (2004). "It will happen again": What SARS taught businesses about crisis management. *Management Decision, 42*(7), 822–836. https://doi.org/10.1108/00251740410550907

Doern, R. (2016). Entrepreneurship and crisis management: The experiences of small businesses during the London 2011 riots. *International Small Business Journal, 34*, 276–302.

Doern, R., Williams, N., & Vorley, T. (2019). *Special issue on entrepreneurship and crises: Business*. https://doi.org/10.1056/NEJMe2001126

Emejulu, G., Agbasi, O., & Nosike, C. (2020). Strategic agility and performance of small and medium enterprises in the phase of Covid-19 pandemic. *International Journal of Finance, Accounting, and Management, 2*, 41–50.

Eze, B. U., Agbi, B. D., & Adenuga, A. O. (2021). COVID-19 pandemic: a qualitative evaluation of MSMEs survival strategies in Nigeria, *Harvard Deusto Business Research*, *10*(2), 382–396. https://doi.org/10.48132/hdbr.331

Fatai, A. (2012). *Small and medium scale enterprises in Nigeria: The problems and prospects*. Retrieved on June 20 2022 from https://www.thecje.com/journal/index.php/economicsjournal/article/..../8

GDA (Global Data Analysis). (2020). *Coronavirus (COVID-19) executive briefing*. Global Data.

Ghanemi, A., Yoshioka, M., & St-Amand, J. (2021). Coronavirus Disease 2019 (COVID-19) Crisis Measures: Health Protective Properties? *Medicines, 8*(49).

Gilbert-Saad, A., Siedlok, F., & McNaughton, R. B. (2018). Decision and design heuristics in the context of entrepreneurial uncertainties. *Journal of Business Venturing Insights, 9*, 75–80.

Hadi, S., & Supardi, S. (2020). Revitalization strategy for small and medium enterprises after Corona virus disease pandemic (covid-19) in Yogyakarta. *Journal of Xian University Architectural Technology, 12*, 4068–4076.

Hans, V. B. (2018). Business environment—Conceptual framework and policies. *International Educational Scientific Research Journal, 4*(3), 67–74.

Henschel, T. (2009). *Risk management practices of SMEs. Evaluating and implementing effective risk management systems.* https://www.researchgate.net/publication/259812085

Herbane, B. (2010). Small business research: Time for a crisis-based view. *International Small Business Journal, 28*, 43–64.

Huang, C., Wang, Y., Li, X., Ren, L., Zhao, J., & Hu, Y. et al. (2019). Clinical features of patients infected with 2019 novel coronavirus in Wuhan, China. *Lancet* 2020. https://doi.org/10.1016/S01406736(20)30183-5

Ibidunni, A. S., Chidubem, M., & Adebanji, A. W. (2020). Entrepreneurial characteristics among university students: Insights for understanding entrepreneurial intentions among youths in an emerging economy. *Education+Training*, https://doi.org/10.1108/ET-09-2019-0204

Ibidunni, A. S., Ibidunni, O. M., Olokundun, M. A., Hezekiah Falola, O., Salau, O. P., & Borishade, T. T. (2018). Data article on disposition towards enhancing SMEs' performance through entrepreneurial orientations: Perspectives from a developing economy. *Data in Brief, 18*, 1009–1012.

Ibidunni, A. S., Ogunnaike, O. O., & Abiodun, A. J. (2017a). Extending the knowledge strategy concept: Linking organizational knowledge with strategic orientations. *Academy of Strategic Management Journal, 16*(3), 1–11.

Ibidunni, A. S., Olokundun, M. A., Oke, A. O., & Nwaomonoh, I. C. (2017b). Enhancing the performance of agro-based SMEs: The role of entrepreneurship competencies. *Covenant Journal of Entrepreneurship, 1*(1), 44–51.

IDAN. (2007). *Entrepreneurship management; student study guide of the Institute of Development Administration of Nigeria (IDAN).*

Kaufman, A. C. (2020). *If we bail out airlines, it better come with climate rules. Newstex Blogs—The Huffington Post*. Retrieved from http://advance.lexis.com/api/document?collection=news&id=urn:contentItem:5YG4-R6S1-F03R-N4KY-00000-00&context=1516831

Khayri, S., Yaghoubi, J., & Yazdanpanah, M. (2011). Investigating barriers to enhance entrepreneurship in agricultural higher education from the perspective of graduate students. *Procedia Social and Behavioural Sciences, 15*, 2818–2822.

Korber, S., & McNaughton, R. B. (2018). Resilience and entrepreneurship: A systematic literature review. *International Journal of Entrepreneurial Behaviour & Research, 24*, 1129–1154.

Kuckertz, A., Brändle, L., Gaudig, A., Hinderer, S., Morales Reyes, C., Prochotta, A., Steinbrink, K., & Berger, C. (2020). *Journal of Business Venturing Insights*, in press.

Li, Q., Guan, X., Wu, P., Wang, X., Zhou, L., & Tong, Y. (2020). Early transmission dynamics in Wuhan, China, of novel coronavirus-infected pneumonia. *New England Journal of Medicine, 2020*. https://doi.org/10.1056/NEJMoa2001316

Martinelli, E., Tagliazucchi, G., & Marchi, G. (2018). The resilient retail entrepreneur: Dynamic capabilities for facing natural disasters. *International Journal of Entrepreneurial Behaviour and Research, 24*, 1222–1243.

Morse, J. M. (2000). Determining sample size. *Qualitative Health Research, 10*(1), 3–15. https://doi.org/10.1177/104973200129118183

Munoz, P., Kimmitt, J., Kibler, E., & Farny, S. (2019). Living on the slopes: Entrepreneurial preparedness in a context under continuous threat. *Entrepreneurship & Regional Development, 31*, 413–434.

Nyikos, G., Soha, B., & Beres, A. (2021). Entrepreneurial resilience and firm performance during the COVID-19 Crisis—Evidence from Hungary. *Hungarian Central Statistical Office: Budapest, Hungary, 11*, 29–59.

Obi, J., Ibidunni, A. S., Atolagbe, T., Olokundun, M. A., Amaihian, A. B., Borishade, T. T., & Peter, F. (2018). Contribution of small and medium enterprises to economic development: Evidence from a transiting economy. *Data in Brief, 18*, 835–839.

Perlman, S. (2020). Another decade, another coronavirus. *New England Journal of Medicine*. https://doi.org/10.1056/NEJMe2001126

Rashid, S., & Ratten, V. (2021). Entrepreneurial ecosystems during COVID-19: The survival of small businesses using dynamic capabilities. *World Journal of Entrepreneurship, Management and Sustainable Development, 17*, 457–476.

Robin, M., Toby, H., & Savage, M. (2020). Don't bet on vaccine to protect us from Covid-19, says world health expert| World news| The Guardian. The Guardian.Com. Retrieved the 17th of May, 2020, from https://www.theguardian.com/world/2020/apr/18/dont-bet-on-vaccine-to-protect-us-from-covid-19-says-world-health-expert

Runyan, R. C. (2006). Small business in the face of crisis: Identifying Barriers to recovery from a natural disaster. *Journal of Contingencies and Crisis Management, 14*, 12–26.

Sarasvathy, S. D. (2001). Causation and effectuation: Toward a theoretical shift from economic inevitability to entrepreneurial contingency. *Academy of Management Review, 26*, 243–263.

Small and Medium Enterprises Development Agency (SMEDAN). (2019).

Smallbone, D., Deakins, D., Battisti, M., & Kitching, J. (2012). Small business responses to a major economic downturn: Empirical perspectives from New Zealand and the United Kingdom. *International Small Business Journal, 30*, 754–777.

SMEDAN. (2013). Medium, Small and Micro Enterprises Survey—Summary Report. https://www.smedan.gov.ng

Smith, Y., & Watkins, J. (2012). A literature review of small and medium enterprises (SME) risk management practices in South Africa. *African Journal of Business Management, 6*(21), 6324–6330. http://www.academicjournals.org/AJBM, https://doi.org/10.5897/AJMB11.2709

Soludo, C. (2020). COVID-19: Can Africa afford lockdowns? Premium Times accessed on 25th April 2020.

Turo, N. K., & Kubik, A. (2021). Business innovations in the new mobility market during the COVID-19 with the possibility of open business model innovation. *Journal of Open Innovation Technology, Market, Complexity, 7*, 195.

Ucbasaran, D., Shepherd, D. A., Lockett, A., & Lyon, S. J. (2013). Life after business failure: The process and consequences of business failure for entrepreneurs. *Journal of Management, 39*(1), 163–202.

Uche, C., & Familusi, L. C. (2018). The adoption of agripreneurship as a mitigating measure to unemployment in Nigeria: A topical review. *Global Journal of Management and Business Research: G Interdisciplinary, 18*(2), 25–31.

Wang, C., Horby, P., Hayden, F., & Gao, G. (2020). A novel coronavirus outbreak of global health concern. *The Lancet.* 2020.

WHO (2020). Novel Coronavirus—China 2020. https://www.who.int/csr/don/12-

Williams, T. A., Gruber, D. A., Sutcliffe, K. M., Shepherd, D. A., & Zhao, E. Y. (2017). Organizational response to adversity: Fusing crisis management and resilience research streams. *Academy of Management Annals, 11*, 733–769.

World Health Organization. Hand Hygiene for Health Workers Caring for Ebola Patients. Available at https://www.who.int/csr/disease/ebola/hand-hygiene/en/. Accessed on the 26th of April, 2020.

Wyns, A. (2020). *How our responses to climate change and the coronavirus are linked*. Accessed April 28th 2020 from https://www.weforum.org/agenda/2020/04/climate-change-coronavirus-linked/

Zhu, N., Zhang, D., Wang, W., Li, X., Yang, B., Song, J., et al. (2020). A novel coronavirus from patients with pneumonia in China, 2019. *New England Journal of Medicine, 382*(8), 727–733.

4

Motivating Entrepreneurial Activities to Achieve Sustainable Development in Sub-Saharan Africa

Chioma Onoshakpor and Oyedele Martins Ogundana

4.1 Introduction

One of the sustainable development goals introduced by the United Nations is SDG 1 which is targeted at ending poverty in all its forms everywhere—especially in a developing economy (Quagrainie et al., 2021). This is because the issue of poverty often results in the lack of education, social exclusion and high vulnerability to diseases (Quagrainie et al., 2021). Poverty is also linked to health and well-being challenges (Currie & Goodman, 2020). Evidence from the developing economies (including Ghana) reveals that chronic malnutrition and anaemia are associated with household poverty levels (Anim-Somuah et al., 2013;

C. Onoshakpor (✉)
Robert Gordon University, Aberdeen, Scotland
e-mail: c.onoshakpor1@rgu.ac.uk

O. M. Ogundana
Nottingham Trent University, Nottingham, UK
e-mail: oyedele.ogundana@ntu.ac.uk

A. S. Ibidunni et al. (eds.), *Innovation, Entrepreneurship and the Informal Economy in Sub–Saharan Africa*, Sustainable Development Goals Series,
https://doi.org/10.1007/978-3-031-46293-1_4

Damilola et al., 2020). Many studies have argued that entrepreneurship and entrepreneurial activities are crucial means for reducing the proportion of poverty especially within the developing economy (IFC, 2014; Misango & Ongiti, 2013; Quagrainie et al., 2021). For instance, the Global Entrepreneurship Monitor (GEM) reported that entrepreneurial activities in Africa reduce poverty by generating about 1million jobs in Angola; 4million in Nigeria; 1.08million in Burkina Faso; and 1.64million in Zambia (GEM, 2014, 2015). Moreover, GEM (2017) reported that entrepreneurial activities would create more jobs as 30% of all business owners in East, North and sub-Saharan Africa are projected to hire six or more employees in 5 years. The employment projection within GEM's report entrepreneurial activities will reduce unemployment and poverty in Africa by an average of 6% (GEM, 2017). Aside from their contribution to the reduction of poverty and unemployment, entrepreneurial activities have reduced the number of child trafficking and prostitution in Nigeria (Ogundana, 2020); improved the rate of child education in Ghana and the Republic of Niger (Chea, 2008; Otoo et al., 2012); improved family nutritional rates by 33% in Botswana (Ama et al., 2014); reduced the level of crime by 23.3% in Ogun State Nigeria (Iyiola & Azuh, 2014); and played a crucial role in alleviating hunger and poverty in Kenya (IFC, 2014; Misango & Ongiti, 2013). These are some of the benefits derivable from engaging in entrepreneurial activities. Yet, the percentage of population involved in business start-ups is still very low in Africa compared to other continents including the developed world (Statista, 2022).

Studies have shown that individuals are motivated into becoming entrepreneurs for different reasons including financial success, status, self-realization, marriage break-up and the existence of an opportunity (Kirkwood, 2009; Manolova et al., 2008). These entrepreneurial motivation factors are generally categorised into push and pull factors (McClelland et al., 2005; Schjoedt & Shaver, 2007; Segal et al., 2005). Push factors are often used to categorise those factors that have negative connotations including lack of job, economic challenges and poverty

(Amit & Muller, 1995; Carsrud & Brannback, 2011; Kirkwood, 2009), while pull factors refer to those positive aspects that attract people to entrepreneurship including seeing an opportunity (Dawson & Henley, 2012; Kirkwood, 2009; Manolova et al., 2008). Some studies opined that pull factors are more prevalent than push factors (see for instance Segal et al., 2005; Shinnar & Young, 2008). However, these studies are mostly from the developed economies and might not apply to the developing economies where push factors (i.e., economy challenges and absence of jobs) are more likely to abound than pull factors (i.e., opportunities). Besides, it is still unclear whether there are gender differences in the way push and pull motivations influence women and men into becoming an entrepreneur in a developing economy. Highlighting these gender differences is needed especially as women manage their businesses in ways different from their male counterparts (Kirkwood, 2009; Ogundana et al., 2020). Thus, this chapter is underlined by 2 research questions:

1. *What motivates people to get involved in entrepreneurial activities in a developing economy—Nigeria?*
2. *How do the motivating factors for women differ from their male counterparts in a developing economy—Nigeria?*

To address these 2 questions, we conducted 10 in-depth interviews, consisting of 5men and women entrepreneurs who operate a range of business enterprises in Nigeria. These interviews were transcribed verbatim and analysed using thematic analysis. The findings are presented using textural and structural descriptors. After this introductory section, we review push and pull factors, social feminist theory and provide insights into the Nigerian context as a backdrop for this study. This is followed by the discussion of the research method employed in this study. The chapter concludes by discussing the research and policy implications of the research findings.

4.2 Theoretical Background

Push and Pull Factors

Generally, in the entrepreneurship literature, the factors that motivate individuals into entrepreneurship are mainly categorised into 2—push and pull factors (Amit & Muller, 1995; Carsrud & Brannback, 2011). Different terminologies, which mean the same thing, have been used to substitute the push and pull division. For instance, Reynolds et al. (2001) utilised the term 'opportunity-based' and 'necessity-based' to describe the pull and push factors. Dawson and Henley (2012) described them in their own words as 'positive' and 'negative' factors. Nonetheless, though studies have used different terms, they mean the same thing. As such, in this study we stick to the push and pull descriptor to reduce discrepancy. Push factors are those factors that have negative connotations including the lack of white-collar employment, job dissatisfaction, unemployment, poor salary, inflexible work schedule, economic challenges and poverty (Kirkwood, 2009; Ogundana, 2022a; Segal et al., 2005). Entrepreneurs who are motivated by push factors are often described as necessity-focused and survival-oriented (Carsrud & Brannback, 2011; Reynolds et al., 2002). Such people who were pushed into entrepreneurship are mostly concerned with avoiding failure, which could mean starvation (Carsrud & Brannback, 2011). The central motivation of an individual pushed into entrepreneurship is often to earn enough money to support themselves and their family (Ogundana, 2022b). In other words, pushed entrepreneurs are often focused on survival which means that they are frequently likely to miss or oftentimes ignore opportunities that have a longer payback period (Carsrud & Brannback, 2011). This is mainly because this category of entrepreneurs is frequently unable to wait to achieve a bigger goal as they are concerned that they might starve to death waiting (Carsrud & Brannback, 2011). Thus, an enterprise born out of push factors is often risk averse as they are likely to assume that failing could mean death, a risk not worth taking (Carsrud & Brannback, 2011). On the other hand, pull factors include those positive aspects that attract individuals to entrepreneurship including the existence of a business opportunity, seeking independence, self-fulfilment and wealth

(Dawson & Henley, 2012; Kirkwood, 2009; Manolova et al., 2008). Individuals who were pulled into entrepreneurship are often described as opportunistic entrepreneurs as they are often driven by the achievement of success through exploiting an opportunity for some form of gain often measured in economic terms (Reynolds et al., 2002). Such individuals are attracted to become entrepreneurs because they want to earn money, power, prestige and/or status (Carsrud & Brannback, 2011).

There is inconsistency in the current entrepreneurship literature regarding how the push and pull factors interact with one another to motivate individuals into entrepreneurship. Many of the existing studies seem to suggest that the push and pull factors might motivate individuals separately and individually (Brünjes & Diez, 2013; Segal et al., 2005; Zgheib, 2018). While some other categories of studies suggest that the push and pull factors are likely to operate together, neither of them would have a dominant role (Carsrud & Brannback, 2011; Dawson & Henley, 2012; Kirkwood, 2009). In developing their argument for an intertwined relationship between push and pull factors, Carsrud and Brannback (2011: 14) claimed that "in biotechnology, the search for a cure for a disease is often a far more powerful motivator than personal wealth creation". Furthermore, there are also inconsistencies regarding whether women and men are equally motivated by similar motivators (Dawson & Henley, 2012; Kirkwood, 2009). On the contrary, the social construction of gender suggests that women are less likely than men to be motivated to become entrepreneurs in the developing economies (Solesvik et al., 2019). Furthermore, there are differences in the motivational factors for men and women to become entrepreneurs, with more women stating personal and family-related issues as motivators; while their men counterparts are more likely to state financial reasons (Dawson & Henley, 2012; Taylor & Newcomer, 2005). Although Brush and Cooper (2012) have questioned whether entrepreneurship actually offers an improved work-family balance for women considering starting a business for familial reasons. This might explain why some women entrepreneurs exit from entrepreneurship after some few years (Brush & Cooper, 2012; Dawson & Henley, 2012; Solesvik et al., 2019). Kirkwood (2009) stated that researchers have paid little attention to gender differences in the push and pull motivations for becoming an entrepreneur. This omission Kirkwood claims is not new, as entrepreneurship research still lacks gender comparative analysis. As such, Dawson and Henley (2012) posited that "pull" and "push" factors should be considered along the lines of current contemporary economic conditions and differential personal circumstances of both genders. This suggests that observable differences in motivation between men and women may be due to sociocultural factors which would differ from context to context.

Social Feminist Theory and Entrepreneurial Motivation

The social feminist theory assumes that women and men differ from one another inherently (Fischer, 1993; Szymanski, 2005). The source of the assumed gender differences is located within the early and ongoing different socialisation processes that women and men are exposed to throughout their lives that often condition them to view the world in fundamentally different ways (DeTienne & Chandler, 2007; Johnsen & McMahon, 2005; Orser et al., 2011). Accordingly, several entrepreneurship studies that have compared women and men on socialised traits and values are consistent with the social feminist assumption (see for instance: Ampofo, 2001; Solesvik et al., 2019). Several studies have observed many consistent gender differences (Dawson & Henley, 2012; Marlow & Martinez, 2018; Szymanski, 2005; Taylor & Newcomer, 2005). For instance, women—who are often conditioned by societal praxis—are often taught to assume domestic roles and possess traits such as gentleness, sensitivity, compassion, submissiveness and deference (Onoshakpor et al., 2023a; Ogundana et al., 2018; Simba et al., 2022; Verheul et al., 2006). On the other hand, men are socialised to express toughness, stoicism, self-sufficient attitudes, lack of emotional sensitivity and a more dominant role in male–female relationships (Ampofo, 2001; Izugbara, 2005; Ogundana et al., 2022b). The gender socialisation processes are more dominant in the developing country context where deviation from them is often frowned at, and culprits stigmatised (Ogundana et al.,

2022a; Simba et al., 2022). Besides, in a developing country region such as Ghana, social expectations are "reinforced by direct instruction, punishments, and by observation of female acceptance of male dominance among parents" (Ampofo, 2001: 16).

Gender socialisation and traits also shape the way both women and men operate their businesses (Manolova et al., 2012; Christopher Weber & Geneste, 2014). For instance, Manolova et al. (2012) observed that women entrepreneurs in the USA desired non-financial forms of success compared to their male counterparts who preferred financial successes. In a study of gender-related perceptions of success in business, Christopher Weber and Geneste (2014) found that women entrepreneurs preferred intrinsic success (i.e., non-financial: lifestyle and perceived success); while their male counterparts preferred extrinsic forms of successes in business (i.e., sales, number of employees and profit). Similarly, in his study, Smith (2000) concluded that male entrepreneurs were motivated by financial and instrumental concerns while women were motivated by relational and social concerns. A recurring conclusion from these prior studies (i.e., Manolova et al., 2012; Smith, 2000; Christopher Weber & Geneste, 2014) is that women are more inclined towards non-financial gains while their men counterparts prefer financial forms of successes. Indeed, there are assumptions that women's preference for non-financial successes is linked to their feminine traits of gentleness, sensitivity, compassion, submissiveness and deference; while men are linked to financial successes because of their masculine traits of self-sufficiency and competitiveness (Manolova et al., 2012; Christopher Weber & Geneste, 2014). However, these conclusions are mostly gleaned from studies that are based on the developed country contexts including the USA. This might not apply in the developing country region that mostly possesses a unique business, social and institutional context (Welter, 2011). Besides, different individuals have started to switch their feminine traits for masculine attributes— vice versa—because of the psychosocial and environmental challenges that characterise our world (Ogundana et al., 2022b). For instance, men have started to take up the responsibilities of child-care and women have become breadwinners of the home (Miller, 2022). Thus, it is difficult, if not impossible, to propose what factors would motivate women and men into entrepreneurship in the developing economies.

The Nigerian Entrepreneurship Context

Existing studies have shown that entrepreneurial activities drive economic growth and create employment opportunities, and wealth (Brush & Cooper, 2012; Huggins et al., 2018). Studies show that in a developing economy like Nigeria, entrepreneurial activities play an important role, not only in economic development but in steering the socio-economic landscape of the country. In a report by the National Bureau of Statistics (2014), entrepreneurship in Nigeria is seen to account for 97% of the total businesses in the country, contributing 87.9% of the net jobs and 48% of the industrial output in terms of value-addition (Olukayode & Somoye, 2013). Besides, SMEs also contribute 48% of the country's GDP (UNDESA, 2019). According to GEM (2012), Nigeria is considered one of the world's most entrepreneurial countries as 35 out of 100 Nigerians are engaged in some kind of entrepreneurial activity or the other. As such, the Nigerian government, indeed the government of other developing economies, has introduced numerous programmes to support the development and growth of enterprises in the developing economies (Onoshakpor et al., 2022; Ajayi, 2016; Ogundana et al., 2018). Notable among them are the National Directorate of Employment (NDE), Small and Medium Enterprises Development Agency of Nigeria (SMEDAN Peoples Bank of Nigeria (PBN), National Bank of Commerce and Industry, Microfinance Banks, National Economic Reconstruction Fund (NERFUND) and the National Economic Empowerment and Development Scheme (NEEDS). However, studies have observed that many of these policy interventions aimed at motivating individuals into entrepreneurship have recorded failures due to poor implementation, corruption, excessive red tapes and bureaucracy (Igwe et al., 2018; Ihugba et al., 2013; Thaddeus, 2012). Yet, individuals continue to stream towards entrepreneurship despite the limited support system in place to motivate potential entrepreneurs to start businesses (UNDESA, 2019). Yet, it is still unclear what factors motivate individuals to venture into entrepreneurship and how these motivating factors differ by gender.

4.3 Research Methodology

This study is interpretive in nature, resting on the epistemological assumption that the focus of this research is inconsistent with what is obtained in the natural sciences terrain (Mason, 2010). This discrepancy is driven by the growing recognition that the way entrepreneurship eventuates will vary depending on its historical, institutional, spatial and social contexts (Welter, 2011). By adhering to an interpretive research paradigm, this study unravelled push and pull motivational factors that are unique to male and female entrepreneurs operating within the Nigerian entrepreneurial context. Besides, the interactionist nature of a qualitative research framework enabled this study to identify gender-specific motivational factors and those applicable to both male and female entrepreneurs (Hesse-Biber 2007). We utilised the purposive and snowballing sampling techniques to recruit respondents for this study. These sampling techniques were useful for obtaining the information we required from those respondents that possessed such information (Hamilton, 2006; Yin, 2012). Overall, we interviewed 10 business owners (5 male and 5 female entrepreneurs) who own and operate businesses within different economic sectors of Nigeria (see Table 4.1). The interview sessions lasted between 30 and 40minutes and were tape-recorded and transcribed verbatim for analysis.

Table 4.1 displays the overview of the respondents, age of their businesses, sector of operation, marital status and specifically their gender. This helps to provide useful information about the demographics of the respondents. The age of the respondents' businesses ranges between 3 and 18 years showing they fall within the range of micro and small enterprises according to SMEDAN's categorization of MSMEs. The number of employees engaged within these enterprises ranged between 1 and 350 employees. We started the analysis by reading and re-reading each of the transcripts to get acquainted with the data analysis process (Glaser, 1978). With the aid of NVivo, we coded important

Table 4.1 Characteristics of interview participants

Respondents	Gender	Marital Status	No. of employees	Sector of operation	Years of operation
1	Male	Married	10	Real Estate	10
2	Female	Single	5	Real Estate	3
3	Female	Married	7	Food/ accommodation	10
4	Male	Married	35	Food/ accommodation	12
5	Female	Single	1	Real Estate	3
6	Male	Married	1	Real Estate	3
7	Female	Married	40	Food/ accommodation	18
8	Male	Single	1	Food/ accommodation	4
9	Male	Married	350	Real Estate	7
10	Female	Married	25	Food/ accommodation	17

Source Authors' idea based on data collection

remarks within each interview transcript using data-driven and theory-driven codes derived from the existing entrepreneurship literature. The evolving codes, commentaries and their interpretations are presented using textural and structural descriptions of factors that motivate male and female individuals into starting a business.

4.4 Finding

Factors Motivating Female Entrepreneurs in Nigeria

The findings showed that women were pushed and pulled into entrepreneurship (See Table 4.2a and b). Furthermore, our findings show that female entrepreneurs in Nigeria are more likely motivated by external economic conditions such as job insecurity in the Nigerian labour market (push factors). In that regard, R2 explained that:

> … you know the job insecurity uncertainties in the private sector is something else, so you always need a backup plan…

Table 4.2a Sample quotes, second-order codes and over-arching themes

Over-arching theme	Second-order codes	Sample quotes (Male)	Sample quotes (Female)
Push factors	Financial motivation	…other reasons of obvious reasons so you know we want to literally enjoy what you earn you know…R1	…it was just trying to make ends meet because initially I was working in the private sector and it was really hectic …R2
	External economic conditions		… you know the job insecurity uncertainties in the private sector is something else so you always need a backup plan…R2

(continued)

Table 4.2a (continued)

Over-arching theme	Second-order codes	Sample quotes (Male)	Sample quotes (Female)
	Non-pecuniary and internal motivations	… … so one of the reasons that made me, you know try to choose this part was to create an opportunity for people…R1 … you know just to take a couple of people off the streets by giving them you know jobs and opportunities to make ends meet…R1	
	Self-employment	…a long-time dream from when I was 12 years old, my mother was a trader, seeing what she does and assisting her in what she does make me what to do this…. it birthed in me such passion to want to do this…R4 …entrepreneurship is something that runs in my blood you know all my life that's what I've been wanting to be to run my business because while I was growing up you know I was suing I was a tailor you know so I'm just a normal tailor and I grew the business to a point where I was wearing clothes and taken them to the UK…. R9	

Table 4.2b Sample quotes, second-order codes, and over-arching themes

Over-arching theme	Second-order codes	Sample quotes (Male)	Sample quotes (Female)
Push factors	Seeking greater autonomy or independence	believe I can I would have job satisfaction if I am an employee I understand so I noticed that job satisfaction is what made me yeah…. R6 you know me as an executive chef running several restaurants for people at some point, I felt that I also need to have something for myself right to at least uh stand as a backup that was the initial plan but in the long run I started developing more interesting growing the business because I also need to stand as a brand…R8	…okay I have a lot of energy and when I started out with the nine to five I would sit at my desk literally do everything I'm asked to do and will try to generate more work to do and still get done with it and still have so much idle time, I'm someone who wants to give a hundred per cent of myself to anything I'm doing so while I was working for my bosses I didn't feel right to also do things on the side…R3 ……and I like the fact that my time is mine I decide how I do it and I decide what I do when I do which is what only an enterprise can do…. R7

(continued)

Table 4.2b (continued)

Over-arching theme	Second-order codes	Sample quotes (Male)	Sample quotes (Female)
	Regaining excitement/ satisfaction in one's work	basically, to be employed to find satisfaction in the workplace…R4	…okay my initial motivation I would say, I have always had a desire to provide better housing for the less privileged right, I've always had that desire to because I don't feel that because you cannot afford a certain amount of money you should not be able to live in a comfortable environment at least averagely so that has always been my desire since I was quite young …R2
	Identifying a gap in the market	… and then being from the Northern part of Nigeria, I saw how food was scarce and the need to cultivate homegrown food, without using sophisticated manure…R4	…. those yeah okay I mean for me I see an opportunity I'm thinking what I can do here right and how can I take advantage…. R5 I found out I was basically cooking for almost all my friend's events so I could as well be paid while doing the job. I was working for free had I actually was working in an office and doing that part-time when they have events, I cook I pack I save…. R10

The issue of job insecurity is an issue that is prevalent in the Nigerian economy irrespective of gender. However, the findings from the interview results reveal that mostly women entrepreneurs were affected by the issue of insecurity in employment. This suggests that there are more reasons specific to the way the feminine gender is constructed that make the issue of job insecurity specific to women. This is consistent with prior studies (including Devine, 1994; Winn, 2004) that revealed that due to a continuing lack of progress within the workplace, women may be lured into entrepreneurship. Similarly, about half of the women including respondent R2 identified that the presence of a 'glass ceiling' hindering their career development in an employee's role was another factor that pushed them into entrepreneurship—mostly as a backup plan.

Our findings showed that female entrepreneurs are also motivated by the need to gain greater autonomy (pull factors). In that regard, R3 laments:

> ….okay I have a lot of energy and when I started out with the nine to five I would sit at my desk literally do everything I'm asked to do and will try to generate more work to do and still get done with it and still have so much idle time, I'm someone who wants to give a hundred per cent of myself to anything I'm doing so while I was working for my bosses I didn't feel right to also do things on the side…

The above comment shows a need for achievement by the female entrepreneur, a trait uncommon in the general literature. For instance, women's interest in achievement defies the existing assumption that women are generally reserved, unambitious and unenterprising. (Kandeland Massey, 2002; Shen, 2019).

The findings also revealed that some women, including respondent R7, were motivated into starting an enterprise because of the flexibility entrepreneurship offers. This is mainly because women are often more likely to be faced with the need to juggle together family and work responsibilities, thereby needing total autonomy to be able to manage both together (Fierrman, 1990; Zellner, 1994). According to Respondent R7:

> ......and I like the fact that my time is mine I decide how I do it and I decide what I do when I do which is what only an enterprise can do...

The comment made by R7 aligns with the conclusions made by Konrad and Langton (1991) and Morris et al. (1995) who posit that family issues and responsibility can influence the career choices of women because it is important to them. Family-related factors such as family policies and family obligations (DeMartino & Barbato 2003; Dean et al., 2019), domestic commitments (Greenfield & Marlow, 2002; Nayak 1992) and the need for work-family balance (Kirkwood & Tootell, 2008; Onoshakpor et al., 2023b) have been found to be important for the female entrepreneur. These factors though labelled as push factors, according to Verheul et al. (2006), are important entrepreneurship motivation factors irrespective of gender.

Other female respondents claimed to have started their businesses because they identified a gap in the market (pull factors). For example, R5 and R10 commented respectively.

> ... okay I mean for me I see an opportunity and I'm thinking what can I do here right and how can I take advantage;
> .... I found out I was basically cooking for almost all my friend's events so I could as well be paid while doing the job.

These commentaries by R5 and R10 can be categorised as 'pull factor'. Furthermore, contrary to prior studies (Kandeland Massey, 2002; Shen, 2019) that indicate that only male individuals have the ability to identify business opportunities in the market, this research shows that a female entrepreneur possesses the opportunistic tendency that a typical male entrepreneur possesses. Besides, our findings disagree with extant literature on the indications that women are mainly pushed into entrepreneurship; and as such set up businesses mostly in the service (Kuratko & Hodgetts, 1995).

Factors Motivating Male Entrepreneurs in Nigeria

Our findings revealed that respondents in this study were motivated by a complex system of interacting factors that included both push and pull factors (*See* Table 4.2a and 4.2b). Male respondents were majorly motivated by the idea of being self-employed. This is supported by prior literature where entrepreneurship is often described as a male domain (Ahl, 2006; Holmquist & Sundin, 1989; Ljunggren & Alsos, 2001; Verheul et al., 2012). In that regard, respondent R4 and R9 stated respectively that:

> ...a long-time dream from when I was 12 years old, my mother was a trader, seeing what she does and assisting her in what she does make me what to do this.... it birthed in me such passion to want to do this... R4; ...entrepreneurship is something that runs in my blood you know all my life that's what I've been wanting to be- to run my business because while I was growing up you know I was sewing, I was a tailor you know and I grew the business to a point where I was sewing clothes and taking them to the UK to sell....R9.

This indicates that men might consider that entrepreneurship is a sector mainly for men. Besides, men are mostly introduced to the business world early in their lifetime. Parents in the developing economy region will normally introduce the family business to their male children because they believe the male child is more superior to the female child and he can handle the business better than the female child. On the contrary, a female child is expected to get married and will change her surname in the process. Women are often not introduced to the family business because in an instance where the business becomes successful, the goodwill and accolades will be transferred to the husband and his family; meaning the wealth and the glory will be transferred to the wife's family. Thus, a family will not introduce their female children to business because they fear that the business might be transferred to the spouse's family. Rather, a male child will keep the business within the immediate family.

Male respondents are also motivated by other factors including non-pecuniary and internal motivations. For instance R1 explained:

> … … so one of the reasons that made me, you know try to choose this part was to create an opportunity for people… … you know just to take a couple of people off the streets by giving them you know jobs and opportunities to make ends meet …R1.

This is new especially as the present literature mainly posit that non-pecuniary motivators are mainly linked to women entrepreneurs only (see for instance: Manolova et al., 2012; Christopher Weber & Geneste, 2014). Also, Dawson and Henley (2012) posit that social entrepreneurs and/or entrepreneurs who provide goods and services in the environmental/sustainability industry are primarily motivated by non-pecuniary factors, this research shows otherwise that R1 operates in the real estate sector and belongs to the male gender, states pecuniary reasons as his motivating factor though secondary to financial motivation.

4.5 Discussion and Conclusion

This chapter investigated what motivates people to start a business in a developing economy and whether these motivational factors for women differ from their male counterparts. Doing this will enable policymakers to better understand how to inspire individuals to become entrepreneurs, especially in a developing economy context where governments continue to struggle with reducing the significant proportion of unemployment, poverty and contributing towards achieving sustainable development in sub-Saharan Africa.

The findings indicate that women and men are mostly motivated into entrepreneurship by both pull and push factors. This is contrary to some existing studies that suggested that the push and pull factors motivate individuals separately and individually (Brünjes & Diez, 2013; Segal et al., 2005; Zgheib, 2018). In the developing economy, individuals are motivated by a mixture of both pull and push factors. Indeed, all contexts will have both pull and push factors operating within them, although either of the categories of motivator will assume a dominant role (Carsrud & Brannback, 2011; Dawson & Henley, 2012). In that regard, women are both pulled and pushed into entrepreneurship—but mostly pulled into entrepreneurship— in the developing country region. This is contrary to prior studies that suggest that women are mostly pushed into entrepreneurship because of the challenges they often encounter within the developing economy. Indeed, women are pushed into entrepreneurship, but they mostly make their career choice based on the sector where opportunities lie and abounds—pull factors. Besides, women are less pushed into entrepreneurship because they are less likely to be breadwinners of their families. For the men, they seem to be equally pushed and pulled into entrepreneurship. However, men are more likely to be pushed into entrepreneurship because they often experience a higher familial pressure in their role as heads and providers for their families. This explains why men experience more push factors than their women counterparts.

In conclusion, this study contributed to the literature on entrepreneurship. It investigated the factors motivating women and men into entrepreneurship. In addition, the study also highlighted how these factors vary based on the gender of the entrepreneur. Besides, the study explained the underlying issue behind the observed differences between the factors motivating women and men entrepreneurs. Thus, we conclude that although women and men in the developing economy encounter push and pull motivators, yet the degree to which they experience both categories of motivators differs. This difference is largely because women are groomed to provide support for their spouses; thus, they often experience less pressure to meet the need of their families and demand from the home front. On the other hand, men are primarily responsible for financing their families, and thus are more likely to experience more of the push motivators than the pull motivators. The implication of this is that women are different from their male counterparts. As such, we recommend that policymakers should focus on developing support mechanisms that are gender-specific rather than generic. By doing that, governments are more likely to develop policy mechanisms that can have a more effective impact on women and men entrepreneurs in the developing economies. For future studies, we recommend that researchers should consider a comparative study of motivators in other developing economies. Future studies should also consider whether the findings of this study will differ for women who are the breadwinners of their homes. Such studies will further broaden the perspective of this chapter.

References

Adom, K., Asare-Yeboa, T., Quaye, M., & Ampomah, A. O. (2018). A critical assessment of work and family life of female entrepreneurs in Sub-Saharan Africa: Some fresh evidence from Ghana. *Journal of Small Business and Enterprise Development, 25*(3), 405–427.

Ahl, H. (2006). Why research on women entrepreneurs needs new directions. *Entrepreneurship Theory and Practice, 30*(5), 595–621.

Ajayi, B. (2016). The impact of entrepreneurial orientation and networking capabilities on the export performance of Nigerian agricultural SMEs. *Journal of Entrepreneurship and Innovation in Emerging Economies, 2*(1), 1–23.

Ama, N., Mangadi, T., & K. and A. Ama, H. (2014). Exploring the challenges facing women entrepreneurs in informal cross-border trade in Botswana. *Gender in Management: An International Journal, 29*(8), 505–522.

Amit, R., & Muller, E. (1995). "Push" and "pull" entrepreneurship. *Journal of Small Business & Entrepreneurship, 12*(4), 64–80.

Anim-Somuah, H., Henson, S., Humphrey, J., & Robinson, E. (2013). *Strengthening agri-food value chains for nutrition: mapping value chains for nutrient-dense foods in ghana* (No. Evidence Report; 2). Institute of Development Studies (IDS).

Christopher Weber, P., & Geneste, L. (2014). Exploring gender-related perceptions of SME success. *International Journal of Gender and Entrepreneurship, 6*(1), 15–27.

de Beauvoir, S. (1953). *Must we bum De Sude?* Nevill.

Biever, J. L., Bobele, M., & North, M. (1998). Therapy with intercultural couples: A postmodern approach. *Counselling Psychology Quarterly, 11*(2), 181–188.

Braches, B., & Elliott, C. (2017). Articulating the entrepreneurship career: A study of German women entrepreneurs. *International Small Business Journal, 35*(5), 535–557.

Bruni, A., Gherardi, S., & Poggio, B. (2004). Entrepreneur-mentality, gender & the study of women entrepreneurs. *Journal of Organizational Change Management, 17*(3), 256–268.

Brünjes, J., & Diez, J. R. (2013). 'Recession push'and 'prosperity pull'entrepreneurship in a rural developing context. *Entrepreneurship & Regional Development, 25*(3–4), 251–271.

Brush, C., & Cooper, S. (2012). Female entrepreneurship and economic development: An international perspective. *Entrepreneurship & Regional Development, 24*(1–2), 1–6.

Brush, C. G. (1992). Research on women business owners: Past trends, a new perspective and future directions. *Entrepreneurship Theory and Practice, 16*(4), 5–30.

Burr, V. (1995). *An Introduction to Social Constructionism.* Routledge.

Carsrud, A., & Brännback, M. (2011). Entrepreneurial motivations: What do we still need to know? *Journal of Small Business Management, 49*(1), 9–26.

Chea, A. C. (2008). Entrepreneurial venture creation: The application of pattern identification theory to the entrepreneurial opportunity-identification process. *International Journal of Business and Management, 3*(2), 37–53.

Currie, J., & Goodman, J. (2020). Parental socioeconomic status, child health, and human capital. In *The economics of education* (pp. 239–248). Academic Press.

Damilola, O., Deborah, I., Oyedele, O., & Kehinde, A. A. (2020). Global pandemic and business performance. *International Journal of Research in Business and Social Science* (2147–4478), 9(6), 01–11. https://doi.org/10.20525/ijrbs.v9i6.906

Dawson, C., & Henley, A. (2012). "Push" versus "pull" entrepreneurship: an ambiguous distinction? *International Journal of Entrepreneurial Behavior & Research, 18*(6), 697–719.

Dean, H., Larsen, G., Ford, J., & Akram, M. (2019). Female entrepreneurship and the metanarrative of economic growth: A critical review of underlying assumptions. *International Journal of Management Reviews, 21*(1), 24–49.

Demartino, R., & Barbato, R. (2003). Differences between women and men MBA entrepreneurs: Exploring family flexibility and wealth creation as career motivators. *Journal of Business Venturing, 18*(6), 815–832.

DeTienne, D. R., & Chandler, G. N. (2007). The role of gender in opportunity identification. *Entrepreneurship Theory and Practice, 31*(3), 365–386.

Devine, T. J. (1994). Characteristics of self-employed women in the United States. *Monthly Lab. Rev., 117*, 20.

Durojaye, E., & Owoeye, Y. (2017). Equally unequal or unequally equal: Adopting a substantive equality approach to gender discrimination in Nigeria. *International Journal of Discrimination and the Law, 17*(2), 70–85.

Ekoja, G., Agbaeze, E., Namah, E., & Ajoku, O. (2020). Female Entrepreneurship and Socioeconomic Development: From the Social Feminist Theory (SFT) Versus Theory of Need of Achievement (TNA) of Entrepreneurial Personality Trait and Intention Perspective. *International Journal of Management, 11*(9), 1296–1306.

Fierman, J. (1990). Why women still don't hit the top. *Fortune, 122*(3), 40–47.

Fischer, A. H. (1993). Sex differences in emotionality: Fact or stereotype? *Feminism & Psychology, 3*(3), 303–318.

Galbin, A. (2014). An introduction to social constructionism. *Social Research Reports, 6*(26), 82–92.

Garba, A. S. (2011). Stumbling block for women entrepreneurship in Nigeria: How risk attitude and lack of capital mitigates their need for business expansion. *European Journal of Economics, Finance and Administrative Sciences, 36*, 38–49.

GEM, (2014). Global Report [online]. *Global Entrepreneurship Monitor*. http://www.babson.edu/Academics/centers/blank-center/globalresearch/gem/Documents/GEM%202014%20Global%20Report.pdf

GEM, (2015). *Special Report Women's Entrepreneurship [online]. GEM*. http://www.babson.edu/Academics/centers/blank-center/globalresearch/gem/Documents/GEM%202015%20Womens%20Report.pdf

GEM, (2017). *Women's Entrepreneurship Report [online]. GEM*. https://www.gemconsortium.org/report/gem-20162017-womens-entrepreneurship-report

Gergen, K. J. (2004). The Sage encyclopedia of social science research methods. *Methods, 1*, 183–185.

Gergen, K. J., & Gergen, M. (2012). Therapeutic communication from a constructionist standpoint. *Discursive perspectives in therapeutic practice*, pp. 65–82.

Glancey, K., Greig, M., & Pettigrew, M. (1998). Entrepreneurial dynamics in small business service firms. *International Journal of Entrepreneurial Behavior & Research, 4*(3), 249–268.

Glaser, B. G. (1978). *Theoretical sensitivity*. The Sociology Press.

Global Entrepreneurship Monitor GEM (2012). 2012 Global Survey Report: GEM.

Greenfield, S., & Nayak, A. (1992). The management information needs of very small businesses: Gender differences. *Small businesses and small business development-A practical approach, 2.*

Hamilton, P. (2006). *Visual research methods*. Sage.

Henry, C., Foss, L., Fayolle, A., Walker, E., & Duffy, S. (2015). Entrepreneurial leadership and gender: Exploring theory and practice in global contexts. *Journal of Small Business Management, 53*(3), 581–586.

Hesse-Biber, S. N. (2007). *The cult of thinness*. Oxford University Press.

Hesse-Biber, S, N., & Piatelli, D. (2007). Truth and truths in feminist knowledge production. In Hesse-Biber (Ed.), *Handbook of feminist research: Theory and praxis* (469–491). Sage.

Hisrich, R., & Brush, C. (1984). The woman entrepreneur: Management skills and business problems. *University of Illinois at Urbana-Champaign's Academy for Entrepreneurial Leadership Historical Research Reference in Entrepreneurship.*

Holmquist, C., & Sundin, E. (1989). The growth of women's entrepreneurship: Push or pull factors, *EIASM Conference on Small Business, University of Durham Business School* 1989.

Huggins, R., Thompson, P., & Obschonka, M. (2018). Human behaviour and economic growth: A psychocultural perspective on local and regional development. *Environment and Planning a: Economy and Space, 50*(6), 1269–1289.

Hurley, A. E. (1999). Incorporating feminist theories into sociological theories of entrepreneurship. *Women in Management Review, 14*(2), 54–62.

IFC, (2014). *Women-Owned SNEs: A business opportunity for financial institutions [online]*. International Finance Corporation. http//www.ifc.org

Igwe, P. A., Amaugo, A. N., Ogundana, O. M., Martin, O., & Egere, J. A. A. (2018). Factors Affecting the Investment Climate, SMEs Productivity and Entrepreneurship in Nigeria. *European Journal of Sustainable Development, 7*(1), 182–200.

Igwe, P. A., Odunukan, K., Rahman, M., Rugara, D. G., & Ochinanwata, C. (2020). How entrepreneurship ecosystem influences the development of frugal innovation and informal entrepreneurship. *Thunderbird International Business Review, 62*(5), 475–488.

Ihugba, O. A., Bankong, B., & Ebomuche, N. C. (2013). The impact of Nigeria microfinance banks on poverty reduction: Imo state experience. *Mediterranean Journal of Social Sciences, 4*(16), 97–114.

Iyiola, O., & Azuh, D. E. (2014). Women entrepreneurs as small-medium enterprise (SME) operators and their roles in socio-economic development in Ota, Nigeria. *International Journal of Economics, Business and Finance, 2*(1), 1–10.

Izugbara, C. O. (2005). The socio-cultural context of adolescents' notions of sex and sexuality in rural south-eastern Nigeria. *Sexualities, 8*(5), 600–617.

Jennings, J. E., & McDougald, M. S. (2007). Work-family interface experiences and coping strategies: Implications for entrepreneurship research and practice. *Academy of Management Review, 32*(3), 747–760.

Johnsen, G. J. & McMahon, R. G. (2005). Owner-manager gender, financial performance and business growth amongst SMEs from Australia's business longitudinal survey. *International Small Business Journal, 23*(2), 115–142.

Kandel, W., & Massey, D. S. (2002). The culture of Mexican migration: A theoretical and empirical analysis. *Social Forces, 80*(3), 981–1004.

Kirkwood, J. (2009). Motivational factors in a push-pull theory of entrepreneurship. *Gender in Management: An International Journal, 24*(5), 346–364.

Kirkwood, J., & Tootell, B. (2008). Is entrepreneurship the answer to achieving work–family balance? *Journal of Management & Organization, 14*(3), 285–302.

Konrad, A. M., & Langton, N. (1991). Sex differences in job preferences, workplace segregation, and compensating earning differentials: The case of Stanford MBA's. *Academy of Management Proceedings* 1991. *Academy of Management Briarcliff Manor, NY, 10510*, 368–372.

Korsgaard, S. (2007). *Social constructionism: And why it should feature in entrepreneurship theory.* CORE, Department of Management Aarhus School of Business, Denmark.

Kuratko, D. F., & Hodgetts, R. M. (1995). *Entrepreneurship: A contemporary approach.* Dryden Press.

Ljunggren, E., & Alsos, G. A. (2001). '*Media expressions of entrepreneurs: Frequency, content and appearance of male and female entrepreneurs*', paper presented at the Babson College-Kauffman Foundation Entrepreneurship Research Conference, Jönköping, June

Lorber, J., & Farrell, A. (1991). *The social construction of gender.* Sage Newbury Park.

Makama, G. A. (2013). Patriarchy and gender inequality in Nigeria: The way forward. *European Scientific Journal, 9*(17), 115–144.

Manolova, T. S., Brush, C. G., Edelman, L. F. & Shaver, K. G. (2012). One size does not fit all: Entrepreneurial expectancies and growth intentions of

US women and men nascent entrepreneurs. *Entrepreneurship & Regional Development, 24*(1–2), 7–27.

Manolova, T. S., Eunni, R. V., & Gyoshev, B. S. (2008). Institutional environments for entrepreneurship: Evidence from emerging economies in Eastern Europe. *Entrepreneurship Theory and Practice, 32*(1), 203–218.

Marlow, S. (2002). Self-employed women: A part of or apart from feminist theory? *International Journal of Entrepreneurship and Innovation, 2*(2), 83–91.

Marlow, S., & Martinez Dy, A. (2018). Annual review article: Is it time to rethink the gender agenda in entrepreneurship research? *International Small Business Journal, 36*(1), 3–22.

Mason, M. (2010, August). Sample size and saturation in PhD studies using qualitative interviews. In *Forum qualitative Sozialforschung/Forum: Qualitative social research, 11*(3).

Mcclelland, E., Swail, J., Bell, J., & Ibbotson, P. (2005). Following the pathway of female entrepreneurs: A six-country investigation. *International Journal of Entrepreneurial Behavior & Research, 11*(2), 84–107.

Miller, R. D. (2022). *Breadwinner Mothers of School-Aged Children During COVID-19: An Interpretative Phenomenological Analysis* (Doctoral dissertation, University of Missouri-Saint Louis).

Misango, B., & Ongiti, K. (2013). Do women entrepreneurs play a role in reducing poverty? A case in Kenya. *International Review of Management & Business Research, 2*(1), 87.

Morris, M. H., Neumeyer, X., & Kuratko, D. F. (2015). A portfolio perspective on entrepreneurship and economic development. *Small Business Economics, 45*(4), 713–728.

National Bureau of Statistics (2014). "Statistical report on women and men in Nigeria".

Nnabugwu F. (2015). (Business News). https://www.vanguardngr.com/2021/05. [30] 1.

OAKLEY, Ann (1972). *Sex gender and society*. New York Harper and Row, Inc.

Ogundana, O. (2020). *Factors influencing the business growth of women-owned sewing businesses (WOSBs) in Lagos-State, Nigeria: A gender-aware growth framework*. Nottingham Trent University (United Kingdom).

Ogundana, O. (2022). Obstacles facing women-owned enterprises: A case for Sub-Sahara African women. *World Review of Entrepreneurship, Management and Sustainable Development, 18*(5–6), 529–544.

Ogundana, O., Galanakis, K., Simba, A., & Oxborrow, L. (2018). *Women-owned sewing businesses in Lagos-State, Nigeria: A study of the factors influencing their business growth.* In BAM 2018 Conference proceedings. London: British Academy of Management. https://irep.ntu.ac.uk/id/eprint/38368/1/1237540_Ogundana.pdf

Ogundana, O., Galanakis, K., Simba, A., & Oxborrow, L. (2022a). Growth perception amongst women entrepreneurs: An emerging economy perspective. *International Journal of Entrepreneurship and Small Business, 47*(1), 109–127.

Ogundana, O., Simba, A., Dana, L. P., & Liguori, E. (2022b). A growth model for understanding female-owned enterprises. *Journal of the International Council for Small Business*, pp.1–10.

Okafor Amuche, C. (2015). Gender inequality in Nigeria. *Journal of Research in Arts and Social Sciences, 4*(1), 69–80.

Okoli, I. (2008). The role of business education in promoting gender equality and women empowerment. *Association of Business Educators of Nigeria Book of Readings, 1*(8), 178–183.

Olukayode, R., & Somoye, C. (2013). The impact of finance on entrepreneurship growth in Nigeria: A cointegration framework, ACRN.

Omodara, D., Ikhile, D., Ogundana, O., & Akin-Akinyosoye, K. (2020). Global pandemic and business performance: Impacts and responses. *International Journal of Research in Business and Social Science, 9*(6), 1–11.

Onoshakpor, C., Cunningham, J., & Gammie, E. (2022). Female entrepreneurship in Nigeria and access to finance: A comparative study. In Proceedings of 36th British Academy of Management conference 2022 (BAM 2022): Reimagining business and management as a force for good, 31 August–2 September 2022, British Academy of Management [online]. https://www.bam.ac.uk/conference-proceedings.html

Onoshakpor, C., Cunningham, J., & Gammie, E. (2023a). Contextualizing female entrepreneurship and financial inclusion in Nigeria. In Harrison, C. and Omeihe, K.O. (eds.) Contextualising African studies: Challenges and the way forward. Bingley: Emerald, chapter 2, (pp.13–36). https://doi.org/10.1108/978-1-80455-338-120231002

Onoshakpor, C., James, I., Ibukun, T., & Irene, B. (2023b). Entrepreneurial motivation in the global south: Addressing gender marginalization. *International Journal of Entrepreneurship, 26*(6).

Orser, B. J., Elliott, C., & Leck, J. (2011). Feminist attributes and entrepreneurial identity. *Gender in Management: An International Journal, 26*(8), 561–589.

Otoo, M., Ibro, G., Fulton, J., & Lowenberg-Deboer, J. (2012). Micro-entrepreneurship in Niger: Factors affecting the success of women street food vendors. *Journal of African Business, 13*(1), 16–28.

Quagrainie, F. A., Adams, S., Kabalan, A. A. M., & Dankwa, A. D. (2021). Micro-entrepreneurship, sustainable development goal one and cultural expectations of Ghanaian women. *Journal of Entrepreneurship in Emerging Economies, 13*(1), 86–106.

Reynolds, P. D., Bygrave, W. D., Autio, E., Cox, L. W., & Hay, H. (2002). *Global entrepreneurship monitor, 2002 executive report*. Babson College, London Business School and Kauffman Foundation.

Risman, B. J. (2004). Gender as a social structure: Theory wrestling with activism. *Gender & Society, 18*(4), 429–450.

Schjoedt, L., & Shaver, K. G. (2007). Deciding on an entrepreneurial career: A test of the pull and push hypotheses using the panel study of entrepreneurial dynamics data. *Entrepreneurship Theory and Practice, 31*(5), 733–752.

Segal, G., Borgia, D., & Schoenfeld, J. (2005). The motivation to become an entrepreneur. *International Journal of Entrepreneurial Behavior & Research, 11*(1), 42–57.

Shen, Y. (2019). *Beyond tears and laughter: Gender, migration, and the service sector in China*. Springer.

Shinnar, R. S., & Young, C. A. (2008). Hispanic immigrant entrepreneurs in the Las Vegas metropolitan area: Motivations for entry into and outcomes of self-employment. *Journal of Small Business Management, 46*(2), 242–262.

Simba, A., Kalu, E. U., Onodugo, V., Okoyeuzu, C. R., & Ogundana, O. (2022). Women entrepreneurs in Nigeria. In M. Dabić, L.-P. Dana, D. Modestus Nziku and V. Ramadani, eds., *Women entrepreneurs in Sub-Saharan Africa: historical framework, ecosystem, and future perspectives for the region*. Springer. ISBN 9783030989651 (Forthcoming).

Solesvik, M. (2019). Entrepreneurial competencies and intentions: The role of higher education, *Forum Scientiae Oeconomia* , Wydawnictwo Naukowe Akademii WSB, pp. 9–23.

Solesvik, M., Iakovleva, T., & Trifilova, A. (2019). Motivation of female entrepreneurs: A cross-national study. *Journal of Small Business & Enterprise Development, 26*(5), 684–705.

Statista. (2022). *Early-stage entrepreneurial activity rate in the Americas by country 2021*. [online]. https://www.statista.com/statistics/315492/percentage-of-population-involved-in-business-start-ups-in-latin-america-and-caribbean/

Taylor, S. R., & Newcomer, J. D. (2005). Characteristics of women small business owners. *International Handbook of Women and Small Business Entrepreneurship, 17*, 31.

Thaddeus, E. (2012). Perspectives: Entrepreneurship development & growth of enterprises in Nigeria. *Entrepreneurial Practice Review, 2*(2), 31–35.

UNDESA. (2019). *World urbanization prospects: The 2018 revision (ST/ESA/SER.A/420)* [Google Scholar].

Van Der Zwan, P., Verheul, I., & Thurik, A. R. (2012). The entrepreneurial ladder, gender, and regional development. *Small Business Economics, 39*(3), 627–643.

Verheul, I., Stel, A. V., & Thurik, R. (2006). Explaining female and male entrepreneurship at the country level. *Entrepreneurship and Regional Development, 18*(2), 151–183.

Welter, F. (2011). Contextualizing entrepreneurship—conceptual challenges and ways forward. *Entrepreneurship Theory and Practice, 35*(1), 165–184.

West, C., & Zimmerman, D. (1987). Doing gender. *Gender & Society, 1*(2), 125–151.

West, C., & Zimmerman, D. (1991). Doing gender. In J. Lorber & S. A. Farrell (Eds.), *The social construction of gender* (pp. 13–37). Sage.

Winn, J. (2004). Entrepreneurship: Not an easy path to top management for women. *Women in Management Review, 19*(3), 143–153.

Yin, R. K. (2012).Case study methods.

Zellner, W. (1994, April 18). *Women Entrepreneurs, Business Week.*

Zgheib, P. (2018). Multi-level framework of push-pull entrepreneurship: Comparing American and Lebanese women. *International Journal of Entrepreneurial Behaviour and Research, 24*(3), 768–786.

5

Informality in Africa in Relation to Sustainable Development Goals 8 and 9: Framework for Innovation and Sustainable Industrialization

Muhammed Olawale Hakeem Amuda

5.1 Introduction

The centrepoint of United Nations' SDGs 8 and 9 resolves around making life better for mankind irrespective of gender and social status to build a more equitable and inclusive world order. In achieving this objective, SDG 8 is concerned with promoting full and productive employment through decent work for all to generate economic growth. SDG 9 on the other hand, focuses on building resilient infrastructure to promote inclusive and sustainable industrialization anchored on innovation. Arguably the accomplishment of SDG 8 rests on the success of SDG 9. A probe into the performance of countries in the implementation and milestones in meeting the SDGs suggests that African countries have not achieved much probably, save for South Africa and Egypt (www.sdg.iisd.org, 2020). It is therefore not surprising that the poverty rate is

---

M. O. H. Amuda (✉)
Department of Metallurgical and Materials Engineering, University of Lagos, Lagos, Nigeria
e-mail: mamuda@unilag.edu.ng

A. S. Ibidunni et al. (eds.), *Innovation, Entrepreneurship and the Informal Economy in Sub–Saharan Africa*, Sustainable Development Goals Series,
https://doi.org/10.1007/978-3-031-46293-1_5

increasing in this part of the world, particularly in Nigeria which is the most populous country on the continent.

Though the United Nation's 17 SDGs provide the blueprint to accomplish a better and more sustainable future for all people and the world, the African context is more complex because of the absence of a clear strategy for integrating both the formal and informal sectors towards achieving the objectives of the SDGs. Indeed, it appears that except SDG 9 is specifically achieved, the possibility of accomplishing all other SDGs remains a mirage, particularly among African countries. It then presupposes that building a resilient infrastructure to drive sustainable and inclusive industrialization anchored on innovation provides the surest route to promoting a better and more sustainable future for the people of Africa and the world. This strategy would not only engender inclusive and sustainable economic growth but facilitate the realization of the goal of full and productive employment, and decent work for all resulting in the accomplishment of other SDGs, particularly that relating to good health and wellbeing (SDG3).

At an event held at the United Nations Headquarters in 2015 just after the ratification of the SDGs by member states, participants identified the industrialization of Africa as a way to accomplish the broad objectives of the SDGs (www.unido.org/who-we-are/unido-and-sdgs/africa-and-sdg-9, 2015). Yet, the communiqué at the end of the event fell short of elucidating a clear roadmap for Africa's industrialization, other than that Africa must embark on a skills revolution programme, particularly in the areas of science, technology, engineering and mathematics (STEM). So, while the United Nations aptly recognize the industrialization of Africa as a way to accomplish the broad objectives of the SDGs, it is clear that the continent lacks the innovation capacity and infrastructure to transit from its predominantly informal economy to a formal economy. It is almost seven years after the summit, it is still not clear what paradigm African countries would adopt to accelerate industrialization in Africa.

The African economic space is characterized by a composite formal–informal system across almost every sector and activity (Peter, 2021). Every industrial activity in Africa from infrastructure, manufacturing, construction and service delivery presents this composite identity. Available data suggest that the informal sector in Africa employs about 66% of Africa's non-agricultural labour force and contributes nearly 35% of continental Gross Domestic Products (GDP) (Medina et al., 2017); with the formal sector accounting for the balance of 34%. Even at that, service requirements in the formal sectors are often outsourced to Foreign Service providers denying the informal sector the opportunity to improve capacity and drive economic growth. This statistic provides insight that the strategy for accomplishing SDG 9 to accelerate industrialization in the African continent must involve a deliberate framework to incorporate the 66% non-agricultural labour force in the informal sector into the industrialization process based on innovation. Incidentally, a higher proportion of this informal sector activities is concentrated outside the city centres which has fueled the urban–rural migration dichotomy (Onwe, 2013). Thus, an industrialization architecture that accommodates this sector in its economic framework may offer a route to emplace inclusive and sustainable full employment towards accelerating economic growth. Such a framework may additionally assist greatly in addressing urban–rural migration since urban migration is mainly pushed by the pursuit of economic opportunity in the city centre with its attendant strain on city infrastructure and facilities.

Although there exists an avalanche of literature (Esaku, 2021; Etim & Daramola, 2020; Khuong et al, 2021) that have made attempts to characterize the features of informality in relation to economic activities in sub-Saharan African countries, none of these literatures relates their interventions to the nexus between informality and the accomplishment of SDGs 8 and 9. Arising from this inadequacy, therefore, this paper sought to deconstruct the characteristics of informality in Africa in relation to economic activities in the continent as it relates to the accomplishment of SDGs 8 and 9.

5.2 Informality in African Industrialization and Economy: Character and Spread

The concept of informality in economic activities and enterprise across the African continent comes with complex characteristics as different countries present different scenarios and situational perspectives. Incidentally, the term "the informal sector" or "informality" was coined by Hart (1973) and the International Labour Organization (ILO) in 1973 to describe the range of employment and income-generating activities occurring outside of formal businesses that were very evident in African countries then which still subsists till today some 48 years after. Hart and the ILO elucidated informal economy in terms of a dualist model of income opportunities among the urban labour force by making a distinction between wage employment and self-employment. The concept of informality was therefore applied to those in self-employment. Additional studies conducted by ILO later in 1973 on the dynamic nature of the informal sectors related informality to poverty implying that people in self-employment exhibited a higher tendency to be poor. Also, Becker (2004) defines the informal sector as the unregulated, non-formal portion of the market economy that produces goods and services for sale or for other forms of remuneration. Thus, the term informal economy refers to all economic activities by workers and economic units that are not covered or are insufficiently covered by formal arrangements. Chen et al. (2005) in their study established that workers in informal employment earned less, had more unstable incomes, lacked access to basic public services and protection and were exposed to higher risks of poverty relative to those in formal employment.

The concept of informality in economic activity equally encompasses production and services employment relationships that are not governed by formal economic regulations and/or basic legal and social protections (ILO, 2002). More often than not, this is the representative nature and character of economic activities in developing countries, particularly in sub-Saharan Africa. In some countries such as Kenya and Senegal (Bocquier, 2005; Federation of Kenyan Employers, 2021; Mbaye et al., 2020) however, the informal and formal sectors intermix such that it may be difficult to properly make a distinction between the two sectors. Labour Statisticians recognized this challenge and at their 1993 15th International Conference of Labour Statisticians (ICLS) adopted a framework for defining the informal sector which could apply across countries. The following criteria were adopted for defining informal sectors (Hussmanns & du Jeu, 2002):

a. "Legal organization of the enterprise. Informal enterprises are private unincorporated enterprises for which no consistent set of accounts are available that would allow the financial activities of the enterprises to be separated from those of the owners. In most cases, informal enterprises are owned and operated by household members, although informal partnerships and cooperatives, whose ownership structures may extend across households, are also included.
b. Market production. A portion of the goods or services produced by the informal enterprise must be sold or bartered in market transactions. Household activities that produce exclusively non-market goods or services do not constitute informal enterprises.
c. Size and/or registration. Informal enterprises are frequently defined in terms of the number of paid employees—for example, if the number of employees in the enterprises falls below a given threshold as determined by national regulators. Alternatively, informal enterprises may be defined in terms of their registration status with respect to national regulatory frameworks and legislation.
d. In 2003, the 17th ICLS expanded the criteria to include the concept of "employment in the informal sector" with a jobs-based concept of "informal employment." The new framework broadens the definition of informality by including workers in informal employment relationships, not only workers in informal enterprises. The ICLS framework for defining informal employment includes (Hussmanns, 2004):

    - Informal own-account workers, employers, and members of producer cooperatives. These categories of workers or employers are engaged in informal employment if the enterprise in which they work or operate is informal. This category of informal employment corresponds to the definition of employment in the informal sector.

- Contributing family workers. All contributing family workers are classified as being engaged in informal employment since this form of employment is rarely regulated by legal and social protections.
- Paid employees in informal jobs. Employees are considered to work in informal jobs if those jobs lack enforceable contracts, social protections and/or if the employment relationship is not subject to national labour regulation or taxation.
- Own-account workers producing goods for own use. Own account workers producing goods for their (or their households') own final use are defined as working informally if they are also considered to be employed.

It must, however, be reiterated that in most cases, the size criterion and/or the registration criterion are the primary indicators used to identify informal enterprises."

Invariably within the sub-Sahara African space, the informal sector is characterized by economic activities being undertaken outside a regulated framework or being employed in a business enterprise that operates outside a regulated framework in terms of legal and social protections for the employees. Incidentally, this sector accounts for more than two-thirds of employment and economic activities in Africa. The ILO (1973) characterizes the informal sector in the African continent as exhibiting the following features:

i. The non-agricultural employment in the informal economy represents 66% of total employment in sub-Saharan Africa and 52% in North Africa. Nearly eight out of ten employed persons in sub-Saharan Africa are in vulnerable forms of employment. Accordingly, the vulnerable employment rate—the share of own-account workers and unpaid family workers in total employment—was estimated at 76.6% in 2014, significantly higher than the global average of 45.3%. This is a clear indication that the informal sector in Africa is not anything near accomplishing SDG 8 for a decent work environment and full employment.
ii. The share of women in informal employment in non-agricultural activities outnumbers that of men. In sub-Saharan Africa, 74%

of women's employment (non-agricultural) is informal, in contrast with 61% for men. Female vulnerable employment (typically unpaid family work) was also considerably higher than the rate for males, at 84.3% compared with 70.1% for males in 2014 in Sub-Saharan Africa. Statistics such as this indicate that the informal sector in Africa though employs a greater number of women, but the nature of employment is sub-optimal and cannot guarantee the accomplishment of SDG 8 which is focused on inclusive and sustainable economic growth, full and productive employment and decent work for all.

iii. Informal employment is the standard condition among most youths in Sub-Saharan Africa where at least eight in ten young workers fall into the category of informal employment. The feminization of poverty, combined with discrimination by gender, age, ethnicity or disability, also means that the most vulnerable and marginalized groups tend to end up in the informal economy and this is especially the case for women and young people, who have no other choice than the informal economy for their survival and livelihood. This is another impediment to inclusive economic growth and full employment.

iv. Self-employment constitutes a greater share of informal employment (non-agriculture) than wage employment. It accounts for as much as 53% of non-agricultural employment in sub-Saharan Africa and 31% in North Africa.

Informality in economic activities is of varying degrees depending on the nature of the economic environment such that informal activities do transit to formal status. Such transition provides the only sure way to ensure inclusive full-employment and sustainable economic growth that can guarantee decent wellbeing. Becker (2004) developed a matrix to illustrate the gradual transition from informal sector to formal status. The degree of informality of informal economic activities is shown in Table 5.1.

The structure of economic activities in five selected sub-Saharan African countries is presented in Table 5.2. The data in the table provides a glimpse into the character of the economies of the selected countries.

Table 5.1 Degree of informality in business enterprises adapted from Onwe (2013)

	Informal Sector ⟶		Formal Sector
	Subsistence Enterprises	*Unofficial Enterprises*	*Official Enterprises*
Degree of Informality	100%	High proportion of sales undeclared and workers not registered	Some proportion of sales undeclared and workers unregistered.May use outside the official purview (e.g., internet to deliver software)
Type of Activity	Single street traders, cottage/micro-enterprises,subsistence farmers	Small manufacturers, service providers, distributors, contractors	Small and medium manufacturers, service providers, software firms
Technology	Labour intensive	Mostly labour intensive	Knowledge and capital Intensive
Owner Profile	Poor, low education, lowlevel of Skills	Poor and non-poor, well educated, high level of Skills	Non-poor, highly educated, sophisticated level of Skills
Markets	Low barriers to entry, highly competitive, high product homogeneity	Low barriers to entry, highly competitive, some Product differentiation	Significant barriers to entry, established market/product niche
Finance Needs	Working capital	Working capital, some investment capital, supplier credit	Investment capital and working capital, lettersof credit, supplier credit
Other Needs	Personal insurance, socialProtection	Personal and perhaps business insurance	Personal and business insurance, business development services
Least dynamic Completely informal ⟶			**Highly dynamic Partially formal**

The table reveals that formal employment represents a small fraction of total employment in most sub-Saharan African countries, except South Africa because of its level of economic development. Formal economic activities in most sub-Saharan African countries are less than 20% of all employment data in each specific country. The estimate is 13.6% in Kenya, 8.7% in Ghana, 10.9% in Mali and 6.8% in Madagascar while it is about 62% in South Africa. The table shows that informal self-employment is the most single significant source of economic activities in many sub-Saharan African countries. Curiously, these countries with predominant informal economic sectors account for greater poor economic conditions in the African continent.

Table 5.2 Structure of employment in five African countries: Distribution of formal and informal sectors (Heintz &Valodia, 2008)

Economic Sector	Kenya (2005)	Ghana (1998/99)	Mali (2004)	Madagascar (2005)	South Africa (2004)
Formal Employment (%)					
Formal, private wage employment	6.9	1.0	n/a	2.5	40.8
Formal, public wage employment	5.4	4.1	n/a	2.7	16.5
Total formal wage employment	12.3	5.1	5.8	5.2	57.3
Formal, self-employment	1.3	3.6	5.1	1.6	4.2
Informal Employment (%)					
Informal wage employment	18.0	9.3	11.0	9.3	22.8
Informal self-employment	64.8	81.6	78.1	83.8	14.4
Other/undeclared	3.6%	0.4	0.0	0.0	1.3
TOTAL	100	100	100	100	100
...of which... (%)					
Agricultural wage employment	n/a	1.2	0.9	3.3	10.6
Agricultural self-employment	50.0	52.3	41.2	77.2	4.7

Further disaggregation of economic activities in the five selected countries by gender using the same structural forms adopted in Table 5.2 indicates that in all the five countries, formal wage employment accounts for a larger share of men's employment than women's employment whereas, in the informal sector, women's employment accounts for the larger share than men's employment (see Table 5.3). Some general conclusions can be drawn from Tables 5.2 and 5.3 that are indicative of the structure of economic activities in many sub-Saharan African countries and by extension other African countries recognizing that South Africa is an exemption in many areas. First, the two tables reveal that the informal sector accounts for a significantly larger share of total economic activities in many African countries than the formal sector. Second, women appear to disproportionately work in the informal sector and are more often in vulnerable forms of informal employment. Third, men tend to have greater access to wage employment—both formal and informal than women. This was the condition a decade and a half ago and recent data has not shown a dramatic change in this pattern.

The dominant activities in the informal sector in the three countries of Ghana, Kenya and Madagascar are summarized in Table 5.4. At any rate, the variety of activities associated with the informal economy is quite diverse cutting across construction, manufacturing, transportation, services and trade. The Nigerian situation is not expected to be significantly different from the scenario in Ghana for instance. Indeed, it appears that the informal sector in Nigeria is steadily growing in recent times.

There is a lot of heterogeneity in the character of the informal sector across different countries in the African continent. Yet, despite its providing employment and means of livelihood to more than 60% of the labour force operating in non-agriculture sector, the sector does not have the structural framework to promote sustainable and inclusive economic growth and guaranteed sustainable full employment and decent work for all.

5.3 Factors Driving Informality in Africa's Economy and Industrialization

The drivers of informality in the African continent are complex but related to some key factors prominent in African economies in the last few decades (Heintz & Valodia, 2008); particularly the lack of economic development and inconsistency in economic policies geared towards accelerating indigenization of the conversion of natural resources to drive economic prosperity. Economic and labour organizations such as the ILO and the Organization for Economic Cooperation and Developments (OECD) through several commissioned studies have identified some interrelated and at times overlapping factors driving the growth of the informal sector in the sub-Saharan African economy and industrialization. Some of these factors include:

Table 5.3 Distribution of men's and women's total employment by economic sector (Heintz & Valodia, 2008)

	Kenya		Ghana		Mali		Madagascar		South Africa	
	M	F	M	F	M	F	M	F	M	F
Formal Employment (%)										
Formal, private wage employment	8.1	2.6	1.4	0.3	n.a	n.a	4.3	3.4	44.1	36.9
Formal, public wage employment	5.5	3.1	6.5	2.0	5.5	5.4	3.2	1.6	14.4	18.3
Total formal wage employment	13.6	5.7	7.9	2.3	5.5	5.4	7.5	5.0	58.5	55.2
Formal, self-employment	1.3	1.0	3.5	3.6	7.1	2.2	4.7	8.5	5.1	3.1
Formal, agricultural	2.5	1.3	0.5	<0.1	0.5	0.1	0.3	0.1	4.9	2.1
Informal Employment (%)										
Informal wage employment	22.8	11.3	14.9	4.5	12.3	9.2	9.7	6.4	18.7	23.2
Informal self-employment	58.2	76.5	72.7	89.2	74.6	83.1	77.8	79.8	12.7	16.3
Of which ... (%)										
...informal own-account	34.7	47.4	61.6	66.4	n.a	n.a	53.8	12.6	8.9	14.0
...informal unpaid family	22.2	28.5	9.4	21.2	17.1	9.4	24.0	67.2	n.a	n.a
Informal employer	1.3	0.6	n.a	n.a	n.a	n.a	n.a	n.a	3.8	2.3
Others/ undeclared	1.6	4.2	0.5	0.4	0.0	0.0	4.1	0.2	0.1	0.1
TOTAL	100	100	100	100	100	100	100	100	100	100
Informal agricultural wage employment	8.3	3.7	2.3	0.3	1.0	0.1	3.2	2.9	3.2	2.1
Informal agricultural self-employment	45.3	63.8	55.7	49.2	41.2	49.6	76.3	78.1	2.7	3.4

Table 5.4 Most significant activities in non-agricultural informal sector (Heintz & Valodia, 2008)

Country	Employment Category	Dominant Activities
Ghana	Informal wage employee	Manufacturing, construction, fabrication, transportation, services
	Informal self-employment	Manufacturing, trade and services
Kenya	Informal wage employee	Trade, transportation, domestic work/laundries
	Informal self-employment	Trade, various services
Madagascar	Informal wage employee	Various services, construction, transportation
	Informal self-employment	Trade, various services

i. *Low economic growth and rapid urbanization:* sub-Saharan African countries have not been able to create employment opportunities to match the increasing population, particularly the upsurge in new entrants into the labour space. Many of these unengaged labour forces made recourse to the informal economy to generate incomes. Also, several studies have equally linked the growth in the urban labour force to a rapid increase in urbanization. Many of these workers living in urban slum areas around major cities (e.g., Makoko, Ilaje both in Lagos Mainland, Lagos, Nigeria) earn their livelihoods in the informal sector (Adeosun & Popogbe, 2021; Ajayi et al., 2019).

ii. *Globalization and redundancies:* The integration of African countries into global trading treaties such as the Free Trade Agreements world has seen manufacturing sectors in the continent undermined by cheaper imports (Onwuka & Udegbunam, 2019). The decline in textile manufacturing in many African countries due to cheaper clothing imports from Asia (Renne, 2019) is a classic example of this regard. Additionally, the structural adjustment programmes implemented by many African countries in the last few decades in which many African governments privatized state holdings in companies, as well as reduced public sector employment, forced many disengaged workers to embrace the informal economy for employment.

iii. *Institutional and legal barriers*: business licensing and registration procedures often fail to cater to the peculiarities of the informal sector. Such institutional and legal barriers make it burdensome for small-scale informal businesses to formalize their activities. In most cases, the costs of formalization exceed the benefits thereof such that workers in the informal sector who earn below the poverty threshold may find it difficult to operate formally.
iv. *Lack of government support and weak institution*: Absence of governmental support and incentives to grow the capacity of the informal sector economic activities and facilitate their transition to formal status. Policy initiatives, service provision, investment in infrastructure and access to the formal financial sector to support the informal sector are scarce. Also, African countries lack the benefit of strong institutions to provide training capacity and other support incentives to drive structural reforms for the informal sector to transit to formal status.
v. *Conflicts and social crisis*: In quite some African countries, economic activities are conducted in an environment characterized by a high level of violence and war resulting in ruined infrastructure and seriously disrupting the possibilities for formal remunerative economic activity. Conflicts and social crisis not only undermine economic activity but also displace large numbers of Africans who, as political refugees, would have to earn their livelihoods in the informal economy.
vi. *Gender disequilibrium*: The women folks in African countries are concentrated in the informal sectors because they are disadvantaged in the labour market (Heintz & Valodia, 2008). For many women in Africa, disadvantaged in the education system and discriminated against in the formal economy, the informal economy offers the only opportunity for income generation.
vii. *Adoption of capital-intensive manufacturing process*: Modern manufacturing practices favour machine-intensive processes in comparison to labour-intensive processes. Also, globalization which encourages multinational companies to move across borders has not helped in the absorption of the surplus-labour. The integration has constantly favoured capital over labour, especially lower-skilled

workers that find it difficult to migrate. Ultimately, these workers find alternative employment in the informal economy.

5.4 Innovating Informality to Drive Industrialization in Africa

Industrialization has many sides to it but in the context of the present discourse, it is used to connote a rapid transformation in the significance of manufacturing about all other forms of production and work undertaken within national or regional economies (O'Brien, 2015); particularly, those production activities driven beyond mere primary extraction of raw materials to the valorization of the raw materials. Such a state in any given society is often accompanied by technological and organizational change resulting in higher levels of productivity, improved living standards, population growth, urbanization, cultural changes and shifts in the balance of power among nations. Innovation on the other hand implies the adoption of a creative paradigm to respond to a pressing challenge. Therefore, innovation in the context of informality and industrialization in Africa is constructed in terms of adopting a new creative paradigm to address the problem of industrialization in Africa associated with the prevalence of the informal sector to provide inclusive and sustainable full employment and ensure a decent living.

It has been stated earlier that the economic landscape of many African countries is pervasively informal accounting for 66% of non-agricultural income-generating employments (www.ilo.org/africa/whats-new/WCMS_377286/lang--en/index.html). The implication of this is that the informal sector is crucial in any framework that is geared towards the accomplishment of objectives of SDGs 8 and 9 and must be accommodated. Surely, economic development and a sustained, broad-based increase in living standards on the African continent are significantly connected to the capacity of African economies to create decent jobs (SDGs 8 and 9) at a rate that keeps up with the rapid growth of the workforce. This, in turn, depends on the ability of governments in African countries to develop innovative, tailor-made strategies towards transiting informal sector economies to formal status. This requires governments to recognize the importance of informality and develop strategies around it to promote industrialization and job creation.

Therefore, it is clear that innovating the informal sector to drive industrialization provides a smart and deliberate strategy to ensure that the growing labour force is continually engaged in inclusive and sustainable full employment while earning a decent living. The strategy involves using the informal sector as the springboard for industrialization which would necessarily encompass some elements of formality. It is not unusual to assume that once the drivers of informality are taken off, those in the informal sector would naturally migrate to the formal sector. But, this is not the case (Lakemann & Jay, 2017); so a better approach is to use the informal sector as centrepoint for industrialization. The informal sector can be innovated to drive industrialization in the following ways:

a. Upscale skill and training: A major limitation inhibiting sustainability in the informal sector is the poor skill level and education of the actors in the sector which has made the migration to formal status near impossible. Many players in the informal sector are often graduates of traditional apprenticeships whose skills are not well valued and as such, their capacity to partake in skill-intensive jobs and bargain for higher earnings is severely limited. Additional education and training to acquire advanced skills open up opportunities to improve productivity and earnings.
b. Standardization of products and protocols of informal sectors: Many products and services from the informal sectors are not quality-checked even though they can deliver. For instance, the ingenuity and competence of local fabricators in Nigeria to deliver in many instances of sub-contracting in major infrastructural projects have well been acknowledged. But, many of them have not received regulatory approvals because they have not been able to obtain relevant industry standard certifications such as those of the International Standard Organization (ISO), American Petroleum Institute (API) and American Society of Mechanical Engineers (ASME). Yet, these informal sector players are contracted in a non-formal arrangement

for the job at quite below the industry rate. This practice promotes underemployment in contrast to the spirit of SDG 8.

c. Pooling of resources by informal sector: The informal sector should be encouraged to pool their resources together to operate in the formal sector thus benefiting from the economy of scale. Such pooling of resources would make them eligible to partake in big infrastructural projects such as the multi-billion-dollar Dangote Refinery and Petrochemical, the 615 km Ajaokuta-Kaduna-Kano (AKK) natural gas pipeline, the railtrack modernization projects, Liquefied Natural Gas (LNG) Train 7 project, etc.
d. The government should adopt a deliberate state policy to assist and empower a select group of informal sector players to offer their products and services to multi-nationals on the continent rather than the current wholesome practice of capital importation into the continent. The Nigerian Government implemented this strategy in the nation's Oil and Gas industry with the Nigerian Content Development Act which was enacted in 2010. Arising from the success recorded by the Act in the Oil and Gas industry, the government is contemplating extending it to all spheres of the Nigerian economy. Other African countries can adopt a similar strategy.
e. A major signature of the informal sector is skill mismatch: Many players in the informal sector find themselves in that sector because of the unavailability of jobs in the formal sector. Therefore, the informal sector is pervasive of skill mismatch with many workers doing jobs outside their primary competencies. This wide range of skill mismatch provides an opportunity for building an ecosystem of skill sets that can be deployed to grow the informal sector to transit to formal status.
f. Policy issues on legal and institutional environments: Governments should moderate the legal and institutional environments to leverage on the potential inherent in the informal sectors. Conditions for access to credit facilities and government guarantees and support should be liberalized to enable the informal sector to transit to active players in the formal sectors of the economy. This will accelerate the industrialization of the informal sector for goods and services and

engender the achievement of full and productive employment, and decent work for all.

5.5 Conclusion

Informality in the African economy setting is a pervasive phenomenon driving the low industrialization character of the continent except for South Africa. The sector accounts for two-thirds of non-agricultural informal sector employment which indicates that unless the informal sector is innovatively integrated into the economic framework, it may be difficult to accomplish the goals listed in SDGs 8 and 9. Several factors fueling informality on the African continent are identified and these include: low economic growth and rapid urbanization, globalization and redundancies, institutional and legal barriers, lack of government support and weak institution, conflicts and social crisis, gender disequilibrium and adoption of capital-intensive manufacturing process. Structural frameworks for innovating the informal sector to drive industrialization on the African continent include skill upscaling and training, standardization of products and protocols of informal sectors, pooling of resources by the informal sector and a deliberate state policy to support the informal sector. Among these identified policy initiatives, the formation of an ecosystem of diverse skill sets through the innovative pooling of the inappropriately deployed expertise in the informal sector provides a quickly implementable policy option to transform the informal sector in the African continent.

References

Adeosun, O. T., & Popogbe, O. O. (2021). Severity of poverty amongst entrepreneurs in slum settlement: A case of Makoko Community, Lagos State, Nigeria. *Crawford Journal of Business & Social Sciences, 11*(1), 81–91.

Ajayi, O., Soyinka-Airewele, P., & Edewor, P. A. (2019). Imperatives for Sustainable Development in Makoko, Lagos State, Nigeria, In *Proceedings of INTCESS 6th International Conference on Education and Social Sciences*, Dubai, U.A.E. 1361–1368.

Becker, K. F. (2004). The informal economy: A fact-finding study. Swedish International Development Cooperation Agency (SIDA). Stockholm Sweden.

Bocquier, P. (2005). Informal sector versus informal contracts in Nairobi, Kenya.

Chen, M., Vanek, J., Lund, F., Heintz, J., Jhabvala, R., & Bonner, C. (2005). *Progress of the World's Women 2005: Women, work, and poverty*. UNIFEM.

Esaku, S. (2021). Has the low level of economic growth spurred informal sector activities in Uganda? An empirical analysis. *African Journal of Economic and Management Studies*.

Etim, E., & Daramola, O. (2020). The informal sector and economic growth of South Africa and Nigeria: A comparative systematic review. *Journal of Open Innovation: Technology, Market, and Complexity, 6*(4), 134.

Federation of Kenyan Employers. (2021). The informal sector in Kenya. A publication in partnership with International Labour Organization. https://www.ilo.org/empent/Publications/WCMS_820312/lang--en/index.htm

Hart, K. (1973). Informal income opportunities and urban employment in Ghana. *Journal of Modern African Studies, 11*(1), 61–89.

Heintz, J., & Valodia, I. (2008). Informality in Africa: A review. Background paper for the Swedish International Development Cooperation Agency (SIDA), Unpublished Working Paper.

https://sdg.iisd.org. (2020). SDG index measures all countries' progress since 2015. Accessed February 4, 2022: 12.55 pm WAT.

https://www.ilo.org/africa/whats-new/WCMS_377286/lang--en/index.html. Five facts about informal economy in Africa. Accessed February 4, 2022: 1.52pm WAT.

Hussmanns, R., & du Jeu, B. (2002). ILO compendium of official statistics on employment in the informal sector. *International Labour Organization* (p. 67).

Hussmanns, R. (2004, February 2–4). Statistical definition of informal employment: Guidelines endorsed by the 17th International Conference of Labour Statisticians. A Paper prepared for the 7th Meeting of the Expert Group on Informal Sector Statistics (Delhi Group).

ILO. (1973). Employment, incomes and equality: A strategy for increasing productive employment in Kenya. International Labour Office.

ILO. (2002). Resolution concerning decent work and the informal economy.

Khuong, N. V., Shabbir, M. S., Sial, M. S., & Khanh, T. H. T. (2021). Does informal economy impede economic growth? Evidence from an emerging economy. *Journal of Sustainable Finance & Investment, 11*(2), 103–122.

Lakemann, T., & Lay, J. (2017). Services, informality and productivity in Africa. Accessed from https://oecd-development-matters.org/2017/10/03/services-informality-andproductivity-in-africa on February 4, 2022: 1.55 pm WAT.

Mbaye, A. A., Golub, S., & Gueye, F. (2020). *Formal and informal enterprises in francophone Africa: Moving toward a vibrant private sector*. IDRC.

Medina. L., Jonelis, A., & Cangul, M. (2017). The informal economy in Sub-Saharan Africa: Size and determinants. International Monetary Fund (IMF).

O'Brien, P. K. (2015). Industrialization, typologies and history of. In J. D. Wright (Ed.), *International Encyclopedia of social and behavioural sciences* (2nd ed., pp. 872–878). Elsevier Ltd.

Onwe, O. J. (2013). Role of the informal sector in development of the Nigerian economy: Output and employment approach. *Journal of Economics and Development Studies, 1*(1), 60–74.

Onwuka, O. N., & Udegbunam, K. C. (2019). The African continental free trade area: Prospects and challenges. *Conflict Trends, 2019*(3), 3–10.

Peter, C. (2021). Social innovation for Sustainable Urban Developmental Transitions in Sub-Saharan Africa: Leveraging economic ecosystems and the entrepreneurial state. *Sustainability, 13*(13), 7360–7378.

Renne, E. P. (2019). United Nigerian Textiles Limited and Chinese-Nigerian textile-manufacturing collaboration in Kaduna. *Africa, 89*(4), 696–717.

www.unido.org/who-we-are/unido-and-sdgs/africa-and-sdg-9. (2015). Africa and SDG 9. Accessed February 4, 2022: 10.40 am WAT.

Part II

Innovations in Entrepreneurship Practices in Sub-Saharan Africa

6

Towards an Integrative Model of Innovative Entrepreneurship Education for Institutional Sustainability

Mercy Ejovwokeoghene Ogbari, George Uzoma K. Chima, Favour Oluwabukola Olarewaju, Maxwell Ayodele Olokundun, and Daniel E. Ufua

6.1 Introduction

World over, the innovative entrepreneurship culture is increasingly gaining wide-spread relevance as a critical success factor not just for entrepreneurship practice but also for pedagogy in entrepreneurship education (Faltin, 1999, 2001). Up until now, majority of its attention,

M. E. Ogbari · M. A. Olokundun · D. E. Ufua
Department of Business Management, Covenant University, Ogun State, Ota, Nigeria
e-mail: mercy.ogbari@covenantuniversity.edu.ng

M. A. Olokundun
e-mail: maxwell.olokundun@covenantuniversity.edu.ng

D. E. Ufua
e-mail: daniel.ufua@covenantuniversity.edu.ng

G. U. K. Chima · F. O. Olarewaju (✉)
Legacy Associated Consults Ltd, Lagos, Nigeria
e-mail: flrewaju@memphis.edu

A. S. Ibidunni et al. (eds.), *Innovation, Entrepreneurship and the Informal Economy in Sub–Saharan Africa*, Sustainable Development Goals Series,
https://doi.org/10.1007/978-3-031-46293-1_6

which is largely triggered by competition, is being channelled to Small and medium sized enterprises (SMEs) and rapidly growing companies that are technology based. No doubt, entrepreneurship is rather complex and multidimensional. As such, entrepreneurial innovativeness does not solely emerge from intensified competition but emanates from identifying prevalent social issues and secure opportunities in existent market. However, discoveries from Vesper (1993), Csikszentmihalyi (1999), and Olarewaju and Olurinola (2021) show that an individual's background (education, social demography, and experiences) naturally opens up platforms and maximises potentials for developing sound and innovative entrepreneurial ideas that are based on well researched factors (SWOT—strengths, weaknesses, opportunities, and threats) which are not easily imitable by other competitors. So, being able to adapt and imbibe societal tenets and communal problems critically helps in successfully executing given innovative ideologies of an entrepreneur. de Jong & Marsili (2015) buttress the major argument of Block et al. (2017) that just very few entrepreneurs can truly be said to be innovative.

Shane (2003) agrees that an individual's experience and knowledge determines how well and efficiently opportunities are identified and exploited, hence the need for properly educating potential entrepreneurs. Surprisingly, there are a plethora of thriving innovative entrepreneurs whose educational background involves them dropping out of school. For instance, founder of Microsoft, Bill Gates dropped out of Harvard whereas the founder of NIKE, Phil Knight received his BSc in Business Administration from University of Oregon, and Master's degree from Stanford Business School. This triggers questions about the relationship between higher educational attainment and innovative entrepreneurship. Can innovation be adequately practised in college? How can universities and colleges actively help students to imbibe innovative entrepreneurial skills? Such inquisitions have resulted in institutional stakeholders revisiting educational practices to examine its efficacy in motivating students' innovative desires for proffering solutions to ongoing issues that extend into future generations. Although some studies such as Akhmetshin et al. (2019) and Undiyaundeye (2015) have evaluated the importance of entrepreneurship education in the schooling system of developing nations including Nigeria, there appears to be a gap and disconnect of reality from expectations of innovative entrepreneurship in Nigerian schools, which this article seeks to address.

For one, in developing countries like Nigeria, graduates seem not to be strong enough in their personal capacity, resolve and drive to becoming independent entrepreneurs, perhaps because of fear, inertia, and unwillingness to take-risk (Lawal et al., 2018; Ukenna, 2009). These are evident in the increasing number of young graduates seeking jobs and the high failure rate of newly established small businesses (Adegbuyi et al., 2018). Such shortcomings in Nigerian graduates somewhat suggest that prevailing innovative entrepreneurship educative models may be pedagogically defective, hence a crucial gap which this study aims to bridge. For one, the Design Thinking Approach, D.I.S.R.U.P.T, and Experiential learning theoretical models do not specifically consider the context of students within educational settings transitioning into real-life entrepreneurial environment, particularly with respect to pedagogical curriculum, technological and institutional peculiarities. It is important to note that policies pertaining to innovation are key in affecting innovative feats. However, they must be designed to cater for the specific needs and institutional structures of each peculiar nation (OECD, 2005). This is otherwise known as the national innovation system—NIS (OECD, 1997) which will be elaborated upon alongside these 3 main theories observed in this research.

Accordingly, it is imperative to posit an integrative model that eliminates the elements of fear, inertia, and weak risk-taking attitude at the tertiary educational levels that concomitantly translate into fostering institutional sustainability through innovative entrepreneurial practices. This theoretical paper seeks to address the research question: what integrative model of innovative entrepreneurship education can guide pedagogy, curriculum development, and practice in innovative entrepreneurship for the context of developing economies—particularly Sub-Sahara African regions like Nigeria? As such, developing such integrative model is impossible without synergising the pertinent theories discussed in this paper, which not only bridges existing gaps but has the potential of providing future researchers in the area of innovative entrepreneurship research with an array of ideas to guide their research. In addition, the model can provide an insight for innovative entrepreneurship practice and training. The rest of the paper discusses the following themes: literature review, methodology, finding, and discussion of proposed model, followed by conclusion and implications.

6.2 Innovative Entrepreneurship

The concept of entrepreneurship has three major approaches: entrepreneurial function that pertains to dynamic actors including managers and intrapreneurs who undertake crucial choices on production, research and development (R&D), location, innovation, and investment. This highlights originality, creativity, dynamism, and innovativeness which are at the core of entrepreneurship. The second aspect entails enterprise performance where firm strategies and capabilities are focused upon, from individual to state ownership, joint ventures, multinational subsidiaries, and so on (Goedhuys & Sleuwaegen, 2010). The third strand deals with owner-operated enterprises, which is a main subset of firms which often targets self-employment and small and SMEs (Szirmai et al., 2011).

Innovative entrepreneurship is a derivative of the first strand of the broad concept of entrepreneurship. The field of innovative entrepreneurship amalgamises two concepts—innovation and entrepreneurship. From the plethora of existing definitions, innovation is turning an idea into a solution that adds value from a customer's perspective. It is something newly introduced, such as a new method or device. Modern thinking in innovation synthesises technologies and continues to challenge conventional techniques. Agreeably, innovation requires technological changes in the form of new era of equipment, machineries, and better educated workers. So, technological advances sometimes emerge from on-the-job training, capabilities, R&D, formal and informal investment forums (Helpman, 2004). Usually, innovation is measured by the magnitude of patents or venture capitalist dollars received. Despite the various perceptions of innovation, including defining it as procedures of inventing new products for modification to satisfy clientele preferences before production and sales, one thing remains common across all definitions, innovation encompasses value creation (Tidd et al., 1997). Inserting the concept of innovation to entrepreneurship leads to producing new items or services or developing uniquely new techniques to manufacture or deliver commodities at lower cost (Baumöl et al., 2007a). This is very contrary to a replicative entrepreneur who imitates what already exists in the market and probably adopts an already existent business model that best suits their personal interests rather than that of the customer base. Cantillon (1755), Say (1827), Schumpeter (1936), and Kirzner (1973) are few authors who first distinguish between replicative and innovative entrepreneurship.

Baumöl (2010) explores bringing innovative entrepreneurship into micro-theory of value. In his book, it was conceded that right from time; entrepreneurs have been acknowledged for their contribution to the general welfare of economies, although it has gradually progressed from entrepreneurs being relegated to the background to eventually coming into the limelight and gaining more obvious global recognition. Entrepreneurship goes beyond hard work and self-employment to utilising its full capacity of creativity, developing ideas (Faltin, 2001). Generation of such entrepreneurial ideas is characterised by rising educational levels which give the necessary forum to compare societal and economic values. Subsequently, it has been envisioned that such culture of innovative entrepreneurship can incorporate social, artistic, and economic activities to human embodiments of creativity. Hence, sound entrepreneurial idea is the foundation to successful innovative entrepreneurship.

Going back to Schumpeter's definition, entrepreneurial functionalities do not entail invention but are more concerned with awakening and re-defining knowledge into physical form in marketplaces. Such invasion and disruption of prevalent market equilibrium with groundbreaking innovation, otherwise termed "creative destruction" is made possible through better effective allocation of resources and a competitive environment (Chima, 2016; Schumpeter, 1993). Hinterhuber (1992) notes the importance of attaching missions or purpose to innovative entrepreneurial ideas such as Stephen Wozniak and Steven Jobs whose visions were to democratise computers such that the greater part of the populace can afford it. In this way, innovative entrepreneurship differs from the traditional business motive/objective of primarily making profit. Additionally, Timmons (1994) sees entrepreneurship as a human creative ability to build something from nothing. Curiosity and an optimistic attitude that there are much more opportunities to be discovered helps to foster innovative entrepreneurship

Another traditional conceptualisation of an innovative entrepreneur is that such a person must be knowledgeable in basically every aspect: bargaining with clients and suppliers, coordinating employees, fostering team spirit, accounting, maintaining inventory and business equipment, handling tax collectors' demands, and other legalities involved. However, such an individual that is generally qualified and perfect is not just difficult to locate but to train from the inception, not to mention that having all these qualifications is rather scary for ordinary people. This does not mean that an entrepreneur should not be vast. Contrarily, it implies that successful innovative entrepreneurship requires basic knowledge and comprehension of these different areas to allow for flexibility as it is literally impossible to be perfectly or fully skilled in every subject matter (Faltin, 2001). This is where the topic of specialisation and division of labour comes in which is advantageous for saving time and energy such that an innovative entrepreneur can focus on turning his vision into reality.

6.3 Interconnection Between Innovation and Entrepreneurship Education

The importance of innovation for entrepreneurship education cannot be overemphasised because coupled with the rising educational levels, customers are getting more sophisticated in their preferences and tend to desire uniquely outstanding products or services (Adegbuyi et al., 2018). This partially arises from broader awareness about how businesses are generally conducted. Thus, asides top notch innovative ideas, having the right team of committed people and resources are additional ingredients that are intertwined in order to achieve innovative entrepreneurship. Embedded within these resources is the entrepreneur's education and experiences, which help to develop persistence and perseverance through the difficult points of possible failure (Ogbari et al., 2019; Olokundun et al., 2018a, 2018b). However, for these factors to work, a thoroughly refined business model is necessary. Undeniably, the process involved in formulating innovative entrepreneurial ideas is critical component of business models. Such models must include synergetic strategies that account for societal values and problems which are common to all or most individuals within any given society; else this might backfire due to its inability to attract the public (Morgan, 1991).

Baumöl (2004) and Ogbari et al. (2019) observe that educating innovative entrepreneurs at the university level is a deliberate process to prevent excessive dependence on imitating traditionally confining thoughts which hamper creative behaviours and attitudes that are important for innovation-oriented activities. Researchers have argued over time on the realistic possibility of teaching entrepreneurship that is innovative, rather than replicative and whether such personality skills including risk-taking are natural (in-born) or nurtured (learnt at an early age) or a synergy of both. Ukenna (2009) advocates for how to overcome risk inertia and cultivate skills towards risk-taking. Some persons believe that one either possesses this entrepreneurship skill or does not, others such as Baumöl, Litan and Schramm (2007b) are of the opinion that training, and education are vital contributors to innovativeness of entrepreneurs.

Modern conditions of professional educational institutions feature rising competitiveness; thus, modern teachers should practise innovative and entrepreneurial dexterity in addition to applied professional competence (Ivanov et al., 2011; Olokundun et al., 2018a, 2018b). Unfortunately, majority of teachers are not focusing on the innovative aspect of business and remain unready for its active implementation (Osipov, 2006). This is probably because most modern educators have not developed their innovative entrepreneurial competence well enough.

Models of entrepreneurial activities span across consulting, inventory, commercial, investment, market-games, acquisition, intermediary and institutional models. So, productivity level of competent innovative and entrepreneurial formation is related to readiness to innovate, dynamism, and the level of teachers' openness/receptiveness to new approaches of doing things. Active involvement in conferences, innovative ideas, grants, projects, and systematic publications also help in boosting teacher's efficiency with regard to innovative entrepreneurship. Cooperating with relevant research institutes, technologies, and developmental projects helps to ensure the integrity of innovative processes of entrepreneurial efficacy (Ivanov et al., 2015).

However, it is apparent that the existent educational structure has not completely succeeded in encouraging a sufficient innovative entrepreneurship approach to tackling overall real-life challenges (Klatt, 1988; Moses et al., 2015). As a matter of fact, most educational schemes that should combine education with real-life production activities do not actually reflect the intricacies of the market. Meanwhile, diverse experiences and lessons can be gotten from being involved in the real functionality of markets, starting from entrepreneurial ideas to pricing and quality which must be favourable to consumers' demands. Also, building dependable network and people-relationships as well as learning to effectively deal with both formal and informal power structures of society is a vital asset that goes beyond the theoretical teachings of schools (Mayhew et al., 2012). In training students for undertaking entrepreneurial ventures that are innovative in nature, higher technical education which combines legal and economic knowledge with practical exposure.

Hence, entrepreneurship education is much beneficial than Intrapreneurship where in the latter, job seekers usually present their educational certificates (most likely without practical experience and vocational training) and wait for employers to accept potential employee's offers of practicalising their own ideologies for organisational gains. However, this stifles innovative entrepreneurship as the entrepreneur is restricted or saved from the burden of personally seeing to the establishment of his own business enterprise. The reality is that for youths to cultivate essential entrepreneurial skills, they must actively participate in developmental programmes that have strong pedagogical accentuation on encouraging creativity, building leadership and problem-solving skills for taking the initiative, dealing with negotiations, decision making amongst other key life skills (Gibb, 1996a).

Baumöl (2004) recommends that universities adopt an integration of two methods in training innovative entrepreneurs: students should choose research projects that allow practical proficiency in prevalent analytical techniques coupled with a liberal imaginative process that is unorthodox. Nonetheless, balancing the provision of sufficient training technicalities with attempts to evade regularised and ordinary thinking approaches remains a crucial obstacle to designing quality schooling curricula for potential innovative entrepreneurs. So, it is much needed for such pedagogy to be imbibed within educational curriculum context that extends to even non-business students that demonstrate flair and interest in such. This is preferable to being restricted to business environment or special trainings in business administration. A vivid illustration is the rising pattern of involving science, arts, and engineering students in the entrepreneurship process (Kuratko, 2005). In fact, the Kauffman Panel on Entrepreneurship Curriculum in Higher Education (2008) is a strong proponent of teaching innovative entrepreneurship as this is not a case of one size fits all, thereby cutting across all disciplines. Therefore, for students to effectively learn how to implement innovative entrepreneurial operations, there must be proper interaction with their teachers.

6.4 National Innovation Systems (NIS) and Institutional Sustainability

Carlsson et al. (2002) note that the concept of innovation system encompasses the operations of public and private actors, interlinkages as well as the roles of institutions and policies. Hence, NIS stems from R&D activities undertaken by research institutes, government agencies, and universities which go beyond traditional inputs such as R&D expenditures, number of research manpower, and patent-related outputs. Lundvall et al. (2002) observe innovation systems from two angles: its structure (in terms of what is produced and the most developed competencies) and institutional setup (that is, the process/manner by which learning, innovation, and production occurs). Lundvall (1992) pinpoints the narrow and broad perspectives of innovation system where the former directly focuses upon those kinds of institutions which are major innovation sources that intentionally aid the attainment and spread of implicit cognition. The broader innovation approach acknowledges that this narrow perspective of institutions is contained within a much larger socio-economic system. This innovation concept has even gained popularity globally including EU and OECD economies.

Interestingly, innovation goes beyond invention, which mainly pertains to R&D and encapsulates modern innovation theory that emphasises innovation as a mechanism of transferring new knowledge. Intriguingly, policy measures for stimulating innovative entrepreneurship are quite different from those that foster general entrepreneurship. Block et al. (2017) explore the magnitude of innovative entrepreneurship by investigating 102 empirical works that were published in the primary economics and management journals. This enabled adequate synthesis of existent research, thereby aiding knowledge, awareness, and support of encouraging more innovative entrepreneurship.

Many empirical works have concentrated on replicative entrepreneurs and their associated educational experiences. Nonetheless, there are recent studies which investigate the interconnectivity of educational exposition and innovative entrepreneurship (Colyvas & Powell, 2007; Mars & Lounsbury, 2009; Mars et al., 2008; Ndofirepi, 2016). A research survey on entrepreneurship education between 1985 and 1994 confirms that entrepreneurship is teachable given the positive influences of educational programmes upon a person's entrepreneurial prowess (Gorman et al., 1997). Similarly, Kourilsky and Walstad (2000) and Chilosi (2001) provide evidence of instances where education has positively led to successful entrepreneurial undertakings, which expand from start-up initiatives to facilitating mass self-employment opportunities. This stems from increased confidence to assume risks that are implicit to such innovative businesses.

Additionally, degree attainment has been affirmed to be correlated with successful performance indicators like earnings, profits, and growth. Van der Sluis et al. (2005) opine that higher educational level aids greater performance of the concerned entrepreneurial ventures. Weaver, Dickson and Solomon (2006) strongly support this assertion in belief that highest entrepreneurship levels are connected to people that possess a minimum of college education; regardless, education that exceeds bachelor's degree is not totally established to have positive linkages with entrepreneurship.

Kourilsky and Esfandiari (1997) explore the New Youth Entrepreneur curriculum that had 12 educational units of coursework that were channelled to teach students major entrepreneurial nuggets. After teaching this syllabus for one period everyday throughout the semester, it was seen that it had substantial positive impact on African American high school students from lower social classes as they were equipped with basic entrepreneurial understanding and dexterity. Other authors establish that such curricular schemes enable the acquisition of creative thinking capacity, developing new products, insights into technological innovations, leadership, and negotiation via related taught courses (Chima, 2016). These subsequently boost awareness of entrepreneurial platforms (Donckels, 1991), likely problems to be encountered (Plaschka & Welsch, 1990), traits of an innovative entrepreneur's personality (Scott & Twomey, 1998), building tolerance levels (Ronstadt, 1987), methods such as patents for safeguarding ideas (Vesper & McMullan, 1988), funding sources for entrepreneurial ventures (Zeithaml & Rice, 1987). Rabbior (1990) goes on to posit that entrepreneurship courses should also boost self-esteem and confidence by enlightening them on how it works in communities, of which communal integration and out-of-the-box thinking is very helpful. Gibb (1996b) recognises the place of addressing students' self-efficacy.

Mayhew et al. (2012) explore the link between innovative entrepreneurship educational experiences by executing series of assessment to 3,700 undergraduate seniors who graduated in 2007 spring. Their findings reveal that undertaking entrepreneurial courses as pedagogical approaches was substantially connected to innovation intentions after controlling for political, educational, demographic, and personality covariates. This buttresses the research of Olarewaju and Olurinola (2021) who recognise the importance of socio-demographic factors combined with the sound health of concerned individuals to impact the level of education attained via hands-on-training and practical experiences. Therefore, synthesising pedagogy-related information from diverse empirical and anecdotal sources makes it obvious that teaching based on real-life experiences yields the best outcomes. Whereas experience-based techniques incorporate developing business plans, field trips, consulting and holding interview sessions with on-the-field entrepreneurs, giving chances for students to actually start-up businesses (Hills, 1988; Solomon et al., 1994); non-experiential approach includes behavioural simulations (Brawer, 1997; Stumpf et al., 1991).

6.5 Review of Previous Models Relating to Innovative Entrepreneurship Education

In this section, some selected models that are relevant to this study's objectives are examined. This will help to inform the model that will eventually be projected by this paper.

A. **Design Thinking Approach**

Originally conceptualised by professional designers and architects, the Design Thinking (DT) approach is argued to be a critical success factor that should form the basis of thinking pattern for modern entrepreneurs and managers. Rauth et al. (2015) note that DT is a management concept derived from a way of working with innovation mainly. They further argue that everyone can learn from the way that designers think and work to come up with better ideas and enable the development of more innovative offerings. Today, DT is being implemented in various organisational settings often through executive education and consultancy projects as it so useful in fuzzy front end of innovation and product development. Consequently, it is developed into a management concept that is now taught at numerous business schools as it being applied in a variety of management contexts (Rauth et al., 2015).

Notably, embedding the DT approach into innovative entrepreneurship education requires primarily the integration of the ten design thinking tools as identified by Liedtka, King and Bennett (2013):

- **Visualisation:** envisioning possibilities to translate into reality.
- **Journey mapping:** reviewing existent experiences from the perspective of the customers.

- **Value chain analysis:** analysing the current value that is most beneficial to the clientele.
- **Mind mapping:** coming up with fresh insights from exploring past and prevalent activities to develop new design criteria.
- **Brainstorming:** formation of new opportunities and alternative business models which are unique and sustainable.
- **Concept development:** gathering innovative components in an orderly manner to solve and evaluate existing problems.
- **Assumption testing:** experimenting and validating major presumptions that will determine a concept's success or failure.
- **Rapid prototyping:** representing new conceptualisations in tangible forms such that it can be tested and refined.
- **Customer co-creation:** engaging customers to generate solutions that best satisfy their needs/demands.
- **Learning launch:** executing an affordable experiment that enables clients to experience modernised solutions over elongated time periods in order to verify main tenets of market data.

However, Randall and Liedtka (2014) note that all these tools can only work after answering four critical questions: What is? What if? What wows? And what works? This corresponds to the opinions of Liedtka et al. (2013). Moreover, these tools are somewhat re-emphasised by Dijksterhuis and Silvius (2017) somewhat re-emphasises these tools by reiterating the importance of focusing on the needs of the concerned users in addition to promoting visual aids. However, this DT approach does not accommodate for learning within academic institutes. Thus, such thinking approach could be helpful when aiming to boost the competence of education for innovative entrepreneurship such that it translates into institutional sustainability. Therefore, a robust model, which this paper seeks to propose, is expected to integrate the DT tools and values.

B. **D.I.S.R.U.P.T Model**

This model is also considered in striving to achieve innovative approach for teaching entrepreneurship. Disrupt is a new way of thinking which generates new ideas of how to meet clients' needs through the provision of either a product or a service, in this case being entrepreneurship education for innovative entrepreneurship and institutional sustainability. Disrupt is an acronym which stands for the following:

i. **D—Derive:** That is, to base a concept on another concept by either extending an original concept or modifying it to create a new one. Bring something new out or slightly change from the original existing product or service to producing a new one.
ii. **I—Include:** This has to do with making something new thing to a business process to add value and make it different from the original.
iii. **S—Separate:** This entails removing connection between people or things and creates a new product or service idea.
iv. **R—RePurpose:** To change something in a product or service to use the change product or service for a different thing.
v. **U—Unite:** This combines two products to create a new product
vi. **P—Personalise:** Designing or producing something to meet someone's or individual requirements.
vii. **T-Transplant:** Transplant is expressed when an idea that works in one place is taken and introduced in another place, which can be a country or a different customer segment.

The disruptive model emerged from the conceptualisation of disruptive innovation. A disruptive innovation is an innovation that creates a new market and value network and eventually disrupts an existing market and value network, displacing established market-leading firms, products, and alliances (Christensen, 2006). The term was defined and first analysed by the American scholar Clayton M. Christensen and his collaborators beginning in 1995. According to (Christensen, 2006), disruptive innovations tend to be produced by outsiders and entrepreneurs in start-ups, rather than existing market-leading companies. The business environment of market leaders does not allow them to pursue disruptive innovations when they first arise, because they are not profitable enough at first and because their development can take scarce resources away from sustaining innovations (which are needed to compete against current competition).

Nonetheless, the context of learning and transitioning from educational institutes is generally not considered in the DISRUPT model which mostly focuses on entrepreneurial realities in business scenarios. However, in terms of this paper's focus, the thinking of DISRUPT model can be built into the teaching of innovative entrepreneurship to attain sustainable institutions. The present teaching of innovative entrepreneurship has focused on sustaining innovation and not on disruptive innovation. Christensen (2006) explained that the goal of sustaining innovation is to improve existing product performance. On the other hand, he defines a disruptive innovation as a product or service designed for a new set of customers, which is critical to innovative entrepreneurship and institutional sustainability.

C. **Experiential Learning Theory/Model**

The critical defect of most entrepreneurship curriculum and pedagogy is the absence of experience on the part of the students. This has given rise to the knowledge-practice gap, which has resulted to low risk-taking attitude and general fear when the students face the real world. This has triggered the need to pedagogically bridge gap integrating experiential learning component in the innovative entrepreneurship education model. Thus, insights are drawn from the Experiential Learning Theory (ELT) posited by Kolb (1984).

According to McCarthy (2016), generally, there are four approaches to learning have (1) personality (2) information processing, (3) social interaction, and (4) instructional preferences. The second approach—information processing, examines how students absorb and use new information. David Kolb's experiential learning model and learning styles inventory (LSI) is the most prominent theory and instrument used (McCarthy, 2016). Depicted in Fig. 6.1, the experiential learning model is a four-stage circular process where for effective learning to occur, the learner must experience the entire cycle. Most students favour one part of the cycle over other parts hence their learning style preference.

Experiential learning, or "learning by doing" has resulted in positive outcomes. Most experts agree that when students take an active role in the learning process, the student's learning is optimised (McCarthy,

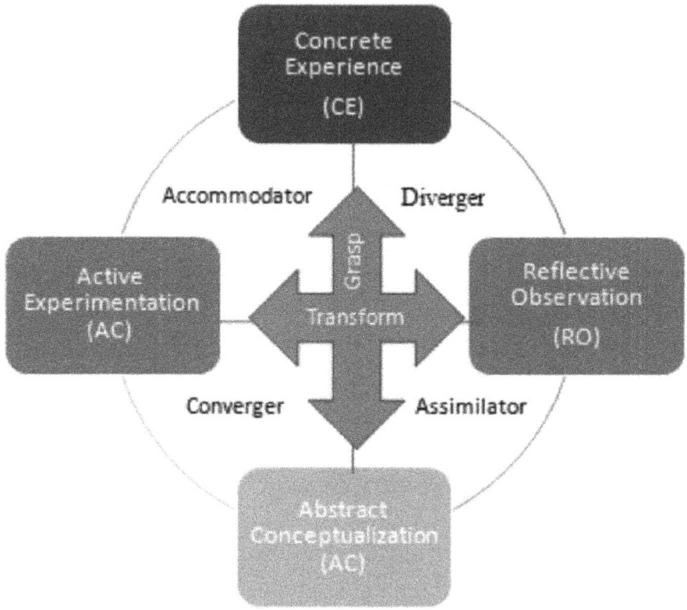

Fig. 6.1 The experiential learning cycle and basic learning styles (Kolb, 1984)

2016 citing Smart & Csapo, 2007). The ELT has important implications for innovative entrepreneurship education (Dhliwayo, 2008). Primarily by understanding experiential learning theory and linking to practise in the classroom, educators are better equipped to promote learning (McCarthy, 2016; Olokundun et al., 2017).

ELT is intended to be a holistic adaptive process on learning that merges experience, perception, cognition, and behaviour. ELT defines learning as "the process whereby knowledge is created through the transformation of experience. Knowledge results from the combination of grasping and transforming experience" (Kolb, 1984, p. 41). The experiential learning model is a cyclical process of learning experiences. For effective learning to transpire, the learner must go through the entire cycle. The four-stage learning model depicts two opposite dimensions of grasping experience—concrete experience (CE) and abstract conceptualisation (AC), and two polar dimensions of transforming experience—reflective observation (RO) and active experimentation (AE).

Experiential learning is a process of constructing knowledge that involves a creative tension amongst the four learning abilities. The learner must continually choose which set of learning abilities to use in a specific learning situation (Kolb, 1984).

The Learning Style Inventory (LSI), the instrument used to assess the individual learning styles, identifies four types of learners based on their approach to obtain knowledge—Diverger, Assimilator, Converger, and Accommodator (see Fig. 6.1).

Divergers prefer to approach learning through Concrete Experience (CE) and to process it through Reflective Observation (RO). Divergers are best at viewing existing situations from many different points of view. Individuals perform better in situations requiring generating new ideas and brainstorming. Their strength lies in imaginative ability and awareness of meaning and values. Accommodators also prefer to take in knowledge through concrete experience, however they favour processing it through active experimentation ideas (Kolb, 1984; McCarthy, 2016). Accommodators are capable of learning from primarily "hands-on" experience. They enjoy carrying out plans and involving themselves in new and challenging experiences. The assimilator prefers to approach knowledge through abstract conceptualisation and to process it through reflective observation.

The converger also approaches knowledge through abstract conceptualisation however the converger favours processing it through active experimentation. Convergers prefer to deal with technical tasks and problems rather than with social and interpersonal issues. (Kolb, 1984). Although ELT is more accommodating of various learning techniques, it does not narrow down to transitioning mechanisms of students imbibing practical entrepreneurial exposure. Obviously, the ELT provides critical insight in any conceptualisation of an integrative model to guide understanding of innovative entrepreneurship education. Such an integrative model incorporates an experiential component that supports students to allay fear and triggers appropriate risk-taking behaviour when engaging in real-world situation, which this paper seeks to develop.

6.6 Findings and Discussion of Proposed Model

Guided by the conceptual framework of Ukenna & Nkamnebe (2017) and National Innovation Systems Approach by Organisation for Economic Cooperation and development—OECD (1997), this study involved a wide range of peer reviewed academic journal articles aimed at addressing the issues and cognate models on innovative entrepreneurship education (IEE). This process led to the conceptualization and formulation of the variables or elements that constitute the proposed Integrative Model of Innovative Entrepreneurship Education (IMIEE). The elements of fear, inertia, no risk-taking (Lawal et al., 2018; Ukenna, 2009) that seems to have partly triggered the increasing number of young graduates seeking jobs and the high failure rate of newly established small businesses owned by young entrepreneurs (Adegbuyi et al., 2018) seems to question the adequacy of prevailing models of innovative entrepreneurship education. Accordingly, we posit the Integrative Model of Innovative Entrepreneurship Education (IMIEE) depicted in Fig. 6.2. Therefore, the IMIEE we propose is expected to guide effectively teaching and other pedagogical activities in innovative entrepreneurship across schools, high schools, and universities alike such that institutional sustainability will be the ultimate result. In addition to the above discussed three key models (i.e., DT Approach, Disruptive Model, and Experiential Learning Theory) that build upon the NIS approach to inform the conceptualisation of IMIEE. Other informative cognate works are sparks of innovation by Hoffman (2005) and entrepreneurship culture and climate by Gabr and Hoffman (2006).

The IMIEE seeks to contribute to the understanding of innovative entrepreneurship in two ways. First, it gives insight to curriculum design and pedagogy in innovative education and second, it provides managerial tool for both potential and current entrepreneurs who seek deepened knowledge that strengthens their innovative drive. Accordingly, IMIEE comprises four critical components or constructs—entrepreneurship education (EE), sparks of innovation drivers (SID), stimulants of innovative entrepreneurship (SIE) culture, and NIS & institutional sustainability.

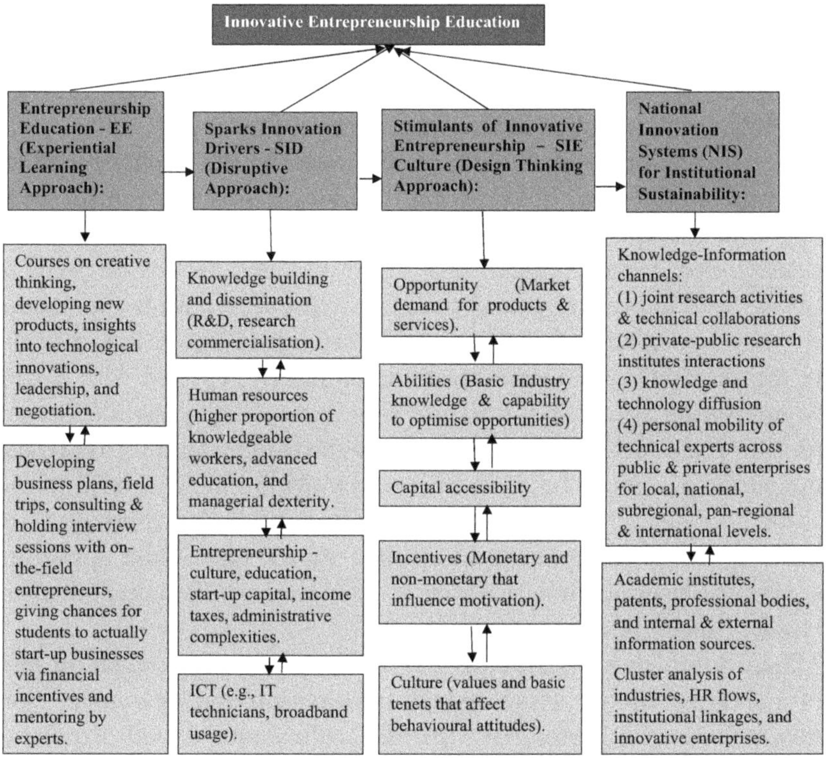

Fig. 6.2 The Integrative Model of Innovative Entrepreneurship Education—IMIEE. Authors' Compilation (2021)

The first construct, entrepreneurship education (EE), in this context is conceptual from the experiential learning prism. The EE construct is strongly underpinned by the Experiential Learning Theory (ELT), as it is believed that the EE projected must be hands-on giving the students opportunities to acquire experience. Hence, it involves two distinct but interrelated parts: the creative development of their products or business idea; and the actual execution of such ideas into micro start-ups within and outside campus. This is bridged by this paper's propositions of more practical-oriented courses, field trips, interview sessions, monetary rewards for outstanding performances, developing business plans, learning the ropes of negotiation by groups of students working closely with assigned successful entrepreneurial mentors. This is a departure from prior teachings in EE, which are theoretical-loaded thereby making EE too abstract, and seemingly increasing inertia, fear, and wider knowledge-practice gap due to non-experiential lessons.

The second construct, SID, is underpinned by the Disruptive Model of innovation building. It is expected that during teaching, instructors are to provoke disruptive and outside-the-box entrepreneurial mind-set. For instance, on-campus competitions, incentives, and awards can exist for students who are able to conceptualise entrepreneurial ideas and sustainably solve school-related challenges. Christensen (2006) maintained that the approach of sustaining innovation should be replaced with disruptive innovation approach if start-ups seek institutional sustainability and survival. The third construct, SIE, argues that innovative entrepreneurship education must be strengthened by wide-spread and firm-wide culture and climate of innovation through sound design thinking across main nuggets of entrepreneurial-inclined values, identifying opportunities via SWOT evaluations, abilities & resources, capital accessibility, and pecuniary incentives.

These 3 models form the basis and build upon NIS approach for institutional sustainability which entails information and knowledge flows across private–public research institutes, collaborations with experts on local, national, sub-regional, pan-regional, and international platforms. Thus, this informs the integrative model of innovative entrepreneurship education (IMIEE) for pedagogical institutes and schools to be sustainably well-equipped for real-life entrepreneurial realities.

6.7 Conclusion and Implications

This study sought to explore innovation entrepreneurship from the perspective of entrepreneurship education. Therefore, the paper investigates diverse approaches to determine how best innovative entrepreneurship can be taught to aspiring entrepreneurs regardless of their disciplines. This entails an overall restructuring of school curriculum and pedagogy such that more practical and hands-on experiences can be gained. This has informed the need of proposed IMIEE, which we conclude will guide curriculum development and other pedagogical issues in innovative entrepreneurship education. It is concluded that an innovative entrepreneurship education that is pedagogically effective through insight from IMIEE can strongly translate into successful entrepreneurial practice, as it is expected to incubate future practitioners.

This study recommends using this paper's proposed integrative model for cluster analysis of specific educational institutes to investigate entrepreneurial-related curriculums and how effective their mechanisms have been in translating into successful real-life entrepreneurs. For instance, future researchers could consider academic institutes without or with very little practical entrepreneurial activities as control group whereas universities and colleges with more practical trainings pose as the experimental group to allow for effective comparisons and informative findings. This would be a build-up of four (4) existing research avenues on NIS but beyond OECD's scope of advanced countries: mapping institutional linkages, human resource (HR) flows, industrial clusters, and innovative firms within the context of chosen African nation(s) or developing countries to achieve sustainable integrated innovative entrepreneurship education.

References

Adegbuyi, A. A., Adegbuyi, O. A., Ogunnaike, O. O., Ibidunni, A. S., & Fadeyi, O. I. (2018). Role of learning orientation on Smes' performance: Empirical evidence from SMEs in Nigeria. *Journal of Entrepreneurship Education, 21*(4), 1–6.

Akhmetshin, E. M., Mueller, J. E., Yumashev, A. V., Kozachek, A. V., Prikhodko, A. N., & Safonova, E. E. (2019). Acquisition of entrepreneurial skills and competences: Curriculum development and evaluation for higher education. *Journal of Entrepreneurship Education, 22*(1), 1–12.

Baumöl, W. J. (2004). Education for innovation: Entrepreneurial breakthroughs vs. corporate incremental improvements. *Working Paper 10578*. National Bureau of Economic Research.

Baumöl, W. J., Litan, R. E., & Schramm, C. J. (2007a). *Good capitalism, bad capitalism, and the economics of growth and prosperity*. Yale University Press.

Baumöl, W. J., Litan, R. E., & Schramm, C. J. (2007b). Sustaining entrepreneurial capitalism. *Capitalism and Society, 2*(2), Article 1. http://www.bepress.com/cas/vol2/iss2/art1

Baumöl, W. J. (2010). *The microtheory of innovative entrepreneurship*. Princeton University Press.

Block, J. H., Fisch, C. O., & Van Praag, M. (2017). The Schumpeterian entrepreneur: A review of the empirical evidence on the antecedents, behaviour, and consequences of innovative entrepreneurship. *Industry and Innovation, 24*(1), 61–95.

Brawer, F. B. (1997). Simulation as a vehicle in entrepreneurship education. *Digest No. 97–1, Center for Entrepreneurial Leadership Clearinghouse on Entrepreneurship Education*. Kauffman Center for Entrepreneurial Leadership.

Carlsson, B., Jacobsson, S., Holmén, M., & Rickne, A. (2002). Innovation systems: Analytical and methodological issues. *Research Policy, 31*, 233–245.

Cantillon, R. (1755). *Essai sur la Nature de Commerce en General*. Chez Fletcher Gyles.

Chilosi, A. (2001). Entrepreneurship and transition. *MOCT-MOST: Economic Policy in Transitional Economies, 11*, 327–357.

Chima, G. U. K. (2016). *New leadership approach: Paradigm shift* (1st ed). Lumen Impact Communication 2084089. ISBN: 978-978-953-790-7.

Christensen, C. M. (2006). The ongoing process of building a theory of disruption. *Journal of Product Innovation Management, 23*, 39–55.

Colyvas, J. A., & Powell, W. W. (2007). From vulnerable to vulnerated: The institutionalization of academic entrepreneurship in the life sciences. *Research in the Sociology of Organizations, 25*, 219–259.

Csikszentmihalyi, M. (1987). *Das flow-Erlebnis: jenseits von Angst und Langeweile: im Tun aufgehen (The flow experience: beyond fear and boredom: immerse yourself in the action)*. Klett-Cotta.

de Jong, J. P., & Marsili, O. (2015). The distribution of Schumpeterian and Kirznerian opportunities. *Small Business Economics, 44*, 19–35.

Dhliwayo, S. (2008). Experiential learning in entrepreneurship education: A prospective model for South African tertiary institutions. *Education+ training, 50*(4), 329–340.

Dijksterhuis, E., & Silvius, G. (2017). The Design Thinking approach to projects. *The Journal of Modern Project Management, 4*(3).

Donckels, R. (1991). Education and entrepreneurship experiences from secondary and university education in Belgium. *Journal of Small Business and Entrepreneurship, 9*(1), 35–42.

Faltin, G. (1999). Competencies for innovative entrepreneurship. *M. Singh, Adult Learning and the Future of Work*, 189–197.
Faltin, G. (2001). Creating a culture of innovative entrepreneurship. *Journal of International Business and Economy, 2*(1), 123–140.
Gabr, H., & Hoffman, A. (2006). A general policy framework for entrepreneurship. *FORA, Division for Research and Analysis*. Ministry of Business and Economic Affairs.
Gibb, A. (1996a). The Role of Education and Training in Small and Medium Enterprise (SME) Development (manuscript).
Gibb, A. A. (1996b). Entrepreneurship and small business management: Can we afford to neglect them in the twenty-first century business school? *British Journal of Management, 7*(4), 3.
Goedhuys, M., & Sleuwaegen, L. (2010). High-growth entrepreneurial firms in Africa: A quantile regression approach. *Small Business Economics, 34*(1), 31–51.
Gorman, G., Hanlon, D., & King, W. (1997). Some research perspectives on entrepreneurship education, enterprise education and education for small business management: A ten-year literature review. *International Small Business Journal, 15*(3), 56–78.
Helpman, E. (2004). *The mystery of economic growth*. Harvard University Press.
Hills, G. E. (1988). Variations in university entrepreneurship education: An empirical study of an evo field. *Journal of Business Venturing, 3*, 109–122.
Hinterhuber, H. H. (1992). *Strategische Unternehmensführung*.
Hoffman, A. (2005). Innovation monitor 2005: Denmark's innovation capacity – from benchmarking to policy priorities. FORA, Division for Research and Analysis, Ministry of Business and Economic Affairs.
Ivanov, V. G., Akhmetgareev, R. A., & Varaksin, V. E. (2011). Competence model of formation of readiness for future professionals to innovative professional activities in the "high school - the troops." *Herald Kazan State Technological University, 4*, 242–244.
Ivanov, V. G., Shaidullina, A. R., Drovnikov, A. S., Yakovlev, S. A., & Masalimova, A. R. (2015). Regional experience of students' innovative and entrepreneurial competence forming. *Review of European Studies, 7*, 35.
Kauffman Panel on Entrepreneurship Curriculum in Higher Education. (2008). Entrepreneurship in American higher education. Kauffman Foundation.
Kirzner, I. M. (1973). *Competition and entrepreneurship*. University of Chicago Press.

Klatt, L. A. (1988). A study of small business/entrepreneurial education in colleges and universities. *The Journal of Private Enterprise, 4*, 103–108.

Kourilsky, M. L., & Esfandiari, M. (1997). Entrepreneurship education and lower socioeconomic black youth: An empirical investigation. *The Urban Review, 29*(3), 205–215.

Kolb, D. A. (1984). *Experiential learning: Experience as the source of learning and development*. Prentice-Hall, Inc.

Kourilsky, M. L., & Walstad, W. B. (2000). *The E generation: Prepared for the entrepreneurial economy?* Kendall/Hunt Publishing Company.

Kuratko, D. F. (2005). The emergence of entrepreneurship education: Development, trends, and challenges. *Entrepreneurship Theory and Practice, 29*(5), 577–597.

Lawal, F. A., Iyiola, O. O., & Adegbuyi, O. A. (2018). Exploring alternative financing for entrepreneurship development in Nigeria: Surmounting challenges. *Journal of Entrepreneurship Education, 21*(2), 1–11.

Liedtka, J., King, A., & Bennett, K. (2013). Solving problems with design thinking: Ten stories of what works. Columbia University Press.

Lundvall, B. A. (Ed.). (1992). *National systems of innovation: Towards a theory of innovation and interactive learning*. Pinter Publishers.

Lundvall, B., Johnson, B., Andersen, E. S., & Dalum, B. (2002). National systems of production, innovation and competence building. *Research Policy, 31*, 213–231.

Mars, M. M., & Lounsbury, M. (2009). Raging against or with the private marketplace? Logic hybridity and eco-entrepreneurship. *Journal of Management Inquiry, 18*(1), 4–13.

Mars, M. M., Slaughter, S., & Rhoades, G. (2008). The state-sponsored student entrepreneur. *The Journal of Higher Education, 79*(6), 638–670.

Mayhew, M. J., Simonoff, J. S., Baumöl, W. J., Wiesenfeld, B. M., & Klein, M. W. (2012). Exploring innovative entrepreneurship and its ties to higher educational experiences. *Research in Higher Education, 53*(8), 831–859.

McCarthy, M. (2016). Experiential learning theory: From theory to practice. *Journal of Business & Economics Research, 14*(3), 91–99.

Morgan, G. (1991). Emerging waves and challenges: The need for new competencies and mindsets. In J. Henry (Ed.), *Creative Management*.

Moses, C., Akinbode, M., Olokundun, A. M., & Agboola, M. G. (2015). Entrepreneurship education and action-oriented pedagogical approaches. *International Journal of Educational Science and Research, 5*(5), 53–60.

Ndofirepi, T. M. (2016). *The impact of technological creativity and entrepreneurship education on the entrepreneurship intentions of students at particular tertiary institutions in Zimbabwe and South Africa.* Doctoral dissertation. Central University of Technology, Free State.

OECD. (1997). *National Innovation Systems.*

OECD. (2005). Innovation policy and performance: Across-country comparison. Author.

Ogbari, M. E., Olokundun, A. M., Ibidunni, A. S., & Obi, J. N. (2019). Imperatives of Entrepreneurship Development Studies on University Reputation in Nigeria. *Journal of Entrepreneurship Education, 22*(2), 1–10.

Olarewaju, F. O., & Olurinola, I. O. (2021). Educational Attainment and Health Outcomes in Nigeria: A Survey from NDHS (2008 & 2013). *Scholars Journal of Science and Technology, 2*(1), 247–257.

Olokundun, A. M., Ibidunni, A. S., Peter, F., Amaihian, A. B., Moses, C., & Iyiola, O. O. (2017). Experiential pedagogy and shared vision: A focus on identification of business opportunities by Nigerian University Students. *Journal of Entrepreneurship Education, 20*(2), 1–12.

Olokundun, M., Iyiola, O., Ibidunni, S., Ogbari, M., Falola, H., Salau, O., Peter, F., & Borishade, T. (2018a). Data article on the effectiveness of entrepreneurship curriculum contents on entrepreneurial interest and knowledge of Nigerian university students. *Data in Brief, 18*, 60–65.

Olokundun, M., Moses, C. L., Iyiola, O., Ibidunni, S., Ogbari, M., Peter, F., & Borishade, T. (2018b). The effect of non-traditional teaching methods in entrepreneurship education on students' entrepreneurial interest and business startups: A data article. *Data in Brief, 19*, 16–20.

Osipov, P. N. (2006). Vocational education and labor market: Cooperation. *Kazan Pedagogical Journal, 2*, 10–13.

Plaschka, G. R., & Welsch, H. P. (1990). Emerging structures in entrepreneurship education: Curricula designs and strategies. *Entrepreneurship Theory and Practice, 14*(3), 55–71.

Rabbior, G. (1990). Elements of a successful entrepreneurship/economics/education program. In C. A. Kent (Ed.), *Entrepreneurship education: Current developments, future directions* (pp. 53–65). Greenwood Publishing Group.

Rauth, I., Carlgren, L., & Elmquist, M. (2015). Making it happen: Legitimizing Design Thinking in large organizations. *Design Management Journal, 8*(3), 47–60.

Randall, R., & Liedtka, J. (2014). Innovative ways companies are using design thinking. *Strategy & Leadership.*

Ronstadt, R. (1987). The educated entrepreneurs: A new era of entrepreneurial education is beginning. *American Journal of Small Business, 7*(4), 37.

Say, J. B. (1827). A treatise on political economy. 1803 (C. R. Prinsep & C. C. Biddle, Trans., 3rd American edition). John Grigg.

Schumpeter, J. A. (1936). The theory of economic development. 1911 (R. Opie, Trans.). Harvard University Press.

Schumpeter, J. (1993). Theorie der wirtschaftlichen Entwicklung. 8th Edition (unchanged version of the fourth edition, which was published in 1934). Berlin.

Scott, M. G., & Twomey, D. F. (1998). The long-term supply of entrepreneurs: Student's career aspirations in relation to entrepreneurship. *Journal of Small Business Management, 26*(4), 5–13.

Solomon, G. T., Weaver, K. M., & Fernald, L. W., Jr. (1994). Pedagogical methods of teaching entrepreneurship: A historical perspective. *Simulation and Gaming, 25*(3), 338–353.

Stumpf, S. S., Dunbar, L., & Mullen, T. P. (1991). Simulations in entrepreneurship education: Oxymoron or untapped opportunity? *Frontiers of Entrepreneurship Research, 11*, 681–694.

Szirmai, A., Naudé, W., & Goedhuys, M. (Eds.). (2011). Entrepreneurship, innovation, and economic development. Oxford University Press.

Tidd, J., Bassat, J., & Pavitt, K. (1997). *Managing innovation. Chichester*. John Wiley & Sons.

Timmons, J. (1994). New Venture Creation. Entrepreneurship in the 1990s (4th ed.). Boston.

Ukenna, S. (2009). Entrepreneurship: Overcoming the risk inertia. *Madonna University Journal of Research in Business Administration and Management, 1*(1), 61–68.

Ukenna, S. I., & Nkamnebe, A. D. (2017). Sustainable consumption behavior in Sub-Saharan Africa: A conceptual framework. *Thunderbird International Business Review, 59*(1), 33–50.

Undiyaundeye, F. (2015). Entrepreneurship skills acquisition and the benefits amongst the undergraduate students in Nigeria. *European Journal of Social Science Education and Research, 2*(3), 9–14.

van der Sluis, J., van Praag, M., & Vijverberg, W. (2005). Entrepreneurship selection and performance: A meta-analysis of the impact of education in developing economies. *The World Bank Economic Review, 9*(2), 25–261.

Vesper, K. H. (1993). *New Venture Mechanics. Prentice Hall.*

Vesper, K. H., & McMullan, W. E. (1988). Entrepreneurship: Today courses, tomorrow degrees? *Entrepreneurship: Theory & Practice, 13*, 7–13.

Weaver, M., Dickson, P., & Solomon, G. (2006). Entrepreneurship and education: What is known and not known about the links between education and entrepreneurial activity. In *The small business economy for data year 2005: A report to the president* (pp. 113–156). U.S. Small Business Administration.

Zeithaml, C. P., & Rice Jr, G. H. (1987). Entrepreneurship/small business education in American universities. *Journal of Small Business Management, 25*(1), 44.

7

Entrepreneurial Ecosystem and the Role of Telecom Multinationals in Achieving SDG 9 in Developing Economies

Ugbede Umoru, Justin Udie, and Victor Udeozor

7.1 Introduction

Entrepreneurship is vital to the sustenance of local economy of any country, hence the need for an entrepreneurial ecosystem consisting of a network of government, Multinational Enterprise (MNEs), start-ups and other institutional bodies task to contribute to entrepreneurial innovation and shape the creation of new businesses (Adler & Hashai, 2007; Bhawe & Zahra, 2019; Fuller-Love & Akiode, 2020; Hong &

U. Umoru (✉) · V. Udeozor
Nottingham Business School, Nottingham Trent University, Nottingham, UK
e-mail: ugbede.umoru@ntu.ac.uk

V. Udeozor
e-mail: victor.udeozor@ntu.ac.uk

J. Udie
Transport Consultancy and Advisory, Atkins Réalis, London, UK

A. S. Ibidunni et al. (eds.), *Innovation, Entrepreneurship and the Informal Economy in Sub–Saharan Africa*, Sustainable Development Goals Series,
https://doi.org/10.1007/978-3-031-46293-1_7

Snell, 2013). However, how MNEs, contribute to entrepreneurial ecosystems and innovation in developing countries to achieve sustainable development goals is often ignored.

Nevertheless, only recently has research emerged to highlight the important role banks, venture capitalists and government agencies play in financing entrepreneurial activities in developing countries (Bhawe & Zahra, 2019; Fuller-Love & Akiode, 2020). Yet, the role MNEs play in creating a sustainable entrepreneurial ecosystem has continued to receive little or no attention notwithstanding its importance in economic prosperity of developing countries where Nigeria is an example. It is contended that MNEs could intervene through policy appraisal and review for entrepreneurship expansion mechanism, investment portfolio through foreign direct investment (FDI), research and development (R&D), IT services, marketing and advertising options and improved collaboration (Audretsch & Belitski, 2017; Meyer & Peng, 2016; Spencer, 2008; Spigel & Harriso, 2018). MNEs could contribute to building a reliable entrepreneurial ecosystem through the provision of direct funding and knowledge sharing for the creation and co-creation of new business frontiers (Adler & Hashai, 2007; Hong & Snell, 2013).

Furthermore, supporting the building of strong entrepreneurial ecosystems drives economic prosperity and leads to the achievement relevant to the United Nations Sustainable Development Goals (UN SDGs), such as reducing poverty and hunger (goals 1 and 2), decent work and economic growth and partnership (goals 8 and 19), building resilient infrastructure and fostering innovation that produces economic development (goal 9). Therefore, local entrepreneurs and relevant stakeholders in host countries must form critical factors to take responsibility to actualise these goals; for example, telecom MNEs, because of their influence in their market spaces, can support entrepreneurs with technological know-how (Dunham et al., 2006; Tapang & Bassey, 2017; Umoru, 2019).

This chapter is a case study investigation conducted on four telecom MNEs operating in Nigeria. Twenty (28) in-depth interviews from case companies and government agencies as well secondary documents were collected across Nigeria. Three contributions are drawn from the case study. First, a novel model that illuminates how telecom MNEs could support the entrepreneurial ecosystem in host country is developed. Second, mainstreaming the model, a guiding framework for policy makers and practitioners on the needed assessment and achievement of SDGs within the host country as it suggests a positive sum-game for all stakeholders. Finally, a methodological framework that draws valuable insights from case companies' executives could serve as a reference for MNEs, Entrepreneurs and policymakers in understanding the Chief Executive's decision-making process.

The balance of this chapter examines the role of MNEs in entrepreneurial ecosystem within the lens of stakeholder theory and the nexus between this theory and MNEs' approaches to achieving relevant SDGs. The methodology adopted for this study is robustly illustrated while the findings, discussion and conclusion are presented in the end.

7.2 Literature Review

Entrepreneurial Ecosystem and MNEs' Influence in Achieving SDG 9

Entrepreneurial ecosystem broadly refers to the community of several stakeholders that provides the needed supportive environment for new venture creations (Cao & Shi, 2021; Isenberg, 2014; Spigel & Harrison, 2018). It is argued that the distinguishing factor between an entrepreneurial ecosystem and others is the important role stakeholders, including government and large private enterprises like the MNEs, play in entrepreneurship development (Haines, 2016; Isenberg, 2011; Motoyama & Knolton, 2014; Rice et al., 2014; Stam, 2008; Spencer et al., 2005). For example, Spigel and Harrison (2018) highlighted subsidies and grants provided by the UK government in support of entrepreneurship as an example of entrepreneurial ecosystem interplay. Similarly, Audretsch and Belitski (2017) examined 70 European cities in the context of entrepreneurship ecosystem and found that infrastructure and incentives such as human and financial resources from government, non-governmental organisations (NGOs) are crucial needs that support entrepreneurship ecosystems. In addition, contemporary investigations on the subject found that private enterprises, especially MNEs, could also provide the support that spurs the creation of new businesses (Groth et al., 2015; Luo et al., 2011). For example, Ryan et al. (2021) demonstrate how high-tech industrial clusters transformed into highly profitable local entrepreneurial ecosystems in Ireland. The study also suggests that multiple new ventures sprout through the support of MNEs subsidiaries to become critical research and development partners. However, evidence also shows that MNEs can inhibit local entrepreneurs from creating new ventures (Liu et al., 2009; Spencer, 2008). This is due to having more access to resources and building capabilities, thus out competing local entrepreneurs (Ryan et al., 2021).

Despite the mix, albeit burgeoning scholarship on entrepreneurial ecosystem (EE), contemporary scholarly arguments are more focused on providing a supportive environment for EE in developed economies than in developing economies (Audretsch & Belitski, 2017; Groth et al., 2015; Isenberg, 2014; Motoyama & Knolton, 2014; Rice et al., 2014; Stam, 2008). Yet, it is important to investigate the developing economies as literature attributes the lack of entrepreneurial ecosystem development, particularly in Sub-Saharan Africa to several challenges that militate a thriving entrepreneurial ecosystem. These include underdeveloped market supporting institutions such as capital markets, labour markets, strong legal system and the absence of large multinationals' participation in the entrepreneurial ecosystem (Atiase et al., 2018; Bhawe & Zahra, 2019; Cao & Shi, 2021; Ogundana, 2020; Umoru, 2019).

Given the significant role MNEs play in resources, knowledge and technology transfer, literature is capturing a more coordinated and targeted approach that leverages the UN SDGs to support entrepreneurship in developing countries. This is an effort toward closing the gap if compared with developed economies (Esmaeilpoorarabi et al., 2021; Nylund et al., 2021). It is believed that entrepreneurship activities within the entrepreneurial ecosystem can contribute to achieving some of the SDGs (Fig. 7.1) (Bischoff & Volkmann, 2018; Volkmann et al., 2021; Wagner et al., 2021). However, evaluating the link between entrepreneurship and sustainability is still at an early stage as past literature are either conceptually driven or regionally based studies (Audretsch & Belitski, 2017; Bischoff, 2021; Sussan & Acs, 2017).

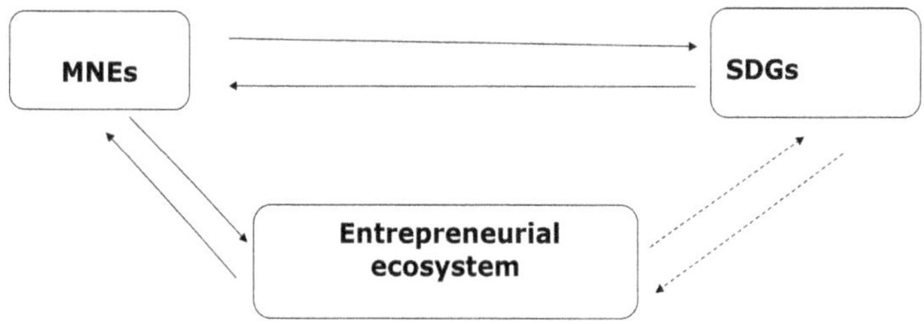

Fig. 7.1 MNEs, Entrepreneurial ecosystem and achieving SDGs

Equally, emerging research in international business has increasingly argued for MNEs' contribution toward achieving SDGs (Halme et al., 2020; van Tulder et al., 2021; van Zanten & Tulder, 2018). However, how MNEs' role in the entrepreneurial ecosystem in the context of a developing country help achieve SDGs has been neglected in current empirical literature. We unpack this topical issue by focusing on the link (see Fig. 7.1) between MNEs, entrepreneurial ecosystem and SDGs from the perspective of Nigeria, with particular emphasis on SDG 9. SDG 9 focuses on building resilient infrastructure, promoting inclusive and sustainable industrialisation and fostering innovation (United Nations, 2015). We propose that the role telecom MNEs play as important stakeholders in the technology ecosystem in Nigeria can foster innovation amongst entrepreneurs. This has been overlooked in current literature (Bischoff & Volkmann, 2018; Sussan & Acs, 2017; Volkmann et al., 2021; Wagner et al., 2021).

Theoretical Perspective

Stakeholder theory refers to any group or individual who can affect or is affected by the operations of an enterprise (Freeman, 1984; Hasnas, 1998). Stakeholder theory assumes that long term profitability, as well as the success of an organisation, is predicated on its ability to satisfy interested stakeholders' needs (Bischoff, 2021; Voss et al., 2005). Within the entrepreneurial ecosystem, the role of stakeholders, including MNEs, is considered important as entrepreneurs require engagement and insights from such key stakeholders to accomplish goals (Bishoff, 2021; Bishoff &

Volkmann, 2018; Spence et al., 2011). Drawing on resource base view theory (Barney, 2001), stakeholders can provide tangible and intangible resources sufficient for an entrepreneur and thereby ensure success for the organisation (Choi & Shepherd, 2005; Simatupang et al., 2015), which then leads to the attainment of competitive advantage (Barney, 2001).

An entrepreneurial environment whose stakeholders provide support can guarantee engagement while also influencing the start of new ventures (Bishoff, 2021; Jain & Ali, 2013; Motoyama & Watkins, 2014). We applied stakeholder theory to interrogate the important role telecom MNEs can play in the Nigerian technology entrepreneurial ecosystem. We propose that MNEs could leverage their resources and capabilities to create an enabling environment that can stimulate growth and facilitate development innovation amongst entrepreneurs in the Global South, Nigeria for example.

7.3 Methodology

The research context of our study is the Nigerian telecom sector. The Nigeria telecom sector comprises mobile operators, original equipment manufacturers, subscribers and other stakeholders. Mobile operators are firms that provide voice calls and internet access services. There are four main mobile operators, two main OEM suppliers and 150 million subscribers in the Nigeria telecom sector (Euromonitor, 2021; Nigeria Communication Commission, 2022). For our study we focus on three mobile operators and one OEM.

In addition to the context being new, the telecom sector has experienced exponential growth over the last two decades. There are about one hundred thousand telecom masts and telecom base stations (TBS) built over the last twenty years. There are thousands of servicing related jobs and dozens of innovative start-up companies linked to the sector (Nigeria Communications Commission, 2022). As such, we argue, this context has an opportunity to potentially contribute new knowledge on how MNEs have contributed to the entrepreneurial ecosystem.

Method

We adopt an exploratory case approach. Exploratory study is appropriate because this research focuses on understanding how telecom MNEs support entrepreneurial ecosystem to help achieve the UN SDGs within the context of Nigeria (Duboise & Gadde, 2002; Welch et al., 2011). The decision to adopt a Case study approach was based on the need to understand how humans interact within a social context like Nigeria with specific reference to the telecom sector (Miles et al., 1994; Welch et al., 2011; Yin, 1993, 2012, 2014). Exploratory research goes beyond description and focuses on understanding and shedding more light on how a particular phenomenon occurred (Collis & Hussey, 2014). It provides the opportunity to contribute to theory building and extension (Doz, 2011). We identified 4 cases for analysis comprising three mobile operators and one OEM, headquartered in India, UAE, South Africa and China, respectively, and government regulatory & enforcement agencies in the host country (see Table 7.1). The case were selected via a purposive sampling. This method involves theoretical replication rather than sampling logic, so the basis for the selection is theoretical, not statistical (Eisenhardt & Graebner, 2007; Patton, 2002).

Data Collection

The data collection process was carried out between September and December 2016 and repeated in August of 2021 in Nigeria to ascertain changes within the study context. Four to seven candidates were interviewed for all case units for about forty-five minutes each. Candidates for interviews were highly experienced senior managers in the sector. We selected these candidates because they are in a better position to understand the strategic decisions their firms make or policies that may shape the decisions of firms within the sector. A total of twenty-eight interviews were conducted. We stopped at this number of interviewees because we noticed reoccurring themes, which implies saturation (Saunders et al., 2016).

Table 7.1 Description of research of interviewees

Case Group	Sector	Respondents ID	Position	Years of experience
Case A MNE From India	Mobile Operator	Respondent 1	Regional Operations Director	7
		Respondent 2	Senior Manager Licencing and Compliance	6
		Respondent 3	Area Business Manager	7
		Respondent 4	Radio Access Network Architecture Manager	5
Case B MNE From United Arab Emirates (UAE)	Mobile Operator	Respondent 5	Head Technical Project Delivery	8
		Respondent 6	Senior Manager Compliance and Regulations	8
		Respondent 7	Senior Manager, Design and Value Engineer	7
		Respondent 8	Senior Manager, Design and Value Engineer	5
		Respondent 9	Area Service Manager (Regional)	5
		Respondent 10	Manager, Economic & Technical Regulation	8
		Respondent 11	Head monitoring and supervisory Team	6

Case Group	Sector	Respondents ID	Position	Years of experience
Case C MNE From China	Original Equipment Manufacturer	Respondent 12	Head Government Relations	8
		Respondent 13	Senior Account Manage	7
		Respondent 14	Senior Customer Project Manager	5
		Respondent 15	Procurement Manager	5
		Respondent 16	Senior Account Manager	7
Case D MNE From South Africa	Mobile Operator	Respondent 17	Senior Manager Government and Community Relations Nation Wide	7
		Respondent 18	Project Manager	7
		Respondent 19	Regional Manager Enterprise Solution	6
		Respondent 20	Regional Sales Manager	5
		Respondent 21	Regional Service Manager 2	6
		Respondent 22	Analytic Based Commercial Senior Strategic Manager 2	6

(continued)

Table 7.1 (continued)

Case Group	Sector	Respondents ID	Position	Years of experience
Government	Regulations and Enforcement Agency	Respondent 28	Assistant Director, NCC 2	5
		Respondent 29	Senior Manager and Adviser on Legal, NCC	5
		Respondent 30	Senior Legal Officer, NCC	5
		Respondent 31	Personal-Assistant to the Director-General (NESREA)	6
		Respondent 32	Assistant Director, NASS	5
		Respondent 33	Head, Enforcement and Compliance	5

(NCC: National Communications Commission; NESREA: National Environmental Standard and Regulations Enforcement Agency; NASS: National Assembly)

Interviewees were recorded using a tape recorder and notes were also taken to ensure details were not lost. Interviews were conducted in four states in Nigeria. These states include Lagos, Rivers, Kano and the Federal Capital Territory, Abuja. In addition, senior executives responsible for telecom infrastructure deployment and expansion, authorised to make decisions on behalf of their headquarters across the country, were interviewed. Examples of questions asked of interviewees at the case companies include: what they do for the business community; how their company benefit people; how do the telecom companies provide support for small businesses in the communities. In addition to the interviews, documents including annual reports, minutes of meetings and the government gazette were analysed and used to triangulate data.

The Cases

Case A

Case company A is a mobile operator headquartered in India. It was established in 1995. Besides Nigeria, it currently has a presence in several African countries, including Congo, Ghana, Kenya, Madagascar, Malawi and Rwanda. The companies offer 2G, 3G and 4G technologies using mobile, voice and data solutions (Market Line, 2021). The company has a subscriber base of 471.3 million, 216,901 telecom network towers and 606,783 mobile broadband base stations across Africa and Asia (Euromonitor, 2021; Market Line, 2021).

Case B

Case B is a mobile operator headquartered in the United Arab Emirate (UAE). It was founded in 1976 in UAE. Case B has an international presence in fourteen countries, including the Middle East, Asia and Africa. In the last ten years, it has grown to become the 15th largest mobile network operator in the world, with a total subscriber base of 135 million (Market Line, 2021). Since its expansion in the last two decades into Africa and Asia, it has grown to 63 million subscribers in

Africa and Asia. It has a presence in the following countries: Afghanistan, Benin, Burkina Faso, Cote Voire, Sri Lanka, Central African Republic, Egypt, Gabon, India, Mali, Morocco, Mauritania, Niger, Pakistan and Togo.

Case C—OEM

Case C is an Original Equipment Manufacturer founded in 1987 in China. It has a presence in 170 countries and regions, including Europe, Africa, the Middle East, Asia and the Americas. It has a company size of 180, 000 employees globally. The firm offers information and communication technology solutions and services to telecommunication operators (Market Line, 2021). The firm is engaged in the development and manufacture of equipment and products in telecommunication and information technology Case C has three business segments including carrier, consumer and enterprise businesses. The carrier network business manufactures a range of wireless and fixed networks for telecommunication operators. The consumer business segment develops smartphones, mobile broadband devices and applications. The enterprise segment develops integrated information, communication and technology (ICT) solutions and products including enterprise network infrastructure and enterprise information securities (Market Line, 2021).

Case D

Case D is a mobile operator founded in 1994 in South Africa. The company has an employee size of 19, 913 across twenty-two countries. The company offers a range of communication, entertainment and content services in addition to voice calls and messaging services; its services are offered to over 232.5 million people in 22 countries across Africa and the Middle East (Annual Report, 2016; Market Line, 2021). The company mostly internationalises to foreign markets through the acquisition of the telecommunication spectrum licensed by host countries.

Data Analysis

Data collected was coded using QSR Nvivo, a qualitative data analysis programme to identify emerging themes. We proceeded to identify relevant concepts and arrange these into categories ensuring "terms and languages adequate at the level of meaning of the informants" (Gioia, Price and Hamilton, 2010: 8). Themes were allowed to emerge until further analysis failed to reveal additional themes (Gioia et al., 2010). Final statements of findings are made at this 1st order stage (see Appendix III) if corroborated across multiple participants (Gioia et al., 2013). Further analysis was carried out to see if abstract theoretical levels of themes and phrases could be formulated according to participants' terms. As a result, we came up with phrases such as "rural infrastructure technology expansion", and "the importance of technology to start-ups". We investigated further to see if these new emerging concepts can be aggregated into an umbrella theme. For example, we categorised concepts such as rural infrastructure technology expansion and technology support for start-ups as providing technology infrastructure to support start-up business communities. This provided the basis to build a data structure (Fig. 7.2), which then allowed us to configure the themes and concepts developed into a visual representation (Fig. 7.3) (Gioia et al., 2013).

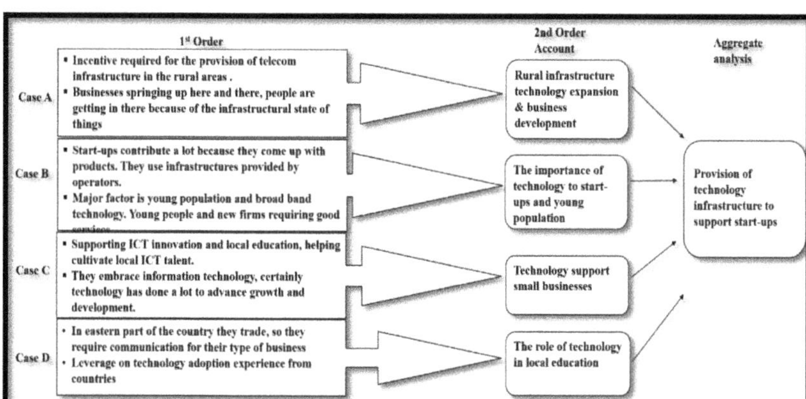

Fig. 7.2 Data structure

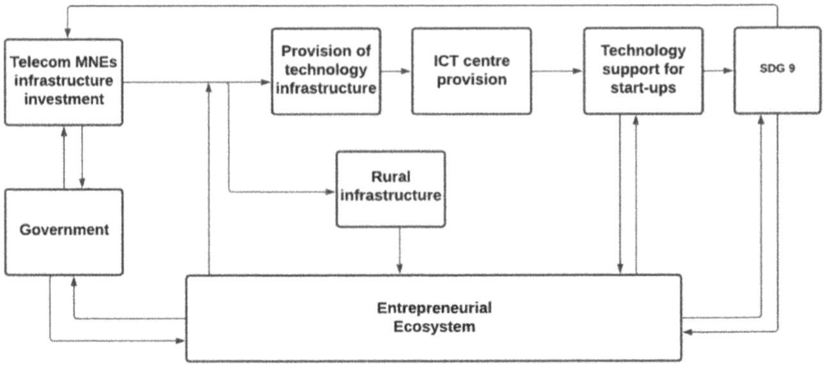

Fig. 7.3 A model showing the Nigerian technology entrepreneurial ecosystem and MNEs influence in achieving SDG 9

7.4 Findings

Provision of Technology Infrastructure to Support Start-ups

Data analysis shows exciting findings regarding the contributions of the telecom MNEs in the entrepreneurial ecosystem that suggest a strong indication toward achieving SDG 9. The goal focuses on building resilient infrastructure, promoting inclusive and sustainable industrialisation and fostering innovation. The business model of telecom MNEs is such that they are required to build telecom technology infrastructure across Nigeria, which seems to be in line with SDG 9. This, therefore, means that areas that lack telecom infrastructure began to have access to several alternative means of communication technology. To clarify how the case companies were contributing to building telecom infrastructure technology, interviewees at Telecom MNEs stated:

> Provision of infrastructure in the rural areas, most of the urban areas have been covered. So, there should be serious incentives for people to go into rural areas with new technology. (Senior Manager Licencing and Compliance, Case A)

Comments above suggest that given that telecom infrastructure technology has already been provided in urban areas, Telecom MNEs started to provide infrastructure to the rural areas to boost economic development. Although this move potentially halted the movement of people out of the rural areas, a rather noticeable increase to the rural areas began to be witnessed. Rural technology diffusion has increased economic development potential (Hübler, 2016), consequently reducing rural–urban migration.

Additionally, the provision of telecom infrastructure led to positive externalities (Adler & Hashai, 2007; Hong & Snell, 2013; Montiel et al., 2021). For example, the provision of communication networks by the MNEs facilitated new businesses amongst young Nigerians and start-ups in both urban and rural areas. Furthermore, start-ups in electronic payment systems, popularly known as point-of-sale (POS) machines, became common, which is an evidence that supports the proliferation of financial technology across Nigeria. The machine facilitates bill payment, cash withdrawals and deposits. Additionally, phone booths and kiosks managed by individuals began to be widely noticed.

> So there are lots of people that up-scale their businesses because of technology. Businesses springing up here and there, people are getting in there because of the infrastructural state of things. (Area Business Manager, Case A)

The findings show the extent to which target 9.3 of the UN SDG 9 is accomplished. Target 9.3 encourages increased access for small-scale industrial and other enterprises, especially in developing countries. Analysis of the data collected from Case B, C and D suggest the following comments:

> Start-ups contribute a lot because starts would come up with a product that will change the face of one particular segment in the industry. Then, these start-ups would ride on the technology infrastructures of the telecom operators. (Senior Manager, Design and Value Engineer, Case B)
> Major factor is young population and broadband technology. Young people require new phone, good services, and new firms coming up. (Manager, Economic & Technical Regulation, Case B)

> Companies can leverage on technology experience within their group from other countries. For example, our company is part of a larger business group, where they have 22 operations in other countries asides Nigeria. (Regional Manager Enterprise Solution, Case D)

The findings above provided compelling evidence to show how telecom companies support start-ups and other small business groups within the entrepreneurial ecosystem. First, opportunities are provided for start-ups to develop products and services that target several segments of the industry. Then, the telecom MNEs provide the technology to support their (start-up) development (Groth et al., 2015; Luo et al., 2011). As a result, MNEs play a substantial role in creating sustainable innovation that can lead to sustainable business practices (Bischoff, 2021; Nylund et al., 2021). A recent publication in Financial Times (2021) captures the importance of small businesses that operate point-of-sale machine services, which reduces the amount of time spent in traditional banks for their services, such as the transfer of funds and withdrawals. Additionally, support is also provided for start-ups that enter into partnerships (Bhawe & Zahra, 2019) with telecom companies and banks to facilitate online payment systems, including start-ups such as Flutterwave, which was recently valued at one billion dollars (Munshi, 2021). A conglomeration of start-ups in a community can help build innovation districts (Esmaeilpoorarabi et al., 2021).

Interestingly, the telecom MNEs leverage on their experience of operating abroad to introduce such innovative technology to multiple start-up communities. A good example from our findings is the evidence produced from the analysis conducted on Case D. According to interviewees:

> Telecom is a technology-dependent industry, so you can't use it if you don't have experience with technology. We use it in South Africa and it gave us this advantage, please bring it to Nigeria, so we could leverage on it. (Regional Manager Enterprise Solution, Case D)

The comments above suggest that given that the industry relies on technology innovation, a company that has experience using it in another country can easily leverage that appearance in Nigeria. This can potentially give the company a competitive advantage. Furthermore, Case D operates across twenty-two African and Middle Eastern countries, hence the benefit of tapping into several technology collaborations. The implication of this is that start-ups can therefore have access to such global technology similar to MNEs.

The Role of Government as an Exogenous Factor Contributing to SDG Commitment

The role of government was found to be an exogenous factor that contributed to the provision of telecom infrastructure across Nigeria. This is because one of the responsibilities of the regulator, as stated in the 2003 telecom Act, is to oversee the expansion of the telecommunication network through the Universal Service Provision Fund (USF). The USPF is a fund set aside by the government in the form of subsidies, monitored through the Nigerian Communications Commission (NCC) to help the expansion of the telecommunication network throughout the country, particularly in the underserved rural areas. This fund is allocated to the Telecom MNEs, granting them additional resources to provide telecom infrastructure. In addition, interviewees reported that government agents and officials enforce the Act by monitoring their activities.

> You have powerful governors in government who want a base station mounted in villages to support businesses. There are quite a number of things that come from the political environment that influence us. (Regional Operations Director, Case A)
>
> To fulfil government regulation that says all operators must cover certain location as part of license requirement, so they try to deploy state of the art infrastructure. (Head monitoring and supervisory Team, Case B)
>
> The government is serious and desirous of advancing the growth of its populace. They embrace information technology, certainly technology has done a lot to advance growth and development as well. (Head Government Relations, Case C)

The comments above illustrated the actions of government to actualise the telecom infrastructure expansion across Nigeria. In addition, interviewees suggested that the condition of their licence is that they are responsible for the provision of certain network coverage across the country. Overall, the findings demonstrate that government action facilitates telecom infrastructure availability in the country. This is in line with goal nine of the UN sustainable development goals (United Nations, 2015).

7.5 Discussion

This chapter set out to understand the link between MNEs, the support they provide entrepreneurial ecosystems and how it translates to achieving SDGs. In line with stakeholder theory, existing literature postulates that MNEs are important stakeholders that play an important role in the development of entrepreneurial ecosystem (Isenberg, 2014; Ryan et al., 2021; Spigel & Harrison, 2018; Voss et al., 2005). Equally, current literature on entrepreneurship suggests that entrepreneurship fosters sustainability (Audretsch & Belitski, 2017; Bischoff, 2021; Sussan & Acs, 2017). Therefore, we argue that a more targeted involvement of MNEs in entrepreneurial ecosystem can engender sustainable entrepreneurship and thus achieve SDGs.

We use the context of the Nigerian telecom sector to show how telecom MNEs support the entrepreneurial ecosystem and thus achieve SDG 9 in two fundamental ways. First, MNEs provided telecom infrastructure that supports communication networks in both rural and urban areas. This has led to infrastructure development in rural areas because of the technology diffusion and therefore enhanced technology inclusiveness (Hübler, 2016; Umoru, 2019; United Nations, 2015).

Additionally, telecom MNEs contributed to building ICT centres to educate members of rural communities. This is an important contribution to achieving SDG 9.c, which calls for urgent rural literacy investment in developing countries. In particular, the goal identified that more effort was required to increase access to ICT and affordable access to the internet. The evidence we found speaks to how telecom MNEs are increasingly contributing to the digitalisation of rural communities through providing resources that enable their learning (Awoyemi et al., 2021; Montiel et al., 2021). The economic implication for the company is that they can benefit from a pool of educated workforce that can be recruited in the future into the company (Kano, 2018; Wei & Liu, 2006; Winthrop et al., 2013). As such, ICT training made available for the people could benefit the MNEs in the future.

Secondly, in the process of performing this core mandate of providing telecom infrastructure, they contributed to positive externalities (Hong & Snell, 2013; Nylund et al., 2021), including new business ventures and start-ups, thus contributing to existing literature that has called for more empirical studies regarding the relevance of MNEs to entrepreneurial ecosystem (Ryan et al., 2021) from a developing country perspective (Cao & Shi, 2021). The new business ventures and start-up SMEs leverage the support of the telecom MNEs to provide innovative services, including online payment systems and the provision of point-of-sale machines. Current literature found evidence to suggest that MNEs engage more with SDGs targets that are actionable within their operations than those outside of it (van Zanten & Tulder, 2018; Voegtlin & Scherer, 2017). Our findings suggest contrary evidence as the telecom MNEs supported the growth of start-ups and other small businesses outside of their core operations (Bhawe & Zahra, 2019; Nylund et al., 2021).

We also found evidence to suggest that entrepreneurs within the ecosystem also benefited from overseas experience and knowledge of the telecom MNEs (Hong & Snell, 2013). This is because the telecom MNEs leverage the experience of using technology in overseas subsidiaries in their operations in Nigeria. In particular, findings on Case D support extant studies as the company draws from the innovations in other 22 countries across Africa and in the Middle East to provide services to their Nigerian customers. In addition, literature on entrepreneurship suggest that entrepreneurs can benefit from the knowledge transfer of MNEs in support of entrepreneurial growth and development (Audretsch & Belitski, 2017; Hong & Snell, 2013).

Figure 7.3 shows the contributions of MNEs to the entrepreneurial ecosystem in Nigeria and how SDG 9 is beginning to be achieved. The

MNEs and the government are seen as significant elements that provide the necessary support that enables technology infrastructure to support the entrepreneurial ecosystem. These findings contribute to enriching extant studies on the role of MNEs in entrepreneurial ecosystem. Literature on entrepreneurship-stakeholders relations suggests that government and MNEs are key stakeholders and their involvement can increase economic growth and development (Atiase et al., 2018; Armanios et al., 2017; Bhawe & Zahra, 2019). Therefore, entrepreneurs that are stakeholders oriented found it easier to execute operations in a conducive environment than those that do not (Smulowitz et al., 2020).

7.6 Conclusion

This chapter aimed to contribute to the ongoing discussion on entrepreneurial ecosystems from a developing country perspective, particularly Nigeria. Extant literature suggests that MNEs as a stakeholder within the entrepreneurial ecosystems are well placed to support entrepreneurs due to access to knowledge and resources. However, we argued that a more targeted approach of MNEs' support in entrepreneurial ecosystems can foster entrepreneurship growth and development, leading to sustainable development. We provided evidence from our investigation of four telecom MNEs operations in Nigeria.

We make three important contributions to extant literature. First, our findings introduce empirical nuances by developing a model that demonstrates that telecom MNEs support the entrepreneurial ecosystem by providing telecom infrastructure technology to rural areas. The increasing support for start-ups and SMEs in the entrepreneurial ecosystem help to achieve SDG 9. However, these contributions are underscored by an exogenous factor—the government. Second, mainstreaming the model, a guiding framework for policy makers and practitioners on the needed assessment and achievement of SDGs within the host country as it suggests a positive sum-game for all stakeholders. Further, we make a methodological contribution as we adopted a qualitative case study to understand the perspective of senior executives of telecom MNEs and the role of business and host communities in the context of Nigeria. Finally, the evidence produced and the model developed have important policy implications and practitioners in the industry. The government should understand their role as enablers in creating a favourable environment to enable MNEs to enhance the entrepreneurial ecosystem that can foster economic growth and development and help achieve SDGs. While we have made an effort to show an exogenous factor that explains the contributions of MNEs, we encourage future research to consider possible endogenous factors that may hinder or enable MNEs' role in the entrepreneurial ecosystem in achieving SDGs.

References

Adler, N., & Hashai, N. (2007). Knowledge flows and the modelling of the multinational enterprise. *Journal of International Business Studies, 38*(4), 639–657.

Atiase, V. Y., Mahmood, S., Wang, Y., & Botchie, D. (2018). Developing entrepreneurship in Africa: Investigating critical resource challenges. *Journal of Small Business and Enterprise Development, 25*(4), 644–666.

Audretsch, D. B., & Belitski, M. (2017). Entrepreneurial ecosystems in cities: Establishing the framework conditions. *The Journal of Technology Transfer, 42*(5), 1030–1051.

Awoyemi, S. O., Adejuwon, O. O., & Ogundari, I. O. (2021). An assessment of technological capabilities and deposit-mobilisation technologies in selected micro-finance banks in Southwestern Nigeria. *Journal of Banking and Financial Technology*, 1–11.

Barney, J. B. (2001). Is the resource-based "view" a useful perspective for strategic management research? *Yes. Academy of Management Review, 26*(1), 41–56.

Bhawe, N., & Zahra, S. A. (2019). Inducing heterogeneity in local entrepreneurial ecosystems: The role of MNEs. *Small Business Economics, 52*(2), 437–454.

Bischoff, K. (2021). A study on the perceived strength of sustainable entrepreneurial ecosystems on the dimensions of stakeholder theory and culture. *Small Business Economics, 56*, 1121–1140.

Bischoff, K., & Volkmann, C. K. (2018). Stakeholder support for sustainable entrepreneurship-a framework of sustainable entrepreneurial ecosystems. *International Journal of Entrepreneurial Venturing, 10*(2), 172–201.

Cao, Z., & Shi, X. (2021). A systematic literature review of entrepreneurial ecosystems in advanced and emerging economies. *Small Business Economics, 57*, 75–110.

Choi, Y. R., & Shepherd, D. A. (2005). Stakeholder perceptions of age and other dimensions of newness. *Journal of Management, 31*(4), 573–596.

Collis, J., & Hussey, R. (2014). *Business Research-a practical guide for undergraduate and postgraduate students*. Palgrave Macmillan Higher Education.

Doz, Y. (2011). Qualitative research for international business. *Journal of International Business Studies, 42*(5), 582–590

Dubois, A., & Gadde, L. E. (2002). Systematic combining: An abductive approach to case research. *Journal of business research, 55*(7), 553–560.

Dunham, L., Freeman, R. E., & Liedtka, J. (2006). Enhancing stakeholder practice: A particularized exploration of community. *Business Ethics Quarterly, 16*(1), 23–42.

Eisenhardt, K. M., & Graebner, M. E. (2007). Theory building from cases: Opportunities and challenges. *Academy of Management Journal, 50*(1), 25–32.

Esmaeilpoorarabi, N., Yigitcanlar, T., Kamruzzaman, M., & Guaralda, M. (2020). How can an enhanced community engagement with innovation districts be established? Evidence from Sydney. *Melbourne and Brisbane. Cities, 96*, 102430.

Euromonitor International (2021). *Technology Nigeria: developing middle class drives E- commerce growth*. Euromonitor International.

Freeman, R. E. (1984). Strategic management: A stakeholder approach. Boston: Pitman. As cited in Mitchell, R. K., Agle, B. R., & Wood, D. J. (1997). Toward a theory of stakeholder identification and salience: defining the principle of who and what really counts. *Academy of Management Review, 22*(4), 853–886.

Fuller-Love, N., & Akiode, M. (2020). Transnational entrepreneurs dynamics in entrepreneurial ecosystems: A critical review. *Journal of Entrepreneurship and Innovation in Emerging Economies, 6*(1), 41–66.

Gioia, D. A., Corley, K. G., & Hamilton, A. L. (2013). Seeking qualitative rigor in inductive research: Notes on the Gioia methodology. *Organizational Research Methods, 16*(1), 15–31.

Gioia, D. A., Price, K. N., Hamilton, A. L., & Thomas, J. B. (2010). Forging an identity: An insider-outsider study of processes involved in the formation of organizational identity. *Administrative Science Quarterly, 55*(1), 1–46.

Groth, O. J., Esposito, M., & Tse, T. (2015). What Europe needs is an innovation-driven entrepreneurship ecosystem: Introducing EDIE. *Thunderbird International Business Review, 57*(4), 263–269.

Halme, M., Rintamäki, J., Knudsen, J. S., Lankoski, L., & Kuisma, M. (2020). When is there a sustainability case for CSR? Pathways to environmental and social performance improvements. *Business & Society, 59*(6), 1181–1227.

Hasnas, J. (1998). The normative theories of business ethics: A guide for the perplexed. *Business Ethics Quarterly, 8*(1), 19–42.

Hong, J. F., & Snell, R. S. (2013). Developing new capabilities across a supplier network through boundary crossing: A case study of a China-based MNC subsidiary and its local suppliers. *Organization Studies, 34*(3), 377–406.

Hübler, M. (2016). Does migration support technology diffusion in developing countries? *World Development, 83*, 148–162.

Isenberg, D. (2011). Introducing the entrepreneurship ecosystem: Four defining characteristics. *Forbes*. Retrieved on May, 25 2011.

Isenberg, D. (2014). What an entrepreneurship ecosystem actually is. *Harvard Business Review*. Retrieved on May, 12 2014.

Jain, R., & Ali, S. W. (2013). Self-efficacy beliefs, marketing orientation and attitude orientation of Indian entrepreneurs. *The Journal of Entrepreneurship, 22*(1), 71–95.

Kano, L. (2018). Global value chain governance: A relational perspective. *Journal of International Business Studies, 49*(6), 684–705.

Liu, X., Wang, C., & Wei, Y. (2009). Do local manufacturing firms benefit from transactional linkages with multinational enterprises in China? *Journal of International Business Studies, 40*(7), 1113–1130.

Luo, Y., Zhao, H., Wang, Y., & Xi, Y. (2011). Venturing abroad by emerging market enterprises: A test of dual strategic intents. *Management International Review, 51*, 433–459.

Market Line. (2021). Company Profile.

Madichie, N. O., Mpofu, K., & Kolo, J. (2017). Entrepreneurship development in Africa: Insights from Nigeria's and Zimbabwe's telecoms. In *Entrepreneurship in Africa* (pp. 172–208).

Meyer, K. E., & Peng, M. W. (2016). Theoretical foundations of emerging economy business research. *Journal of International Business Studies, 47*(1), 3–22.

Miles, M. B., Huberman, A. M., Huberman, M. A. & Huberman, M. (1994). *Qualitative data analysis: An expanded sourcebook*. Sage.

Montiel, I., Cuervo-Cazurra, A., Park, J., Antolín-López, R., & Husted, B. W. (2021). Implementing the United Nations' sustainable development goals in international business. *Journal of International Business Studies, 52*(5), 999–1030.

Munshi, N. (2021, August 19). Explosion in electronic payments powers start-up boom in Nigeria. *Financial Times* [online] https://www.ft.com/content/5fa49678-9eed-45e8–9c3d-6e19a2237b81

Nigeria Communication Commission. (2022). Operator Data [Homepage of Nigeria Communication Commission], [Online]. Available: https://consumer.ncc.gov.ng

Nylund, P. A., Brem, A., & Agarwal, N. (2021). Innovation ecosystems for meeting sustainable development goals: The evolving roles of multinational enterprises. *Journal of Cleaner Production, 281*, 125329.

Ogundana, O. (2020). *Factors influencing the business growth of women-owned sewing businesses (WOSBs) in Lagos-State, Nigeria: A gender-aware growth framework*. Nottingham Trent University (United Kingdom).

Patton, M. Q. (2002). Designing qualitative studies. *Qualitative Research and Evaluation Methods, 3*, 230–246.

Rice, M. P., Fetters, M. L., & Greene, P. G. (2014). University-based entrepreneurship ecosystems: A global study of six educational institutions. *International Journal of Entrepreneurship and Innovation Management, 18*(5–6), 481–501.

Ryan, P., Giblin, M., Buciuni, G., & Kogler, D. F. (2021). The role of MNEs in the genesis and growth of a resilient entrepreneurial ecosystem. *Entrepreneurship & Regional Development, 33*(1–2), 36–53.

Saunders, M., Lewis, P., & Thornhill, A. (2016). Research methods for business students (Vol. Seventh). Pearson Education.

Smulowitz, S. J., Rousseau, H. E., & Bromiley, P. (2020). The behavioral theory of the (community-oriented) firm: The differing response of communityoriented firms to performance relative to aspirations. *Strategic Management Journal, 41*(6), 1023–1053.

Stam, E. (2008). Entrepreneurship and innovation policy. In B. Nooteboom & E. Stam (Eds.), *Microfoundations for innovation policy* (pp. 135–172). Amsterdam University Press.

Simatupang, T. M., Schwab, A., & Lantu, D. C. (2015). Building sustainable entrepreneurship ecosystems, Introduction. *International Journal of Entrepreneurship and Small Business, 26*, 389–398.

Spence, M., Gherib, B. B., & J., & Ondoua Biwolé, V. (2011). Sustainable entrepreneurship: Is entrepreneurial will enough? A north–south comparison. *Journal of Business Ethics, 99*(3), 335–367.
Spencer, J. W. (2008). The impact of multinational enterprise strategy on indigenous enterprises: Horizontal spillovers and crowding out in developing countries. *Academy of Management Review, 33*(2), 341–361.
Spencer, J. W., Murtha, T. P., & Lenway, S. A. (2005). How governments matter to new industry creation. *Academy of Management Review, 30*(2), 321–337.
Spigel, B., & Harrison, R. (2018). Toward a process theory of entrepreneurial ecosystems. *Strategic Entrepreneurship Journal, 12*(1), 151–168.
Spigel, B. (2016). Developing and governing entrepreneurial ecosystems: The structure of entrepreneurial support programs in Edinburgh, Scotland. *International Journal of Innovation and Regional Development, 7*(2), 141–160.
Sussan, F., & Acs, Z. J. (2017). The digital entrepreneurial ecosystem. *Small Business Economics, 49*, 55–73.
Tapang, A. T., & Bassey, B. E. (2017). Effect of corporate social responsibility performance on stakeholder's perception of telecommunication companies in Nigeria (a study of MTN, Globalcom & Etisalat). *Journal of Business and Management, 19*(6), 39–55.
Umoru, U. (2019). *Institutional factors influencing the internationalisation of developing market telecommunication firms in Nigeria*. Nottingham Trent University (United Kingdom).
United Nations, (2015). Resolution adopted by the General Assembly on 25 September 2015.
Van Tulder, R., Rodrigues, S. B., Mirza, H., & Sexsmith, K. (2021). The UN's sustainable development goals: Can multinational enterprises lead the decade of action? *Journal of International Business Policy*, 1–21.
Van Zanten, J. A., & Van Tulder, R. (2018). Multinational enterprises and the Sustainable Development Goals: An institutional approach to corporate engagement. *Journal of International Business Policy, 1*(3), 208–233.
Voegtlin, C., & Scherer, A. G. (2017). Responsible innovation and the innovation of responsibility: Governing sustainable development in a globalized world. *Journal of Business Ethics, 143*(2), 227–243.
Volkmann, C., Fichter, K., Klofsten, M., & Audretsch, D. B. (2021). Sustainable entrepreneurial ecosystems: An emerging field of research. *Small Business Economics, 56*(3), 1047–1055.

Voss, Z. G., Voss, G. B., & Moorman, C. (2005). An empirical examination of the complex relationships between entrepreneurial orientation and stakeholder support. *European journal of Marketing*.

Wagner, M., Schaltegger, S., Hansen, E. G., & Fichter, K. (2021). University-linked programmes for sustainable entrepreneurship and regional development: How and with what impact? *Small Business Economics, 56*(3), 1141–1158.

Wei, Y., & Liu, X. (2006). Productivity spillovers from R&D, exports and FDI in China's manufacturing sector. *Journal of International Business Studies, 37*(4), 544–557.

Welch, C., Piekkari, R., Plakoyiannaki, E., & Paavilainen- MäntymäkI, E. (2011). Theorising from case studies: Towards a pluralist future for international business research. *Journal of International Business Studies, 42*(5), 740–762.

Winthrop, R., Bulloch, G., Bhatt, P., & Wood, A. (2013). *Investment in global education: A strategic imperative for Business*. Center for Universal Education Working Paper, 11. p. 101899.

Yin, R. K. (2009). Case Study Research: Design and Methods. Essential guide to qualitative methods in organizational research (Vol. 5). In The Information Systems Research Challenge (Harvard Business School Research Colloquium). Sage.

Yin, R. K. (2014). *Case study research: Design and methods*. Fifth edition. edn. SAGE Publications.

Yin, J., & Jamali, D. (2016). Strategic corporate social responsibility of multinational companies subsidiaries in emerging markets: Evidence from China. *Long Range Planning, 49*(5), 541–558.

8

Transportation and Economic Development: Advancing Technological Innovation and Sustainability in the Transportation Sector of a Developing Nation

Toyin Samuel Olowogbon, Segun B. Fakayode, and Adebisi Oloruntoba Luke

8.1 Introduction

Worldwide, as the population is increasing, so is urbanization. In developing nations, emerging challenges attributed to urbanization include inefficient transportation systems. An efficient transportation system is focal to achieving economic development as it is directly responsible for the movement of humans, goods, and services. In recent times, emerging technologies are transforming how transportation systems operate. The engagement of information communication technology (ICT) has been identified as a significant driver of economic development and job

T. S. Olowogbon (✉)
Centre for Sustainable Agricultural Empowerment, Ilorin, Nigeria
e-mail: solowogbon@csaempowerment.com

S. B. Fakayode
Department of Agricultural Economics, Federal University, Oye-Ekiti, Nigeria

A. O. Luke
Agricultural and Rural Management Training Institute, Ilorin, Nigeria

A. S. Ibidunni et al. (eds.), *Innovation, Entrepreneurship and the Informal Economy in Sub–Saharan Africa*, Sustainable Development Goals Series,
https://doi.org/10.1007/978-3-031-46293-1_8

creation in all areas (World Bank, 2021). It has also been determined that digital solutions are the critical path to achieving sustainable mobility for all (World Bank, 2020a).

In the case of Nigeria, with an estimated population of over 195 million (World Bank, 2020b Poverty is a major issue in Nigeria, with over 86.9 million (50%) of her population living in extreme poverty (World Poverty Clock, 2018). Further evidence revealed that over 50% of the Nigerian population are youths aged 15–35. 55.4% of these youth were unemployed or under-employed (National Bureau Statistics, 2018). It is possible to harness the vast potential of these youths by engaging in technological innovations. As the Nigerian population is rapidly growing, efficient transportation is needed to enhance the nation's development. However, rapid urbanization has exposed the weakness of the transportation systems in the country. Various digital technologies are being integrated into the nation's transportation systems to facilitate efficient services and management. Like other countries, digital innovations are expected to make transportation services easier and provide more access to secured services, reduce fuel costs, provide a better customer experience, and reduce waiting and processing time, among others. Other likely advantages included transportation-aided financial inclusion, job creation, and enhanced well-being among citizens. Evidence of the impact of technology integration on development outcomes in developing nations is rare. This has provided no policy impetus in this regard. This study addressed this evidence gap and advanced issues relating to technological sustainability rather than solely innovation.

8.2 Literature Review

Transport infrastructure plays a crucial role in economic growth and development. Many theoretical and empirical studies have recognized it necessary to maintain and promote economic growth, especially when incorporating information and communication technology (ICT). It has been recognized that information and communication technology (ICT) functions as the nerve system of a multimodal transport chain and leads to multiple benefits to organizations. For example, ICT helps to provide real-time visibility, efficient data exchange, and better flexibility to react to unexpected changes during delivery (Moldabekova et al., 2020; Som & Anyigba, 2022). Though the use of ICT in transport and logistics started long ago, in the 1960s, the primary functions were inventory management systems, transport routing, scheduling, distribution Requirement Planning, and billing systems.

Transport infrastructure is a significant asset in advancing the world's economies; it is considered the pivot of any economic activity (Okechukwu et al., 2021). Also, transport infrastructure is categorized as a productive public expenditure (Clarke & Batina, 2019) because the economy can benefit from transport facilities by speeding up access to the services and encouraging international investors, and broadening the trade between common resources by increasing the market and labors mobility, reducing the wealth gaps, improving social welfare such as saving time and reducing business costs (Valila, 2020). In addition, transport infrastructure plays an essential role in industrial development. It has apparent spillover effects on regional advancement, factor re-assignment, and manufacturing efficiency, which fosters the accumulation of industry, population, and the economy (Yin & Yu, 2019). Furthermore, the integration of ICT into transportation and logistics systems has advanced supply chain and logistics operations by increasing competitiveness (Mubarik et al., 2019), supply chain integration and performance (Xu et al., 2022), cost reduction, visibility and tracking, exchange, and real-time information (Sorker, 2019), efficiency and responsiveness (Karl et al., 2018), and effective collaboration among the relevant stakeholders and actors (Abboubi, 2022).

Despite the benefits accrued to the incorporation of ICT into the transportation system, the uptake of ICT advancements has been low in developing countries which was discovered in the study by Molero et al. (2019) to be due to the following (a) user-related barriers, (b) economic and financial factors, (c) operation related barriers, (d) management capability, (e) technology-related barriers, (f) collaborators influence, and (g) policy-related barriers. Some of these issues are common in the Nigerian transport and logistics industry due to the persistent infrastructural deficits, lack of innovation skills, digitally divided regions, and lack of government support for innovation (Tob-Ogu et al., 2018).

The extent of the effect of transport systems incorporated with ICT on domestic and regional economics differs in rural and urban areas; and is subject to economic growth. However, transportation infrastructure adds primarily to the development of the economy and productivity, but not consistently over time. Transport infrastructure encourages economic growth, cuts commodity prices, offers access to global producers and customer markets, and makes global manufacturing more cost-effective by decreasing transport costs and increasing accessibility (Meersman & Nazemzadeh, 2019) (Fig. 8.1).

In all sectors of the economy, especially in developed countries, the growth of transport infrastructure has been established and its relationship with economic development. Smith's economic vision centered on the evolution of transport infrastructure: "No roads meant no transport, no trade, no skills, no economies of scale, no growth in productivity and no development" (Okechukwu et al., 2021). A study by Cigu et al. (2018) has revealed that investment in transport infrastructures permits businesses to extend their presence and transport facility to enjoy access

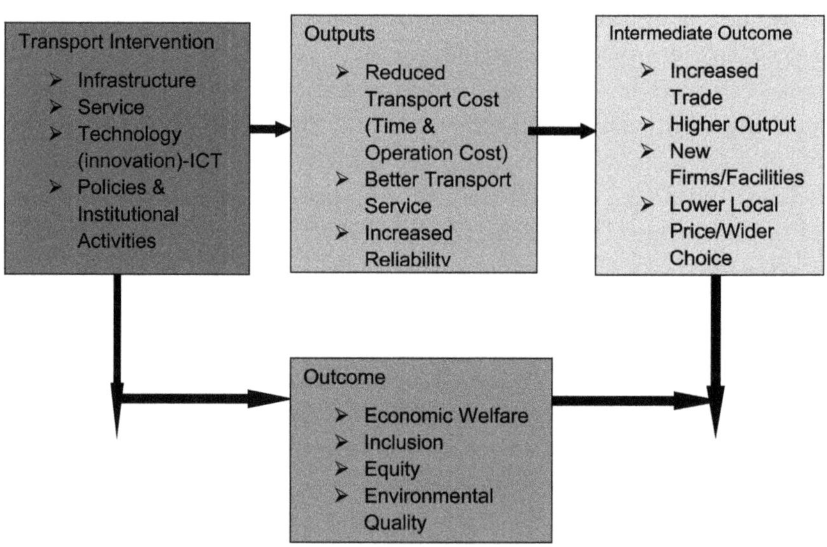

Fig. 8.1 Effect of transport invention and innovation on the economy (*Source* Adapted from Meersman and Nazemzadeh [2019])

to goods, distribution channels, and customer base. All of these relate to economic clusters and promote economic growth. But in many developing countries, like Nigeria, economic development policies indicate weaknesses in depicting the connection between transport infrastructure investments and economic growth; and how the change can occur at different stages of development (Lemes et al., 2020; Lindsey & Santos, 2020).

8.3 Analytical Framework

Several studies have examined the effect of transport on economic growth. However, most of them are limited to one-way analysis, while several scholars noted that an interaction exists between transportation and economic improvement. Studies have also accessed the effect of ICT on transportation systems and the factors influencing its adoption.

Lenz et al. (2018) estimated the effects of transport infrastructure (road and rail) on economic growth in Central and Eastern EU member states using data for the 1995–2016 periods. The study utilized panel data with three standard estimators: pooled ordinary least squares, fixed effects, and random effects and found positive results in the case of all estimated variables such as road infrastructure, gross fixed capital formation, population growth, and trade openness, except the railway infrastructure where the effects seem to be negative. Their results also illustrated the long-standing problem of inefficient and outdated railway infrastructure.

Walid (2020) investigated how ICTs interact with road freight transport to affect environmental quality by reducing CO_2 emissions. The author employed a two-step GMM technique on a dataset from 2002 to 2014 in 43 countries. First, he found that ICTs decrease road freight transport and negatively impact environmental sustainability. Also, he discovered the interactions of mobile phones and fixed telephone technologies with road freight transport are more efficient in reducing pollution than using internet networks.

Adeyi (2018) examined the linkage between transportation and economic development using both theoretical models as econometrics models (ordinary and least square [OLS] of multiple regression) as the data were sourced from secondary sources and found a positive relationship between transportation and economic development.

Park et al. (2019) examined the role of various types of transport infrastructure in OECD and non-OECD countries by employing the hybrid production approach that combines macroeconomic growth with the supply of and demand for transportation. They used the panel two-stage least squares method to estimate the parameters of economic growth and supply and demand functions, where a principal component represents transportation demand. Their finding shows a more substantial significance of maritime transportation in economic growth than air and land transport. Also, the need for transportation is driven by other social and economic factors apart from prices.

Cigu et al. (2019) examined the link between the transport infrastructure and the economic performance in the EU-28 countries over the period 2000–2014, using panel data methods (production function and factor analysis). Their results showed significant effects from transport infrastructure components even after institutional and other factors are controlled for. They also discovered the unidirectional long-run causality relationship between growth, transport infrastructure, and Public Sector Performance. Transport infrastructure status (measured through index of transport) significantly impacts economic development with a coefficient estimate.

Ma et al. (2020) investigated the relationship between GDP and freight turnover for economic zones of stationary series and non-stationary sequences using the vector autoregressive (VAR) and the vector error correction models (VECM). They used the data on freight transportation and GDP in China from 2003 to 2018 and conducted an impulse response analysis and variance decomposition to verify the effectiveness of the models. They also carried out a Granger causality test to find the relationship between transportation and economic development in each economic zone. Their results showed that freight turnover and GDP in the Northeast economic zone are bidirectional. At the same time, a unidirectional relationship exists between freight turnover and GDP in the Circum Bohai-Sea, the Pearl River, Middle Part, Southwest, and Northwest zones.

Listiono (2018) examined the correlation between freight and economic growth experienced by 1990 countries between 1980 and 2014 using the simultaneous equation model for estimation. Results revealed a two-way causal relationship between economic growth and the transport of goods in high-income and low-income countries. Unfortunately, the concurrent equation model did not integrate the lagged effect into the model. Therefore, the models did not capture the dynamic relationship between transportation and economic improvement. Tong and Yu (2018) examined the interaction between economic growth and freight transport. The results showed a two-way Granger causality between them in the underdeveloped central and western zones.

Pradhan (2019) used the vector error correction model (VECM) to study the interaction between transport infrastructure and economic growth in G-20 countries from 1961 to 2016. The results showed that transportation infrastructure promotes economic growth and vice-versa. These studies focus on the relationship between economy and transportation improvement. Nevertheless, there is a lack of application in the economic zone of developing nations.

Similarly, Tob-Ogu et al. (2018) utilized multiple case studies and in-depth interviews to map ICT adoption in road freight transport in Nigeria. Their findings show that levels of ICT adoption are mainly determined by local contextual factors (competitiveness, safety, and regulation) and firm size.

Concisely, our study engages microdata to advance insight into the dynamic and relationship between transportation and economic development through promoting technological innovation in a developing nation scenario focusing on Nigeria.

8.4 Methodology and Program Background

We engaged a quasi-experimental approach to estimate the impact of the O-pay technological innovation in transportation services on development outcomes using Kwara State, Nigeria, as a case study. The project covered transportation engagement with Cabs, tricycles, and motorcycles. However, the most prominent in the metropolis is that of the

O-rider (Motorcyclist). Therefore, we focused on using technology to connect O-riders (motorcyclists) to their respective customers in the study area, leveraging Google Maps. At inception, the O-pay company signed interested commercial motorcyclists in the Ilorin metropolis into the project. They were duly registered with home address verification and guarantor. With this registration, they were automatically enrolled on the e-wallets account platform with facilities such as savings/deposits, e-payments for utility bills-electricity/TV, airtime, loans, data purchase, QR merchant, etc.

The entry criteria included being an experienced motorcyclist, having a functional motorcycle, the ability to use an Android phone with the O-pay mobile app, and having a basic literacy level. They were given an Android phone with the O-pay app installed. They were provided with lemon-colored helmets and jackets. They were invited for about 2 hour of training on the use of the O-pay mobile application. The cost of the package at inception was ₦27,000 naira (USD 75). This fee covers the phone, helmet, jacket, and other administrative fees. O-riders were expected to pay back the installment of 300 naira daily (0.833 USD). With the help of a Google Map, the O-Pay mobile app connects a potential customer to the motorcyclist through the order platform. The customer also needs to have a registered O-pay account with the company, which allows them to be financially included with services such as e-wallets, e-payments, e-investments, e-wealth, etc. As soon as the O-rider takes the customer to their booked destination, the customer pays using the O-pay electronic payment platform to the O-riders' account. The O-pay company will then add bonuses to the account of the O-rider. For this study, we randomly sampled 100 O-riders (motorcyclists under the O-pay project) and 60 motorcyclists who were not under the O-Pay project. The intervention effects were evaluated in the short term (3 months post-intervention). The project was initiated in July 2019. We collected our data in October/November 2019. Data engaged in the first data collection covered activities from August to October 2019. Baseline data were collected retrospectively since the project initiation was short at the time of data collection. The problem of memory loss was not an issue. Structured questionnaires and interviews were used for data collection. In October 2020, the long-term intervention interview was conducted.

8.5 Statistical Methods

Descriptive statistics and a difference in difference estimator were used for analysis. The difference in difference estimator was used in estimating the effects of the project on the O-riders' welfare:

$$Y_{it} = \alpha + \beta_1 \text{Treat}_i + \beta_2 \text{Post}_t + \beta_3 (\text{Treat} \cdot \text{Post})_{it} + _{it} \tag{8.1}$$

Y_{eit} is the outcome variable for an individual i at time t, is the constant, Treat_i is the dummy equals 1 if treated and 0 if not treated, and Post_t is the dummy equals 1 if data collected at post-intervention, 0 if at baseline, the $\text{Treat} \cdot \text{Post}$ is the interactive effect, β_1, β_2, and β_3 are the coefficients. However, α measures the average treatment outcome before the program.

β_1 measures the difference between treatment and control before the program (selection effect)
β_2 measures changes across time in the outcome variable common to both groups
β_3 measures the average treatment effect of the program on the outcome variable.

Variable measurements: Outcome variables were collected daily and multiplied by the number of workdays per week to arrive at weekly estimates. Variables were collected engaging this method to overcome memory recall issues among respondents.

Average weekly savings: Average amount saved per week
Average weekly income: Average income from bike riding saved per week
Average weekly health expenditure: Average out-of-pocket expenses on health issues

Average weekly fuel cost/ expenditure: Average expenses on bike fueling per week
Average weekly labor productivity was calculated by weekly income/ weekly work hours

8.6 Results and Discussion

As shown in Table 8.1, we found that the average age of motorcyclists in both groups was 35 years. This implied these motorcyclists were mainly youths, and both groups had comparatively of the same age group. This result agrees with the findings of Jibrilla and Fashola (2018), which indicated that the youth majorly occupied the motorcycle business. Furthermore, we found that the average number of schooling years for O-riders was 13 years, while motorcyclists who were not under the O-pay project had 8 years of schooling on average. This showed that the majority of the riders had at least primary education as there was a statistical difference in the mean of the two groups, attributed to the fact that basic education is required for participation in O-ride projects. The low level of motorcycle operator's education might be responsible for some operators' inability to participate in O-ride projects, as literacy will aid the use of the mobile application among users.

Table 8.1 Socio-economics of respondents

Socio-economics	Treated (N = 100) Mean	Control (N = 60) Mean	t-test for difference in mean (p-value)
Age	35 years	35 years	0.3 (0.7)
Household size	5.0 persons	5.3 persons	0.5 (0.7)
Schooling years	13 years	8 years	4.5 (0.0)*

*A statistical difference of 1% was recorded for schooling years among the group. This is attributed to the fact that basic literacy was an entry criterion for the O-pay participants
Source Survey 2019

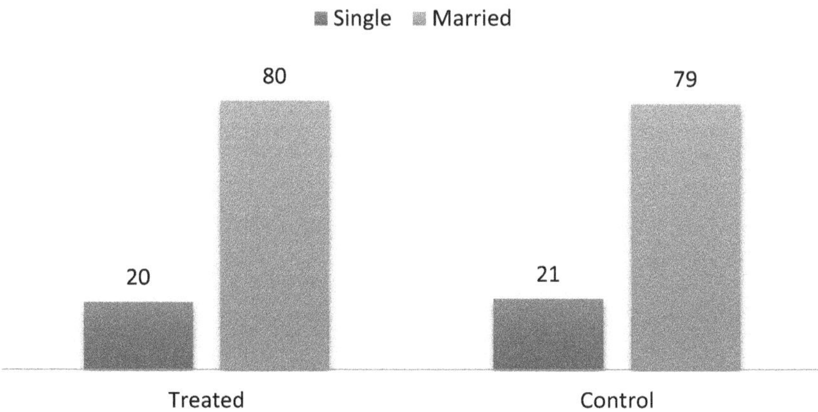

Fig. 8.2 Marital status of respondents

As shown in Fig. 8.2, findings revealed that there was no significant difference in the marital statuses of respondents, as the respondents under the O-pay project had 80% of them married. In comparison, those that were not under the project had 79% of them as married.

Table 8.2 shows the outcome variables for both groups at baseline. We found that weekly work hours, weekly fuel cost, labor productivity, and income were not statistically significant at baseline. However, weekly savings and health expenditures were found to be statistically significant. Since bike income was generated, productivity and fuel costs for both groups at baseline were not statistically different. These statistical differences observed in the savings and health expenditure may be attributed to literacy differentials between the groups, which may have influenced saving culture and the amount spent on health. Literacy level or level of education is expected to impact savings and health expenditure. This is corroborated with the findings (Mohammed, 2020) that education positively affects savings, as respondents having education were 3 times more likely to save than their uneducated counterparts. This could also be linked to the awareness level of health care for educated folks is expected to be high accordingly.

Table 8.2 Outcome variables for both groups at baseline

Outcome variables	Treated ($N = 100$) Mean	Control ($N = 60$) Mean	*t*-test for difference in mean (p-value)
Weekly bike income	24,200 Naira ($67)	22,050 Naira ($61)	1.25 (0.009)
Weekly savings	10,720 Naira ($30)	4875 Naira ($14)	2.94 (0.000)*
Weekly health expenditure	1415 Naira ($3.9)	670 Naira ($1.9)	2.69 (0.000)*
Labor productivity	323 Naira/hour ($0.9/h)	389 Naira/hour ($1.08)	1.61 (0.920)
Weekly fuel cost	5360 Naira ($14.9)	6020 Naira ($16.7)	1.44 (0.130)
Weekly work hours	79 hours	67 hours	1.86 (0.285)

*Statistical difference at 1%
Source Survey 2019

8.7 Impact of the Project on Selected Development Outcome Variables

Our findings showed that at ($p < 0.01$); the generated average weekly income increased by 137% for O-riders compared to the motorcyclists who were not under the O-pay project (₦30,220 [US$84[1]] from ₦22,050 [the US$61] at baseline). This showed that in the short term, technology engagement in transportation management significantly impacted the O-riders' income compared to the non-O-pay participants. Which will consequently improve their livelihood (Table 8.3).

The average weekly savings of O-riders increased by 355% (₦4875 [$14] to ₦17,309 [$48] at baseline) at ($p < 0.01$). This also indicates an enhanced saving culture, which enhanced financial well-being attributed to technological integration in the process. This also has a strong relationship with the welfare of the respondents. Therefore, an increase in savings indicates improved welfare gains in the short term attributed to technological innovation (Table 8.4).

Job quality; is measured by assessing the productivity level of a worker by engaging the ratio of the input per hour to the output

[1] At the time of research, a US dollar was 360 naira. This was used for the conversion.

Table 8.3 Average program effect on average weekly income (Naira)

The difference in difference estimates		
Y average weekly income	Co-efficient	*t*-value
Treatment	2150	1.60
Time trend	−4550	−4.21
DID (Interaction)	30,220*	11.57
Constant	22,050	25.84

*Represent significance at 1% level
Source Survey 2019

Table 8.4 Average program effect on average weekly savings (Naira)

The difference in difference estimates		
Y average weekly savings	Co-efficient	*t*-value
Treatment	5845	4.62
Time trend	−2225	−9.69
DID (Interaction)	17,309*	6.41
Constant	4875	36.48

*Represent significance at 1% level
Source Survey 2019

(wages). We found an increase in average weekly labor productivity at 160% (625.06 Naira/hour [$1.7] from ₦389.6/hour [$1.1] at baseline). This implied an enhanced job quality attributed to digital integration in the transportation system. This finding agrees with the report of Jedwab and Moradi (2014), which reported that transportation technology could produce economic change by reducing trade costs and integrating markets, thereby increasing long-term productivity. Additionally, Meng et al. (2015), Rodrigue et al. (2016) reported that an efficient transportation network contributes to socio-economic development and the increased quality of life by generating inter- or intra-city connections during urbanization (Meng et al., 2015; Rodrigue et al., 2016) (Table 8.5).

As shown in Table 8.6, we also found that the weekly health expenditure was reduced by 145% (₦974 [$2.7] out of ₦670 [$1.86]) compared with those that were not under the project. Of course, motorcyclists who are not under the project will have to roam around till passengers

Table 8.5 Average program effect on average weekly labor productivity (Naira/hours)

The difference in difference estimates		
Y average weekly labor productivity	Co-efficient	*t*-value
Treatment	−66.32	−1.80
Time trend	−117.2	−3.64
DID (Interaction)	625.06*	11.29
Constant	389.6	13.78

*Represent significance at 1% level
Source Survey 2019

Table 8.6 Average program effect on average weekly health expenditure (Naira)

The difference in difference estimates		
Y average weekly health expenditure	Co-efficient	*t*-value
Treatment	745	4.13
Time trend	130	1.66
DID (Interaction)	−974*	−4.29
Constant	670	13.83

*Represent significance at 1% level
Source Survey 2019

are picked up. Still, for the O-riders, digital technology engagement has helped reduce workplace stress and fatigue as motorcyclists do not need to roam around but move when an order notification is received.

Further evidence in Table 8.7 showed that at $p < 0.05$, the weekly fuel cost was reduced by 21% (₦1254 [$3.48] out of ₦6020 [$16.7]) when compared with the non-O-pay participants. This result is so because the O-riders only move from their location when an order is received, which helps fuel management. Technological innovation has contributed to fuel consumption among the O-riders. This may also have contributed to the reduction in greenhouse gases from fossil fuels attributed to the invention. This was responsible for the reduced fuel expenditure attributed to technological innovation. This agrees with the findings of Jedwab and Moradi (2014), which reported that technology engagement contributed to reduced trade costs.

Table 8.7 Average program effect on average weekly fuel cost

The difference in difference estimates		
Y average weekly fuel cost	Co-efficient	*t*-value
Treatment	−660	−1.67
Time trend	−650	−1.22
DID (Interaction)	−1254**	−2.08
Constant	6020	20.46

**Represent significance at 5% level
Source Survey 2019

Ninety percent of the O-rider respondents reported poor internet services affecting their operations. This result may be linked to deficient digital infrastructure, which leads to business disruptions. About 85% of the O-riders also noted inconsistencies in the host company policies as the organization kept modifying some of its terms and conditions of engagement to the detriment of the O-riders. Eighty percent of the respondents also noted that the company failed to secure the motor bicycle unions to support the project. This leads to rivalry among the participating riders and non-participating riders. Most participating riders stopped paying the daily dues to the association with the claims that they were no longer union members but O-pay riders. This indicates a need to develop contextualized strategies for advancing relevant innovation to enhance inclusivity (Table 8.8).

Table 8.8 Constraints to efficient utilization of smart transportation ($N = 100$-O-riders only)

S/N	Constraints	%
1.	Poor internet services	90
2.	Inconsistency in policies of the host company	85
3.	Poor support from the bike unions	80

Source Survey 2019

8.8 Conclusion and Recommendations

From the evidence, in the short term, we concluded that digital integration in the transportation sector has significantly contributed to enhancing the welfare of the O-pay participants. The study also showed that the O-pay digital project enhanced job efficiency and quality vis-a-vis productivity while reducing resource wastage, fuel, and health expenditure. However, the long-term intervention data collection showed the project was not sustained as the service no longer exists in less than a year of start-up. Reasons range from poor managerial sustainability of innovation to poor user integration at the project design stage. However, evidence in the short term revealed that technological integration in the transportation system has the potential to address significant development issues, including poverty, unemployment, financial exclusion, and poor health and well-being. Furthermore, our findings showed that technological innovations are enablers for sustainable development goals (SGDs). Therefore, to sustain the technological intervention impact, development efforts should focus on innovating digital solutions and sustaining digital innovations in developing nations to harness its full benefits.

Practical implications: There is a need to integrate project managerial sustainability skills focus right from the project design stage. Future innovation designs should engage participatory and user-centered approaches and stakeholders' engagement to aid the sustainability of digital innovations in developing economies for inclusive prosperity. Investing in digital infrastructure is also necessary to engage innovative transportation solutions efficiently.

Theoretical implications: Most innovations are usually designed on case-dependent basis to address particular social problems with the business goal of making profits while solving such problems. Future efforts should also include a development focus to aid uptake and sustainability. This has implications for principles and theory in the design and sustainability models in technological innovations in the transport sector, especially in the emerging economy context.

8.9 Limitations of the Study and Future Research Opportunities

The study was a modest effort to evaluate the impact of digital innovation in the transportation sector on development outcomes engaging micro-level data. A limitation of this study is that technology's impact on welfare was examined in the short term as comprehensive data were not available to estimate the long-term effect, making it difficult to investigate the trend. We suggest a similar study be carried out to examine the impact of digital innovations in the transportation sector with a broad range of development variable outcomes in a developing nation using an experimental model such as randomized control. The study should also study the development variables' outcomes in the short and long run to advance relevant recommendations.

References

Abboubi, M. E. L. (2022). The perilous path toward supply chain integration addressed from social capital perspective. *International Journal of Accounting, Finance, Auditing, Management and Economics, 3*(1–1), 32–57.

Adeyi, E. O. (2018, August). The impact of transportation on economic development in Nigeria. *International Journal of Contemporary Applied Researches, 5*(8). ISSN: 2308-1365. www.ijcar.net

Cigu, E., Agheorghiesei, D. T., Gavrilut, A. F., & Toader, E. (2018/2019). Transport infrastructure development, public performance and long-run economic growth: A case study for the EU-28 countries. *Sustainability, 11*, 67. https://doi.org/10.3390/su11010067

Clarke, C., & Batina, R. G. (2019). A replication of "is public expenditure productive?" (Journal of Monetary Economics, 1989). *Public Finance Review, 47*(3), 623–629. https://doi.org/10.1177/1091142117736606

Jedwab, R., & Moradi, A. (2014). *Transportation technology and economic change: The impact of colonial railroads on city growth in Africa* (Working Paper Series IIEP-WP-2014-3). Institute for International Economic Policy. www.gwu.edu/~iiep

Jibrilla, H. M., & Fashola, O. M. (2018). Impact of commercial tricycle operation on income of youths in Mubi North Local Government Adamawa State, Nigeria. *IDOSR Journal of Humanities and Social Sciences, 2*(3), 56–72.

Karl, A. A., Micheluzzi, J., Leite, L. R, & Pereira, C. R. (2018). Supply chain resilience and key performance indicators: A systematic literature review. *Production*. https://doi.org/10.1590/0103-6513.20180020

Lemes, A., Ferreira, G., Antonio, A., Junior, B., & Larson, W. D. (2020). Effects of land use and transportation policies on the spatial distribution of urban energy consumption in Brazil. *Energy Economics, 90*. https://doi.org/10.1016/j.eneco.2020.104864

Lenz, N. V., Pavlić Skender, H., & Mirković, P. A. (2018). The macroeconomic effects of transport infrastructure on economic growth: The case of Central and Eastern E.U. member states. *Economic Research-Ekonomska Istraživanja, 31*(1), 1953–1964. https://doi.org/10.1080/1331677X.2018.1523740

Lindsey, R., & Santos, G. (2020). Research in transportation economics addressing transportation and environmental externalities with economics: Are policymakers listening? *Research in Transportation Economics, 82*(October 2019), 100872. https://doi.org/10.1016/j.retrec.2020.100872

Listiono, L. (2018). The relationship between transport, economic growth, and environmental degradation for ninety countries. *Journal of Environmental Sustainability, 2*, 1–64.

Ma, Y., Zhu, J., Gu, G., & Chen, K. (2020). Freight transportation and economic growth for zones: Sustainability and development strategy in China. *Sustainability, 12*, 10450.

Meersman, H., & Nazemzadeh, M. (2019). The contribution of transport infrastructure to economic activity: The case of Belgium. *Case Studies on Transport Policy, 5*(2), 316–324. https://doi.org/10.1016/j.cstp.2017.03.009

Meng, L., Li, L., & Liu, S. (2015). Research on the relationship between regional railway freight volume and GDP. In *Proceedings of 4th International Conference on Logistics, Informatics and Service Science* (pp. 345–350). Springer.

Mohammed, A. U. (2020). Impact of financial literacy on individual saving: A study in the Omani context. *Research in World Economy, 9*(2), 123–128. https://doi.org/10.5430/rwe.v11n5p123

Moldabekova, A., Zhidebekkyzy, A., Akhmetkaliyeva, S., & Baimukhanbetova, E. (2020). Advanced technologies in improving the management of logistics services: Bibliometric network analysis. *Polish Journal of Management Studies, 21*, 211–223.

Molero, G. D., Santarremigia, F. E., Poveda-Reyes, S., Mayrhofer, M., Awad-Núñez, S., & Kassabji, A. (2019). Key factors for the implementation and integration of innovative ICT solutions in SMEs and large companies involved in the multimodal transport of dangerous goods. *European Transport Research Review, 11*, Article 28.

Mubarik, M., Rasi, R. Z., & binti, R. M. (2019). Triad of big data supply chain analytics, supply chain integration and supply chain performance: Evidences from oil and gas sector. *Humanities and Social Sciences Letters, 7*(4), 209–224. https://doi.org/10.18488/journal.73.2019.74.209.224

National Bureau of Statistics (NBS). (2018, December). *Labour force statistics. Unemployment and underemployment report* (Vol. 1).

Okechukwu, N., Sizwe, M., & Adedotun A. (2021). *The effect of transportation infrastructure on economic*. Proceedings of the 2nd African International Conference on Industrial Engineering and Operations Management Harare, Zimbabwe, December 7–10, 2020.

Park, J. S., Seo, Y. J., & Ha, M. (2019). The role of maritime, land, and air transportation in economic growth: Panel evidence from OECD and non-OECD countries. *Research in Transportation Economics, 78*, 100765. https://doi.org/10.1016/j.retrec.2019.100765

Pradhan, R. P. (2019). Investigating the causal relationship between transportation infrastructure, financial penetration and economic growth in G-20 countries. *Research in Transportation Economics, 78*, 100766.

Rodrigue, J.-P., Comtois, C., & Slack, B. (2016). *The geography of transport systems*. Taylor & Francis.

Som, J. O., & Anyigba, H. (2022). Examining the effects of information systems usage and managerial commitment on supply chain performance: The mediating role of supply chain integration. *SAGE Open*. https://doi.org/10.1177/21582440221091251

Sorker, F. (2019). *Investigation on reverse logistics of end of life cars in the UK*. eprints.mdx.ac.uk

Tob-ogu, A., Kumar, N., & Cullen, J. (2018). ICT adoption in road freight in Nigeria—A case study of the petroleum downstream sector. *Technological Forecasting & Social Change, 131*, 240–252.

Tong, T., & Yu, T. E. (2018). Transportation and economic growth in China: A heterogeneous panel co-integration and causality analysis. *Journal of Transport Geography, 73*, 120–130.

Valila T. (2020). An overview of economic theory and evidence of public-private partnerships in the procurement of (transport) infrastructure. *Utilities Policy, 62*(November 2019). https://doi.org/10.1016/j.jup.2019.100995

Walid, C. (2020). Information and communication technologies, road freight transport, and environmental sustainability. *Environmental Economics, 11*(1), 124–132. https://doi.org/10.21511/ee.11(1).2020.11

World Bank. (2020a, May 29). *Three emerging digital technology for the new normal in transport*. World Bank Blogs. Retrieved on 10 August 2021 from www.blogs.worldbank.org/transport/three-emerging-digital-technology-for-the-new-normal-in-transport

World Bank. (2020b). Disability Inclusion in Nigeria: A Rapid Assessment. © World Bank. http://hdl.handle.net/10986/34073. License: CC BY 3.0 IGO.

World Bank. (2021, May 12). *How digital integration has transformed Kenya's transportation sector*. The World Bank feature Story. Retrieved on 10 August 2021 from www.worldbank.org/news/feature/2021/05/12/how-digital-integration-has-transformed-Kenya-s-transportation-sector/

World Poverty Clock. (2018, June). *Nigeria has become the poverty capital of the world*. Retrieved on 15 December 2019 from www.qz.com/Africa

Xu, L., Li, B., Ma, C., & Liu, J. (2022). Supply chain finance and firm diversification: Evidence from China. *Australian Journal of Management*. https://doi.org/10.1177/03128962221075366

Yin, C. & Yu, S. (2019). Social benefit of urban infrastructure: An empirical analysis of four Chinese autonomous municipalities, *Utilities Policy, 58*(16–26). ISSN 0957-1787. https://doi.org/10.1016/j.jup.2019.03.001

9

Drivers of Eco-Innovation Among Manufacturing Firms in Nigeria

Olufemi Adebola Popoola
and Grace Oluwatofunmi Popoola

9.1 Introduction

Innovative economic growth routes and a thorough grasp of nation-specific technical problems are essential for economically sustainable development (Sanni, 2017). There have been increasing concerns from stakeholders and the international community on the commitment of firms to the adverse impact of industrial activities on the environs (Choi et al., 2018). As a consequence of rising environmental expectations from society, stakeholder groups, and regulatory authorities, companies have

O. A. Popoola (✉)
Innovation and Technology Policy Department, Nigerian Institute of Social and Economic Research (NISER), Ibadan, Nigeria
e-mail: adebolastephens@gmail.com

G. O. Popoola
Department of Agricultural Economics, Bowen University, Iwo, Nigeria

A. S. Ibidunni et al. (eds.), *Innovation, Entrepreneurship and the Informal Economy in Sub–Saharan Africa*, Sustainable Development Goals Series,
https://doi.org/10.1007/978-3-031-46293-1_9

continuously adopted innovations to decrease the impact of their operations on the environment (Rothenberg & Zyglidopoulos, 2003). The level and rate of adoption, however, differ across firms.

Kemp and Pearson described eco-innovation as the development, assimilation, or exploitation of a product, process, service, management, or business techniques novel to the firm that results in a decrease in environmental risk, pollution, or other negative consequences (Kemp & Pearson, 2008). Eco-innovation has gained traction in the literature (Runnings, 2000) as a means of enhancing corporate competitiveness and facilitating the transition to a more sustainable society (Carrillo-Hermosilla et al., 2010; Machiba, 2010). This sort of innovation does not have to be new to the world; nevertheless, it should be original to the firm or organization that implements or accepts it (OECD-EUROSTAT, 2005).

Africa's rapid industrial growth requires that there be sustained policies toward environmental protection. As a result of industrial and domestic activities, the country's emission rate is increasing. The carbon output rate exceeds 10 metric tons of carbon per year (WDI, 2018), making the country one of Africa's top CO_2 emitters. The poor business environment in the country encourages such pollution by firms. Non-enforcement of environmental regulations by authorities has also led to inappropriate means of disposing of industrial waste. The manufacturing sector is dominated by small-sized firms (Efobi et al., 2018) and the attendant effects of these firms on pollution cannot be undermined. For instance, the country's regulatory system for environmental protection is inadequate. Nigeria's 2015 National Renewable Energy Efficiency (NREE) policy of increasing the usage of green energy has not yielded its intended objectives. Furthermore, the country's efforts toward the management of industrial waste and other types of pollution have been ineffective. Despite these attempts, research suggests that policy enforcement is lacking (World Bank, 2016). This indicates that legislation enacted by government agencies alone may not be sufficient to minimize industrial pollution. Innovative solutions and more environmentally friendly technologies should be developed to minimize or mitigate the effects of such challenges. Eco-innovation is a novel approach of dealing with such environmental problems. According to the literature, it is believed that the adoption of eco-innovation presents positive gains for both the economy and the environment (Belin et al., 2011). This is in terms of making the country competitive and sustaining the environment. It will also help businesses in improving performance while protecting the environment.

This study further examines the innovation activities in the manufacturing sector in order to better understand the nature of eco-innovation and drivers of eco-innovation. This will aid in the development of self-regulatory regulations that will benefit these firms and ensure environmental sustainability.

Moreover, research has established that African nations would be the most affected by human-caused climatic and environmental changes (Asongu, 2018). According to Environmental Protection Agency of the United States, the principal contributor in 2018 was the combustion of fossil fuels for generating energy for use domestically and industrial sector. In Nigeria, the majority of industrial operations rely on a strong demand for government-subsidized replacement fossil fuels for power (Asongu et al., 2016).

Nigeria must adopt eco-innovation policies if it is to achieve sustainable industrial growth (UNIDO, 2011). Understanding how companies embrace eco-innovation might help policymakers design green industrialization strategies for the industrial sector. This will aid in the development of self-regulatory rules that encourage businesses to adhere to better environmental standards. Additionally, the Agenda 2063 of the African Development Bank (AfDB) and the Sustainable Development Goals (SDGs) of the United Nations of achieving industrialization while ensuring that the environment and health of the people are improved.

Several empirical evidences exist on eco-innovation from developed countries (Cainelli et al., 2012; del Río et al., 2016), but the evidence is limited for developing countries like Nigeria with the exception of Adelegan et al. (2010) and Sanni (2017). Adelegan et al. (2010) examined eco-innovation and corporate performance of firms in the pulp and paper industry in Nigeria. Sanni (2017) examined drivers of eco-innovation in Nigeria's manufacturing sector using a 2005/2007 innovation data. This study builds on these studies by using the latest available nationally representative innovation data for Nigeria—the World Bank Innovation Survey and further examines the drivers of product and process eco-innovations. Understanding how businesses in Nigeria's manufacturing sector are adopting eco-innovation might help policymakers build economic tools to support its development and acceptance throughout the country's industrial sector. The objective of this study is to examine the drivers of adoption of eco-innovation by firms in Nigeria's manufacturing sector. Specifically, the study identified the factors influencing firm's decision to adopt product and process eco-innovations.

9.2 Literature Review

Theoretical Framework: *Dynamic Capabilities Theory*

This study is premised on the dynamic capabilities' theory (Teece, 2007; Zahra et al., 2006). This idea is a development of the resource-based approach (Barney, 2001; Teece et al., 1997). They defined dynamic capabilities as "the firm's ability to incorporate, create, and adapt to the changing environments." Dynamic capabilities were defined by Eisenhardt and Martin (2000) as unique and recognizable processes, while Nelson and Winter (2002) defined them as predictable behavioral patterns through which an organization manages its resources with the goal of achieving corporate success. Teece (2007) also points out that those organizations' skills allow them to produce innovation. As a result, dynamic capabilities involve the management of all areas of a company's skills and resources with the goal of gaining a competitive edge.

Conceptualizations of Eco-Innovation

Different authors have defined the concept of eco-innovation. Carrillo-Hermosilla et al. (2010) defined it as a form of innovation that ensures the production of products and services that are sustainable and environmentally safe. Kemp (2010) and Rennings (2000) define the concept as products, processes, and services or organizational shifts that promote reduction in pollution and ensures economic sustainability. In addition, Doran and Ryan (2016) explains it as creating new business opportunities through product innovation or new practices that benefit the environment.

Key Elements of Eco-Innovation

According to Arranz et al. (2019), eco-innovation improves the environment, adds value, creates new business niches, or improves competitive behavior while also implying a benefit to the environment. Kemp and Foxon (2007) divided eco-innovation into four categories: green system innovations; environmental organizational innovation; environmental technologies; and environmental product and process innovations.

All pollution control and cleaning technologies that address pollutants discharged in the natural environment are referred to as environmental technologies. This comprises waste management equipment and cleaner process technologies (i.e., new industrial methods that are less polluting and/or more resource efficient than related alternatives). Monitoring and instrumentation of the environment, green energy, and noise and vibration management are all included. Environmental organizational innovation is the development of organizational strategies and management systems that solve environmental issues that occur throughout the manufacturing process. Organizational techniques comprise all pollution control measures aimed at preventing pollution through input substitution, more efficient process operation, and minor adjustments to industrial plants. Environmental management and auditing systems comprise all formal environmental management systems that involve measurement, reporting, and responsibility for material consumption, energy, water, and waste. Product and service innovation that improves the environment: All new or improved commodities, as well as environmentally useful services, are instances of environmentally beneficial product and service innovation.

Financial goods and services that are low-pollution and resource-intensive (such as eco-lease or climate mortgages) are examples (car sharing, for example). Green system advancements: Green system innovations are innovative production and consumption systems that are less harmful to the environment than existing ones. Biological agriculture and renewable energy systems are examples of green system innovation.

Drivers of Eco-Innovation in the Manufacturing Sector

Regulation, market conditions, technology, and company-specific processes are the four types of eco-innovation drivers identified by Horbach et al. (2012) and Kowalska (2014). Other writers argue that eco-innovation did not arise solely as a systematic reaction to law and that other variables (market circumstances, technology) had a significant role in its growth. Although the manufacturing process conforms with environmental regulations, the final product is significantly costlier (del Rio, 2013).

Mazzanti and Zobloi (2008) found a number of factors that influence eco-innovation in Italy. These include the company's structural factors, sustainability-focused research and development, adherence to environmental regulatory requirements, and technology research. According to Maçaneiro et al. (2013), there are a few important factors that have a big impact on achieving good outcomes. These aspects include environmental legislation and incentives, leadership support and the company's community reputation, technical research, and environmental formalization.

Pacheco et al. (2017) provided a concise review factors identified by many writers in the literature as driving eco-innovation. The researcher identified 23 factors of eco-innovation in small- and medium-sized businesses from the literature on the subject. The variability of the research, on the other hand, cannot be used to draw conclusions about the predominance of specific elements in a certain field. Furthermore, virtually all of the studies are new and insufficient to draw a meaningful judgment. Some literature has also identified supply, demand, and law and Policy as factors affecting eco-innovation (Belin et al.,

2011; Horbach, 2014). Firstly, external factors include the organization's knowledge, skills, experience, and technical capabilities. The second pertains to customers' environmental awareness as well as the need and duty to evade pollution. The final strand focuses on environmental regulatory instruments, institutions, and legislation engaged in environmental protection.

Furthermore, Belin et al. (2011) and del Rio (2013) highlighted the importance of company scale and external information sources. Small businesses see innovation as a method to break into new markets, but giant corporations have a secure market position and do not prioritize exploring new prospects. As a result, while dealing with the size of firms, eco-innovation factors demand specific consideration, especially because small businesses account for a substantial portion of the economy in many nations. Furthermore, in order to enhance eco-innovation, established firms pay close attention to information supplied by various institutions, while young companies are on the opposite end of the spectrum (Alvarez & Iske, 2015). There are no major variations in age between the firms since those who have recently entered the market are not more eco-innovative than those who have been there longer.

Many businesses have participated in eco-innovation for a variety of reasons. An increase in company performance has been one of the important variables (Adelegan et al., 2010; Bansal & Gao, 2006). According to one of the few articles on eco-innovation in Nigeria's industrial sector, the pulp and paper industry indicated a strong correlation between green technology usage and financial performance (Adelegan et al., 2010). Environmental management strategies or eco-innovation activities were found to be positively related to financial outcomes and operational efficiency by Darnall et al. (2008) and Ahmad and Schroeder (2003). Businesses that adopt eco-innovative management practices, according to some writers, are more competitive because they decrease costs, improve quality, and offer new processes and products (Shrivastava, 2008; Yang et al., 2010). Apart from these factors, environmental management systems like as ISO 14001 are said to influence market share, brand image, risk portfolios, organizational efficiency, and growth in global sales (Jacobs et al., 2010; Zeng et al., 2008).

Review of Empirical Studies

A number of elements have been identified as having an influence on the emergence of eco-innovations in the literature. Service capabilities (Fernando et al., 2019), dynamic capabilities (Wu et al., 2016), human resource considerations (Jabbour et al., 2015), and training (Neto et al., 2014) are all aspects to consider, as well as absorptive capacity (Neto et al., 2014; Zhang et al., 2020). Technology push, market pull, regulatory push–pull, and firm-specific variables were highlighted by Zubeltzu-Jaka et al. (2018) as influencing eco-innovation. They discovered that teamwork and care for the environment among businesses improve the possibility of eco-innovation. They also stressed the importance of technology.

Pacheco et al. (2017) carried out a comprehensive literature analysis to investigate eco-innovation drivers in manufacturing small- and medium-sized businesses, a segment of businesses for which they feel there is a dearth of research. Among the critical determinants identified were policies and regulations that support the development and implementation of eco-innovations, resource availability (i.e., people, technology, and knowledge), perception of eco-innovations' strategic relevance, technological advisory geared toward the environment, product, and process eco-innovation-oriented methods, and cooperation and partnership within supply networks. The literature on the association between eco-innovation uptake and company performance is equivocal (Doran & Ryan, 2016; Tang et al., 2018). While some research has shown a negative link between eco-innovations and business performance (e.g., Driessen et al., 2013; Liu et al., 2011), others have found a positive link (Dangelico, 2016).

Guoyou et al. (2013) looked at the impact of stakeholders on the adoption of eco-innovations by Chinese manufacturing firms. They discover that, whereas international customers have a significant impact on businesses' eco-innovation efforts, community and regulatory stakeholders have none. Cai and Zhou (2014) looked at the internal and external determinants of eco-innovations in China across numerous industries. Their findings highlight the importance of the demand side for environmental eco-innovations and legislation, as well as the significance of internal drives as a link between the two (Cai & Zhou, 2014; Kesidou & Demirel, 2012). Peng and Liu (2016) examined how managerial attitudes (such as managerial environmental risk awareness and managerial cost–benefit awareness) and resource acquisition (from corporate and political networks) influenced eco-management, eco-process, and eco-product innovation activities. Their main contribution is the notion that eco-innovation is influenced by managers' perceptions and interpretations of their surroundings, rather than the external environment.

9.3 Methodology

Data Sources and Description

The World Bank Enterprise and Innovation Surveys for 2014/2015 was used in this study. The enterprise survey and the innovation survey were sampled for the same enterprises, as such the two datasets were combined using the unique firm identification to provide a rich dataset for the empirical analysis. The description of variables is presented in Table 9.1.

9.4 Analytical Techniques

The factors influencing firm's decision to adopt eco-innovation were determined using the logit regression model. It is applicable because the dependent variable is a binary variable that assumes the value of 1, if the firm has developed any environmental-compliant product or process in the last fiscal year, and 0 otherwise.

The regression model is expressed as follows in Eq. (9.1):

$$\begin{aligned} \text{eco\_inv}_i = {} & \beta_0 + \beta_1 X_1 + \beta_2 X_2 + \beta_3 X_3 \\ & + \beta_4 X_4 + \cdots + \beta_n X_n + \varepsilon_i \end{aligned} \tag{9.1}$$

Table 9.1 Description of variables

Variable	Description
Eco-innovation	Whether a firm developed any environmental-compliant product/ process in the last fiscal year = 1; and 0 otherwise
Innovativeness	
Organizational innovation	1 = introduction of a new and significantly improved organizational structure in the last 3 years, 0 otherwise
Marketing innovation	1 = introduction of new or significantly improved marketing method in the last three years, 0 otherwise
Demand-pull factors	
Satisfy customer demand	1 = Satisfy customer demand, 0 otherwise
Enter new market	1 = firm enters a new market or increases market share; and 0 otherwise
Increase the quality of products or services	1 = increase quality of products/ services, 0 otherwise
Increase the speed of production or offering service	1 = increase speed of production, 0 otherwise
Extend product range	1 = Whether the firm extends product range; and 0 otherwise
Domestic competition	1 = Whether completion is highly relevant and; 0 otherwise)
Technology-push factors	
Sources of knowledge	
Domestic academic or research institutions;	1 = Enterprise acquired information from domestic academic or research institution and 0 otherwise
Foreign firms;	1 = Enterprise acquired information from foreign firms and 0 otherwise
Private consulting company/individuals;	1 = Enterprise acquired information from private consulting companies/individuals and 0 otherwise
Public research institutes as sources of knowledge	1 = Enterprise acquired information for the public research institute, 0 otherwise

(continued)

Table 9.1 (continued)

Variable	Description
Training	1 = Enterprise engaged in training of personnel and 0 otherwise
Control variables	
	Age of firms (years)
	Firm size

where eco_ inv_i is defined as

$$\text{eco\_ inv}_i = \begin{cases} 1 & \text{if firm } i \text{ has developed any environmental compliant product or process} \\ 0 & \text{Otherwise} \end{cases}.$$

The explanatory variables are presented in Table 9.1.

However, Eq. (9.1) can be rewritten as:

$$\text{eco\_inv}_i = \beta_0 + \beta_1 X_i, \tag{9.2}$$

where X_i represents all the independent (explanatory) variables.

Following Maddala (1983), the structure of the logit regression model derives from the relations in Eqs. (9.1) and (9.2) as shown in Eq. (9.3):

$$\text{Prob}(y_1 = 1) = \text{Prob}(\varepsilon_i > -\beta' x_i) = 1 - F(-\beta' x_i) \tag{9.3}$$

If the cumulative probability function of the error term ε_i is assumed to have a logistic distribution, we have the logit model:

$$F(-\beta' x_i) = \frac{\exp(-\beta' x_i)}{1 + \exp(-\beta' x_i)} = \frac{1}{1 + \exp(-\beta' x_i)} \tag{9.4}$$

Hence,

$$1 - F(-\beta' x_i) = \frac{\exp(-\beta' x_i)}{1 + \exp(-\beta' x_i)} \tag{9.5}$$

The above logit model was estimated using a non-linear maximum likelihood method.

9.5 Results and Discussion

Firm Characteristics

This section presents the characteristics of firms in Nigeria's manufacturing sector. Table 9.2 presents the region where the sampled firms were located. As expected, about 20.7% of the firms are located in Lagos. This is followed by firms located in Anambra (12.5%), Kano (10.8%), and Abuja (10.8%). About 46% of these firms are located in the main business city. These would have an effect on the likelihood of adopting eco-innovation. It is believed that belonging to a specific geographical area encourages the adoption and development of innovation (Cooke et al., 2005).

Considering location of the firms in an export processing zone or industrial cluster, slightly above one-third of the firms are located either in an industrial park or an export processing zone. When firms are concentrated or clustered in a region (either in an industrial park or economic zone), learning, knowledge transfer, and collaboration promotes eco-innovation (De Marchi, 2012; Melander, 2018). The average age of firms was about 17.6 years with firms being as young as 2 years and the oldest being 102 years. With respect to innovation, previous studies have supported the inverse relationship between innovation and the age of the firm (Ayyagari et al., 2012). Younger firms have a higher propensity to innovate (Barasa et al., 2016) on account of their greater flexibility (Yusof & Mohd, 2011). This is to say that age is not

Table 9.2 Region of establishment

Region	Frequency/percentage
Abuja	45 (10.8)
Abia	41 (9.9)
Anambra	52 (12.5)
Cross-river	35 (8.4)
Enugu	43 (10.4)
Kaduna	35 (8.4)
Kano	45 (10.8)
Lagos	86 (20.7)
Oyo	33 (8.0)

a barrier for firms in the sector to adopt eco-innovation. Rehfeld et al. (2007) also supports that age is not an obstacle for firms to eco-innovate.

Majority of firms are owned by private domestic individuals (83.1%), although there are still a number of firms owned by foreign individuals/ companies (see Table 9.3). This could also have implications whether a firm adopts eco-innovation or not. The manager has about 14 years of experience working in the sector. Moreover, about 46.2% of these managers have at least some University training, though a considerable proportion (35%) had only secondary education (see Table 9.4). This implies that the manager is most likely to be equipped with the requisite skills and knowledge that will facilitate the adoption of eco-innovation. Schilirò (2010) asserted that the experience of the manager is a key input for innovation.

The capacity utilization of firms is about 77.7% and works an average of 64 hours per week. The average firm size of about 55 full-time employees. The size of the firm is an indication that most of the firms in the sample are medium-sized firms based on SMEDAN and NBS (2013) firm size classification and therefore should be able to eco-innovate. Triguero et al. (2013) posit that firm size is a major influencing factor in the adoption of eco-innovation. Larger firms are more likely to adopt eco-innovation than smaller firms because of the investments needed and complexity of such innovation. Only 9% of sampled firms had international quality certification. IQC 9% and 14% used foreign-licensed technology. About 21.4% of sampled firms spend on R&D. The low proportion of firms that spend on R&D could significantly affect firm's capacity to eco-innovate.

Drivers of Eco-Innovation

This section presents a descriptive analysis of the drivers of eco-innovation in Nigeria's manufacturing sector. Because enterprises in emerging nations, particularly Nigeria, have had to compete with imported goods from rich countries, this section is essential. It is therefore important to know these drivers so as to be able to compete favorably. Capability of firms to produce eco-innovative products is a

Table 9.3 Firm characteristics

	Observations	Mean	Standard deviation	Minimum	Maximum
Age	377	17.6	11.6	2	102
Owned by private domestic individuals/ companies	395	83.1	33.6	0	100
Owned by private foreign individuals/ companies	395	3.3	12.6	0	100
Owned by government/ state	395	1.7	7.4	0	100
Manager's years of experience working in the sector	384	13.5	9.2	1	72
Capacity utilization	257	77.7	28.1	0	100
Firm size	383	54.5	244.7	1	3500
International quality certification	389	0.09	0.28	0	1
Use of foreign-licensed technology	317	0.14	0.36	0	1
Spend on R&D	402	0.214	0.411	0	1
Located in the main business city	415	0.460	0.499	0	1
Located in an export processing zone or industrial park	394	0.352	0.478	0	1
Log of sales productivity	343	12.4515	2.456966	5.991465	23.13121
Hours of operation per week	313	64.4	34.7	7	168

Table 9.4 Education of top manager

Education of top manager	Frequency/percentage
Primary	18 (4.5)
Incomplete secondary education	16 (4.0)
Secondary	141 (35.0)
Vocational Training	41 (10.2)
Some university training	37 (9.2)
Tertiary (BA, BSc)	117 (29.0)
Tertiary (MSC, MBA, PhD)	33 (8.2)
Total	*403*

function of their competence to combine product and process innovations with environmental goals (Oltra & Saint Jean, 2005). In that light, this section first examines the proportion of firm that adopted eco-innovation product and/or process, and it is presented in Table 9.5. The results showed that about 68.2% of firms have adopted product eco-innovation while 72.2% adopted process eco-innovation. This is further explained by whether this eco-innovation product or process is new to the local market, new to the national, and new to the international market. This is shown in Table 9.6. Results showed that about 57.4% of eco-innovative product are new to the local market, followed by 25.5% new to the national market. Similarly, most process innovations are new to the local market (56.3%), while a significantly low proportion are new to the international market (7.7%). This evidence is not far-fetched because the firms in the country still operate at a low technology frontier and capacities to innovate are limited. This is further constrained with very low or no investment in research and development. Moreover, for a country like Nigeria, which is still trying to catch-up with frontiers of knowledge and technology, it is most reasonable that innovation among firms will most likely be new to the local market and in some cases new to the national market but rarely new to the global market.

The categorization of drivers of eco-innovation in this study is presented under three headings. They are innovativeness, demand-pull factors, and technology-pull factors. This is shown in Table 9.7. For innovativeness, about 39.3% of the firms have a new or significantly improved organizational structure, while a higher proportion (54.8%) of the firms have a new or significantly improved marketing method.

Table 9.5 Adoption of eco-innovation

	Product eco-innovation	Process eco-innovation
Yes	219 (68.2)	288 (72.2)
No	102 (31.8)	111 (27.8)
Total	321 (100)	399 (100)

Table 9.6 Categories of eco-innovation

	Product eco-innovation	Process eco-innovation
New to local market	53 (57.4)	54 (56.3)
New to national market	26 (25.5)	24 (24.7)
New to international market	7 (7.3)	7 (7.7)

Four variables were examined for demand-pull considerations. They are meeting customer demand, entering new markets, expanding product lines, and offering the same products as competitors. Results showed that 66.4% of firms developed innovative products to satisfy customer demand, 74.4% to enter new markets, 92.7% to extend product range, and 77.9% developed products to maintain competitive edge with domestic competitors.

Furthermore, considering technology-push factors, the factors considered were time to develop new ideas, engagement in formal training, and sources of knowledge. About 45.8% of firms give time to their employees to develop new ideas. About 27.9% of firms engage in formal training of employees. With respect to sources of knowledge, five sources of knowledge were considered. The question asked was whether firms interacted with foreign firms, domestic academic or research institutions, foreign academic or research institutions, private individuals/companies, and the government as sources of knowledge in their firms. Results showed that only 10.1% of sampled firms interact with private individuals and companies, 5.7% of firms interact with domestic academic and research institutions, and 4.2% and 4% with foreign firms and government respectively. It is evident that firm interactions are mostly with private individuals and companies, other sources of knowledge are almost non-existent. One can infer that research–industry linkage is weak and even almost nonexistent. This aligns with the findings of

Table 9.7 Distribution of drivers of eco-innovation

Eco-innovation drivers	Observations	Mean	Std. Dev.	Min	Max
Develop environmental-compliant product	148	0.6891892	0.4643971	0	1
Innovativeness					
Organizational innovation	407	0.3931204	0.4890444	0	1
Marketing innovation	407	0.5479115	0.4983117	0	1
Demand-pull factors					
Satisfy customer demand	149	0.6644295	0.4737821	0	1
Enter new market	149	0.7449664	0.4373502	0	1
Extend product range	150	0.9266667	0.2615562	0	1
To offer products or services already offered by competitors	145	0.7793103	0.4161491	0	1
Technology-push factors					
Time to develop new ideas	400	0.4575	0.4988144	0	1
Formal training of full-time employees	398	0.2788945	0.44902	0	1
Sources of knowledge					
Any foreign firms or a foreign-owned patent firm	405	0.0419753	0.2007808	0	1
Domestic academic or research institutions	402	0.0572139	0.2325403	0	1
Foreign academic or research institutions	403	0.0148883	0.1212566	0	1
Private consulting company or individuals	405	0.1012346	0.3020122	0	1
Government	402	0.039801	0.195735	0	1

Adeoti et al. (2010) in the book titled tackling innovation deficit, an analysis of university-firm interaction in Nigeria that university-firm interaction is weak in the country. The study added that economies that lag behind are characterized by relatively low capacity to generate and use technological innovation and economically relevant knowledge. Meanwhile, Horbach (2008) asserted that managerial and technological capabilities are important for product eco-innovation. On the other hand, it is believed that process innovation is internally generated at the firm level, therefore making the technological capabilities within the firm a crucial driver of process eco-innovation. The role of collaboration with Universities and research agencies was also emphasized (Horbach et al., 2012).

Factors Influencing Firm's Decision to Adopt Eco-Innovation

Product Eco-Innovation

We report results for firms adopting product eco-innovation. The drivers of product eco-innovation presented in Table 9.8 were regressed with product eco-innovation (as to whether a firm developed any environmental-compliant product or not). The model was significant at 1% with the log-likelihood of −53.461642 and LR χ^2 (13) = 33.68. Three factors significantly influenced firm's decision to adopt product eco-innovation. These factors are satisfying customer demand, offering products or services already offered by competitors and custom regulations.

The probability for product eco-innovation increases as firms try to satisfy customer demands and this was positive and significant at 1%. This implies that the need to satisfy customer demands by firms makes it imperative for firms to adopt product eco-innovation. This probability increases by 28.2 percentage points. This is because customers now value eco-friendly products and for increasing health concerns in recent times.

In addition, offering products or services already offered by competitors decreases the probability of adopting eco-innovation. This was negative and significant at 5%. This implies that as firms try to compete by offering the same products and services as their competitors, the probability of product eco-innovation decreases. This probability decreases by 26.7 percentage points. It has been established that competitors' activities toward environmental performance (Dai et al., 2015). Cai and Li (2018) also found that firm's competitive environment drives eco-innovation, even more than regulatory pressure. This probability increases by 24.7 percentage points.

Table 9.8 Factors influencing firm's decision to adopt product eco-innovation

				Marginal effects		
	Coefficient	Standard error	*z*	Coefficient	Standard error	*Z*
Innovativeness						
Organizational innovation	0.4702	0.5469	0.86	0.0830	0.0981	0.85
Marketing innovation	−0.4156	0.5905	−0.70	−0.0686	0.0926	−0.74
Demand-pull factors						
Satisfy customer demand	1.4462***	0.5526	2.62	0.2815**	0.1146	2.46
Enter new market	0.2199	0.6197	0.35	0.0395	0.1149	0.34
Extend product range	0.2046	1.0998	0.19	0.0373	0.2092	0.18
To offer products or services already offered by competitors	−2.0918**	0.9633	−2.17	−0.2668***	0.0802	−3.33
Technology-push factors						
Formal training for permanent full-time employees	−0.1162	0.5729	−0.20	−0.0205	0.1019	−0.20
Domestic academic or research institutes	0.2199	1.0591	0.21	0.0363	0.1656	0.22
Regulatory framework						
Custom and trade regulations						
Minor obstacle	−0.0937	0.5569	−0.17	−0.0165	0.0986	−0.17
Moderate obstacle	1.7647**	0.7949	2.22	0.2469***	0.0871	2.83
Major obstacle	1.4822	1.2250	1.21	0.1752*	0.0915	1.91
Firm age	−0.0055	0.0222	−0.25	−0.0010	0.0039	−0.25
Firm size	0.0013	0.0023	0.55	0.0002	0.0004	0.56

(continued)

Table 9.8 (continued)

				Marginal effects		
	Coefficient	Standard error	z	Coefficient	Standard error	Z
Constant	1.0146	1.1343	0.89			
Number of observations = 114						
Prob > χ^2 = 0.0013						
Log likelihood = −53.461642						
LR χ^2 (13) = 33.68						

*, **, and *** represent 10%, 5%, and 1% levels of statistical significance

Governments and regulatory bodies constitute crucial factors when it comes to firms' environmental performance (Darnall et al., 2010; Zhu et al., 2017). Furthermore, as more of custom and trade regulations become an obstacle to firms, the more likely these firms are likely to eco-innovate. The likely reason for this is that stricter trade regulations will ensure that firms comply with environmental regulations and thus will produce products that are eco-friendly.

Process Eco-Innovation

This section presents the factors influencing firm's decision to adopt process eco-innovation. We report results for firms adopting process eco-innovation. The drivers of process eco-innovation presented in Table 9.9 were regressed with the dependent variable as to whether a firm developed any environmental-compliant process or not. The model was significant at 1% with the log-likelihood of −63.530412 and LR χ^2 (17) = 75.51. Five factors significantly influenced firm's decision to adopt process eco-innovation. These factors are organizational innovation, customs and trade regulations, increasing the quality of products or services, increasing the speed of production or offering service, and source of knowledge (private consulting company/individuals).

The probability for process eco-innovation increases as firms introduce a new or organizational structure and this was positive and significant at 1%. This means that as firms improve and introduce new organizational structures, the probability of adopting process eco-innovation increases. This probability increases by 25.8 percentage points.

Customs and trade regulations were positive and significant. As customs and trade regulations become obstacles, the probability of adopting process eco-innovation increases. This finding is consistent with Del Río et al. (2015) and Liao (2018) who posited that the creation and implementation of eco-innovation is aided by regulatory pressure. However, according to Zhu et al. (2017), the severity and effect of regulatory pressures varies by country.

The probability of adopting process eco-innovation increases as firms try to increase the quality of products and services and also as firms try

Table 9.9 Factors influencing firm's decision to adopt process eco-innovation

				Marginal effect		
	Coefficient	Standard error	*z*	Coefficient	Standard error	*z*
Innovativeness						
Organizational innovation	1.4889***	0.5280	2.82	0.2579***	0.0956	2.70
Marketing innovation	−0.6470	0.6253	−1.03	−0.1007	0.0882	−1.14
Regulatory framework—customs and trade regulation						
No obstacle	0.9668*	0.5557	1.74	0.1469*	0.0789	1.86
Minor obstacle	2.1286***	0.6950	3.06	0.2671***	0.0773	3.46
Moderate obstacle	2.2569**	0.9458	2.39	0.2234***	0.0644	3.47
Major obstacle	0.3050	1.6466	0.19	0.0473	0.2327	0.20
Demand-pull factors						
To increase the quality of products or services	2.0880*	1.0846	1.93	0.4620*	0.2396	1.93
To increase the flexibility of production or offering service	−0.9071	1.2582	−0.72	−0.1222	0.1277	−0.96
To increase speed of delivery to the customer	0.6013	0.7934	0.76	0.1146	0.1669	0.69

	Coefficient	Standard error	z	Marginal effect Coefficient	Standard error	z
To increase the speed of production or offering service	1.7161*	0.8718	1.97	0.3661*	0.2007	1.82
Technology-push factors						
Formal training	−0.3745	0.5414	−0.69	−0.0657	0.0987	−0.67
Sources of knowledge						
Domestic academic or research institutions	0.2781	1.0079	0.28	0.0440	0.1479	0.30
Foreign firm or foreign-owned patent firm	−0.0720	1.3442	−0.05	−0.0124	0.2361	−0.05
Private consulting company or individuals	2.2827**	1.1258	2.03	0.2382***	0.0683	3.49
Government	1.1524	1.1960	0.96	0.1435	0.1060	1.35
Control variables						
Firm age	−0.0112	0.0260	−0.43	−0.0019	0.0043	−0.44
Firm size	0.0032	0.0047	0.70	0.0005	0.0008	0.74
Constant	−3.4634***	1.2409	−2.79			
Number of observations = 163						
LR χ^2 (17) = 75.51						
Prob > χ^2 = 0.0000						
Log likelihood = −63.530412; Pseudo R^2 = 0.3728						

*, **, and *** represent 10%, 5%, and 1% levels of statistical significance

to increase the speed of production. These variables were positive and significant at 10%. This means that the probability increases by 46.2 and 36.6 percentage points for an increase in the quality of products and speed of production.

Collaboration activities do occur among stakeholders such as universities and research institutions, suppliers, and others with the goal of improving product and process environmental performance (Danese et al., 2019). Participating in eco-innovation collaborations also gives a mechanism to protect against lost investments (Cainelli et al., 2015). This is a source of information for businesses. The source of knowledge in this scenario is a private firm or an individual. With the chance of adopting process eco-innovation, it was positive and significant at 10%. Adoption rises by 23.8 percentage points as a result of this likelihood. This type of cooperation and collaboration is critical for successful eco-innovation engagement and development (Lee & Kim, 2011; Melander, 2018).

9.6 Conclusion and Recommendation

The study examines the drivers of adoption of product and process eco-innovation in Nigeria's manufacturing sector. Although our results are specific to our study context, they contribute to the stream of literature on eco-innovation that investigates the drivers of eco-innovation. Firms in Nigeria's manufacturing sector are eager to adopt product and process eco-innovation in order to meet customer demands and improve the speed of production. The capability of firms to carry out organizational innovation is important for eco-innovation. Engagement with private companies and individuals is critical to firms in the sector to eco-innovate. Eco-innovation strategies should be contextualized and tailored to the realities of the Nigerian technology space. As this will promote the development of environmental technologies affordable and applicable to firms in the sector. It is expected that the adoption of eco-innovation strategies will promote the competitiveness of the sector and the economy at large. This study also provides impetus for Nigeria's Medium-Term National Development Plan (2021–2025) which has a vision to catalyze the potential of the public, private, and social sectors to boost industrialization, and sustainably improve inclusive, holistic development and competitiveness. It is essential for Nigeria at this time to break into the global market and remain there in order to achieve economic transformation and competitiveness. It will also help businesses in improving performance while protecting the environment. Since organizational innovation is crucial to the adoption of eco-innovation, firms should develop organizational strategies and management systems that solve environmental issues that occur throughout the manufacturing process. This could be in the form of pollution control measures, efficient process operation, and minor adjustments to industrial plants. There should be an increasing awareness of customers on eco-friendly products and health issues, which will significantly drive the adoption of both product and process eco-innovations. These awareness campaigns could be done by the Manufacturers Association of Nigeria (MAN), SMEDAN, and other relevant agencies. The issue of trade regulations relating to ensuring that manufactures meet required environmental standards should be put in place and made less stringent by relevant government agencies like NAFDAC, NESREA, customs, and others. Firm capabilities need to be improved especially in the area of ensuring quality products and services while improving the speed at which products and services are delivered. Moreover, organizational innovation needs to be a necessity for firms. These would significantly influence firm's decision to adopt process eco-innovation. Policies that encourage partnerships and interactions of firms with other actors, especially private companies, individuals, and other stakeholders in the innovation system be developed to encourage the adoption of process eco-innovation. Policies should also be put in place in the form of tax holidays for eco-innovative firms so that they could be encouraged to adopt eco-innovation products and processes, thereby reducing the cost of adopting these measures and increasing sales.

References

Adelegan, J. A., Carlsson, B., & Perelli, S. (2010, October 8–9). *Eco-innovation and corporate performance: The African experience*. A Paper Presented at the Berlin Conference on the Human Dimensions of Global Environmental Change, Berlin.

Adeoti, J. O., Odekunle, S. O., & Adeyinka, F. M. (2010). *Tackling innovation deficit: An analysis of university-firm interaction in Nigeria*. Evergreen Publishers.

Asongu, S. A. (2018). CO_2 emission thresholds for inclusive human development in Sub-Saharan Africa. *Environmental Science and Pollution Research, 25*, 26005–26019. https://doi.org/10.1007/s11356-018-2626-6

Ahmad, S., & Schroeder, R. G. (2003). The impact of human resource management practices on operational performance: Recognizing country and industry differences. *Journal of Operations Management, 21*(1), 19–43.

Alvarez, H., & Iske, P. (2015). Internal capabilities and external knowledge sourcing for product innovation in LMT SMEs. *Journal of Innovation Management, 3*(2), 55–70.

Arranz, N., Arroyabe, C. F., & Fernández de Arroyabe, J. C. (2019). The effect of regional factors in the development of eco-innovations in the firm. *Business Strategy and the Environment, 28*, 1406–1415. https://doi.org/10.1002/bse.2322

Asongu, S. A., El Montasser, G., & Toumi, H. (2016). Testing the relationships between energy consumption, CO_2 emissions, and economic growth in 24 African countries: A panel ARDL approach. *Environmental Science and Pollution Research, 23*(7), 6563–6573.

Ayyagari, M., Demirgüc-Kunt, A., & Maksimovic, V. (2012). Firm innovation in emerging markets: The role of finance, governance, and competition. *Journal of Financial and Quantitative Analysis, 46*(06), 1545–1580.

Bansal, P., & Gao, J. (2006). Building the future by looking to the past: Examining research published on organizations and environment. *Organization & environment, 19*(4), 458–478.

Barasa, L., Kinyanjui, B., Knoben, J., Kimuyu, P., & Vermeulen, P. A. M. (2016). *Export and innovation in Sub-Saharan Africa* (DFID Working Paper; p. 35). Radboud University Nijmegen.

Barney, J. B. (2001). Resource-based theories of competitive advantage: A ten-year retrospective on the resource-based view. *Journal of Management, 27*(6), 643–650.

Belin, J., Horbach, J., & Oltra, V. (2011). *Determinants and specificities of eco-innovations—An econometric analysis for the French and German industry based on the community innovation survey*. http://cahiersdugretha.u-bordeaux4.fr/2011/2011-17.pdf (Accessed on 05 March 2017).

Cai, W., & Li, G. (2018). The drivers of eco-innovation and its impact on performance: Evidence from China. *Journal of Cleaner Production, 176*, 110–118. https://doi.org/10.1016/j.jclepro.2017.12.109

Cai, W., & Zhou, X. (2014). On the drivers of eco-innovation: Empirical Evidence from China. *Journal of Cleaner Production, 79*, 239–248. https://doi.org/10.1016/j.jclepro.2014.05.035

Cainelli, G., De Marchi, V., & Grandinetti, R. (2015). Does the development of environmental innovation require different resources? Evidence from Spanish manufacturing firms. *Journal of Cleaner Production, 94*, 211–220. https://doi.org/10.1016/j.jclepro.2015.02.008

Cainelli, G., Mazzanti, M., & Montresor, S. (2012). Environmental innovations, local networks and internationalization. *Industry and Innovation, 19*(8), 697–734.

Carrillo-Hermosilla, J., Del Río, P., & Könnölä, T. (2010). Diversity of eco-innovations: Reflections from selected case studies. *Journal of Cleaner Production, 18*(10), 1073–1083.

Choi, S. B., Min, H., & Joo, H. Y. (2018). Examining the inter-relationship among competitive market environments, green supply chain practices, and firm performance. *The International Journal of Logistics Management, 29*(3), 1025–1048.

Cooke, P., Clifton, N., & Oleaga, M. (2005). Social capital, firm embeddedness and regional development. *Regional Studies, 39*(8), 1065–1077. https://doi.org/10.1080/00343400500328065

Dai, J., Cantor, D. E., & Montabon, F. L. (2015). How environmental management competitive pressure affects a focal firm's environmental innovation activities: A green supply chain perspective. *Journal of Business Logistics, 36*(3), 242–259. https://doi.org/10.1111/jbl.12094

Danese, P., Lion, A., & Vinelli, A. (2019). Drivers and enablers of supplier sustainability practices: A survey-based analysis. *International Journal of Production Research, 57*(7), 2034–2056. https://doi.org/10.1080/00207543.2018.1519265

Dangelico, R. M. (2016). Green product innovation: Where we are and where we are going. *Business Strategy and the Environment, 25*(8), 560–576. https://doi.org/10.1002/bse.1886

Darnall, N., Henriques, I., & Sadorsky, P. (2008). Do environmental management systems improve business performance in an international setting? *Journal of International Management, 14*(4), 364–376.

Darnall, N., Potoski, M., & Prakash, A. (2010). Sponsorship matters: Assessing business participation in government- and industry-sponsored voluntary environmental programs. *Journal of Public Administration Research and Theory, 20*(2), 283–307. https://doi.org/10.1093/jopart/mup014

Del Rio P. (2013). Analysing firm-specific and time-specific determinants of eco-innovation. Available at: http://druid8.sit.aau.dk/acc_papers/199xhmxrvmojaae780urjt1imlt4.pdf (11 March 2017).

Del Río, P., Peñasco, C., & Romero-Jordán, D. (2015). Distinctive features of environmental innovators: An econometric analysis. *Business Strategy and the Environment, 24*(6), 361–385.

Del Río, P., Peñasco, C., & Romero-Jordán, D. (2016). What drives eco-innovators? A critical review of the empirical literature based on econometric methods. *Journal of Cleaner Production, 112*, 2158–2170.

De Marchi, V. (2012). Environmental innovation and R&D cooperation: Empirical evidence from Spanish manufacturing firms. *Research Policy, 41*(3), 614–623. https://doi.org/10.1016/j.respol.2011.10.002

Doran, J., & Ryan, G. (2016). The importance of the diverse drivers and types of environmental innovation for firm performance. *Business Strategy and the Environment, 25*(2), 102–119.

Driessen, P. H., Hillebrand, B., Kok, R. A. W., & Verhallen, T. M. M. (2013). Green new product development: The pivotal role of product greenness. *IEEE Transactions on Engineering Management, 60*(2), 315–326. https://doi.org/10.1109/TEM.2013.2246792

Efobi, U. R., Belmondo, T., Orkoh, E., Atata, S. N., Akinyemi, O., & Beecroft, I. (2018). *Environmental pollution policy of small businesses in Nigeria and Ghana: Extent and impact* (AGDI Working Paper, No. WP/18/050). African Governance and Development Institute (AGDI).

Eisenhardt, K. M., & Martin, J. A. (2000). Dynamic capabilities: What are they? *Strategic Management Journal, 21*(10–11), 1105–1121.

Fernando, Y., Jabbour, C. J. C., & Wah, W.-X. (2019). Pursuing green growth in technology firms through the connections between environmental innovation and sustainable business performance: Does service capability matter? *Resources, Conservation and Recycling, 141*, 8–20. https://doi.org/10.1016/j.resconrec.2018.09.031

Guoyou, Q., Saixing, Z., Chiming, T., Haitao, Y., & Hailiang, Z. (2013). Stakeholders' influences on corporate green innovation strategy: A case study of manufacturing firms in China. *Corporate Social Responsibility and Environmental Management, 20*(1), 1–14. https://doi.org/10.1002/csr.283

Horbach, J. (2008). Determinants of environmental innovation—New evidence from German panel data sources. *Research Policy, 37*(1), 163–173. https://doi.org/10.1016/j.respol.2007.08.006

Horbach, J. (2014). Determinants of Eco/innovation from a European/wide Perspective–an Analysis based on the Community Innovation Survey (CIS). Available at: http://www.sustainability-seeds.org/papers/RePec/srt/wpaper/0714.pdf (07 March 2017).

Horbach, J., Rammer, C., & Rennings, K. (2012). Determinants of eco-innovations by type of environmental impact—The role of regulatory push/pull, technology push and market pull. *Ecological Economics, 78*, 112–122. https://doi.org/10.1016/j.ecolecon.2012.04.005

Jacobs, B.W., Singhal, V. R., & Subramanian, R. (2010). An empirical investigation of environmental performance and the market value of the firm. *Journal of Operations Management, 28*(5), 430–441.

Jabbour, C. J. C., Neto, A. S., Gobbo, J. A. Jr., de Souza Ribeiro, M., & de Sousa Jabbour, A. B. L. (2015). Eco-innovations in more sustainable supply chains for a low-carbon economy: A multiple case study of human critical success factors in Brazilian leading companies. *International Journal of Production Economics, 164*, 245–257. https://doi.org/10.1016/j.ijpe.2014.11.015

Kemp, R. (2010). Eco-Innovation: Definition, measurement and open research issues. *Economia Politica, 27*(3), 397–420.

Kemp, R., & Foxon, T. (2007). Eco-Innovation from an Innovation Dynamics Perspective. *Deliverable 1 of MEI project (D1), Maastricht, 6*, 25 p.

Kemp, R., & Pearson, P. (2008). *Final report of the project measuring eco-innovation.* http://www.merit.unu.edu/MEI/index.php

Kesidou, E., & Demirel, P. (2012). On the drivers of eco-innovations: Empirical evidence from the UK. *Research Policy, 41*(5), 862–870. https://doi.org/10.1016/j.respol.2012.01.005

Kowalska, A. (2014). Implementing eco-innovations. Determinants and effects. *Roczniki (Annals), 3*, 153–158.

Liu, X., Dai, H., & Cheng, P. (2011). Drivers of integrated environmental innovation and impact on company competiveness: Evidence from 18 Chinese firms. *International Journal of Technology and Globalisation, 5*(3/4), 255–280. https://doi.org/10.1504/IJTG.2011.039767

Lee, K.-H., & Kim, J. W. (2011). Integrating suppliers into green product innovation development: An empirical case study in the semiconductor industry. *Business Strategy and the Environment, 20*(8), 527–538. https://doi.org/10.1002/bse.714

Liao, Z. (2018). Institutional pressure, knowledge acquisition and a firm's environmental innovation. *Business Strategy and the Environment, 27*(7), 849–857. https://doi.org/10.1002/bse.2036

Machiba, T. (2010). Eco-innovation for enabling resource efficiency and green growth: Development of an analytical framework and preliminary analysis of industry and policy practices. *International Economics and Economic Policy, 7*(2/3), 357–370.

Maçaneiro, M. B., Cunha, S. K., & Balbinot, Z. (2013). Drivers of the adoption of ecoinnovations in the pulp, paper, and paper products industry in Brazil. *Latin American Business Review, 14*(3–4), 179–208.

Maddala, G. S. (1983). *Limited dependent and qualitative variables in econometrics*. Econometric Society Monographs No. 3, p. 22. Cambridge University Press.

Mazzanti, M., & Zobloi, R. (2008). Environmental innovations, SME strategies and policy induced effects: Evidence for a district-based local system in northern Italy. *ICFAI Journal of Environmental Economics, 6*(1), 7–34.

Melander, L. (2018). Customer and supplier collaboration in green product innovation: External and internal capabilities. *Business Strategy and the Environment, 27*(6), 677–693. https://doi.org/10.1002/bse.2024

Nelson, R. R., & Winter, S. G. (2002). Evolutionary theorizing in economics. *Journal of Economic Perspectives, 16*(2), 23–46.

Neto, A. S., Jabbour, C. J. C., & de Sousa Jabbour, A. B. L. (2014). Green training supporting eco-innovation in three Brazilian companies: Practices and levels of integration. *Industrial and Commercial Training, 46*(7), 387–392. https://doi.org/10.1108/ICT-02-2014-0010

OECD-EUROSTAT. (2005). *Oslo manual: Guidelines for collecting and interpreting innovation data* (3rd ed.). OECD.

Oltra, V., & Saint Jean, M. (2005). The dynamics of environmental innovations: Three stylized trajectories of clean technology. *Economics of Innovation and New Technology, 14*(3), 189–212.

Peng, X., & Liu, Y. (2016). Behind eco-innovation: Managerial environmental awareness and external resource acquisition. *Journal of Cleaner Production, 139*, 347–360. https://doi.org/10.1016/j.jclepro.2016.08.051

Rehfeld, K. M., Rennings, K., & Ziegler, A. (2007). Integrated product policy and environmental product innovations: An empirical analysis. *Ecological Economics, 61*, 91–100.

Rennings, K. (2000). Redefining innovation—Eco-innovation research and the contribution from ecological economics. *Ecological Economics, 32*(2), 319–332.

Rothenberg, S., & Zyglidopoulos, C. (2003, October). *Determinants of environmental innovation adoption in the printing industry. The importance of task environment versus firm specific factors* (No. PICRM-2003-04). A Research Monograph of the Printing Industry Center at RIT. https://scholarworks.rit.edu/cgi/viewcontent.cgi?article=1013&context=books

Sanni, M. (2017). Drivers of eco-innovation in the manufacturing sector of Nigeria. *Technological Forecasting & Social Change*, 1–12. https://doi.org/10.1016/j.techfore.2017.11.007

Schilirò, D. (2010). In Arentsen, M. J., van Rossum, W., Steenge, A. E. (Eds.), *Investing in knowledge: Knowledge, human capital and institutions for the long run growth*, pp. 33–50. Edward Elgar.

Shrivastava, P. (2008). Sustainable organisational technology. *International Journal of Sustainable Strategic Management, 1*(1), 98–111.

SMEDAN and NBS. (2013). *SMEDAN and National Bureau of Statistics collaborative survey: Selected findings.*

Tang, M., Walsh, G. S., Lerner, D. A., Fitza, M., and Li, Q. (2018). Green innovation, managerial concern and firm performance: An empirical study. *Business Strategy and the Environment, 27*(1), 39–51. https://doi.org/10.1002/bse.1981

Teece, D. J. (2007). Explicating dynamic capabilities: The nature and microfoundations of (sustainable) enterprise performance. *Strategic Management Journal, 28*(13), 1319–1350.

Teece, D. J., Pisano, G., & Shuen, A. (1997). *Dynamic capabilities and strategic management. Strategic Management Journal, 18*(7), 509–533.

Triguero, A., Moreno-Mondéjar, L., & Davia, M. A. (2013). Drivers of different types of eco-innovation in European SMEs. *Ecological Economics, 92*, 25–33. https://doi.org/10.1016/j.ecolecon.2013.04.009

United Nations Industrial Development Organization—UNIDO. (2011). UNIDO Green Industry: Policies for supporting Green Industry. UNIDO.

WDI. (2018). *World Bank Development Indicators database.*

World Bank. (2016). *Doing business 2016: Measuring regulatory quality and efficiency*. World Bank.

Wu, K.-J., Liao, C.-J., Chen, C.-C., Lin, Y., & Tsai, C. F. M. (2016). Exploring eco-innovation in dynamic organizational capability under incomplete information in the Taiwanese lighting industry. *International Journal of Production Economics, 181*, 419–440. https://doi.org/10.1016/j.ijpe.2015.10.007

Yang, C. L., Lin, S. P., Chan, Y. H., & Sheu, C. (2010). Mediated effect of environmental management on manufacturing competitiveness: An empirical study. *International Journal of Production Economics, 123*(1), 210–220.

Yusof, N., & Mohd, S. M. W. (2011). Factors affecting housing developers' readiness to adopt innovative systems. *Housing Studies, 26*(3), 369–384.

Zahra, S. A., Sapienza, H. J., & Davidsson, P. (2006). Entrepreneurship and dynamic capabilities: A review, model and research agenda. *Journal of Management Studies, 43*(4), 917–955.

Zeng, S. X., Xie, X. M., Tam, C. M., Wan, T. W., (2008). Competitive priorities of manufacturing firms for internationalization: an empirical research. *Measuring Business Excellence, 12*(3), 44–55.

Zhang, J., Liang, G., Feng, T., Yuan, C., & Jiang, W. (2020). Green innovation to respond to environmental regulation: How external knowledge adoption and green absorptive capacity matter? *Business Strategy and the Environment, 29*(1), 39–53. https://doi.org/10.1002/bse.2349

Zhu, Q., Qu, Y., Geng, Y., & Fujita, T. (2017). A comparison of regulatory awareness and green supply chain management practices among Chinese and Japanese manufacturers. *Business Strategy and the Environment, 26*(1), 18–30. https://doi.org/10.1002/bse.1888

Zubeltzu-Jaka, E., Erauskin-Tolosa, A., & Heras-Saizarbitoria, I. (2018). Shedding light on the determinants of eco-innovation: A meta-analytic study. *Business Strategy and the Environment, 27*(7), 1093–1103. https://doi.org/10.1002/bse.2054

10

Open Innovation Across the Innovation Value Chain: An African Perspective

Lerato E. Mdaka and Mpumelelo Jr. Longweni

10.1 Introduction

Entrepreneurship is crucial to the journey of economic growth and progression in emerging markets. It accounts for a vast contribution to the quality, development and progress of an industry, economy or country. The role of entrepreneurs from an economic perspective is seen as one that informs the market of new elements. Entrepreneurs as innovators identify gaps within the market and are determined to fill these gaps (Hague et al., 2011: 156). In doing so, new economic activities are created and essentially generate jobs, wealth and the country's overall well-being.

L. E. Mdaka (✉) · M. Jr. Longweni
School of Management Sciences, North-West University, Potchefstroom, South Africa
e-mail: lerato.mdaka@nwu.ac.za

M. Jr. Longweni
e-mail: 22965092@nwu.ac.za

A. S. Ibidunni et al. (eds.), *Innovation, Entrepreneurship and the Informal Economy in Sub–Saharan Africa*, Sustainable Development Goals Series,
https://doi.org/10.1007/978-3-031-46293-1_10

Various scholars view that technology innovation or invention is critical for entrepreneurship, SMME development and job creation (Nambisan et al., 2019). In more recent years, innovative strategies such as Open innovation are utilised to stimulate entrepreneurship in Africa. Open Innovation connects solution seekers and solution providers (Diener et al., 2020). Solution providers could be entrepreneurs or inventors with solutions for market or organisational challenges. Small to large businesses as well as the general market could be considered solution seekers. They are looking for solutions to problems in their business and the environment. Open Innovation allows inventors and entrepreneurs to connect with investors, IP lawyers, funders, facilities, associations, standards and other market players (Bigliardi et al., 2021).

Although the successes and benefits of Open Innovation are widely spoken about in literature across the globe, there's very little understanding of the role open innovation plays across the innovation value chain, particularly in African contexts. Additionally, the understanding of the innovation value chain from idea to market mainly focuses on the extreme ends of the innovation value chain: Research and Development on one end and marketing on the other. This implies that a range of activities and processes of the innovation value chain are overlooked (Mohalajeng & Kroon, 2016). This paper seeks to interrogate the existing literature to provide a conceptual model depicting the role of open innovation across the innovation value chain from an African perspective. Investigating the various academic and industry texts regarding open innovation and the innovation value chain leads to an in-depth understanding of what is needed to bridge the gap from invention or idea to market. The model derived helps government stakeholders, industries and entrepreneurs across Africa in making better decisions about what is needed in fostering total early-stage entrepreneurial activity. This chapter is divided into two main sections: the innovation value chain and Open innovation strategies for each stage of the innovation value chain. Firstly, each phase of the innovation value chain will be elaborated, especially how open innovation contributes to each phase. After that, the chapter elaborates on how to support the innovation value chain for success in developing countries.

10.2 The Innovation Value Chain

Innovation and entrepreneurship take place through a sometimes difficult extensive process. Seminal author, Smith (2015: 107), describes this process of taking an idea and turning it into a successful commercial product or service as the innovation value chain.

The innovation value chain occurs when entrepreneurs generate ideas and new knowledge needed for innovation, convert this knowledge into products or services and later exploit such innovations to escalate business growth and the value provided to consumers (Ganotakis & Love, 2012: 840). Therefore, there are several activities involved in turning an invention into successful commercialisation. The innovation value chain is a steady process that helps reduce risk and uncertainty through various phases in the chain (Tidd & Bessant, 2020). The number of phases and how they link to one another depends mostly on the nature of the product or service idea. Developing new innovations is often a complex process that differs from context to context. Even though that is the case, the major phases in the generic innovation value chain show a sequence starting from idea generation and ending with a finished product or service going into the market.

Chen et al. (2020) have concluded that the innovation value chain embodies innovation as a "sequential, three-phase process" comprising of idea generation, idea conversion into a concept and diffusion of the concept into the market. These serve as the key phases in the innovation value chain, although the terminology and steps within each phase may differ across industries.

The following sections of this chapter examine each phase of the innovation value chain. The three phases and the various steps within each phase are elaborated.

Idea Generation: Phase 1 of the Innovation Value Chain

The most basic definition of this phase is found in its title, it simply means generating ideas and knowledge. This phase may occur within a business department, across departments in a business as well as outside the business (Chen et al., 2020; Hansen & Birkinshaw, 2007). The idea generation phases may be divided into two steps: idea generation and idea screening.

Idea Generation

During the idea generation phase, new opportunities for innovation are identified. Seminal author Drucker (2011: 208) explains that sources of innovation stem from unexpected incidences, process needs, demographic and behavioural changes, industry and market trends and new knowledge as a result of individual genius.

- ***Unexpected incidences***: Because they are unplanned and unanticipated, random occurrences give rise to a new awareness; this insight then forms the basis for new ideas that essentially lead to innovations (Kuratko, 2018). Random incidences are the most basic source of innovation opportunities because opportunities, in essence, come from the unexpected. Unexpected successes or failures provide insights into innovation opportunities (Drucker, 2011: 210). Often failure is disregarded and marginalised. Tidd and Bessant (2020) state that accidents may prompt innovation and introduce new ideas. Entrepreneurs can spot these failures and accidents as an opportunity and develop them into innovation.
- ***Process needs***: As a result of the need for improvement, "process needs" are, in some cases, referred to as "pain" in the marketplace (Kuratko, 2018). Frustrations often provide significant signs of change and process needs. Process improvements are more relevant in the public sector since the focus is not necessarily to create wealth but to provide value through service delivery. As demands within various processes increase, solutions to such needs are birthed through the need to innovate. Process needs to stimulate innovation in more mature industries undergoing the pressure of competition. The competitive environment gives rise to the need to keep finding innovative ways to better service or product offerings.

- ***Demographic and perceptual changes***: Drucker (2011: 216) argues that demographics are the utmost dependable sources of innovation outside a business but are often neglected. Innovation opportunities are made possible as changes in age, population size, geographic locality, education and occupation occur. Pursuing entrepreneurship based on demographics is the least risky, and often has the most innovation opportunities (Kuratko, 2018). As demographics change, circumstances are perceived differently. Changes in perceptions do not alter facts but instead change their meaning (Drucker, 2011: 218). People's understanding of concepts and facts serve as a source of innovation. As individuals begin to emphasise the importance of healthy living, opportunities for healthy foods and fitness centres arise. Entrepreneurs have the ability to view perceptions of stakeholders as opportunities for innovation.
- ***Industry and market changes***: Repeated modifications in the marketplace result in structures of the industry and market changing (Kuratko, 2018). Changes in consumer preferences, improvements in technology, as well as the growth in the classification of industries and markets are good sources of innovation and entrepreneurial opportunities (Drucker, 2011: 215).
- ***New knowledge***: The prospects that arise from various scientific research studies form the basis of many innovations (Tidd & Bessant, 2020). Research and development (R&D) departments play an important role in finding new knowledge, problems and challenges that, in essence, serve as innovation opportunities. Continuous investigation and information gathering through extensive reading, attending professional workshops and working with individuals in unrelated fields produces new knowledge (Kuratko, 2018). Accumulating new knowledge regarding problems, challenges or opportunities provide entrepreneurs with an understanding of the manner in which an opportunity can be utilised. Drucker (2011: 219) emphasises that innovations that stem from new knowledge differ from others in that they have lengthy lead times and are unpredictable. These knowledge-based innovations are whimsical and often hard to direct. It can be concluded that innovation requires various kinds of knowledge. New knowledge originates from demographic, perceptual, industry

and market changes. Unexpected incidences and needs within various processes provide new knowledge for innovation. Innovation is multidimensional and has various types.

Ideas are generated in many ways, but these ideas must serve to add value to the end user. The viability of ideas is established through idea screening.

Idea Screening

Once ideas are generated, strong screening mechanisms need to be in place (Chen et al., 2020; Hansen & Birkinshaw, 2007). Idea screening and selection involve filtering the ideas according to the business's innovation strategy and perceived value-creation potential for the consumer. During this stage, the feasibility and viability of ideas are evaluated (Marais & Schutte, 2010: 102). During screening and selection, it is important to ensure that ideas integrate with the various product or service offerings as well as the objectives of the business. The capability of the business to carry out the idea and meet its future demand should be analysed. There are various ways to screen and select ideas before they are further developed. According to Tidd and Bessant (2020), ideas may be screened through the following:

- Ranking: this implies listing the ideas in order of value or worth for business support. Ideas are also ranked according to their forecasted financial costs.
- Profiling: ideas are given scores based on a set of criteria. Ideas that prevail on the majority of the criteria are selected.
- Scenario building: alternative visions of future-based outcomes are played out; ideas yielding different pay-offs in the different outcomes are selected.

There are various methods by which ideas are screened. These methods vary from business to business. The above screening methods are the most commonly used.

Open Innovation Across the Idea Generation Phase and Its Application in Southern Africa

Open Innovation is merging a business' internal assets and resources, with those outside the business to acquire the best value from existing information and available information (Mohalajeng & Kroon, 2016). In African economies, businesses often depend on the support of intermediary services to implement Open Innovation (Ottonicar et al., 2020). These intermediaries are known as Open Innovation Accelerators (OIA) and help accelerate ideas to market.

In the idea generation phase, businesses make use of Open Innovation in various forms. Ideas may be sourced externally from other small businesses within the same industry and even outside that industry (Chen et al., 2020; Hansen & Birkinshaw, 2007). This means ideas may originate from various role players within the triple-helix. With Open Innovation ideas and new knowledge for ideas are generated from suppliers, consumers, competitors, academia, investors, government agencies and independent entrepreneurs.

Open Innovation Accelerators (OIA) in Africa such as The Innovation Hub Open Innovation Solution Exchange in Southern Africa have cross-industry associations, widespread knowledge regarding industry-specific issues and an overall innovation eco-system when generating ideas through collaboration. Large businesses and SMEs participate in open innovation in two ways: (1) Large businesses across the globe tap into the African environment by publishing their request for innovation idea proposals or solutions through the OIA. The OIA invites stakeholders across the triple-helix to submit their solutions or ideas onto their digital platform for selection. (2) Entrepreneurs and SME owners post their technology onto The OIA digital platform; businesses interested in collaborating with these entrepreneurs through their knowledge or technology can then contact the entrepreneurs for collaboration. Entrepreneurs gain surprising returns by integrating their ideas, and concepts into existing innovation value chains (Mohalajeng & Kroon, 2016). Figure 10.1 illustrates how Open Innovation plays a role within the idea-generation phase of the innovation value chain.

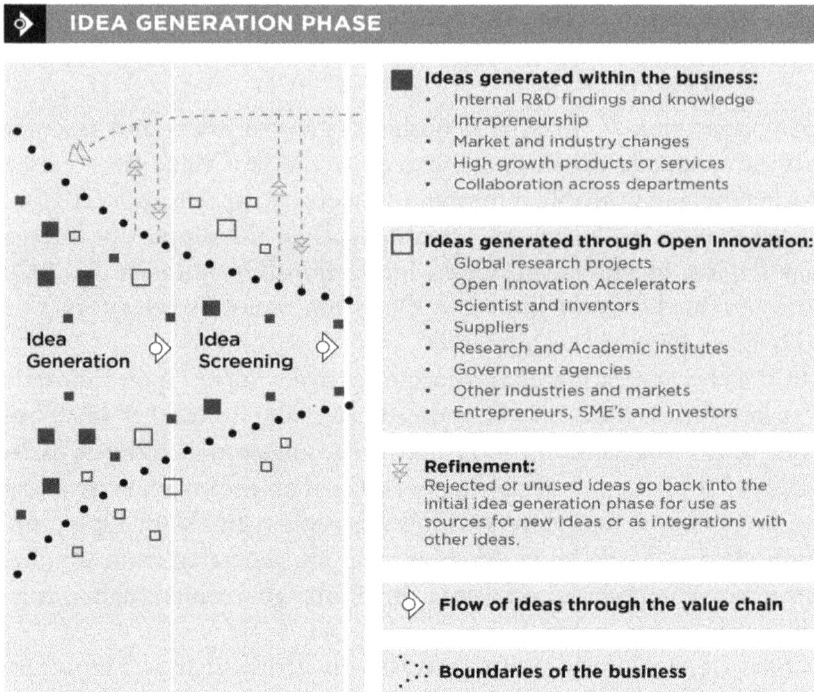

Fig. 10.1 Conceptual graph of the idea generation phase of the innovation value chain using open innovation (*Source* Mohalajeng and Kroon [2016])

Idea Conversion: Phase 2 of the Innovation Value Chain

Once ideas have been generated, the second phase of the innovation value chain begins. Here, selected ideas are converted to products or services (Hansen & Birkinshaw, 2007: 3). This phase comprises all activities involved in taking the chosen idea and converting it into a product or service which will be ready for commercialisation. During this phase, funding, research and development of the selected ideas occur. The steps involved in the idea conversion phase are concept definition, prototype development and business model analysis.

Concept Definition

This step in the idea conversion phase encompasses transforming and combining ideas that have been selected into concepts that are formally defined and have features that add consumer value (Marais & Schutte, 2010: 102). During this step, the various departments or functions within the business collaborate in determining specific concerns and making decisions on the details of the innovation.

The business functions defining the concept include the R&D personnel, designers and marketing departments (Tidd & Bessant, 2020). Knowledge is transferred to these departments and is then translated into innovation outputs. The new knowledge generated from ideas may sometimes form different outcomes than expected from the initial idea (Ganotakis & Love, 2012: 840). The defined concepts are then developed through prototyping and feasibility assessments.

Prototype Development

Once the concept of an idea is defined that concept is then further developed into a model and prototype (Marais & Schutte, 2010: 102). During the idea conversion phase, constructing a model and prototype of the idea is important (Mohalajeng & Kroon, 2016). Models are designed to demonstrate the appearance of the future product to give an impression of the overall look of the invention; they have no functioning capability as yet (Smith, 2015: 111). Modelling can be done through concept drawings and sketches, mock-ups and site models and various simulations.

The concept and model are turned into an invention by prototyping the fundamental working principles of the defined concept. Unlike models, prototypes are designed for functionality to ensure that future product operations are as projected (Smith, 2015). The prototypes are later used when evaluating the performance of the future product. Tidd and Bessant (2020) emphasise that prototypes undergo many iterations as the designers come to learn more about the problem and alternative solutions. Frequent prototyping assists the various role players in better understanding the future product.

Prototypes assist in having reliable assessments of preferences and recommendations. It is important to note that prototyping thus happens continuously. Although the prototype is not ready for entrance into the market, it obtains many final product characteristics (Smith, 2015). It, therefore can be used in the next steps of the idea conversion phase.

Business Model Analysis

Once the prototype has been developed, additional information is used to determine the feasibility of the prototype (Marais & Schutte, 2010: 102). During this step, the fit of the prototype with the overall business model is investigated. A solid business model for the prototype is analysed, meaning the materials used for manufacturing the product and the process by which the product will be manufactured are evaluated (Smith, 2015). Intellectual Property (IP) protection decisions are made as well.

Open Innovation Across the Idea Conversion Phase and Its Application in Southern Africa

During the idea conversion phase, Open Innovation practices in Africa are applied through the use of joint technology development as well as joint product development (Gonyora et al., 2022). Developing the technology with external parties such as customers and suppliers allows the business to understand the public's needs and the limitations the concepts may have. Joint development with suppliers allows businesses to understand the importance of materials and equipment (Gonyora et al., 2022).

Souring external technology through Open Innovation also occurs during the idea conversion phase. Technology discovered or created outside the business may be acquired when defining the concept and developing the prototype through ongoing feasibility studies (Marais & Schutte, 2010: 104). Conversely, prototypes and technologies developed internally during this phase may be transferred out of business through outbound Open Innovation. This situation can occur, for instance, when the business doesn't have the ability to realise sufficient revenue in its own market or when the technology is a spin-off that cannot be used for the core business (von Nell & Lichtenthaler, 2011: 133).

Open Innovation accelerators in Africa manage collaborations through multi-level involvement and governance (Janssen et al., 2014: 19). The Innovation Hub Open Innovation Solution Exchange in Southern Africa, for example, involves their innovation eco-system by ensuring solution seekers (large businesses or SMEs) connected with a variety of possible external technologies which are often new and unknown to the seeker (Diener et al., 2020).

The open innovation in the idea conversion phase is best summarised as part of the innovation value chain in Fig. 10.2.

Idea Diffusion: Phase 3 of the Innovation Value Chain

According to Tidd and Bessant (2020), the idea conversion phase oftentimes overlaps with the diffusion phase. This is because the developed concept still requires buy-in from the rest of the business departs as well as the target market. Chen et al. (2020) emphasise that businesses need relevant units that support and spread new product concepts and business models across all areas within and outside the business. During the idea diffusion phase, concepts are tested and implemented in the market for further development opportunities as feasibility studies. New products and services must be rolled out across various distribution channels and markets. The idea diffusion phase takes place in two steps, namely, testing and commercialisation.

Testing

Products that have come out of the idea conversion phase need to be tested. Testing the products ensures their functionality is as intended and that their performance is what the end-users require (Smith, 2015). The prototypes are tested in various environments and conditions. If the

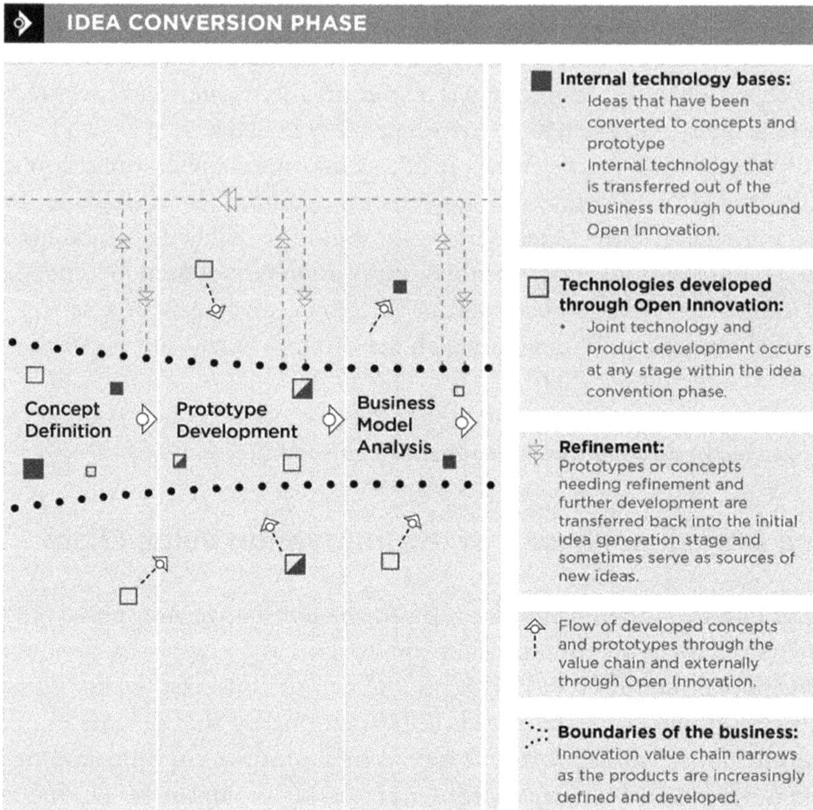

Fig. 10.2 Conceptual graphic of the idea conversion phase of the innovation value chain (*Source* Mohalajeng [2016])

performance of the prototypes is poor during testing, they are sent back for further development and modifications.

Introducing the prototypes to various markets during testing helps identity audiences that are most receptive to the product. When testing the prototypes, the primary and secondary requirements of the consumers should be listed along with any dislikes they may have (Tidd & Bessant, 2020). The relation between the consumers' requirements and the technical characteristics of the prototype should be measured in order to ensure an appropriate design fitting both needs is completed.

During testing, it is imperative that products are projected as profitable to the business in addition to their appeal to the consumer. Refined products after initial testing are retested in order to determine their overall value to the consumer (Smith, 2015). Refinement is an iterative process.

Commercialisation

Once products have been refined, formalised and introduced to the market through testing, the commercialisation step commences (Marais & Schutte, 2010: 103). Commercialisation is the final step in the innovation value chain and involves manufacturing and launching the final product for entrance into the market (Smith, 2015).

After the prototype has been approved, production and manufacturing proceeds; designers help simplify the prototype in order to make it appropriate for manufacturing it in batches. The manufacturing and production that takes place is not full-scale as yet since individuals operating the manufacturing process need to familiarise themselves with the production of the new product (Smith, 2015). During manufacturing and production, a range of components need to be finalised. Businesses need to decide on whether machinery or labour will be used, where raw materials and equipment should be sourced from as well as the various supporting tools and information that should be incorporated (Smith, 2015). During the manufacturing process potential flaws in the product may be picked up; these faults serve as information for further development but may be supplied to the consumers for their perception of the product (Smith, 2015).

The main purpose of commercialisation is generating ideas into new markets and extending the business offerings in existing markets (Marais & Schutte, 2010: 103).

Launching the product or services into the market is another crucial step in commercialisation. Hemert et al. (2013: 438) highlight that continually engaging in the market through meetings with business partners and consumers as well as engaging with various business communities and everyday individuals allows businesses to have an understanding of the market and gain useful insights regarding the overall industry. Launching the product through buy-in from various role-players speeds up the commercialisation process. Market launch requires a substantial input from marketing departments (Smith, 2015). This is due to the fact that most of the activities associated with the launch involve exhibitions, online marketing, advertising, developing product briefs and collaterals as well as ensuring the availability of stock in various outlets.

Once the product has successfully been launched, it then creates financial value for the business and social value for those consuming the product or service. The products, processes and services are continuously evaluated. Knowledge sourced from evaluation then serves as input for improving these processes, products and services through incremental innovation.

Open Innovation Across the Idea Diffusion Phase and Its Application in Southern Africa

During the idea diffusion phase, businesses are able to sell prototypes to external parties as they perceive them as not feasible for the business's own model but may be worthwhile in other industries or markets. This is referred to as outbound or inside-out Open Innovation (Gassmann & Enkel, 2004: 10).

For start-up entrepreneurs, commercialisation through Open Innovation occurs through the identification and implementation of agreements with businesses seeking solutions for commercialisation (Gans & Stern, 2003: 336). Entrepreneurs, therefore, yield returns by commercialising their inventions through existing innovation value chains. Open Innovation strengthens established market power and simultaneously moderates competition in the market.

During the manufacturing and production of the products, through Open Innovation, equipment is shared with external parties and manufacturing may be a joint undertaking (Gonyora et al., 2022). This often occurs when the businesses taking part in Open Innovation are close to one another in manufacturing and equipment sharing are location-sensitive undertakings.

Through Open Innovation as a commercialisation strategy, there is joint access to new markets through co-branding (Gonyora et al., 2022). This helps entrepreneurs lower the cost of identifying and accessing new markets. Strategic alliances with other entrepreneurs; outsourcing agreements as well as entering into supplier–customer relations are typical practices of Open Innovation at the commercialisation stage (Hemert et al., 2013: 436).

For Open Innovation Accelerators in Southern Africa, this stage of the process is placed in the hands of the business and the external party for confidential deal-making (The Innovation Hub, 2022). Open Innovation Accelerators can assist when businesses are seeking ready-to-commercialise products for their markets. Figure 10.3 illustrates how Open Innovation plays a role within the idea diffusion phase of the innovation value chain.

Commercialisation plays an important part in innovation and entrepreneurship. Although it has been depicted as a step within the idea diffusion phase, commercialisation is actually the entire process of taking a raw idea and successfully introducing it to the marketplace. As mentioned previously, what converts a mere invention into an innovation is the commercialisation of that invention (Smith, 2015).

The innovation value chain serves as a generic adaptation of various innovation processes that may take place. Innovation value chains may differ according to the industry, the business and the commercial product.

10.3 Supporting the Innovation Value Chain

Although ideas are screened and become prototypes, many of these inventions are commercial failures and do not make it into the marketplace. Small- and medium-sized businesses (SMEs) across Africa risk falling victim to digital disruption, regulatory requirements and economic shifts that fundamentally change their markets. SMEs have gone out of business due to their inability to innovate in response to these changes and to successfully commercialise their technology. Within the

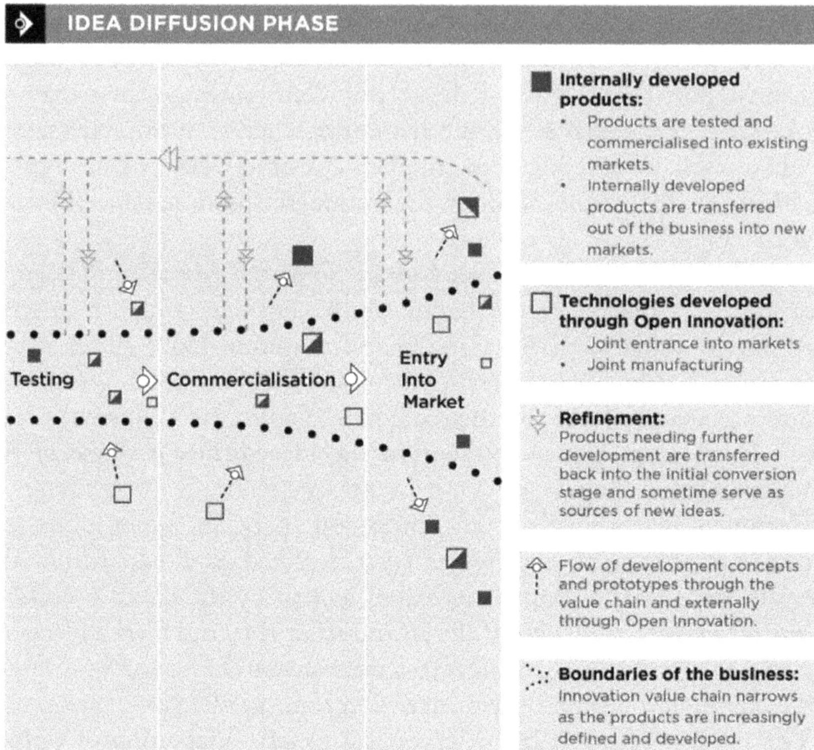

Fig. 10.3 The idea diffusion phase in the innovation value chain (*Source* Mohalajeng [2016])

African context, the innovation value chain requires a number of support activities to ensure the successful commercialisation of inventions.

Marketing activities, funding the innovation as well as protecting intellectual property are three key supporting functions necessary for the success of inventions through Open Innovation. These may pose challenges found in the innovation value chain.

Marketing

Introducing the invention to the public, as either a product or a service, forms part of the innovation value chain. Smith (2015) refers to this as the market launch. There are a number of activities that are required to ensure that the product or service is made known to and desired by the marketplace. These activities tend to pose a challenge because of the inability to acquire input from marketing departments.

Marketing activities should occur during the idea diffusion phase in the innovation value chain. This is because the developed concept requires buy-in from the rest of the business departments as well as the target market. The marketing department needs to be involved through spreading the new product concepts and business models across all functional areas within and essentially outside the business (Hansen & Birkinshaw, 2007: 5). The marketing of a new innovation, product or even entrepreneurial business that occurs through Open Innovation consists of a range of areas that need to be considered.

Selecting the Target Market

In order for the new product or service to succeed, the business and external parties involved through Open Innovation, have to target a specific market. It is important to identify groups of customers within the industry the business and its collaborative party plans to engage with (Barringer & Ireland, 2010). The target market selected should be distinct so that the marketing campaigns appeal specifically to them. In order for the new product or service to appeal to the market it is important to have an understanding of the market and its needs as some businesses make the mistake of launching a new product to a specific market without understanding its customers. The prime challenge faced when selecting a market for new products or services is choosing a market that is attractive enough to be interesting yet different enough that the product or service doesn't disappear into the crowd (Barringer & Ireland, 2010). It is vital that the selected market be in line with the business's background, business model and the skills of its founders.

Establishing a Position

In addition to selecting the right target market, it is the responsibility of the marketing department to establish a position that differentiates the new product or service from potential competitors (Barringer & Ireland, 2010). The position is what the business claims as its own and is what customers use when differentiating between the various products or services in the specific market.

If the business launching the new product already has a well-established target market and position in that market, the marketing department needs to focus on building the brand of the new product or service in line with the business's product range or service offerings.

Building a Brand

Marketing department is responsible for communicating the benefits of purchasing a new product or service. The mistake often made when launching new inventions is that marketing personnel rush to point out the features and specifications that particular invention has rather than just pointing out how the invention would enhance the customer's life (Barringer & Ireland, 2010). Customers buy benefits rather than features.

It is essential that the brand of the new product or service sets out the new product or service attributes. The main purpose of branding new products and services is for product identification, allowing marketers and consumers to distinguish the new products and services from competitors (Lamb et al., 2013: 170).

Lamb et al. (2013: 170) emphasise that marketing departments should consider the customer's loyalty towards a brand; the recognition of the brand; the perceived quality of the business's overall products and services and the associations made with the brand.

Since the new products or services are developed through Open Innovation, other proprietary assets such as patents and trademarks should be considered. Through the high-quality partnerships and agreements made during the conversion and diffusion phases of the innovation value chain, co-branding arrangements may be made. This takes place when the businesses' brands promote one another. The marketing department should consider whether the branding partnership will strengthen the new product or service's brand image and whether lengthening the brand image with an undesirable product will damage the original brand (Gbadamosi et al., 2013: 189).

Marketing Mix

Once the target market, position and brand have been established, the marketing department should now set marketing tools that will be used to yield the response desired from the market (Barringer & Ireland, 2010). Marketing departments arrange their marketing mix into four categories: product, price, place and promotion. These are commonly known as the 4Ps of marketing or the marketing mix and will be illustrated in Fig. 10.4. The 4Ps of marketing are variables that marketing departments can control and merge together in order to satisfy customers in the target market in the best way possible (Anon, 2022a).

In summary, marketing is a crucial step in the commercialisation phase of the innovation value chain. In order to successfully commercialise new products and services, marketers are required to have an extensive understanding of customers and market in which they function. Once this is understood, a position in the market as well as a brand for the new product or service should be established. The purpose of the marketing department should be to convince potential customers of the new product or service's value and benefit to the customer as well as its viability.

Funding

Innovation refers to exploiting ideas and inventions and turning them into commercial products and services. The idea generation and conversion phase of the innovation value chain requires funding. Smith (2015) states that the development of innovation requires an expenditure of funds. This takes place prior to generating an equivalent intake of funds.

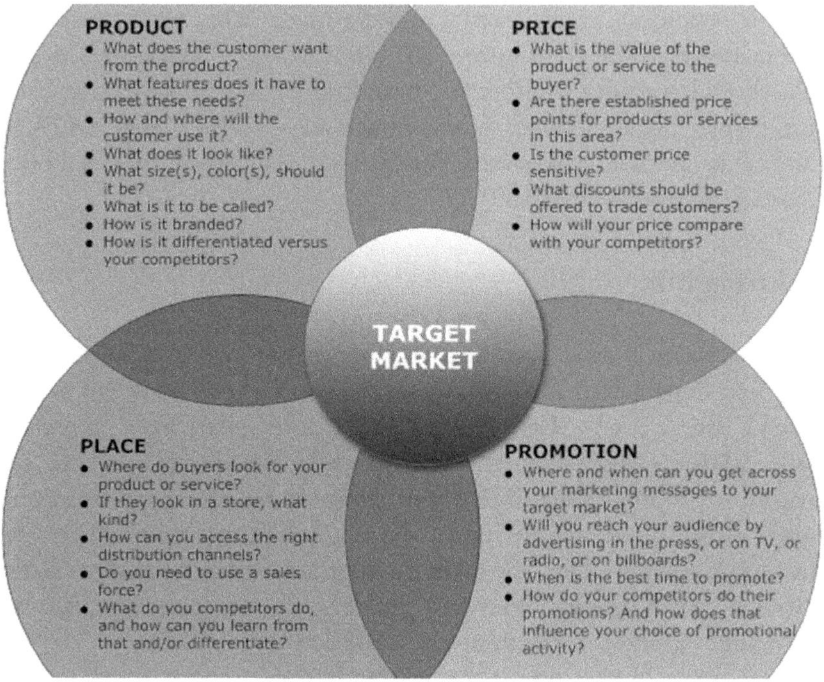

Fig. 10.4 Summary of the marketing mix (*Source* Anon [2022a])

There is subsequently a negative cash flow right through the innovation value chain before funds are generated and cash flow turns positive. The outflow of cash at this stage does not correspond with an inflow of sales. Figure 10.5 summarises the flow of funding throughout the innovation value chain.

From Fig. 10.5, it is clear that there are various kinds of funding that can be obtained. These depend on how far the new product or service is from commercialisation.

Bootstrapping

Spinelli et al. (2014) describe bootstrapping to be an effort to minimise resources or the cost thereof throughout the innovation value chain.

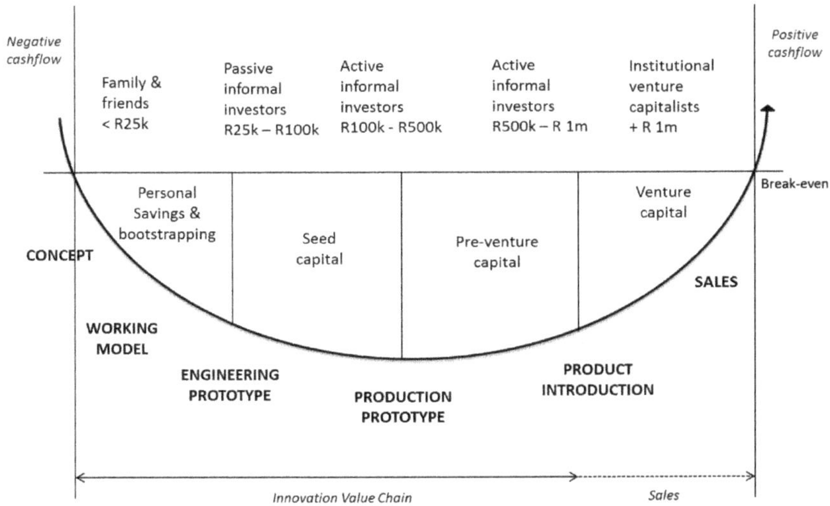

Fig. 10.5 Funding streams in the innovation value chain (*Source* Adapted from Smith [2015])

It involves attempting to accomplish more with minimum expenditure in order to pursue the opportunity. The entrepreneur focuses on finding methods to avoid external funding through cost-cutting, ingenuity and creativity (Barringer & Ireland, 2010). Bootstrapping results in the acquisition of resources for free or much less than one would expect to pay.

Personal financing and the use of family and friends form part of bootstrapping as the "bootstrapper" uses creative ways of receiving funds without the use of banks (Smith, 2015). Friends and family may offer delayed compensation, investments and sometimes financial gifts.

Bootstrapping often occurs at the idea generation stage in the innovation value chain. The funds acquired from bootstrapping as well as friends and family are used in the early stage of the new product or service for the first models as proof of concepts (Smith, 2015). The various idea generators taking part in this initial phase of the value chain may also provide finances in getting the idea into the conversion stage.

Government Funding

There have been a number of government-funded schemes that have been designed to finance innovation around the globe. These schemes aim to develop new marketable technologies that have commercial feasibility (Smith, 2015).

In South Africa, receiving funding is a major stumbling block when attempting to commercialise innovations. However, the government has increased the availability of funding mechanisms in order to overcome this hurdle (van der Merwe, 2013). There are three role-players within the government sector that aim to provide funding for new inventions and business ventures namely the Technology Innovation Agency (TIA), Industrial Development Corporation (IDC) and the Department of Trade and Industry (DTI).

TIA is a government-funded agency which aims to stimulate technological innovation in South Africa. The agency uses South Africa's innovation industries to develop new industries and in essence diversify the economy (Anon, 2022b). TIA provides both non-financial and financial support to various role-players within the triple helix of South Africa. The IDC is a self-funded but government-owned entity. Its development funds aim to enable the conversion of inventions and technology developed in South Africa into commercial products (van der Merwe, 2013). They are particularly interested in high-impact and labour-intensive technologies that potentially lead to the creation of new industries.

South Africa's Department of Trade and Industry also finances innovation. The DTI has launched an online selection and application portal for various funding initiatives therefore making it easier for entrepreneurs to obtain funding (van der Merwe, 2013).

The government serves as a significant contributor to South Africa's increasing venture capital environment. It is the role of the entrepreneur to ensure that they apply for the various funding mechanisms the government offers.

Angel Investors

Barringer and Ireland (2010) define angel investors as individuals investing their own capital in new business or new products and services. These individuals are normally high in net worth, well-educated and have previously succeeded as entrepreneurs themselves. Angel investors seek more than capital returns but are often particularly interested in the growth of the new product or services as well. Because they do not form part of recognised associations and aren't clearly visible in markets, they are seen as informal investors (Smith, 2015).

Angel investors are varied and have a broad range of interests in new business opportunities. Investors may be interested in maximising their wealth, seeking increased income or because of their entrepreneurial mindset (Smith, 2015). Established businesses may also form part of angel investors as they invest in unquoted businesses or products. This is referred to as corporate venturing.

It's concluded that angel investors play quite an invaluable role in the innovation value chain because of their willingness to make relatively small investments into new products and services that don't necessarily require a great deal of money as venture capitalists do. They are often anonymous and are paired up with entrepreneurs through networking and referrals.

Venture Capital

Venture capital arose due to new businesses' inability to find access to long-term risk capital. Smith (2015) explains that venture capital is loaned from acknowledged investors. Venture capitalists form partnerships with wealthy individuals, foreign investors, university grants, pension funds and other similar sources of funding. Through these partnerships, the role of the venture capitalists is to evaluate the risks and growth of the new product or service and ensure that their respective partner would make a capital gain when choosing to withdraw their funds at a later stage (Smith, 2015).

Commercial Banks

Unlike the previously mentioned sources of funding, commercial banks serve as debt funders whereas the previous sources serve as equity funders. With commercial banks, none of the business or new product's ownership is surrendered and any interest payments on the loan are tax deductible rather than dividends being paid out. Although this is the case, banks are not seen as the most viable and practical source of funding a new product or service simply because they need to be repaid in full and also impose particularly strict conditions on their investment (Barringer & Ireland, 2010).

Commercial banks play a role at a later stage in the new products or services' life cycle. It is once the product or service is commercialised that entrepreneurs should consider commercial funding as banks are a significant source of credit for small businesses.

Barringer and Ireland (2010) further mention that commercial banks take an interest in businesses that have audited financials, low leverage, healthy balance sheets and high cash flow which is not necessarily the case for new businesses and new products.

In summary, it is important to consider the various funding mechanisms during the innovation value chain. The lack of finances and finding funding could potentially lead to discontinuing the process of commercialising the ideas generated.

Intellectual Property (IP)

Intellectual property is referred to by the World Intellectual Property Organisation (WIPO, 2012) as any creation born of human intellect with value in the marketplace. It is articulated as an invention, literature, artistic works as well as names, symbols and images used in commerce. When observing creating new products and services, it is imperative that entrepreneurs determine what intellectual property to protect. When doing so the entrepreneur should determine if the intellectual property is directly linked to its competitive advantage and if protecting that IP will increase its value in the marketplace (Barringer & Ireland, 2010).

IP rights make it possible for the entrepreneur to benefit from their originality and inventiveness as well as to prohibit others from exploiting their inventions. There are three main types of IP protection namely copyright, patents and trademarks. Copyright allows a writer to decide how their work is used and to benefit from its profitability. Smith (2015) adds that copyright follows automatically after creating a new work. On the other hand, patents are granted by the government to the entrepreneur, rewarding them for their invention and ensuring them exclusive right to the patent. WIPO (2012: 9) describes a trademark as any graphically representable sign used for identification and the differentiation of a new invention and product from others similar. These methods of IP protection are to be looked into when commercialising new innovations.

In the innovation value chain, it is important that due diligence is completed on new partners and solution providers participating in the Open Innovation process at any of the three phases. Spinelli et al. (2014) explain that due diligence is the process of authenticating the potential partners' credibility. It involves verifying the new partners' and solution providers' backgrounds and facts; the reputations of the key contributors and staff involved; investigating the technical competencies of the new idea, prototype or product and confirming market estimates and proprietary rights.

During the concept definition, prototyping and feasibility steps of the idea conversion phase, it is important to ensure that the IP of the various parties is protected. If the IP rights of the external party (whether an entrepreneur, scientist, start-up business, association, supplier or consumer) are already available, disclosure of the solution is less stressful (Gans & Stern, 2003: 338). This implies that disclosing the solution will not reduce the owner's ability to profit from it. As mentioned previously, sharing IP can pose a number of challenges. A business's competitive advantage may possibly decrease, and future planned products could be blemished (Marais & Schutte, 2010: 106). A business disclosing its ideas or inviting other businesses into its innovation process is often seen as a weakness.

IP protection occurs in various places within the innovation value chain. When new inventions and new useful business processes and improvements are brought about, patents are to be registered therefore giving the inventor exclusive rights to the new invention. The marketing department also needs to consider IP protection of new slogans, names, brochures, logos and jingles through trademarks and copyrights. The various agreements and processes such as contractual forms, PowerPoint slides, new methodologies, employee handbooks and training materials are also to be protected through copyright and trade secrets. Other administrative and informative systems should also be protected. These include website designs, computer software and codes as well as internet domain names (Barringer & Ireland, 2010).

Throughout the innovation value chain, the idea generator and owner of the prototype may choose to sell their IP or license it to the business wishing to commercialise the new product or service.

Figure 10.6 serves to illustrate the entire innovation value chain from idea generation to idea diffusion as well as the supporting activities necessary for the success of the innovation value chain.

10.4 Chapter Summary

For developing countries to attain industrial and economic growth, entrepreneurship and innovation should be at the forefront of the country's priorities. This is because there is a direct relationship between the level of early-stage entrepreneurial activity and per capita income across a range of economies.

Entrepreneurship through innovation, however, does not happen overnight but instead is an extensive process. This process of taking ideas to market through commercialisation is referred to as the innovation value chain. Although the innovation value chain may differ from business to business, it is a sequential three-phase process starting from idea generation, idea conversion and then idea diffusion. Within these three phases are various activities that need to be undertaken.

During the first phase, ideas are generated through the various sources of innovation and are screened and selected according to set. Through Open Innovation ideas may be obtained from external role players. The

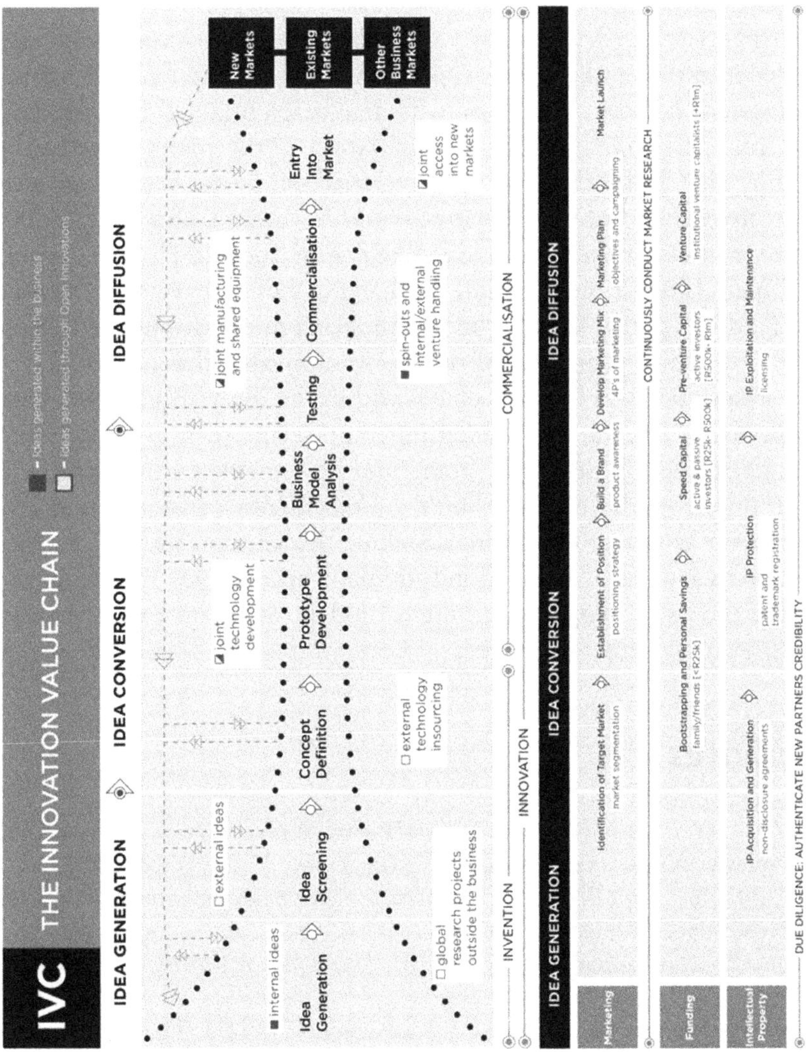

Fig. 10.6 Open innovation across the innovation value chain with support mechanisms (*Source* Mohalajeng [2016])

second phase comprises defining the concepts in order to develop prototypes that serve as tools that will used to analyse the business model. Joint technology and product development takes place through Open Innovation in the second phase. In the last phase, prototypes are tested and further developed. These prototypes are then manufactured and later launched into the market. With Open Innovation, equipment for manufacturing may be shared and products may be co-branded for increased access into new markets. Commercialisation is the main objective of the innovation value chain. It refers to successfully converting an idea into an invention and later an innovation by introducing the product into the market. Open Innovation Accelerators such as The Innovation Hub Open Innovation Solution Exchange, should have the capabilities of ensuring the increase in commercialisation through ensuring collaboration in various parts of the innovation value chain.

It is also imperative that the phases within the innovation value chain are supported. The various marketing components such as considering the target market, building the brand and how the new innovation will be introduced to the market should be taken into consideration. The entrepreneur as well as the business seeking the solution should consider the different sources of innovation funding. These include the economic principle (bootstrapping), government funders, angel investors, venture capitalists and commercial banks.

References

Anon. (2022a). *The marketing Mix: The 4Ps of marketing*. www.smartdraw.com/examples/view/4ps+marketing+mix/ (Accessed on 12 December 2022).

Anon. (2022b). *The Technology Innovation Agency*. www.tia.org.za/about-us (Accessed on 12 December 2022).

Barringer, B. R., & Ireland, R. D. (2010). *Successfully launching new ventures.* Pearson.

Bigliardi, B., Ferraro, G., Filippelli, S., & Galati, F. (2021). The past, present and future of open innovation. *European Journal of Innovation Management, 24*(4), 1130–1161.

Chen, X., Liu, Z., & Zhu, Q. (2020). Reprint of "Performance evaluation of China's high-tech innovation process: Analysis based on the innovation value chain." *Technovation, 94*, 102094.

Diener, K., Luettgens, D., & Piller, F. T. (2020). Intermediation for open innovation: Comparing direct versus delegated search strategies of innovation intermediaries. *International Journal of Innovation Management, 24*(04), 2050037.

Drucker, P. F. (2011). *The discipline of innovation.* Harvard Business Review. The Best of Harvard. Harvard Business School Publishing Corporation.

Ganotakis, P., & Love, J. H. (2012). The innovation value chain in new technology-based firms: Evidence from the UK. *Journal of Product Innovation Management, 29*(5), 839–860.

Gans, J. S., & Stern, S. (2003). The product market and the market for ideas: Commercialisation strategies for technology entrepreneurs. *Research Policy, 32*, 333–350.

Gassmann, O., & Enkel, E. (2004). *Towards a theory of Open Innovation: Three core process archetypes.* https://www.alexandria.unisg.ch/Publikationen/274 (Accessed on 8 January 2014).

Gbadamosi, A., Bathgate, I. K., & Nwankwo, S. (2013). *Principles of marketing: A value-based approach.* Palgrave Macmillan.

Gonyora, A. M., Migiro, S., Mashau, P., & Ngwenya, B. (2022). The impact of open innovation challenges on automotive component manufacturers' competitiveness: An insight from the South African automotive industry. *African Journal of Science, Technology, Innovation and Development, 14*(4), 1139–1148.

Hague, C., Hague, E., & Breitbach, C. (2011). *Regional and local economic development*. Palgrave Macmillan

Hansen, M. T., & Birkinshaw, J. (2007). *The innovation value chain.* Harvard Business Review. Harvard Business School Publishing Corporation.

Hemert, P., Nijkamp, P., & Masurel, E. (2013). From innovation to commercialisation through networks and agglomerations: Analysis of sources of innovation, innovation capabilities and performance of Dutch SME's. *Annual Regular Science, 50*, 425–452.

Janssen, W., Bouwman, H., van Buuren, R., & Haaker, T. (2014). An organisational competence model for innovation intermediaries. *European Journal of Innovation Management, 17*(1), 2–24.

Kuratko, D. F. (2018). *Entrepreneurship* (10th ed.). Cengage Learning.

Lamb, C. W., Hair, J. F., & McDaniel, C. (2013). *MKTG6*. Cengage Learning.

Marais, S. J., & Schutte, C. S. L. (2010). *The development of Open Innovation models to assist the innovation process* (Msc Eng dissertation). University of Stellenbosch, Stellenbosch.

Mohalajeng, L. E. (2016). *Investigating an open innovation platform to accelerate commercialisation* (Doctoral dissertation). North-West University, South Africa, Potchefstroom Campus.

Mohalajeng, L. E., & Kroon, J. (2016). Innovation through accelerators: A case for open innovation. *The Southern African Journal of Entrepreneurship and Small Business Management, 8*(1), 1–9.

Nambisan, S., Wright, M., & Feldman, M. (2019). The digital transformation of innovation and entrepreneurship: Progress, challenges and key themes. *Research Policy, 48*(8), 103773.

Ottonicar, S. L. C., Arraiza, P. M., & Armellini, F. (2020). Opening science and innovation: Opportunities for emerging economies. *Форсайт, 14*(4), 95–111 (Eng.).

Smith, D. (2015). *Exploring innovation* (3rd ed.). McGraw-Hill.

Spinelli, S., Ensign, P. C., & Adams, R. J. (2014). *New venture creation.* McGraw-Hill Ryerson.

The Innovation Hub. (2022). *Open Innovation solution exchange pilot project case study*. The Innovation Hub Management Company. https://www.theinnovationhub.com/innovation-programmes/openix-5. (Accessed on 14 March 2022).

Tidd, J., & Bessant, J. R. (2020). *Managing innovation: Integrating technological, market and organizational change*. Wiley.

van der Merwe, N. (2013, September 10). Getting innovative about funding. *Finweek.* http://finweek.com/2013/09/10/getting-innovative-about-funding/. (Accessed on 6 March 2022).

von Nell, P. S., & Lichtenthaler, U. (2011). The role of innovation intermediaries in the markets for technology. *International Journal of Technology Intelligence and Planning, 7*(2), 128–139.

WIPO. (2012). *What is intellectual property?* World Intellectual Property Organisation. http://www.wipo.int/edocs/pubdocs/en/intproperty/450/wipo_pub_450.pdf (Accessed on 6 January 2022).

11

Empirical Analysis of the Impact of Institutions on Innovative Entrepreneurship in Sub-Saharan African Countries

Muftau Olaiya Olarinde and Shehu Auta

11.1 Introduction

Achieving an appreciable level of development in any economy requires the presence of a vibrant entrepreneurship which is a major driver of structural transformation and economic development (Acs et al., 2012; Audretsch & Keilbach, 2004, 2008; Castano et al., 2015; Minniti, 2008). It is, however, not surprising that in the twenty-first century, policy makers in most countries have now directed public policy measures away from direct government provision of employment towards the promotion of entrepreneurial activities (Shane, 2009). This is because encouraging entrepreneurial activities has the ability for improving economic development (Baumol & Strom, 2007; Bjornskov & Foss, 2013; Estrin et al., 2013). Authors such as Reynolds et al. (1999) have broadly categorized entrepreneurship into two types: opportunity

M. O. Olarinde (✉) · S. Auta
Department of Economics, Usmanu Danfodiyo University, Sokoto, Nigeria
e-mail: Olarinde.muftau@udusok.edu.ng

A. S. Ibidunni et al. (eds.), *Innovation, Entrepreneurship and the Informal Economy in Sub–Saharan Africa*, Sustainable Development Goals Series,
https://doi.org/10.1007/978-3-031-46293-1_11

entrepreneurship (arising from the discovery or innovation of new business ideas) and necessity entrepreneurship (arising from limited job opportunities and harsh economic realities).

Most importantly, innovative entrepreneurs have been adjudged to be the engines behind structural transformation. As such, there is a broad agreement among development economists on the role played by innovative entrepreneurship in structural transformation of economy for sustained economic development (Cararro & Karfakis, 2018). Focusing on innovative entrepreneurship as a promoter of the process of structural transformation, Porter et al. (2002) stated that innovative entrepreneurship plays different roles across three stages of structural economic transformation process (factor-driven-stage, an efficiency-driven-stage and innovative-driven-stage) and across the groups of countries. Building upon this, Acs and Naude (2013) looked at the link between structural economic transformation and innovative entrepreneurship. They confirmed that; in the earlier stages (factor-driven-stage) of structural economic transformation, the level of innovative entrepreneurial activity is low accounting for not more than 5% of economic activities. But it rises to 10% in the efficient-driven-stage and 30% in the innovative-driven-stage. Also, moving onward through the stages, the importance of knowledge accumulation and absorption increases.

However, UNECA (2016) concludes that strong institutions are fundamental prerequisites for a successful achievement of increased entrepreneurial activities and economic development in Sub-Saharan African (SSA) countries. While most of the developed countries record or display a higher score of institutional quality, developing countries ranked very poor in term of institutional quality (Aidis et al., 2008; Drury et al., 2006; Houssa & Megarsa, 2017; Mauro, 1995). Therefore, institutional quality plays a very important role in providing a stable macroeconomic environment necessary for the growth of entrepreneurial activities, as well as facilitating reallocation of resources across sectors that are required for smooth and faster structural transformation and economic development in Sub-Saharan African countries.

The tent of conventional wisdom on strong institutional quality implies market-oriented reforms, effective checks and balances, adequate regulatory/legal framework and strong enforcement mechanisms are critical factors towards efficient and effective growth of entrepreneurial activity and resource reallocation necessary for structural transformation and economic development. Strong institutional quality encourages physical and human capital accumulation through technological improvement, increased investments and lowering of transaction costs. On the other hand, weak institutional quality discourages local/foreign research and development (R&D) implementation, contributes to lock resources in low-productivity sectors and struggles to manage Foreign Direct Investment (FDI) (Aron, 2000; Houssa & Megarsa, 2017). Hence, strong institutional quality will help countries to move resources from sectors where they have lower comparative advantage to sectors with higher comparative advantage and positively influence innovative entrepreneurship.

Therefore, to achieve the desired level of economic development through innovative entrepreneurship, the significant roles of institutions (formal and informal) cannot be left out. The strength of these institutions determines to a large extent, the nature and quality of entrepreneurial activities that will take place in any given environment. These institutions could be legal, social, political, economic and cultural (value-based) in nature. They specify the rules of the game, in terms of how entrepreneurs should carry out their business activities, lower the cost of doing business, instilling confidence in an entrepreneur that is investing is secure, among others (North, 1990). The structural transformation of any economy, particularly the developing countries where lack of capital constraints for investment capital goods depends on the growth of entrepreneurship that requires a sound, efficient and effective environment to flourish. However, providing an enabling and conducive environment for a successful structural transformation and entrepreneurship development depends on strong institutions. Disappointedly, Sub-Saharan African countries' institutions are mostly ineffective in providing the required environment necessary for the growth of entrepreneurship.

There are a number of studies that have investigated the impact of institutions on growth of entrepreneurship across the world (Amoros & Stenholm, 2014; Crnogayi & Hojnik, 2016; Castono et al., 2015; Fuentelsaz et al., 2015; Kocenda & Karen, 2017; Salihu & Yusuf, 2015;

Hussein, 2019 among others). In the case of Hussein, 2019, the study does not specifically focus on Sub-Sahara Africa while Salihu and Yusuf (2015) only include ten selected emerging and developing countries covering the periods 2004 to 2012. This study differs from the existing studies by examining the relationship between innovative entrepreneurship and institutional quality in Sub-Sahara Africa based 2SLS with year fixed effects. Generally, choice of becoming an entreprenuer is predicated upon the economic structure and entrepreneurs' environment and/or circumstances that motivate them to go into a particular type of entrepreneurial activity, rather than taking up a paid job. These factors cannot be looked at in isolation of population, institutions and the environment entrepreneurs find themselves (Mendez-Picazo et al., 2012; Shane & Venkataram, 2000). It is in line with these factors that this study attempts to look at the role of institutional quality as its affects the growth of opportunity entrepreneurship in twenty selected Sub-Saharan African countries using "institutional theory" propounded by North (1990) as its main theoretical framework.

Conceptual and Literature Reviews

Institution has been conceptualized to be constraints which guide conducts and behaviors of economic agents. Hodgson (2006) defines institutions as systems of established and prevalent social rules that structure social interaction, hence institutions in this sense are a habit that exists and known in the society as people interact with one another. This view concurred with Veblen (1919) who conceptualizes institutions as "settled habits of thought common to the generality of men".

Looking at the concepts of institutions from the perspective of social relationships, institutions are seen as persistent systems of established as well as entrenched social rules that program and guide social interactions towards achieving a common goal (Olarinde, 2015). However, the concept of institutions to be conceived as only a social rule was modified, and is now seen in a broader perspective. For instance, North (1990) defined institutions as rules of the game in a society, or more formally the humanly devised constraints that shape human interaction.

In consequence, they structure incentives in human exchange, whether political, social or economic. This definition is wider in scope and more encompassing than the earlier view. This is because North's definition of institutions entails the earlier views of established or settled "social rules" in the society that aim at achieving a common or societal goal. Also, the definition captured the view that institutions provide incentives (positive and negative) in any political, social and economic settings. By this, institutions in modern societies specify the rules of the game on how economic actors behave and define incentives for such economic activities (Acemoglu et al., 2000). Modern societies are a rich web of formal (law and regulation) and informal (culture norms) institutions that differ greatly (Henredson & Johnson; 2010). A properly designed rule of the game either formal or informal that is religiously implemented, obeyed and followed by all will result in the existence of strong formal institutions necessary for entrepreneurial activity and structural transformation. Hence, institutions must be part of a country's production function for the growth of entrepreneurial activity and for structural transformation to occur (Charles, 1995).

Entrepreneurship is the state of being an entrepreneur (Ibru, 2007). An entrepreneur is an individual who owns, organizes and manages a business and in so doing, assumes the risk of either making a profit or losing the investment. Entrepreneurship is often approached as a catalyst and caretaker of national and regional economies. It is seen as the privileged road to enhance the creation of new jobs and increase GDP (Parker, 2000). The OECD (1998) is of the view that as more countries move towards fostering entrepreneurship, the evidence is mounting that implemented comprehensively, entrepreneurship policies represent an effective response for countries wanting to strengthen their adaptability and improve their economy's ability to create jobs.

Therefore, entrepreneurial activities have a positive connection to economic transformation through the creation of innovation. This positive link between entrepreneurship and economic transformation has undoubtedly been established since the early works of Schumpeter (1911). According to Schumpeter (1934), entrepreneurship is about innovation, and as entrepreneurs introduce new combinations of factors of production, the level of economic transformation increases. This positive effect is due to their skills and their ability to innovate. For instance, Belthelt (2001) asserted that entrepreneurs find new combinations of existing assets, new niches and market needs, which enables entrepreneurs to efficiently raise productivity. Also, Acs and Audretsch (1990) are of the view that entrepreneurship increases economic transformation and diversity, new network creation, cooperation, provides a more fluid information exchange and introduces important innovations by entering markets with new products or production processes. Though innovation is a key trait of entrepreneurship, it is not the only trait.

Basically, there are two major types of entrepreneurship in the literature, the necessity and the innovative entrepreneurship. The necessity entrepreneurship is associated with the Austrian school of economics led by Kirzner (1973). The school is of the view that the entrepreneur's main function in the society is to serve as an arbitrage. Kirzner (1973) further argued that markets are perfectly constructed where the entrepreneur is expected to exploit the gaps that exist between and within the market. Thus, an entrepreneur only discovers the price gaps that exist and act on that margin to close the gap. This notion of entrepreneurship is that of necessity type of entrepreneurship. However, Schumpeter's notion of entrepreneurship is that an entrepreneur is an innovator rather than an arbitraged. He rejected that markets are perfectly competitive constructs, but markets are rather dynamic processes driven by creative skills (new combination). Hence, entrepreneurs channel the means of production into previously unexploited markets and attract followers into these new markets. Therefore, entrepreneurship is about being innovative as it involves the ability to break away from routine, overhaul existing structures and move the system away from the ever-circular flow of equilibrium (Duguet, 2004; Schumpeter, 1961).

Schumpeter (1934) emphasized that economic development processes could be divided into three distinct stages. The first stage is the technical discovery stage of new things or new ways of doing things (invention stage). The second stage is the successful commercialization of a new good or service stemming from technical discovery or a new combination of knowledge (innovation stage) while the third is concerned with the adoption and diffusion of new products or processes of the market (imitation stages). Therefore, the concept of innovation and entrepreneurship are closely connected to one another. Entrepreneurs disrupt market equilibrium by introducing new product combinations into a market that meets the dynamic needs of consumers and the environment, as well as crowd out less productive firms as the innovations advance the production frontier (GEM, 2018).

Drawing from the perspective of the Austrian school of economics and Schumpeter (1934) views of an entrepreneur, an entrepreneur identifies and discovers previously unexploited profit opportunities and moves the economy to an economically and /or technologically efficient production point. Also, the entrepreneurial processes shift the production possibility frontier outwards in its discovery of improved technology, leading to increased productivity and thus, structural economic transformation.

Studies have established a linkage between innovative entrepreneurship and institutions. For example, Salihu and Yusuf (2015) examined the linkage between institutions, innovative entrepreneurship and economic growth in ten selected emerging and developing countries covering the periods 2004 to 2012. The study used control of corruption and access to credit facilities as a proxy for informal institution and formal institution respectively, while entrepreneurs that were motivated to pursue perceived business opportunities was used as a proxy for innovative entrepreneurship. The results of the two-stage least square technique revealed that control of corruption is positive and highly significant at a one percent level. This implied that the perception about government's effort at controlling petty and grand forms of corruption had a positive influence on innovative entrepreneurship. The result also indicated that confidence in one's skills and abilities increases the level of innovative entrepreneurship while access to credit has an insignificant positive influence on innovative entrepreneurship. The insignificant impact of access to credit as a proxy for formal institutions might be due to the nature of the entrepreneurs that operate on a small scale, with less expertise in developing a proposal and keeping financial records that are require for loan acquisition.

Hussein (2019) investigated the causality between institutions, innovative and necessity entrepreneurship in factor-driven, efficiency-driven and innovative-driven countries both in the short run and long run, covering the periods 2005 to 2015. Physical property rights, intellectual property right and international property right were used as proxies for institutions. Three-steps method was used while the panel Granger causality test was conducted to test the direction of causality among the series. The author found that in a factor-driven country, there was a unidirectional causality running from entrepreneurship to institutions in both the short run and long run, while in an efficiency-driven country, entrepreneurship equally causes institutions in the short run but in the long run institutions cause entrepreneurship. However, the study established a bidirectional causality between institutions and entrepreneurship in the long run in innovative-driven economies. On average, it could be concluded that institution drives entrepreneurship activities regardless of the nature of the economies.

Williams and Vorley (2017) investigated the effects of direct and indirect informal institutions on performance of innovative entrepreneurial activities in 26 European countries over the periods of 2002 to 2009. Business environment and enterprise performance were used as proxies for informal institutions on the enterprise level. Random and fixed effects estimators were used to analyze the data. The result showed that there was a high correlation between innovative entrepreneurs in any country level with corruption perception index and moderately with cultural values. The author also showed that informal institutions had a positive statistically significant impact on the entrepreneur's innovative behavior and that informal institutions could directly or indirectly affect entrepreneurial behavior.

Fuentelsaz et al. (2015) analyzed and compared the influence that the formal institutions of a country had on the different types of entrepreneurship and their relative presence in 63 developed and developing countries over a period from 2005 to 2012. Using both fixed and random effect estimates to analyze dataset. The result showed that property rights, business freedom, labor freedom financial capital of formal institutions had positive effects on opportunity entrepreneurship and negatively affected necessity entrepreneurship. They also found the presence of positive influences of greater business freedom, educational and financial freedom and the protection of property rights on the ratio of opportunity total entrepreneurship activity (TEA) and necessity total entrepreneurship activity (TEA). This supported the idea that policymakers should direct policies towards entrepreneurial activities with positive effects on economic transformation.

Crnogaj and Hojnik (2016) examined the impact of institutional factors on early-staged entrepreneurial activity in light of 24 countries from factor-driven, efficiency-driven and innovative-driven nations over the periods 2006 and 2010. Political institutions were proxies of Government spending, economic institutions were proxies of property right and social institutions were proxies of freedom from corruption. Ordinary Least Squares (OLS) and econometrics business methods were used to analyze data. The result showed that government spending had a significantly positive impact on early-staged entrepreneurial activity in both innovative and efficiency-driven countries. However, the study indicated a significantly positive impact on the early-stage entrepreneurial activity for property right and freedom from corruption in the innovative-driven countries but negative and not significant impacts in the efficiency-driven countries. The study also revealed that cultural and social norms prevailing in the society had positive and significant impacts on the individual's division for entrepreneurship.

Kocenda and Karen (2017) analyzed institutional quality, GDP per capital and size of the economy on export sophistication entrepreneurship based on a large panel dataset over the periods 2001 to 2005 across 101 emerging and developing countries. Various estimation algorithms were adopted to analyze datasets. The result revealed that weak institutional quality exhibited negative and significant effects on export sophistication entrepreneurship. Also GDP per capital and the size of the economy exhibited significant and positive effects on export sophistication. The authors also found that export sophistication entrepreneurship is path-dependent and stable even during major economic crises, especially for emerging and developing economies.

Amoros and Stenholm (2014) investigated how the quality of institutions affected the necessity-based entrepreneurial activities in 89 economies from both developing and developed countries over periods from 2001 to 2012. The percentage of the country's adult population involved in entrepreneurship was used as a proxy for necessity-based entrepreneurship. Using voice of accountability, political stability, government effectiveness, regulatory quality, rule of law and control of corruption as proxies for institutional quality. Using pooled OLS regressions on cross-sectional time series data for analyses. The result showed that all the qualities of institutional variables had significant and negative influences on necessity-based entrepreneurship. However, when two institutional variables were interacted one with a developed country and one with GDP. The result revealed a positive interactional effect between economic development and institutions. This implied that the negative effects were enhanced when the levels of economic development improved.

Amoros (2009): examined the relationship between three types of entrepreneurial dynamics to different variables relating to the quality of institutions in a panel data of 60 developed and developing countries covering periods between 2002 and 2007. Using does who claimed to be driven by the recognition of a business opportunity as a proxy for opportunity entrepreneurship, the proportion of opportunity-driven undertakings as a proxy for improved entrepreneurship while creating new businesses as the best available option as proxies for necessity-based entrepreneurship. Using voice of accountability, political stability, government effectiveness, regulatory quality, rule of law and control of corruption as proxies for institutional quality. Ordinary least squares (OLS) linear model and random fixed effects were adopted to analyze the dataset. The result revealed that the regulatory quality had a positive and not significant impact, rule of law had a negative and not significant impact and government effectiveness had a negative and significant impact on opportunity entrepreneurship. The result further indicated a positive and significant impact of control of corruption and political stability but negative and significant impact of rule of law and negative and not significant impact of regulatory quality on improved entrepreneurship. The result furthermore indicated a negative and significant impact of rule of law and government effectiveness however a positive and significant impact of regulatory quality on necessity-based entrepreneurship. This suggested that institutional quality had different economic implications on entrepreneurship across developed and developing countries.

Pathak (2016) examined the influence of informal institutions, on the extent of internationalization by early-staged entrepreneurial activities in 39 countries from 2001 to 2008. Performance orientation, self-expression and social desirability of entrepreneurship were used as proxies for informal institutions. Multi-level modeling techniques were used to analyze data. The result showed that high Performance orientation, high self-expression and low social desirability of entrepreneurship in the society had positively influenced the extent of internationalization by early-staged entrepreneurial activity.

Williams and Vorley (2015) examined how changes to the institutional environment impacted entrepreneurial activity in the crisis-hit region of Greece. The result revealed that changes to institutions had a negative impact on entrepreneurial activity, and the impact worsened in the midst of the crisis.

Mauro (1995) on factors that impact entrepreneurs' investment and development in 24 European countries over a period from 1960 to 1985. Using OLS and the two-stage least square (2SLS) method to analyze data, the result showed that corruption had a negative and significant impact on entrepreneurs' investment rate, indicating that the quality of institutions has a significant influence on the growth of entrepreneurship.

Examining the impact of other determinants of entrepreneurship growth, Castano et al. (2015) analyzed social, cultural and economic variables affecting entrepreneurship and entrepreneurs' perception of opportunity using partial least square method for two groups of countries of European, Latin America and Caribbean. The authors found that innovation, openness, economic performance and economic policy measures have a positive influence on the growth of entrepreneurship. This effect was stronger in Latin American and Caribbean Countries when compared to European Countries. They also found that Countries with greater degrees of economic freedom, rule of law, high corruption control and education had significant increases in entrepreneurial activities. This was particularly true for most European economies.

Assessing the impact of socio-economic factors on entrepreneurial activities in Cape Coast, Ghan Rotina, et al. (2017) used samples of 181 entrepreneurs and adopted Partial least square (PLS) method as a technique of data analysis. The results revealed that the inflation rate, religion and lifestyles of entrepreneurs significantly influenced their entrepreneurial activities and performances. The result also confirmed that economic factors had strong and direct impacts on entrepreneurial activities in Cape Coast, Ghana.

Muhsin and Serife (2016) examined the role of financial development and institutional factors on entrepreneurship growth in seventeen emerging market economies over the periods 2004–2009. The study used control of corruption, political stability and corruption perception index as proxy for institutions, private sector credit as proxy for financial development and new registration per thousand people between the ages of 15 to 64 as proxy for entrepreneurship. The result indicated a positive and statistically significant relationship between financial development and entrepreneurship. The study also found a negative and statistically significant relationship between inflation and entrepreneurship. In addition, the result revealed a positive but not statistically significant relationship between institutions and entrepreneurship.

11.2 Methodology

Types and Sources of Data

This study used secondary data to establish the impact of institution on innovative entrepreneurship and structural transformation in Sub-Saharan Africa. To assess the validity of our hypotheses, we gathered a panel dataset comprising twenty (20) Sub-Saharan African countries for periods of 18 years, from 2001 to 2018. Data on innovative entrepreneurship is obtained from the Global Entrepreneurship Monitor's (GEM, 2019). The sectoral employment data was sourced from the World Development Indicators (WDI) of World Bank (2019). Data on economic, political and social institutions such as control of corruption, government stability, and law and order, were obtained from International Country Risk Guide (ICRG, 2019). Data on control variables (inflation rate, openness and financial development) were sourced from World Development Indicator (WDI) of World Bank (2019) and Doing business dataset.

Model Specification

We specified a system of four simultaneous equations to verify our hypotheses.

More specifically, hypothesis (a) will be tested by estimating an entrepreneurial function in which the dependent variable IE_{it} is expressed as:

$$IE_{it} = f(ec_{it}, po_{it}, sc_{it}, c_{it}) \tag{11.1}$$

where IE_{it} represents country i's endowment of innovative entrepreneurship at time t; ec_{it}, is a vector of economic institutional factors such as law and order that influenced total entrepreneurial activities. po_{it} is a political institution factors, such as government stability, which are likely to positively impact entrepreneurship. sc_{it} is a social institutions such as control of corruption, as in line with ICRG (2019). c_{it} is a vector of other controls that may influence innovative entrepreneurship, inflation rate, openness and financial development in an economy is an important factor that influences entrepreneurship.

Variables Definitions and Measurement

The variables captured in the specified model for this study are defined and measured as follows;

Dependent variables

This study has two independent variables, they are;

Innovative Entrepreneurship: Innovative entrepreneurship (INENTP) is defined as a process which involves the deliberate application of information, imagination and initiative in deriving greater or different values from resources. It also includes all processes by which new ideas are generated and converted into useful products (Duguet, 2004). Innovative entrepreneurship is proxy by perceived opportunities of total entrepreneurial activity (TEA) source from GEM (2019). This indicator showed the percentage of entrepreneurs who claimed to be motivated to pursue perceived business opportunities. This is in line with the work of Salihu and Yusuf (2015) and Amoros (2009)

Measures of Independent Variables

One of the independent variables is the quality of institutions which is measured as an index source from political risk service (PRS) dataset of ICRG (2018). It takes a value between 0 and 6. The higher the score, the higher the quality of institutions. The variable is proxy by three different indicators, law and order, government stability and corruption.

I. Law and order: It is an index that entails establishing and protecting property rights; facilitating transactions and permitting economic co-operation and organization (Olarinde, 2015) and is divided into two components. Law sub-component is measured based on the strength and impartiality of legal system, while the Order sub-component is measured based on popular observance of the law, this is used as proxy for economic institutions.

II. Government stability: Government stability is the assessment of the government's ability to carry out its declared program(s) and its ability to stay in office for specified periods of time as enshrined in the constitution of the land without any interruption. It is measured on a 12-point risk rating score with 0 showing weak institutional quality while 12 indicating a strong quality of institution. However, this has been converted to a 6-point scale for ease of analysis. Government stability is used as a proxy for political institution.

III. Corruption: social institutions are enduring patterns of attitudes, practices behaviors and relationships that are approved and preserved by societal norms and values with significant impacts on mans' life (Abdulrahman, 2009). Corruption is a threat to both local and foreign investment because it distorts the economic and financial environment and reduces the efficiency of both government and businesses. It is measured as a 6-point risk rating score with 0 equating to weak quality institutions and 6 strong institutional qualities. Corruption as a proxy for social institution has been used in previous studies such as Mauro (1995).

Control variables

i. Inflation; to account for the impact of macroeconomic uncertainties, we consider an inflation-rate proxy by the ratio of nominal GDP to the ratio of price level. The data for inflation is sourced from the World Development Indicator dataset of the World Bank (2019). A situation of high level of uncertainty in the economy will result in inefficiency of the price mechanism and discourage firms from investing in high-risk projects with higher returns. Thus, a priori negative relationship is expected between inflation and innovative entrepreneurship.
ii. Financial development; a well-evolved financial system aids the availability of funds for capital accumulation and new technologies from highly advanced economies to less developed ones. This is measured as the ratio of credit to private sector to GDP. The data for financial development is from the World Development Indicator dataset of the World Bank (2019). A positive relationship is expected between financial development and entrepreneurship.

Method of Data Analysis and Estimation Procedures

The systems of equations were estimated using ordinary least squares (OLS) and two-stage least squares (2SLS) on an unbalanced panel data of 20 countries that participated in GEM for the periods of 2001 to 2018. Given the heterogeneous nature of the countries in our dataset, we may be concerned that certain socio-economic characteristics of the countries in our sample are correlated with omitted variables at the country's levels. Thus, to reduce the risk of omitted variable bias, the study introduced country and year fixed effects, controlling for unobserved time-constant heterogeneity at the country's levels. The number of observations and the adjusted R^2 of each equation are reported at the foot of each table. Also, given the possible threat of multi-collinearities among the main variables of interest, the study used standard errors that are robust to heteroscedasticity and multi-collinearities. Furthermore, the study computed the Hausmann specification test in order to compare the estimated coefficients of OLS and 2SLS. Where the result failed to reject the null hypothesis that there is no systematic difference in the coefficients of 2SLS and OLS. Thus, the study considered the 2SLS for the purpose of inference, since in the presence of simultaneity, the OLS estimator is biased (Woolridge, 2010).

Hausmann Specification Test

A test for simultaneity which was developed by Hausmann (1978) is essentially a test of whether an endogenous independent variable is correlated with an error term. If it does correlate, the endogeneity problem exists, as such, an alternative to OLS must be found, but if it does not correlate, we can use OLS (Gujarati, 1995). To test for endogeneity, the study used Hausmann's specification error test. We specified our null hypothesis that there is no simultaneity of our OLS coefficient, i.e., the correlation between endogenous independent variable and error term should be zero. Then, if we run the test and find that the test is statistically zero, that is, not significant, we conclude that there is no endogeneity problem but if statistically significant, hence endogeneity problem exists (Gujarati, 1995).

If there is endogeneity, OLS estimators are not consistent. In the presence of endogeneity, the method of two-stage least squares (2SLS) and Instrumental Variables are the most common estimators that are consistent and efficient. Therefore, the econometric solution to endogeneity is to use 2SLS method (Ersado, 2006).

For Eq. (11.1), the study conducted a Hausmann test to compare the coefficient of OLS and that of 2SLS to know which of the techniques of data analysis is most robust for drawing an inference. Based on the chi-square value of 0.91 and its associate probability value of 0.34 obtained from the Hausmann, the study failed to reject the null hypothesis that there is no systematic difference in the coefficients of 2SLS and OLS. Thus, the study considered the 2SLS for the purpose of inference, since in the presence of simultaneity, the OLS estimator is biased (Woolridge, 2010).

11.3 Results and Discussion

This section of the study is divided into two parts: the presentation of inferential results and discussion of results on the impact of institutions on innovative entrepreneurship.

The presentation of inferential statistics commences with the results of the estimated baseline Eq. 11.1 for the impacts of institutions and entrepreneurship using OLS and 2SLS as shown in Table 11.1.

From Table 11.1, the estimated OLS without year fixed effect results indicated that social institution proxy by control of corruption had a positive and significant influence on innovative entrepreneurship. However, estimating the model using OLS with year fixed effects indicated that the coefficient of control of corruption is equally positive but insignificant. Using 2SLS technique, it was further confirmed that control of corruption has a positive and significant influence on innovative entrepreneurship. However, estimating the model using 2SLS with year fixed effects control of corruption maintains its positive influence, however, the impact turns insignificant. This implied that improved efforts towards the control of corruption will boost innovative entrepreneurial activity. This impact was only significant with OLS and 2SLS specification without year fixed effects because the fixed effect model controlled for time-invariant characteristics of the individual entity and assessed the net effect of the predictors on the outcome variable.

Estimating the impact of economic institutions using the OLS technique, the result revealed that law and order was positive and not significant without year fixed effect but negative and not significant with year fixed effects as shown in Models 1 and 2 respectively. However, using the 2SLS technique, it was found that law and order was positive and not significant with or without year fixed effects. This implies governmental

Table 11.1 Institutions and innovative entrepreneurship

	(1)	(2)	(3)	(4)
VARIABLES	OLS	OLS	2SLS	2SLS
Dependent Variable: Perceived opportunities (INENTP.)				
Corruption	5.4727**	2.2874	14.5321**	13.7396
	(2.5009)	(3.5286)	(7.3237)	(8.6529)
Law and order	1.1826	−0.8168	1.0257	0.4270
	(2.3498)	(2.6931)	(2.4481)	(2.2952)
Government stability	−2.4826**	−1.2282	−3.7198***	−3.9214**
	(1.0616)	(1.7299)	(1.3238)	(1.8971)
Financial development	−0.2660***	−0.2269***	−0.3025***	−.2834***
	(0.0292)	(0.0346)	(0.0453)	(0.0533)
Inflation	0.2734**	0.3265	0.3041*	0.3159
	(0.1275)	(0.1953)	(0.1554)	(0.2010)
Year fixed effect	NO	YES	NO	YES
Observations	77	77	77	77
R-squared	0.546	0.676	0.497	0.622

Robust standard errors in parentheses
***p < 0.01,**p < 0.05,*p < 0.1
Source Computed by the Author using Stata Version 14.0

effort at maintaining law and order has the potential of increasing level of innovative entrepreneurship; however this result was not significant for the countries under study.

Furthermore, the result of the impact of political institutions revealed that the coefficient of government stability was negative and significant at 5% level without year fixed effects and negative and not significant with year fixed effects as shown in Table 4.3, Models (1) and (2) respectively. A further look at Table 11.1, Models (3) and (4) revealed that government stability exerts a significant negative influence on the level of innovative entrepreneurship at 1% and 5% respectively. This suggests that unstable polity will hinder entrepreneurial activities and as such discourage more innovative entrepreneurs.

Examining the behaviors of other variables used as control variables, it was revealed that financial development is negative and highly significant at a 1% level with or without year fixed effects and using both OLS and 2SLS estimators. This suggested that financial development is harmful to the innovative entrepreneurship. This might be predicated on high-borrowing rate being charged by most of the financial institutions. Also, macroeconomic uncertainties in developing countries (in particular Sub-Saharan African region) discourages saving and may generate some levels of mistrust in the financial system, which could lead to weak financial to support entrepreneurial ideas based on knowledge or innovation. Also, it was confirmed that the coefficient of inflation using the OLS specification was positive and significant at a 5% level without year fixed effects, and positively insignificant with year fixed effects. However, the results in Table 11.1, Models (3) and (4) indicate that the coefficient of inflation is positive and marginally significant at 10% without year fixed effects, and positive and not significant with year fixed effects using 2SLS specification. This implies that persistent increase in prices of goods and services will boost business profitability and encourage more innovative entrepreneurship activities.

Discussion of Results

On the impact of institutions and entrepreneurship development, the result indicated that institutions significantly encouraged entrepreneurship development in Sub-Saharan African countries. As presented in Table 11.1, the coefficients of control of corruption are positive and significant at a 5% level. This result is in conformity with theoretical assertions that most countries of the world especially the developing countries located within Sub-Saharan Africa perceive corruption as a major threat to entrepreneurship development. This assertion can be supported by the efforts of many governments in Sub-Saharan African countries towards the establishment of anti-corruption agencies to fight all forms of corruption. This finding is in tandem with that of Salihu and Yusuf (2015), Williams and Vorley (2017) and others but contradict the work of Mauro (1995). Also, the positive and insignificant influence of law and order indicates the existence of a weak economic institution in Sub-Saharan African countries. It needs to be noted that a strong economic institution implies the existence of strong property rights that make a country a safe haven for investment and innovative ideas. This finding is in line with the findings of Amoros (2009), but contradicts the work of Castano et al. (2015), Crnogaj and Hojnik (2016) and Rotina, et al. (2017).

Further in the result, the coefficient of government stability is negative and statistically significant at a 1% level. This empirical finding concurred with the findings of Amoros and Stenholm (2014), however, in conflict with that of Fuentelsaz et al. (2015). Although most of the Sub-Saharan African countries have enjoyed uninterrupted democracy over a long period of time, evidences have shown that changes in the mantle of leadership in the region always come along with changes in government policies and focus, resulting in policy inconsistencies. Therefore, lack of continuity of policy in the region may be alluded to this result. The result of the impact of financial development which revealed a significant negative impact on innovative entrepreneurs contradicts the empirical finding by Muhsin and Serife (2016).

Finally, the coefficient of inflation was positive and significant at a 10% level in line with Rotina et al. (2017) but contradicts that of Muhsin and Serife (2016). The result also provides an empirical support for the inflation hypothesis which hypothesize that persistent increase in price level has the tendency of increasing business profitability, thereby encouraging more entrepreneur to venture into the business with new innovation and knowledge. That will lead to an overall increase in the entrepreneurial activity.

11.4 Conclusion and Policy Implication

The study examined how good institutions and innovative entrepreneurship interact with one another to enhance economic development using an unbalanced panel data of twenty (20) Sub-Saharan African countries. We empirically examioned the importance of good institutions in influencing innovative entrepreneurship. Given the heterogeneous nature of Sub-Saharan African regions, the study applied year fixed effects to control for unobserved time-constant heterogeneity at country levels, while Hausmann's specification error test was used to diagnose the presence of endogeneity. To achieve the objective, the study adopted the ordinary least square (OLS) and the two-square least square (2SLS) estimation techniques. The major finding of this study was that Institution has a statistically significant impact on innovative entrepreneurship in Sub-Saharan African countries. This result provided evidence that strong institutions, especially those that seek to control corruption, maintain law and order and ensure government stability will positively impact on entrepreneurial activities in Sub-Saharan Africa.

From the study, it was established that political institution has a negative impact on innovative entrepreneurship in the regions. The implication of this result is that policy and reforms embarked upon by the various governments to provide an enabling environment for entrepreneurial activities to flourish have been ineffective. For instance, due to lack of continuity of policy in the region, various programs like N-power, Young Entrepreneurship Training Programme (YETP), Global Entrepreneurship Network (GEN) and others introduced in Nigeria aimed at empowering youths with entrepreneurship skills in Sub-Saharan African countries only produced a marginal improvement in terms of creation of more innovative entrepreneurs due to lack of sustainability. Therefore, Sub-Saharan African countries seeking to encourage entrepreneurial activities should ensure that there is a strong institutional structure capable of reducing corruption to its barest minimum, protect property rights and ensure continuity in policy implementation. In order to address the negative impact of financial development on entrepreneurship development, government in SSA should introduce financial policy that will further improve the financial capacity of financial institutions and make financial services easily accessible for entrepreneurs.

Lastly, many empirical issues remain to be resolved. First, we may seek to improve our analyses by extending the dataset to include more countries and additional institutional factors that are likely to impact innovative entrepreneurship. Indeed, with a large sample size and additional control variables, it is likely we obtain more precise estimators that allow for a dynamic analysis of the effects of institutions and entrepreneurship. Also, to reduce the risk of omitted variables, including time-varying country-level changes, complicate causal identification, we could seek to gather country-level data. Such micro-empirical analyses are needed to illuminate precise causal channels and design more effective policy responses that are country specific. However, the real challenge in this task lies in getting the appropriate country-level data.

References

Abdulrahman A. D. (2009), Institutions and Organizations. In Salisu A. Abdullahi, Isma'il Z. Muhammed and Conertly Casey (eds.), *Studies in Cultural Sociology*, (pp. 122–128). Foludex printers, Ibadan.

Acemoglu, D., Johnson, S., & Robinson, J. A. (2000). *The colonial origins of comparative development: An empirical investigation*. National Bureau of economic research.

Acs, Z. J., & Audretsch, D. B. (1990). *Innovation and Small Firms*. The MIT press.

Acs, Z. J., & Naude, W. A. (2013). Entrepreneurship stages of development and industralisation. In A. szirmai, W. A. Naude, and L. Alcorta, L. (eds.), *Pathways to industrialization in the 21st century*. Oxford University press.

Acs, Z. J., & Szerb, L. (2007). Entrepreneurship, economic growth and public policy. *Small Business Economics, 28*(2–3), 109–122.

Acs, Z. J., Desai, S., & Klapper, L. F. (2012). What does "entrepreneurship" data really show? *Small Business Economics, 31*(3), 265–281.

Acs, Z. J., & Armington, C. (2006). *Entrepreneurship, geography and American economic Growth*. Cambridge University Press.

Aidis, R., Estrin, S., & Mickiewicz, T. (2008). Institutions and entrepreneurship development in Russia: A comparative perspective. *Journal of Business Venturing., 23*(6), 566–672.

Amoros J. E (2009). *Entrepreneurship and Quality of Institutions*. A developing country approach. UNU-WIDER.

Amoros J. E., & Stenholm, P. (2014). The influence of the Quality Government Institutions on Entrepreneurial Motivation: Exploring the Variance Across Countries Barcelona University, spain.

Aron, J. (2000). Growth and Institutions: A review of the evidence. *The World Bank Research Observer*, pp. 99–135.

Audretsch, D. B., & Keilbach, M. (2004). Entrepreneurship capital and economic performance. *Regional Studies, 38*(8), 949–959.

Audretsch, D. B., & Keilbach, M. (2008). Resolving the knowledge paradox: Knowledge spill-over entrepreneurship and economic growth. *Research Policy, 37*(10), 1697–1705.

Audretsch, D. B., Bönte, W., & Keilbach, M. (2008). Entrepreneurship capital and its impact on knowledge diffusion and economic performance. *Journal of Business Venturing, 23*(6), 687–698.

Baumol, W. J., & Strom, R. J. (2007). Entrepreneurship and economic growth. *Strategic Entrepreneurship Journal, 1*(3–4), 233–237.

Belthelt, H. (2001). Regional competence and economic recovery: Divergent growth paths in Boston's high technology economy. *Entrepreneurship and Regional Development., 3*, 287–314.

Bjornskov, C., & Foss, N. (2013). How strategic entrepreneurship and the institutional context drive economic growth. *Strategic Entrepreneurship Journal., 7*, 50–69.

Braunerhjelm , P. (2010). *Entreprenuership, innovation and economic growth. Past experiences, current knowledge and policy implication.* Working paper 2010, p. 02 Swedish Entrepreneurship Forum. http://www.entrepreneurskapsforum.se

Carraro; A., & Karfakis, P. (2018). *Institutions, Economic Freedom and Structural Transformation in 11 Sub-Saharan African Countries*. FAO Agricultural Development Economics working Paper 18–01, ISSN2521–1838.

Castano, M., Mendez, M., & Galindo, M. (2015). The effect of social, cultural, and economic factors on entrepreneurship. *Journal of Business Research, 68*, 1496–1500.

Casson, Guista, D.M., & Kambhampati, U. S. (2010). *Formal and Informal Institutions and Development, 38*(2), 137–141.

Charles, B. (1995). Strategic innovation, corporate entrepreneurship and matching outside- in to inside out approaches to strategy research. *British Journal of Management, 6*(1), 3–15.

Crnogayi, K., & Hojni, B. B. (2016): Institutional determinants and entrepreneurial action. Review challenges of Europe: Growth, competitiveness and inequality 2015 *Journal of Contemporary Mangement*.

Duguet, E. (2004). Are R&D subsidies a substitute or a complement to privately funded R&D? Evidence from France using propensity score methods for non-experimental data. *Revue D'economie Politique, 114*(2), 245–274.

Drucker, P. (1985). *Innovation and entrepreneurship*. Butterworth-Heineman Elsevier.

Drury, A. Krieckhaus, J., & Lusztig, M. (2006). Corruption, democracy, and economic growth. *International Political Science Review, 27*(2), 121–136.

Ersado, L. (2006). *Income Diversification in Zimbabwe: Welfare Implication from Urban and Rural Areas*. World Bank Policy Research Working Paper 3964.

Estrin, S., Korosteleva, J., & Mickiewicz, T. (2013). Which institutions encourage entrepreneurial growth aspirations? *Journal Business Venturing., 28*, 564–580.

Fuentelsaz, L., Gonzalez, C., Maicas, J.P., & Montero, J. (2015). How different formal Institutions affect opportunity and necessity Entrepreneurship. *Business Quarterly Research*.

GEM, (2018), Global Report 2017/18. Global Entrepreneurship Research Association. http://www.gernconsortium.org/. Cheltenham.

GEM, (2019), Global Report. http://www.gemconsortium.org

Gujarati, D. N. (1995). *Basic econometrics* (3rd ed.). McGRAW-Hill inc.

Hausmann, J. (1978). Specification test in econometrics. *Econometrical., 46*, 1251–1271.

Henredson, M., & Johnsson, D. (2010). Firm growth, institution, IFN Working Paper NO. 820.S Herbig, P., & Dunphy, S. (1998). Culture and innovation. Cross Cultural Management: *An International Journal, 5*(4), 13–21.

Hodgson, G. M. (2006). What are institutions? *Journal of Economic Issues, 40*(1), 1–25.

Houssa, & Megarsa. (2017). Institutional Quality, economic development and the performance of VAT. *Belgian Policy Research Group on Financing Development*. Belgian Development co-operation, Belgian working paper No. 15.Global Entreprenuership Monitor (2018).

Hussein, A. S. (2019). Institutions and entrepreneurship: Unidirectional or bidirectional Causality? Journal of Entrepreneurship Research. *Springer, Heidelberg, 9*(3), 1–16.

Ibru, C. (2007). Entreprenuership and economic development in Nigeria. NES, No 6. Imbs., J., & Wacziarg, R. (2003). Stages of diversification. *The America Economic Review, 93*(1), 63–86.

ICRG. (2019). *Political Risk Guide*. New York: PRS Group http://www.prsgroup.Com. (accessed November 2014).

Johnson, N. (1975). *The place of institutions in the study of politics*. Sage Jounals.

Katarina, M., & Jurkovic, Z. (2013). *Impact of Informal Institutions on Economic Growth and Development Interdisciplinary Management Research.*, *9*, 701–716.
Kirzner, I. M., (1973). *Competitions and Entrepreneurship*. University of Chicago press.
Kocenda, E., & Karen, P. (2017). *Export sophistication: A dynamic panel data approach*. KIER Discussion Paper Kyoto Japan. No.980; 1–28.
Mauro, P. (1995). Corruption and Growth. *Quarterly Journal of Economics, 110*(3), 681–712.
Mendez-Picazo, M. T., Galindo-Martin, M. A., & Ribeiro-Soriano, D. (2012). Governance, entrepreneurship and economic growth. *Entrepreneurship and Regional Development, 24*(9–10), 865–877.
Minniti, M. (2008). The role of government policy on entrepreneurial activity: Productive, unproductive or destructive? *Entrep. Theory Practice, 32*(5), 779–790.
Muhsin, K., & Serifie, D. (2016). *Role of Financial Development on Entrepreneurship in the Emerging Market Economies Eskisehir Osmangizi University.*, *11*(3), 131–152.
North, D. C., & Thomas, R. P. (1973). *The rise of western world: A new Economic History*. Cambridge University. Press.
North, D. C. (1990). *Institutions*. Institutional Change and Economic Performance.
North, D. C. (1991). Institutions. *The Journal of Economic Perspective, 5*(1), 97–112.
Noseleit, F. (2014). Entrepreneurship, structural change, and economic growth. *Journal of Evolution Economics, 23*(4), 735–766.
OECD, (1998). *Fostering Entrepreneurship*. Paris: Organization for Economic Cooperation and Development.
Olanrinde, O. M. (2015). *Analysis of the role of institutions and macroeconomic policy on economic growth: Evidence for panel data 1990–2014*. A PhD Thesis submitted to Usmanu Danfodiyo University Sokoto—Nigeria.
Osabuohein, Efobi., & Salami (2012). *Planning to fail or failing to plan: Institutional Response to Nigeria's Development Question* working paper series no 162 African Development Bank, Tunis, Tunisia.
Osita. G. N., Chinedu. S. I., & Stanley. M. (2014). *Nigeria and the Enigma of Policy Implementation*. Nnamdi Azikiwe University.
Parker, S. C. (2000). *On the dimensionally and composition of entrepreneurship*. Barclays Centre for Entrepreneurship.
Pathak, S. (2016). Informal institutions and international entrepreneurship.

Peng, M. W. (2006). *Global Strategy*. South-western Thomson.

Portor, M. J., Sachs, J., & McArthur, J. (2002). Executive Summary: Competitiveness and Stages of Economic Development. In M. J. Portor, P. K. Sachs, J. W. Cornelius, J. McArther and k Schwab (eds.), *The Global Competitiveness Report 2001–2002*. Oxford University Press, 16–25.

Reynolds, P., Hay, M., & Camp, S. M. (1999). *Global Entrepreneurship Monitor 1999 Executive Report*. Babson College/London BusinessSchool/Kauffman Center for Entrepreneurial Leadership, BabsonPark, MA/London/Kansas City, MO.

Roland, G. (2003). *Understanding Institutional Change: Fast-moving and slow-moving Institutions*. University of Berkley. Retrieved on 2nd August, 2013 from emlob. Berkely. Edu/ngrola/ pubs/gr3.

Rotina, A. G, Nana, Y. Oppong., & Stephen, O. (2017). Effects of socio-economic factors on Entrepreneurship activities in cape coast, Ghana: *Journal of Entrepreneurship and Business, 5*(1), 39–51. ISSN:22898298.

Salihu, K., & Yusuf, A. M. (2015). Institutions and Innovative Entrepreneurship: Are they Relevant in the Development of an Inclusive Growth Framework? NES Conference.

Schumpeter, J. A (1911), Theorie der wirtschaftlichen Entwicklung. Eine Untersuchung Uber Unternehmerge-winn, Kapital, Kredit, Zins und den onjunkturzyklus; translated by R. OPIE, *The theory of economic development*. An inquiry into profits, Capital, Credit, Interest, and the Business Cycle,Oxford University Press (1963) (1934).

Schumpeter, J. A. (1934). *The theory of economic development*. Oxford University Press.

Schumpeter. (1961). *The theory of economic development*. Oxford University Press.

Shane, S. (2003). *A general theory of entrepreneurship: The individual-opportunity nexus*. Edward Elgar.

Shane, S. (2009). Why encouraging more people to become entrepreneurs is bad public policy. *Small Business Economics., 33*, 141–149.

Shane, S., & Venkataraman, S. (2000). The promise of entrepreneurship as a field of Research. *Academy of Management Revie., 25*(1), 217–226.

Soysa, I., & jutting, J,. (2007). *Informal Institutions and Development: Think local, Act Global? International Seminar on Informal Institutions and Development-What do we know and What can we do?* Organized by OECD Development Centre.

Thompson, John. Geoff Alvy., & Ann, L. (2000) Social Entrepreneurship- *A New Look at the People and the Potential in Management Development, 38*(5), 335–338.

UNECA (2016). Domestic Resource Mobilization in Africa: A Focus Government Revenue, Inter-Agency Task Force on Financing for Development, United Nations Economic Commission For Africa, Adis Ababa.

Veblen, T. B. (1919). *The place of science in modern civilization and other essays.* Heubsch.

Venkatarm, S. (1997), The Distinctive Domai of Entrepreneurship Research: An Editor's Perspective, In Katz, J. and Brockheus, R., (eds.), *Advances in entrepreneurship Firm Emergence, and Growth*, JAI Press.

Williams, N., & Vorley, T. (2015). The impact of institutional change on entrepreneurship in a Crisis-hit economy: The case of Greece. *Entrepreneurship and Regional Development*, *27*(1-2), 28–49.

Williams, N., & Vorley, T. (2017). The resilience of entreprenuers and small businesses in the depths of a recessionary crisis. In *Creating Resilient Economies* (pp. 28–40). Edwad Elgar. .

Wooldridge, J. M. (2010). *Econometric analysis of cross-section and panel data* (2nd ed.). MIT Press.

World Bank, (2019). World Development Indicators, 2019. World Bank Policy Research, Washington D.C.

Part III

Economic Impact of Entrepreneurship in Sub-Saharan Africa

12

Microfinance as a Vehicle for Zero Poverty and Gender Equality in Nigeria

Damian Kalu Ude

12.1 Introduction

The overall lack of access to factors of production, especially capital, among the populace in less developed nations may make it difficult to achieve sustainable development goals. This restricts people's capacity for entrepreneurship, particularly the poor. As a result, lost are possible work chances as well as household prospects for increasing wealth and income. One strategy used to solve this issue is microcredit. Its development is a reflection of the failings of the credit markets, particularly in the official financial sector. As a result, the focus has shifted from the traditional banking industry to microfinance, which combines credit and savings. This implies that alternative financial services, other than loans, may

D. K. Ude (✉)
Department of Economics, Michael Okpara University of Agriculture, Umudike, Nigeria
e-mail: dk.ude@mouau.edu.ng

A. S. Ibidunni et al. (eds.), *Innovation, Entrepreneurship and the Informal Economy in Sub–Saharan Africa*, Sustainable Development Goals Series,
https://doi.org/10.1007/978-3-031-46293-1_12

contribute to enhancing the welfare of the underprivileged, particularly women (Vonderlack & Schreiner, 2021).

So, as a response to the state-led and mainstream formal financial system's failure to reach the poor, who were not perceived as bankable clients due to information asymmetry and risk perceptions, microfinance institutions (MFIs) have formed in many countries. It is generally acknowledged that MFI programs can help low-income entrepreneurs grow their businesses and boost their level of living while also making up for some of the shortcomings in emerging capital markets. The notion that microfinance support programs can encourage the success of female entrepreneurs who might not have access to other types of help is particularly intriguing. Microfinance activities take many different forms in Nigeria and are deeply ingrained in the culture of the populace. Microfinance initiatives by nongovernmental organizations have also grown. The Nigerian government launched a Microfinance Policy in 2005, which offers a framework for regulation and supervision (Central Bank of Nigeria, 2005). The policy includes eliminating the gender gap in access to financial services as one of its goals.

Focusing on the underprivileged, microfinance institutions (MFIs) have a strong track record in a number of developing nations, including Tanzania, Ghana, South Africa, and Bangladesh (Ogwu, 2008). Women and the impoverished are two groups in Nigeria that need financial services to expand their enterprises and enhance their standard of living (Ogwu, 2008). They could significantly contribute to the country's economic development, financial inclusion, and efforts to reduce poverty if given more power (Ogwu, 2008). Due to this, these microfinance service providers are required by law to offer microcredits to the impoverished who are actively seeking employment and who are not typically served by traditional banks. Microfinance institutions, like other financial service providers, give loans to women and the disadvantaged to assist them in financing agricultural initiatives like raising chickens, producing food and other animals, etc. The rural populace, impoverished households, and small business owners should also have access to their fundamental financial needs in order to help them transition from subsistence living to future planning, investing in better nutrition, health, children's education, and wealth development. Because of their low levels of literacy and inability to furnish the necessary collateral, among other reasons, traditional financial institutions deny access to financial services to women and the poor. Noting that a well-run microfinance institution that effectively meets the population's capital needs could have a multiplier effect on the country's economic well-being may be stating the obvious.

So, as a response to the state-led and mainstream formal financial system's failure to reach the poor, who were not perceived as bankable clients due to information asymmetry and risk perceptions, microfinance institutions (MFIs) have formed in many countries. It is generally acknowledged that MFI programs can help low-income entrepreneurs grow their businesses and boost their level of living while also making up for some of the shortcomings in emerging capital markets. The potential for microfinance support programs to encourage the success of female entrepreneurs who may not have access to other types of help is particularly intriguing (AIMS, 1997).

Women who are micro and small business owners are increasingly being targeted by microfinance programs. Access to microloans is thought to be a requirement for eradicating poverty, promoting gender equality, and thus, empowering women. Poor women are beginning to attract the attention of traditional financial institutions as it becomes more widely acknowledged that they make better borrowers (Innocent & Elizabeth, 2013). The Nigerian government decided to replicate the microfinance scheme in Nigeria as a strategy for poverty reduction in 2005 as a result of the introduction of Microfinance Institutions (MFIs) in various Asian countries and the subsequent impact of the plan on poverty reduction. According to Awojobi (2014), who looked at the effects of MFIs in Nigeria, clients of MFIs benefited from micro-credit in the areas of income, employment, and household well-being. However, despite the shown benefits of offering microfinance services to the underprivileged and female entrepreneurs, there is still a significant obstacle preventing them from doing so. In order to eliminate poverty and promote gender equality, this study aims to identify and analyze the barriers that prevent women entrepreneurs and poor people in Nigeria from accessing microfinance. It also explores the effects that microfinance banks have on these goals by making it easier for people to access microfinance services.

12.2 Literature Review

Financial experts have emphasized that by making credit facilities accessible, the poor will be able to use them to escape the cycle of poverty. This hypothesis' main conclusion is that poor people can use loans they get from MFIs to improve their lives. For instance, when a female MFI client received a loan, she used it to grow her business. As a result, she will be able to support her family with the money generated by the growth of her firm. Some critics, however, have criticized the loans given to MFI clients because they force them to owe money to the MFIs. The main goal of MFIs is to increase the poor's access to credit by providing them with credit facilities. According to Taha (2012), microcredit to MFI clients has three effects on them: material welfare, social welfare, and women's empowerment. (Chowdhury et al., 2004; Mustafa, 2011) concur that customers who use microcredit can increase their income, expand their asset base, and secure employment. According to Mawa (2008), there is empirical support for the idea that microcredit helps the poor gain skills and start their own businesses so they may make money.

Two theories about poverty and two theories about money are pertinent to this investigation. These include the cyclical interdependency poverty theory, the demand-following and supply-leading hypotheses, and the poverty theories of economic, political, and social distortion. These will all be covered in the paragraph that follows.

(i) **Economic, Political, and Social Distortion Poverty Theory**

This theory looks at the economic and political structures that allow people to have insufficient means to live fulfilling lives rather than the reasons of poverty as being personal. Karl Marx attributed capitalism's creation of a "reserve army of the unemployed" as a means of lowering wages in this context. The economic system is set up in such a way that poor individuals who have the abilities and knowledge to work are not carried along with the economic system, according to pertinent literature. The difficulty of the working poor in obtaining better employment has been attributed to a pay issue connected to a structural barrier prohibiting the poor from obtaining better employment, made more difficult by a lack of employment options and a lack of economic growth (Tobin, 1994).

(ii) **Cyclical Interdependency Poverty Theory**

According to this idea, which was created by Myrdal in 1957, the relationship between the person and the community might result in the underdevelopment of the community if people are jobless in the community, reducing tax, consumption, savings, and income. Since fewer people are paying taxes, the community suffers as a result of people's loss of ability to engage in the economy. Once the cycle has peaked, the interconnection of the causes that cause poverty begins to emerge.

(iii) **Demand-Following and Supply-Lending Hypothesis**

The supply-lending theory deals with the circumstance when financial institutions are located in some location before the demand for their services is taken into consideration, whereas the demand-following financial theory is a sort of financial development that stimulates the economy favorably (Taiwo, 2012). Effective economic development requires the availability of financing facilities for the purchase of capital goods. According to Taiwo, the efficient financial institutions that the financial system offers make the supply-lending and demand-following financial theories pertinent for development. Both ideas were founded on the same principles as microfinance in Nigeria. The provision of financial services to the underprivileged is one of MFIs' goals in Nigeria. This is a direct response to the supply-lending finance theory, which advocated the establishment of MFIs in rural areas to increase access to credit for people who live in rural areas. Contrarily, the majority of microfinance banks in Nigeria are situated in urban areas with pre-existing financial institutions, which is the position predicted by economic theory.

(iv) **Financial Liberalization or Repression Hypothesis**

As one of the requirements for developing countries under the International Monetary Fund's (IMF) Structural Adjustment Programs, governments of developing countries decided to liberalize their financial systems in the 1980s (SAP). The goal was for the government to switch from a socialist to a market-based economy. The primary goal of financial liberalization is to implement the Washington Consensus's agenda, which includes the privatization of public banks, the abolition of credit controls, the easing of restrictions on the private sector's access to domestic financial markets, and capital account liberalization. Shaw (1971) argues that financial liberalization makes money available in the financial markets, paving the way for economic growth, whereas financial repression has a detrimental effect on the economy (Shaw, 1971). In Nigeria, the financial industry was liberalized in the 1980s and 2000s, which resulted in an increase in financial institutions and unethical business practices. In 2010 and 2004, the CBN, respectively, liquidated 224 MFIs and 60 commercial banks. However, the supply-lending finance hypothesis and the dependency of poverty on a cyclical basis form the basis of this study. The reason for this is that only through creating microfinance banks in rural areas can poor rural residents have access to financial services, which is how MFIs can truly break the cycle of poverty.

What is Microfinance? Microfinance, according to CBN (2005), entails offering services to the underprivileged who are typically unmet by regular financial institutions. Additionally, microfinance is the delivery of a relatively limited range of financial services to the underprivileged in order to assist them in seizing new possibilities and engaging in profitable endeavors. Additionally, microcredit is defined as initiatives aimed at providing very poor individuals with tiny loans for self-employment ventures that generate money, allowing them to take care of themselves and their family. The Summit confirms that different countries have their own definitions of microcredit. For instance, size, which indicates that loans are micro or very small in size, target users, which refer to micro-entrepreneurs and low-income households, and utilization, which indicates the use of funds for income generation, enterprise development, as well as for community use (provision of health/education facilities), are some of the defining criteria applied. Others are terms and conditions, which suggests that the majority of terms and conditions for microcredit loans are adaptable, simple to grasp, and appropriate to the local circumstances of the community.

In Nigeria, women-owned enterprises were shown to be positively and significantly influenced by the number of female account holders, financial institution accounts in rural areas, grants or loans to start-up firms, rural areas, and household size, according to Ukwueze (2022). According to Onuka (2021), understanding the contribution that microcredit makes to the informal economy and the reduction of poverty is a crucial first step in formulating an effective microcredit policy that includes the main stakeholders. Even though Eton et al. (2020) show that microcredits cause long-term indebtedness among the rural poor, households lack the skills necessary to manage their finances, which suggests that more financial services would help reduce poverty and educate households on how to use financial credit.

Evidence from the literature demonstrates that good credit helps entrepreneurs perform, which lowers poverty. Gatewood and colleagues (2004), Kuzilwa (2005), Lakwo (2007), Martins (2009), Ojo (2009), and Peter (2011). Improvements in income, output, investment, employment, the welfare of the entrepreneurs, and a decrease in poverty are frequently witnessed as a result of this loan help for business owners, particularly women entrepreneurs (Kuzilwa, 2005; Lakwo, 2007; Martins, 2009, Peter, 2011). According to Jegede et al. (2011), among the many savings clubs and credit societies that can be found all over the world are the "Susus" of Ghana, "Chit Funds" in India, "Tandas" in Mexico, "Arisan" in Indonesia, "Cheetu" in Sri Lanka, "Tontines" in West Africa, and "Pasanaku" in Bolivia. In his own studies on "Credit for the Alleviation of Rural Poverty in Bangladesh" Hossain (1988) found that Grameen members who are poor and landless have an average household of 43% higher than marginal landowners. In their article "Impact of Microfinance on Poverty Alleviation in Nigeria: An Empirical Investigation," Jegede et al. (2011) cited Nwachukwu (2008) as saying that the major obstacles to microfinance in Nigeria include communication gaps and inadequate awareness, inadequate government support, inadequate donor funding, little focus on the financial sustainability of MFIs, a lack of sufficient loan or equity capital to increase loanable funds, and high transaction costs.

12.3 Methodology and Data

The contribution of microfinance banks will help Nigeria achieve gender equality and zero poverty, and these goals will be quantified by descriptive statistics. The descriptive technique works well for enumerating specific traits in a sample. Easy comprehension of population behavior and condensed display of extensive population data are two of this instrument of analysis' benefits, according to Asad (2007). It will be used to compile the study's information from the financial index data for Nigeria.

Econometric Analysis of Zero Poverty and Gender Equality

Aggregate data will be analyzed to evaluate whether economic factors and public policies (such as government social spending and financial development) have any empirical importance in explaining gender equality and zero poverty in Nigeria. The study seeks to identify the traits connected to poverty and gender in Nigeria by taking advantage of changes in poverty indices over time. The basic growth-poverty model proposed by Saruparia, (2014), as modified by Anyanwu, (2013), will be used in the study to estimate gender equality and zero poverty. The relationships that we aim to estimate may be expressed as:

Model 1 (Zero poverty through microfinance)

$$\mathrm{logPhc_t} = \theta_t + \Omega_1\mathrm{log(mc_t)} + \Omega_2\mathrm{log(g_t)} + \Omega_3\mathrm{log(H_t)} + \varepsilon_t \quad (12.1)$$

Model 2 (Gender equality through microfinance)

$$\log Fe_t = \theta_t + \Phi_1 \log(mc_t) + \Phi_2 \log(g_t) + \Phi_3 \log(Ht) + vt \quad (12.2)$$

In the baseline specification, Phc is the measure of poverty in Nigeria at time t (poverty headcount); and Fe is the measure of gender equality, θ_i is a constant factor; Ω_2 is the elasticity of poverty with respect to microfinance credit (*mc*), Φ_1 is the elasticity of gender equality with respect to microfinance credit (*mc*); Ω_2 is the "growth elasticity of poverty" with respect to real per capita GDP given by *g*; $\Phi_{2,}$ is the "growth elasticity of gender equality with respect to real per capita GDP given by *g*. H represents the vector of control variables, including financial deepening *(findp)*, savings per capita *(spc)*, interest rate *(int)*, and ε and v are error terms that include errors in the poverty and gender equality measures.

The dependent variable in Eq. (12.1), which is poverty, is the headcount index of international poverty line at US$1.25 per day. The headcount measure is considerably the most commonly calculated and used poverty measure while the dependent variable in Eq. (12.2) is gender equality dummy. Thus, Eq. (12.2) is a linear probability model (LPM) while Eq. (12.1) is the basic growth–poverty model.

12.4 Results and Discussion

The result on Table 12.1 suggests that microfinance is a veritable tool for poverty eradication in Nigeria. The coefficient implies that an increase in microfinance credit accessibility by the micro, small and medium enterprises (MSMEs) including poor households would significantly reduce poverty to the tune of 56%. More so, gross domestic product per capita and saving per capita are very significant factors to eradicate poverty as suggested by the result of Table 12.1. However, financial deepening and interest rate have insignificant effect on poverty eradication in Nigeria. This is in line with the findings by Bertram et al. (2016) and Onuka (2021).

From the given information in Table 12.2, it is easy to obtain the estimates of the conditional probabilities of gender equality of the various categories. Thus, if we want to find the probability for gender equality, with access to microfinance credit, gross domestic product per capita, financial deepening, savings per capita, and with interest rate, we obtain

Table 12.1 Impact of microfinance on poverty eradication in Nigeria

Dependent Variable: LOG(PHC)				
Variable	Coefficient	Std. Error	t-Statistic	Prob
C	4.541137	0.038029	119.4128	0.0000
LOG(MC)	−56.021514	7.002505	8.000210	0.0000
LOG(GDPPC)	−0.027381	0.008026	−3.411692	0.0019
LOG(FINDP)	0.008860	0.018323	0.483516	0.6322
LOG(SPC)	−0.061529	0.012881	−4.776882	0.0000
INT	−0.001425	0.000957	−1.488627	0.1470

Table 12.2 Probability of gender equality with respect to microfinance in Nigeria

Dependent Variable: FE (Gender equality)				
Variable	Coefficient	Std. Error	t-Statistic	Prob
C	1.953232	0.528705	3.694371	0.0009
LOG(MC)	−0.188113	0.034827	−5.401416	0.0000
LOG(GDPPC)	−0.051230	0.111580	−0.459136	0.6494
LOG(FINDP)	0.526653	0.254741	2.067403	0.0474
LOG(SPC)	−0.358310	0.179076	−2.000876	0.0545
INT	−0.007124	0.013311	−0.535218	0.5964

$1.953232 - 0.188113 - 0.051230 + .526653 - 0.358310 - 0.007124 = 0.875108$. In other words, the probability of gender equality by women with the preceding characteristics is estimated to be about 87 percent. However, gross domestic product and interest rate have an insignificant effect on gender equality in Nigeria. This conforms to the findings by Ukwueze (2022) and Eton et al. (2020) (Fig. 12.1).

The figure suggests that GDP growth rate (GDPGR) fluctuates with the changes in the savings rate per capita (spc). In 1981, savings per capita was 6.96 while GDP growth rate was −1.1. However, in 2009, when spc increased to 23.25, GDPGR also increased to 7.8.

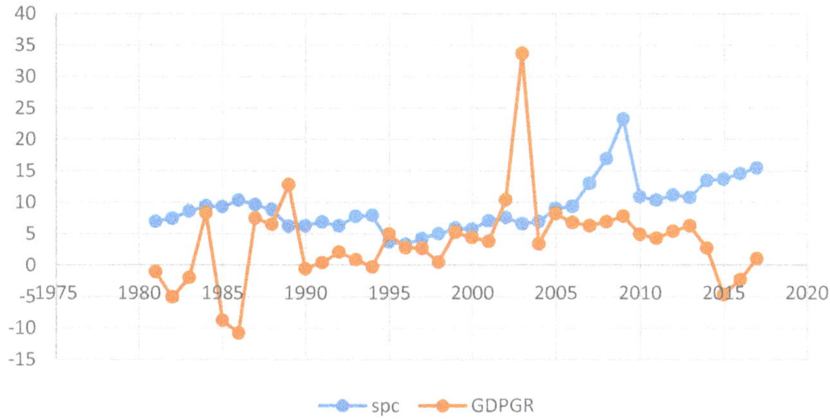

Fig. 12.1 Savings per capita and GDP growth rate in Nigeria (*Data source* The World Bank, World Development Indicators [2020])

Factors Constraining Access to Microfinance Services by Women Entrepreneurs in Nigeria

Table 12.3 lists the varimax rotated factors limiting women business owners in Nigeria's access to microfinance services. Based on the respondents' responses, four criteria were extracted. Only variables with an overlapping variance of 10% or above (Comrey, 1962) were included. Factors 1, 2, 3, and 4 were dubbed "Technical, Economic, Managerial, and Social factors, respectively" based on the clustering of the data. Transportation expense (−0.475), lack of trust (−0.544), diverting funds (−0.464), short payback period (−0.649), loan aimed at certain enterprises (−0.587), and marital status were among the specific constraint variables under factor 1 (technical factor) (0.637). Protocol before obtaining a loan (0.478), high-interest rates on borrowing (−0.431), a small loan amount supplied (0.407), the requirement of collateral (0.505), the unwillingness of MFIs to lend to women entrepreneurs (0.592), and respondents' marital status were loaded under the economic component. The time between application and loan collection (−0.524), the amount given as loan is discretionary (0.489), opening of account as a requirement for microcredit access (0.515), and the educational level of the entrepreneur were among the specific issues with high loading under managerial constraint (0.405). The biggest barriers cited by the business owners under "social issues" were distance (0.405), obtaining a guarantor (0.539), the fact that only those who are in business are receiving loans (0.592), and, finally, the fact that MFIs are receiving more applications than they can handle (0.531). These findings are comparable to those made for South-South Nigeria by Ifelunini and Wosowei (2013) (Fig. 12.2).

The figure suggests that microfinance credit was relatively low till 2003. However, as microfinance credit began to increase from 2005, poverty headcount in Nigeria remained relatively low (Fig. 12.3).

The figure suggests that in 1981 microfinance credit and poverty headcount in Nigeria were 77.1 and 89.2 respectively. However, in 2001 microfinance credit and poverty headcount in Nigeria were 86.5 and 1314.00 respectively. This, however, could suggests that microfinance credit enhances poverty headcount reduction in Nigeria.

Figure 12.4 suggests that in 1981 microfinance credit in Nigeria was 89.2 m while it increased to 144.2 m in 1991. However, it increased to 1314.00 m, 50,928.3 m, and 190,490.05 in 2001, 2011, and 2017 respectively (Fig. 12.5a and b).

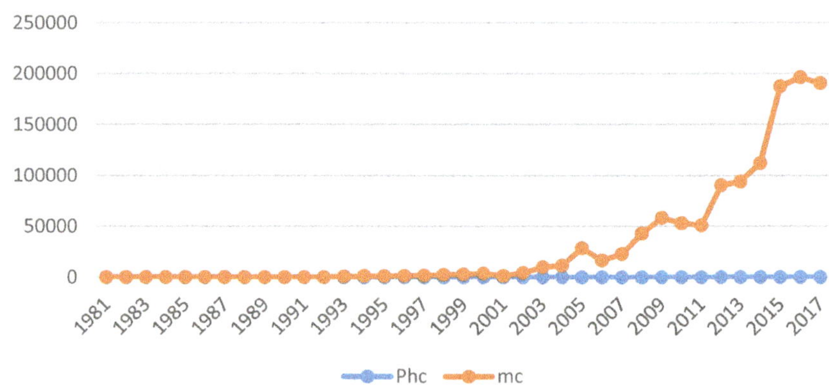

Fig. 12.2 Microfinance credit and poverty headcount in Nigeria (*Data source* The World Bank, World Development Indicators [2020])

Table 12.3 Factors constraining access to microfinance services by women and poor entrepreneurs in Nigeria

Variable	Factor			
	Technical factor (1)	Economic factor (2)	Management factor (3)	Social (4)
Low accessibility of loan	0.179	0.081	**0.590**	0.041
The time lag between application and loan collection	−0.045	0.227	**−0.524**	0.030
Protocol before accessing loans	−0.017	**0.478**	−0.119	0.308
Transportation cost	**−0.475**	−0.081	0.274	−0.004
High-interest rate	0.024	**−0.431**	0.053	−0.090
Limited amount of loan given	0.152	**0.407**	−0.110	−0.008
Lack of trust	**0.544**	−0.035	0.154	0.065
Distance	0.006	0.163	0.176	**0.405**
Stringent condition given	0.015	−0.353	0.166	0.065
The Amount given is discretionary	−0.201	−0.147	**0.489**	0.078
Opening of account as a condition	0.219	−0.144	**0.515**	0.309
Securing of guarantor	−0.188	−0.273	−0.227	**0.539**
Loans are given to only people in business	0.284	−0.006	0.108	**0.592**
Having no knowledge of MFIs	0.229	0.494	0.464	0.034
Provision of collateral	−0.291	**0.505**	−0.025	−0.195
Non-willingness of MFIs to grant loan to women	0.091	**0.592**	−0.136	−0.210
MFIs services are concentrated in the urban centers	−0.237	0.281	−0.100	0.159
Diversion of funds	**−0.464**	0.102	−0.008	−0.320
Attitude of MFIs officials	−0.002	0.057	−0.174	0.112
Too many applications than what MFIs can serve	0.159	0.097	0.106	**−0.531**
MFIs give their loans in stages	−0.110	**0.436**	0.324	−0.190

(continued)

Table 12.3 (continued)

Variable	Factor			
	Technical factor (1)	Economic factor (2)	Management factor (3)	Social (4)
Short payback period	**−0.649**	0.097	0.010	0.289
Loans are targeted at certain businesses	**0.587**	0.108	0.066	−0.189
Education level of the recipient	−0.109	−0.192	0.**405**	−0.068
Marital status of the recipient	**0.637**	−0.006	−0.307	−0.074
Recipient's year of business experience	0.090	−0.439	0.127	−0.422
Recipient's business location	0.372	0.002	0.123	0.146

Principal factor analysis was used to transform the observed variables into scores.
Note Factor loading of 0.4 is used (10% overlapping variance); any variable that loads **more than one** factor is dropped; also, a variable with loadings of **less than 0.40** is dropped

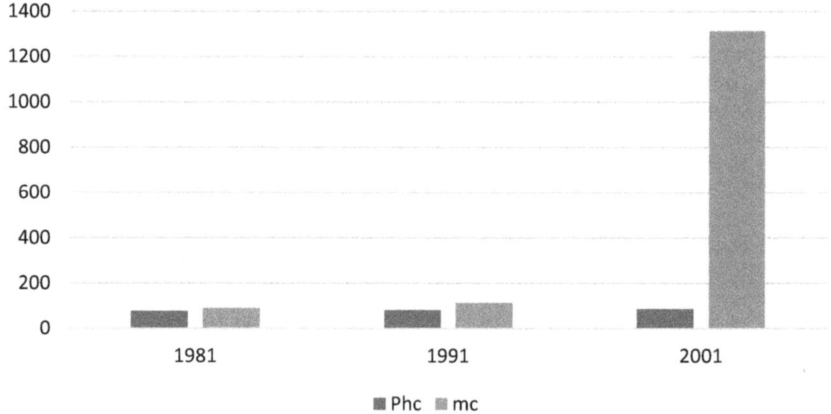

Fig. 12.3 Microfinance credit and poverty headcount in Nigeria (*Data source* The World Bank, World Development Indicators [2020])

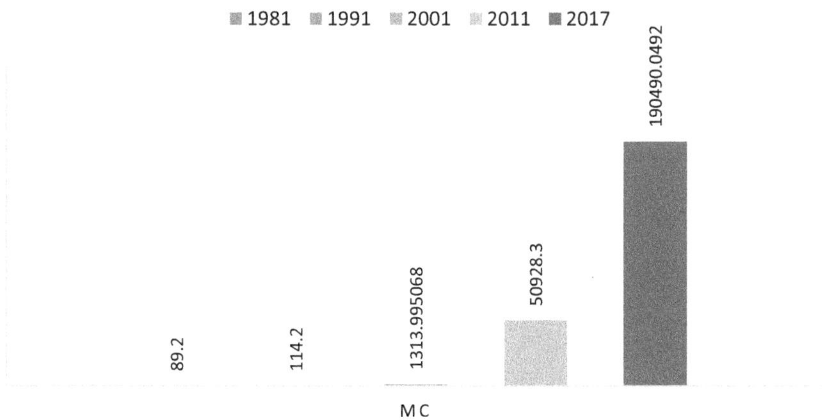

Fig. 12.4 Growth of microfinance credit in Nigeria (*Data source* The World Bank, World Development Indicators [2020])

In 1990 percentage of poverty headcount with respect to access to microfinance credit in Nigeria was 49% to 51% respectively. While it was 2% to 98% in 2020. This suggests that as percentage of microfinance credit increases, poverty headcount percentage reduces in relative terms.

12.5 Discussion and Policy Implication

In Nigeria, microfinance is a real tool for eradicating poverty. According to the findings, poverty in Nigeria would be greatly reduced if micro, small, and medium-sized companies (MSMEs) and poor households had more access to microfinance credit. Additionally, on a broad scale, microfinance services are ways of extending economic participation to marginal groups that have previously been excluded. This makes microfinance institutions effective and has an impact on the economic development of Nigeria by its capacity to reduce poverty, as shown by the analysis's findings. The policy implication is that microfinance is a tool for economically engaged poor individuals to obtain financial services, such as wage earners or business owners of small firms in the informal sector. Government should therefore guarantee appropriate management

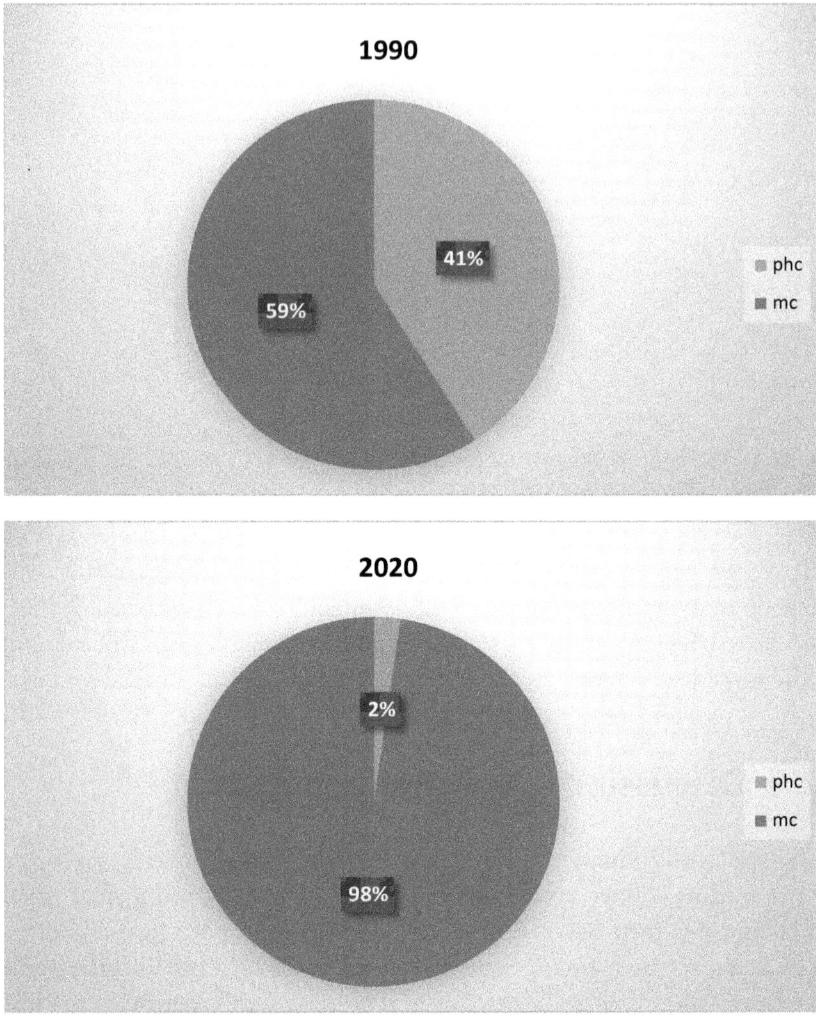

Fig. 12.5 Percentage of poverty headcount and access to microfinance credit in Nigeria (*Data source* The World Bank, World Development Indicators [2020])

and administration of microfinance institution services. Once more, the Central Bank of Nigeria (CBN) needs to implement a better system of microfinance institutions in Nigeria.

According to the study, expanding access to microfinance will likely result in more female-owned firms, which will improve gender equality. The likelihood of gender equality by women who exhibit the aforementioned traits is thought to be high. This suggests that the gender equality gap is likely to widen when female entrepreneurs do not have access to microfinance.

The implication of this is that financial inclusion is essential for women entrepreneurs to operate efficiently, keeping in mind that the more access to capital women entrepreneurs have, the more successful their firms become. This conclusion also has the implication that rural areas, where the majority of women reside, must be developed so that they can have access to financing and other facilities that will support their efforts in business. In order to foster more female-owned enterprises in Nigeria, one policy proposal from this study is that the government establish more effective grant and loan programs specifically for female entrepreneurs in both rural and urban regions. In addition, the study identified four categories of barriers to microfinance access: technical, economic, managerial, and social ones. The study's limitations, it is implied by the results, have the potential to reduce the advantages of microcredit schemes for small investors, particularly women entrepreneurs. Additionally, it would be difficult for more women entrepreneurs to gain from this program. The interest of female entrepreneurs in microfinance incentives may also be impacted.

12.6 Generic Factors that Restraints Poor People and Women Entrepreneurs from Gaining Access to Microfinance in Nigeria

Gender-Specific Constraints: "Structures of constraint" are the social norms and laws that govern connections between various social groups in society and put some in dominant positions over others and differentiate the options open to them, notably in terms of access to and control over resources (Folbre, 1994). Gender-specific structures of constraint are social norms, attitudes, and practices that specify differences in roles and obligations between men and women in societies, generally placing a lesser value on the skills, abilities, and pursuits that are typically associated with women. Gender-specific norms commonly assign males the major wage-earning role and women the duty for reproductive tasks within the family. At the local, institutional, and policy levels, women's concerns and gender-related limitations frequently have a negative impact on the equitable involvement of both sexes. Since the majority of the people is left out or given only restricted possibilities, this may prevent the full potential of human resources for wealth generation from being realized. Compared to other women entrepreneurs, disabled women confront more obstacles, such as restricted mobility, prejudice, myths and unfavorable cultural attitudes, excessive protection, marginalization, and a lack of finance that is specifically tailored to their needs.

Financial and Credit Availability and Accessibility: Numerous studies have identified access to the availability of capital as one of the main hindrances to growth. In a study of NGOs and female small-scale business owners in the Nyeri and Nairobi garment manufacturing sector of the textile industry, it was discovered that women face barriers to obtaining credit due to a lack of start-up (seed) capital, ignorance of available credit options, high-interest rates, drawn-out and rigorous loan application processes, and a lack of collateral security for financing. These elements have grown to be a significant impediment to the potential expansion of female-owned firms. In Kenya, women head more than 25% of households, but just 5% of women are landowners in their own right (Feldman, 1984). An official from the Ministry of Trade and Industry presented an example that amply demonstrated the situation of women during a seminar on "Kenya Gender and Economic Growth Assessment" in May 2006. Due to her husband's refusal to put up the family's land title deeds as collateral, a loan that the Joint Loan Scheme at the Ministry had approved for the woman applicant failed to materialize. Given that property is typically not registered in the names of women entrepreneurs, having title deeds as security to finance development remains a challenge for most of them (Karanja, 1996). However, the Government is working to find a solution to this issue through the 2005 Micro-Finance Bill and Sessional Paper No. 2. In December 2006, the latter was made an Act of Parliament. Even when it is accessible, getting access to start-up funding is a significant barrier for women business owners. Regional disparities are caused by the location decisions made by commercial banks and microfinance institutions (MFIs), which exclude entrepreneurs in rural areas. Delays in accessing initial money are caused by credit requirements when creating groups, paying membership dues, group registration fees, and joining savings plans, which worsens the financial load on women's households (Alila, 2002; Stevenson & St-Onge, 2005). The main obstacle and restraint for women's entrepreneurship in Kenya is currently, however, a lack of imagination, innovation, and responsiveness (on the side of capital suppliers). Despite the fact that many MFIs have sprung up to offer start-up and working funding, relevance and cost-effectiveness are sometimes insufficient to meet the unique needs of aspiring and established women entrepreneurs.

Legal and Regulatory Barriers: The following are some examples of the legal and regulatory obstacles: contracting, getting licenses, registering business names, and complying to statutory requirements. Women entrepreneurs are the least prepared to participate in contractual processes that are essential to conducting business in Kenya as a result of the aforementioned concerns. Contracts entail protracted legal procedures, such as leasing, drafting business contracts, legal representation, and other elements that disfavor female business owners. The majority of MSEs find these procedures tedious and time-consuming, which prevents them from expanding or growing their businesses (K'Obonyo, 2009).

Limited Entrepreneurial Culture and Management Skills: In general, emerging nations lack an entrepreneurial culture. For instance, in Kenya, with a focus on current and prospective female MSE owners and managers. Njeru and Njoka (2008) note that because of patriarchal social authority structures, women received significant family assistance when they first started their enterprises, but that support later on is restricted, curtailed, or withheld out of concern that husbands may lose control over their wives. Additionally, there are numerous sociocultural elements at play in Kenya that have a detrimental effect on the rearing of girls. Girls are socially conditioned by many ethnic communities to develop an attachment demand for affiliation rather than an accomplishment desire. Girls with disabilities are particularly vulnerable because they face barriers to education and are stigmatized as “bad omens” for their families. They are even kept secret from the public by their families.

12.7 Conclusion and Recommendations

This paper has attempted to articulate some contemporary issues in microfinance activities, poverty eradication, and gender equality with a view to appraising the effectiveness of microfinance credit in zeroing poverty and enhancing gender equality in Nigeria. The study revealed that access to microfinance credit is a panacea for zeroing poverty and enhancing gender equality in Nigeria. The barriers to accessing microfinance services and Nigeria’s improvement plans are particularly pertinent at this time. Given the contribution that microfinance has made to economies around the world, such as Bangladesh, and the recent push by the federal government of Nigeria to use small and medium-sized businesses as engines for economic development, microcredit programs have emerged as a key tenet in federal government strategy for accelerating economic growth. Economic growth and poverty alleviation are the two goals of the program. The study thus comes to the conclusion that microfinance is a vehicle for mobilizing savings for entrepreneurship because it has given people, mostly women, in rural areas affordable channels of funding and greatly influenced their activities and standard of living. Its positive impact on reducing poverty in Nigeria has also aided the desire for macroeconomic growth and development. The study also comes to the conclusion that using microfinance services can increase economic involvement for marginalized groups that had previously been excluded, which increases the effectiveness of microfinance institutions by promoting gender equality and the eradication of poverty. The study makes the suggestion that in order to address the need for financing at the micro levels of the economy and achieve our goals of sustainable zero poverty and gender equality now and in the future, microfinance institutions should be adequately capitalized, appropriately regulated, and overseen.

References

Alila, P. O. (2002). *Women street vendors*. University of Nairobi, Nairobi.

Anyanwu, J. C. (2013). *Determining the correlates of poverty for inclusive growth in Africa*. Working Paper Series, Africa Development Bank. No 181.

Asad, K. G. (2007). Measuring the impact of microfinance intervention: A conceptual framework of social impact assessment. *The Singapore Economic Review Conference Journal*. University of Manchester.

Awojobi, O. N. (2014). Microfinance as a strategy for poverty reduction in Nigeria: Empirical investigation. *International Journal of Current Research, 6*(9), 8944–8951.

Bertram, O. A., Gabriel, A. A., & Clifford, E. E. (2016). Micro-Finance institutions: A vehicle for empowerment of rural women and urban poor in Nigeria. *Journal of Policy and Development Studies,* 10(1).

Central Bank of Nigeria (2005). Microfinance Policy, Regulatory and Supervisory Framework for Nigeria. December 2005. Abuja, Nigeria: CBN.

Chowdhury, M., Mosley, P., & Simanowitz, A. (2004). The Social Impact of Microfinance: Introduction. *Journal of International Development, 16*(3), 291–300.

Comrey, A. L. (1962). The minimum residual method of factor analysis. *Psychological Reports, 11*, 15–18.

Eton, M., Basheka, B. C., & Mwosi, F. (2020). Co-operative and saving societies (SACCOS) and poverty reduction in Lango and Kigezi sub-regions of Uganda: A comparative empirical study. *African Journal of Business Management, 14*(9), 278–290.

Feldman, R. (1984). Women's groups and women's subordination: An Analysis of Policies towards Rural Women in Kenya. *Review of African Political Economy, Double Issue, 27*(28), 67–85.

Folbre, N. (1994). *Who takes care of the kids? Gender and the structures of constraint*. Routledge.

Gatewood, E. J., Brush, C. G., Carter, N. M., Greene, P. G. & Hart, M. M. (2004). Women entrepreneurs, growth and implications for the classroom.

USA: Coleman Foundation whitepaper series for the USA Association for Small Business and Entrepreneurship.

Hossain M. (1988). *Credit for the Alleviation of Rural Poverty*. The Grameen bank in Bangladesh. Washington DC IFPRI Research Report No 65 Informal Sector of Managua, Nicaragua.

Ifelunini, I. A. & Wosowei, E. C. (2013). Constraints to women entrepreneurs' access to microfinance in South-South Nigeria. *Research Journal of Finance and Accounting*, *4*(6).

Igbokwe, U. (2012). *Microfinance institutions: A vehicle for empowerment of rural women and urban poor*. A study of Umuchinemere Microfinance Bank. Term Paper submitted to the Department of Banking and Finance, Enugu State University of Science & Technology (ESUT), Enugu.

Innocent, A. I., & Elizabeth, C. W. (2013). Constraints to women entrepreneurs' access to microfinance in South-South Nigeria. *Research Journal of Finance and Accounting*, *4*(6).

Jegede, C. A., Kehinde, J., & Akinlabi, B. H. (2011) Impact of microfinance on poverty alleviation in Nigeria: An empirical investigation. *Journal of Humanities & Social Science*. Journals Bank Inc.

Karanja, A. M. (1996). Entrepreneurship among Rural Women in Kenya. In D. McCormick; P.O. Pedersen (eds.), *Flexibility and networking in an African context* (Kenya, Longhorn).

Khartoum Report. (2009). *Report on Training Program on Microfinance Sector Development for OIC Member Countries*, July 18–21, Sudan.

Kiiru, M. J. & Kenia, M. (2007). The impact of microfinance on rural poor Hohseholds' income and vulnerability to poverty: Case Study of Makueni District, Kenya. http://hss.ulb.unibonn.de/2007/1181/1181.pdf

K'Obonyo, P. (2009). *Complying with Business Regulation in Kenya,* IDS Occasional Paper No. 64, University of Nairobi, Nairobi.

Kuzilwa, J. (2005). The role of credit for small business success: A study of the National Entrepreneurship Development Fund in Tanzania. *The Journal of Entrepreneurship, 14*(2), 131–161.

Lakwo. (2007). Microfinance, rural livelihood, and women's empowerment in Martin (1999), Socio-Economic Impact of Microenterprise Loan Access.

Martins, U. J. (2009). *Microfinance and developing the Nigerian Economy*. CIBN Press, Lagos.

Mawa, B. (2008). Impact of Micro-finance Towards Achieving Poverty Alleviation. *Pakistan Journal of Social Sciences, 5*(9), 876–882.

Microcredit, Summit. (2005). Retrieved from http://www.gdrc.org/icm/what is ms.html. Virtual Library on Microcredit, UNDP.

Mustapha, M. (2011). *Poverty alleviation as a machinery for economic reconstruction in Nigeria.* http://mustaphamuktar.blogspot.de/2011/01/povertyalleviation-as-machinery-for.html

Myrdal, G. (1957). *Economic theory and underdeveloped regions.* Gerald Duckworth and Co.

Njeru, E. H. N., & Njoka, J. M. (2008). *Small scale enterprise in Nairobi: The socio-cultural factors influencing investment patterns among informal sector women entrepreneurs.* University of Nairobi, Nairobi.

Nwachukwu, I. (2008, February 12). Poverty eradication: Looking at microfinance strategy. *Business Day Newspaper*, Lagos: Business Day Publishers.

Ogwu, L. (2008). *Microfinance bank and the village economy.* Financial Standard, March 3rd, Lagos: Financial Standard Publishers.

Ojo, O. (2009). *Impact of microfinance on entrepreneurial development: The case of Nigeria. Faculty of administration and business*, University of Bucharest.

Onuka, O. I. (2021). Microcredit and poverty alleviation in Nigeria in COVID-19 Pandemic. *Asia-Pacific Journal of Rural Development, 31*(1), 7–36.

Peters, O. (2011). *Fundamentals of research methods.* Nelson Clemmy Press.

Saruparia, M. C. (2014). *Financial inclusion for inclusive growth in India.* National Law University.

Shaw, E. (1973). *Financial deepening in economic development.* Oxford University Press.

Stevenson, L., & St-Onge, A. (2005). *Support for growth-oriented women entrepreneurs in Kenya.* International Labour Organization.

Taha, S. A. (2012). *The effectiveness of microcredit programmes on alleviating poverty and empowering women in Cairo*, Egypt pp. 20–21.

Taiwo, N. J. (2012). *The impact of microfinance on welfare and poverty Aalevi-ation in Southwest Nigeria.* http://eprints.covenantuniversity.edu.ng/1149/1/CU03GP0036-Taiwo%20J.%20N.pdf

The World Bank, World Development Indicators. (2020). Domestic credit provided by financial sector (% of Gross Domestic Product). https://databank.worldbank.org/data/reports.aspx?dsid=2&series=FS.AST.DOMS.GD.ZS

Tobin, J. (1994). *Poverty in relation to macroeconomic trends, cycles, policies.* http://econpapers.repec.org/paper/cwlcwldpp/1030r.htm

Ukwueze, E. R. (2022). Women and Entrepreneurship in Nigeria: What Role Does Social Inclusion Play? *Journal of International Women's Studies*, 23(5), 41–62. https://vc.bridgew.edu/jiws/vol23/iss5/4

Vonderlack, R., & Schreiner, M. (2021). Women, microfinance and savings: Lessons and proposals. *Working Paper 01–5, Centre for Social Development*, Washington University at St. Louis.

13

Financial Inclusion and Poverty Reduction in Sub-Saharan Africa Region

Achugamonu Bede Uzoma, Francis Abolade Akintola, Owolabi Folashade, and Isibor Areghan

13.1 Introduction

There has been a gradual but steady transformation of the financial sector in most economies in Africa. The evolution started from providing small credits to the vulnerable poor to rural banking and community banking. In the recent past, emphasis has shifted to micro financing, financial

A. B. Uzoma (✉) · I. Areghan
Department of Finance, Covenant University, Ota, Nigeria
e-mail: uzoma.achugamonu@covenantuniversity.edu.ng

I. Areghan
e-mail: areghan.isibor@covenantuniversity.edu.ng

F. A. Akintola
Department of Finance, Babcock University, Ilishan-Remo, Nigeria
e-mail: akintolaa@babcock.edu.ng

O. Folashade
Department of Accounting, Covenant University, Ota, Nigeria
e-mail: folashade.owolabi@covenantuniversity.edu.ng

A. S. Ibidunni et al. (eds.), *Innovation, Entrepreneurship and the Informal Economy in Sub–Saharan Africa*, Sustainable Development Goals Series,
https://doi.org/10.1007/978-3-031-46293-1_13

inclusion, and financial wellness (Achugamonu et al., 2020). Specific financial inclusion initiatives by government and financial regulatory authorities include: (i) credit inclusion—which involves the provision of micro credits to the vulnerable poor through the establishment of microfinance banks and other microfinance institutions; (ii) pension inclusion—the initiative created by the government in this regard started with the deregulation of the pension market to encourage private participation (Achugamonu et al., 2019). This culminated to the creation of different pension fund administrators (PFA) and allowing employers and employees to choose the PFA to save and invest with through the compulsory contributory scheme initiative (Achugamonu et al., 2019). There is also the micro pension scheme which encourages artisans and other self-employed in rural areas to plan for their retirement; (iii) insurance inclusion—is also an initiative of government and financial regulatory agencies to provide micro insurance services to individuals for their life, health, education and to protect their assets. Some insurance policies also serve as investment vehicles for the policy holder (Achugamonu et al., 2019). The most recent financial inclusion initiative supported by the G-20 group, the World Bank, and other financial regulatory institutions is digital financial inclusion. This involved the deployment of an avalanche of payment channels like point of sale services (POS), automatic teller machines (ATM), mobile banking, and internet banking. It also includes the involvement of private financial technology institutions in the financial intermediation process within and outside the shores of their host countries (Babajide, 2020). The above strategies focused on ensuring that the poor and downtrodden are given commensurable financial access to engage in productive and sustainable economic activities. Investment in financial or real asset by these category of persons in rural communities will engender food and financial security and subsequently reduce poverty.

Financial development will continue to be an illusion if a large number of citizens remain poor due to inability to get the needed financial assistance to create wealth, build capacity, and achieve financial security for themselves and their dependents.

Recent studies like Isibor et al. (2018) have shown that half of the indigent forty percent of the world population in emerging and developing economies have no bank account. Likewise, thirty-five percent of SMEs encounter serious challenges when seeking for loans for investment (Isibor et al., 2018). Also, the segregation between the rich and poor, urban and rural dwellers as well as women and men when accessing financial services is still in existence up to date (Ratna et al., 2015). The survey by the Consultative Group to Assist the Poor (CGAP) in the year 2012 indicated that the number of unbanked active poor in SSA ranked below the world benchmark whereas that of countries in high-income region ranked above it (CGAP, 2012). Specifically, Sub-Saharan Africa and South Asia have the highest number of unbanked households compared to the rest of the world (CGAP, 2012). With an increasing demand for an all-inclusive growth by almost all sovereign nations by 2030 there is an urgent need to eliminate the widening gap between the rich elites that are financially included and the poor that lack financial services especially in rural communities. Financial inclusion is needed for rural and downtrodden masses that are the future growth engine of the economy (Agarwal, 2010).

On the other hand, the report by Enhancing Financial Inclusion and Access (EFInA) in 2018 showed evidence that those SSA countries made visible progress in financial inclusive growth. For instance, between 2012 and 2018, South Africa increased the number of banked adults from 67 to 80% while Namibia rose from 62 to 68% for the same period. Furthermore, Nigeria moved from 33% in 2012 to 40% in 2018. Likewise, Rwanda rose from 23% in 2012 to 26% in 2016, Ghana rose from 34% in 2010 to 36% in 2015, while Kenya rose from 23% in 2009 to 42.3% in 2016. In addition, financial exclusion rate and the number of persons in informal financial sector dropped considerably for all the countries mentioned above. This trend is almost the same for all the countries in the SSA region (EFInA & NBS, 2018). Despite the considerable progress achieved by most countries in this region to drive financial inclusive and economic growth and development, it is perturbing that poverty rate in the same region had been on the increase overtime. This is to the extent that a country in the region (Nigeria) was declared the poverty capital of the world. For instance in 1990, SSA accounted for about 15% of persons living below the world's benchmark of $1.90 per day. In 2013, the number of poor persons rose to 766.6 million representing about 50% more than the world's extreme poor persons, (Anyanwu and Anyanwu, 2017; Kabuya, 2015) in his study projected that SSA region will become the poorest region with the highest percentage of its population living below $1.25 per day by 2030 if the trend continues.

With the abundant resources and government intervention programs at the disposal of most SSA countries it becomes a paradox than reality that poverty still persist and increase at an alarming rate in SSA region. This is despite the efforts by government and international donor agencies (like Melinda and Bill Gates) to drive inclusive financial and economic growth in the SSA region. It is expected that greater financial inclusion should result to tangible economic benefits for the users, such as higher GDP growth and lower income inequality and poverty reduction. When a person or group of person's irrespective of geographical location, political affiliation, religion and social strata receive adequate, cost effective, and sustainable financial support it will help to encourage stable growth by smoothening savings and investment. The result will culminate into efficient and equitable income redistribution from lenders to borrowers. By this development, individuals are able to create wealth for themselves, income level rises and of course poverty is reduced while at the same time the economy is protected from adverse economic shocks, Adigun and Kama (2015). In the light of the aforesaid, this study examined whether financial inclusion truly reduce poverty or whether increase in per capita income will motivate persons in the informal financial sector to embrace formal financial services or products. The objective is to examine the extent to which financial inclusion reduce poverty while the hypothesis in its null form is that financial inclusion does not really reduce poverty or that increase in per capita income does not necessarily drive financial inclusive growth.

13.2 Theoretical Review

Financial System Paradigm Theory

Several development theories were unanimous in their position that financial development drives economic growth which by extension reduces poverty. Chiefly among these theories were the works of McKinnon (1973), Shaw (1973), and Keynes (1937). This study is however hinged on a variant of the Keynesian theory called financial system paradigm. The financial system paradigm was developed in the 1980s to address the financial repression occasioned by the failure of the direct credit approach to finance in developing countries. The theory assumes that the poor can actually create wealth and generate income to service their debts as well as save for the future if given required credit facility. This principle known as "banking with the poor" is based on the assumption that micro finance institutions should provide financial services to the rural poor on a sustainable and widespread basis to enable them to accumulate savings and build assets to protect themselves against risks as well as invest in income generating projects. Some countries like Indonesia, Bangladesh, Bolivia, as well as so many other developing countries have imbibed the concept of "banking with the poor" as a platform for driving sustainable inclusive growth and stability. This theory is relevant to this study as it supports that the poor in the rural communities also have the capacity to service debts, save and accumulate wealth for further investment in the economy. By so doing, poverty will be reduced, inequality gap is bridged, social exclusion is addressed, crime and unemployment rate is reduced, and finally financial stability is achieved. (Hannig et al., 2010) Financial inclusion is an intermediation approach government and its monetary authorities can adopt to destroy asymmetric information and eliminate market frictions preventing the poor from accessing the required credit to build a financial life for themselves and families (Fadun, 2015). When financial inclusive drive is scaled up, it offers a veritable platform to tackle poverty and address sustainable development programs culminating to economic growth and development (Chibba, 2009). Sustainable financial inclusive drive among low-income earners in rural communities will help them achieve financial security and take advantage of investment opportunities in their immediate environment to grow their business. For any development policy to be successful, it must address the financial and economic needs of the vulnerable poor in rural communities. Such policies must engender a rapid and sustainable economic growth that will culminate to financial wellness and security of the society at large (Department for International Development, 2016).

13.3 Empirical Review

According to Asadull and Savola (2018), the number of poor people and gap measures reduced greatly in initially high-income poverty countries when they subscribed to drive the millenium development goals. Another result using dynamic panel estimations found that financial inclusion is positively related to economic growth in Organization of Islamic Cooperation (OIC) countries. The result showed that financial inclusion mutually granger cause economic growth as revealed by the granger causality test conducted on 56 OIC countries.

Achugamonu et al. (2020) examined financial inclusion as a tool for poverty alleviation and income redistribution in Nigeria. The study found that through financial inclusion strategies, the number of excluded individuals was reduced over the study period thereby resulting to poverty alleviation and income redistribution. They therefore recommended that government should increase effort at capturing more persons into the financial net in order to alleviate poverty as well as redistribute income.

Tita and Aziakpono (2017) studied the relationship between financial inclusion indicators and income inequality in SSA. The study found that account ownership and usage, electronic payment, and formal savings have a positive relationship with income inequality. This implies that financial inclusion does not really reduce income inequality. This is a justification that owning a transaction account alone is not enough to gain access to necessary credit that will create wealth and reduce poverty. The reason being that most account owners especially first-timers may suffer from moral hazards and information asymmetry which prevents them from acquiring the needed finance that will enable them to invest in their future and reduce poverty. Choudhury and Bagchi (2016) in their study found that work status, disposition of the family head to finance, education, and location of financial service point are major reasons for increase in financial exclusion rate in India.

Ogunsaki and Fawehinmi (2017) examined financial inclusion as an effective policy tool to ease poverty in Ekiti for the period 1980 to 2015. The study found that the poverty rate was high among women and that unemployment, gender inequality, income level, age, financial discipline education are some of the factors that determine poverty rate in Ekiti State. Ibrahim et al. (2019) investigated how financial inclusion could aid poverty reduction in forty nine SSA countries between 1980 to 2017. The study found that savings, access to credit by the private sector, ownership of debit cards, and digital payment platforms are factors that alleviate poverty whereas interest rate and economic growth worsen poverty in the sampled region.

Hicks and Lanau (2018) investigated the triggers of in-work poverty among households in Britain and found that in-work poverty is momentary than poverty among working-age adults generally. The study further revealed that the number of persons working in every household is a key indicator of in-work poverty in Britain. Findings from this study shows that persons who witnessed in-work poverty are three times more likely to be out of job than non-poor workers. The implication is that gainful employment alone has limitations in serving as a tool toward poverty reduction but lifestyle changes and moderations will reduce income fluctuations by working households, and this was supported by the study of Babajide, Isola et al. (2020).

13.4 Methodology

Research Design

The research design adopted by this study is a relational-based design that follows the intuitive convention that financial stability depends essentially on financial inclusion drive (Batheit and Glucker, 2018). This study used a purposive sampling technique to select 27 countries out of 46 sub-Saharan African countries for the period 2007 to 2017. A simple random sampling technique was adopted in this study for the selection of countries that met the criteria and purpose for this study in terms of the availability of data. A simple random sampling technique is used in research to select the sample (in this case the countries) that meet the criteria of data availability required by the study before selecting such information from the population. It is a probabilistic sampling technique used when the population is very large or resources limited to conduct a survey. This implied that the sample size covers 59% of the population. To engender a robust and thought-provoking analysis and discussion, the 27 sampled countries were disaggregated into: large savings, small savings, and overall samples according to their level of financial deepening and development (see Appendix). The justification for sourcing data from World Bank database for the period 2007–2017 was based on the fact that it covered the pre and post financial meltdown era. The Granger Error Correction Method (ECM) for short panel data specification was adopted to analyze the data whereas the differenced Generalized Methods of Moments (GMM) of Arellanon and Bond (1991) was engaged to address persistency, heterogeneity, and endogeneity problems associated with short panel data. Short panel data are so called when the number of observations (N) is greater than the sampled period (T). For this study the number of observation is 27 whereas the sampled period is 10 years (that is, N > T).

Model Specification

The model shows financial inclusion usage as the dependent variables while poverty represented by per capita income is taken as the independent variable for the ARDL specification as follows:

$$\begin{aligned} \ln dcpa_{it} &= i_0 + i_1 \ln dcpa_{i,t-1} + i_2 \ln dcpa_{i,t-2} + i_3 \ln pci_{it} \\ &\quad + i_4 \ln pci_{i,t-1} + i_5 \ln pci_{i,t-2} + \psi_{t1} + v_{it1} \qquad (13.1) \end{aligned}$$

Table 13.1 Definition of variables

Variable description	Type of data/ source/ measurement	Literature justification	Parameter's a priori
Fin. Inclusion (Usage): dcpa = deposits in commercial banks per 1000 adults	Secondary/World Bank DB This measures the amount of deposits by customers in commercial banks in SSA. It is also a measure of frequency and consistency of usage of financial product	Forgelli et. al. (2016)	Positive: More frequent deposits is an indication of the acceptability of such financial product. dcpa > 0
Poverty (Welfare): Per Capita Income = pci	Secondary/World Bank (DB) Poverty is represented by per capita income (pci). It measures how the financial product affects the living standard of users	Koppensteiner and Olukorede (2016)	Negative: Increase in poverty is an indication that the financial product is not yielding the right dividend. (pci < 0)

Source Author compiled

Equation 13.1 shows the effect of financial inclusion usage and quality with poverty denoted by per capita income (Table 13.1).

13.5 Result

Dynamics of Financial Inclusion and Poverty

This study investigates whether there is a significant influence/causation from financial inclusion to poverty for the overall sample of countries, as well as low and large-saving countries. The results of the investigation are reported in Tables 13.2, 13.3, and 13.4 respectively.

Table 13.2 Long-run and Short-run dynamics of FI and poverty for overall sample

Regressors	Coef	Std. Err	Z-stat	*P*-value
Δ lnfininc1 (−1)	−0.23	0.10	−2.33	0.02**
Δ pci	−0.32	0.23	−1.31	0.19
Δpci (−1)	−0.13	0.55	−0.24	0.81
ECM	−0.20	0.07	−3.09	0.00*
pci(−2)	0.12	0.89	0.13	0.90
Summation of short-run coef		−0.46		
Short-run wald test (*P*-value)		0.57		
Long run coefficient		2.72		
Long run coefficient (*P*-value)		0.71		
Sargan difference test (*P*-value)		0.99		
Sargan test (*P*-value)		0.87		
AR1 (*P*-value)		0.00		
AR2 (*P*-value)		0.92		
Number of observations		270		
Number of countries		27		

Table 13.3 Long-run and Short-run dynamics of FI and poverty for large saving countries

Regressors	Coef	Std. Err	Z-stat	*P*-value
Δ lnfininc1 (−1)	−0.09	0.17	−0.54	0.59
Δ pci	−0.37	1.30	0.29	0.77
Δpci (−1)	0.16	1.97	0.08	0.93
ECM	−0.18	0.11	−1.63	0.10
pci(−2)	0.45	2.91	0.15	0.88
Summation of short-run coef		−0.21		
Short-run wald test (*P*-value)		0.67		
Long run coefficient		1.41		
Long run coefficient (*P*-value)		0.83		
Sargan difference test (*P*-value)		0.01		
Sargan test (*P*-value)		0.91		
AR1 (*P*-value)		0.00		
AR2 (*P*-value)		0.83		
Number of observations		80		
Number of countries		8		

Table 13.2 displays the overall sample result of the short and long-run relationship between financial inclusion and poverty for the sampled 27 SSA countries. The coefficient of the ECM is (−0.20) with a probability

Table 13.4 Long-run and Short-run dynamics of FI and poverty for small saving countries

Regressors	Coef	Std. Err	Z-stat	*P*-value
Δ Infininc1 (−1)	−0.34	0.09	−3.72	0.00
Δ pci	−0.54	0.19	−2.89	0.00
Δpci (−1)	−0.71	0.37	−1.92	0.05
ECM	−0.26	0.05	−4.52	0.00
pci(−2)	−0.87	0.55	−1.59	0.11
Summation of short-run coef		−1.25		
Short-run wald test (*P*-value)		0.43		
Long run coefficient		0.71		
Long run coefficient (*P*-value)		0.24		
Sargan difference test (P-Value)		0.83		
Sargan test (*P*-value)		0.22		
AR1 (*P*-value)		0.00		
AR2 (*P*-value)		0.94		
Number of observations		190		
Number of countries		19		

Note (1) The figures in parentheses are the p-values, *, ** and *** indicate significant at alpha value of 1%, 5% and 10% respectively
(2) Estimation by one step Diff-GMM (Arellano, and Bond)
(4) The Sargan test is based on the assumption that the instruments are not correlated with the residuals
(5) AR1 and AR2 tests are based on the hypothesis that the errors are not serially correlated
(6) The instruments used are the lags of the regressors
(7) Yearly dummies are excluded

value of 0. The result invalidates a priory expectation which suggests the existence of long-run positive relationship between financial inclusion and poverty for the overall sample countries. It was further observed that the ECM coefficient is statistically significant meaning that financial inclusion respond to spatial variations in poverty. However, the negative sign of the ECM coefficient is an indication that the movement is in opposite direction, meaning that a reduction in poverty rate does not necessarily engender financial inclusion of the affected countries. The short-run coefficient (−0.46) is in tandem with a probability value of 57%. This implies that in the short-run poverty does not significantly influence financial inclusion. To this end, increase in poverty by 46% will result in a commensurate reduction in financial inclusion. The long-run coefficient of 2.72 has a probability value of 71 which is very large.

This shows no significant response of financial inclusion to long-lasting changes in poverty for the overall sample of the selected SSA countries.

Table 13.3 shows the result of the influence between financial inclusion and poverty for large savings countries among 27 SSA countries sampled. The ECM which is −0.18 is significant at 10% probability value. This reveals that in the long run, poverty influences financial inclusion and any deviation in the influence will warrant an adjustment of financial inclusion at 18% speed to every unit change in poverty. Furthermore, the short-run coefficient of −0.21 has a probability value of 0.67 which suggests that no significant dynamic relationship exists between financial inclusion and poverty. However, 1% increase in poverty reduces financial inclusion by 21 meaning that the presence of poverty limits the rate at which people visit the bank for deposit and receipt of their money. Likewise, the coefficient of the long-run elasticity is not significant at (1.47) indicating that financial inclusion do not influence poverty for the large sample SSA countries. The instruments used are not weak since the Sargan test is insignificantly different from zero. Similarly, the AR at lag 2 shows the absence of autocorrelation in the residuals, thereby validating the correctness of the model.

Table 13.4 is the result of the interactive relationship between financial inclusion and poverty for small savings countries with an ECM coefficient of (−0.26) with an associated probability value of 0.00. This implies that there is the existence of a long-run dynamic relationship between financial inclusion and poverty at a *p*-value of 1%. In addition, 26% change in the long-run coefficient is corrected within 1 year. The long-run elasticity coefficient is positive at 0.71 but insignificant even at a 10 probability value. The meaning is that just like the large savings countries, financial inclusion does not respond to long-lasting variations in poverty. That is, improvement in the per capita income of the citizens does not culminate in the use of formal financial services. For both samples of small and large countries, the short-run effects are negative and insignificant. The Sargan test and Sargan in difference test accept the null hypothesis for the post-estimation test. Equally, the AR(2) is in support of the absence of autocorrelation, while the AR(1) rejects it.

13.6 Discussion

The result of the ECM is significant for the overall and small savings countries. This is because a change in per capita income will result in noticeable change in financial inclusion. However, the negative coefficient of the variation suggests movement in opposite direction. This implies that improvement in per capita income will necessitate a corresponding reduction in financial inclusion. This discussion is based on the results of the ECM and the negative relationship between financial inclusion and poverty which is not in tandem with the a priori expectation of this study. The implication is that the government should make policies to increase the capacity of citizens to earn income through employment generation and job creation. Specifically, they should encourage financial institutions in rural communities which have the highest number of financially unbanked and underserved persons in the country. Similarly, they should intervention programs in the region that will culminate in more persons using mainstream financial products and services. When such persons are able to create wealth, their ability to use more of bank-sophisticated products will improve. This will culminate to boost in economic activities and an increase in gross domestic products with its resultant effect on poverty reduction and financial system stability. Literature supporting the argument that financial inclusion is a veritable tool deployed to create wealth for the users of financial products and bring them out of extreme poverty includes the works of Asadull and Savola (2018), Chibba (2009), Alexander and Laurent (2016), Anthanansius and Aziakpono (2016).

13.7 Conclusion

This study therefore concludes that although there significant influence between poverty reduction and financial inclusion especially for the overall and small savings countries. Such influence impacts negatively on financial inclusion. That is, increase in per capita income does not necessarily encourage more persons to use mainstream finance in the sampled SSA countries. Other factors like financial literacy, improvement in the payment systems, cost of funds, and digital financial technology may contribute to the integration of more persons into mainstream finance.

Achievement of an inclusive financial system could only be a mirage if more persons remain unbanked and underbanked. It is recommended that the government of the affected countries should develop policies to encourage more persons to be integrated into the formal financial enclave. This can be achieved by mandating banks to create more payment channels, reduce interest rate, collaborate with financial technology companies to promote digital finance, and embark on aggressive financial education to create awareness of the available financial products they can leverage on to improve their financial wellbeing.

13.8 Suggestions for Further Studies

Further studies and other researchers can carry out the same subject matter of financial inclusion and poverty reduction in other developing countries of the world.

Appendix

See Fig. 13.1, Tables 13.5 and 13.6.

The sample includes 27 SSA countries listed in alphabetical order which bears no significance to the result obtained except for identification purpose alone.

Descriptive Statistics: Graphical Method

This study showed the movements and the distribution pattern of the underlying variables over time/across countries using line graphs. Note that each line graph shows the movement of the prescribed underlying variable across countries and overtime among the 27 SSA countries.

Table 13.5 Identification number for each of the countries

S/N	Name of country
1	Angola
2	Burundi
3	Botswana
4	Central African Republic
5	Cameroon
6	Congo Democratic Republic
7	Congo Republic
8	Equatorial Guinea
9	Ghana
10	Guinea
11	Gambia
12	Kenya
13	Liberia
14	Lesotho
15	Madagascar
16	Mozambique
17	Mauretania
18	Mauritius
19	Malawi
20	Namibia
21	Nigeria
22	Rwanda
23	South Africa
24	Seychelles
25	Tanzania
26	Uganda
27	Zambia

From the line graph above, financial inclusion by usage is denoted by fininc. This shows the movements of financial inclusion by usage (represented by the number of deposits in commercial banks per 1000 adults). A high volume of deposits in commercial banks shows that individuals use more of bank products for deposit purpose which is an evidence of high rate of financial inclusion.

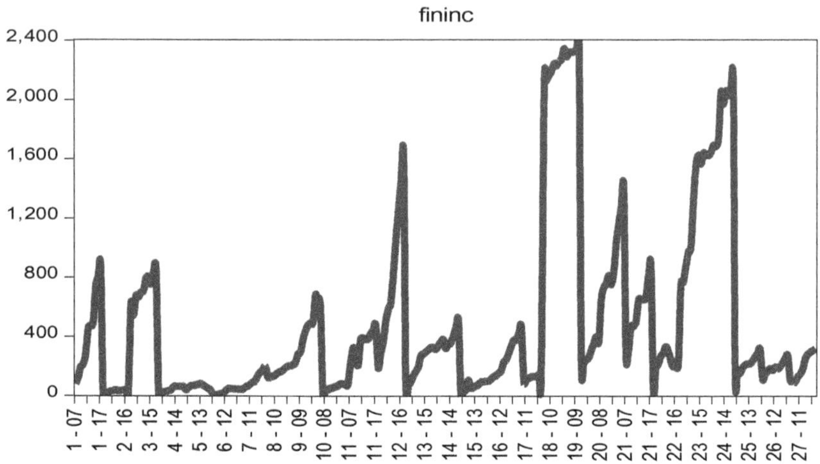

Fig. 13.1 Line graph showing number of deposits in commercial banks per 1000 adults

Table 13.6 Number of deposits in commercial banks per 1000 adults (2007–2017)

I.D no	Name of country	No deposit/1000 adults	Rank
19	Malawi	2,400	High
18	Mauritius	2,350	High
24	Seychelles	2,300	High
25	Tanzania	2,300	High
23	South Africa	1600	Moderate
12	Kenya	1600	Moderate
21	Nigeria	1400	Moderate
3	Botswana	900	Moderate
2	Burundi	500	Low
4	Central African Republic	10	Low
5	Cameroon,	10	Low
7	Congo Republic	10	Low
6	Congo Democratic Republic	10	Low

References

Achugamonu, B. U., Adegbite, E. O., Omankhanlen, A. E., Okoye, L. U., & Isibor A. A. (2019). Dynamics of digital finance and financial inclusion nexus in sub-Saharan Africa. In *Proceedings of the 33rd international business information management association conference, IBIMA 2019: Education excellence and innovation management through Vision 2020.*

Achugamonu, B., Adetiloye, K., Adegbite, E., Babajide, A., & Akintola, F. (2020). Financial exclusion of bankable adults: Implication on financial inclusive growth among twenty-seven SSA countries. *Cogent Social Sciences, 6*(1), 1730046.

Adigun. M., & Kama, U. (2015). *Financial inclusion in Nigeria: Issues and challenges* (CentralBank of Nigeria ocassional paper no. 45).

Agarwal, A. (2010). *Financial inclusion: Challenges & opportunities.* 23rd Skoch Summit 2010.

Alexandra, Z., & Laurent, W., (2016). The determinants of financial inclusion in africa. Review of Development Finance, *6*, 46–57.

Anyanwu, J., & Anyanwu, J. (2017). The key drivers of poverty in sub-saharan africa and what can be done about it to achieve sustainable development Goal. *Asian Journal of Economic Modelling*, *5*, 297–317. www.aessweb.com

Arellano, M., & Bond, S. (1991). Monte Carlo evidence and application to employment equations. *Review of Economic Studies, 58*, 277–297.

Asadull, M. N., & Savola, A. (2018). Poverty reduction during 1990–2013. *Did millennium. Development goals adoption and state capacity matter? Effective state and inclusive development Research Center (ESID)* (Working Paper No. 93). Retrieved May 20, 2020 from http://www.effective-states.org/wp-content/uploads/working_papers/final-pdfs/esid_wp_93_asadullah_savoia.pdf

Babajide, I., Okafor, I., Achugamonu., & Osuma. (2020). Financial inclusion among low-income groups in Nigeria: Triggers and barriers. *Academy of Entrepreneurship Journal*, *26*(2).

Babajide, A. A., Oluwaseye, E. O., Adedoyin, L. I., & Isibor, A. A. (2020). Financial technology, financial inclusion and msmes financing in the south-west of Nigeria. *Academy of Entrepreneurship Journal, 26*(3), 1–17.

Barrell, R., Davis, H., Karma, V., & Liadze, I. (2010). Credit booms, banking crises and the current account. *Federal Reserve Bank of Dallas Publication: Globalization & Monetary Policy Institute* (workshop paper no. 178) http://www.dallasfed.org/assets/documents/institute/wpapers/2014/0178.pdf

Batheit, H., & Glucker, J. (2018). Relational research design in economic geography. *The New Oxford Handbook of Economic Geography.* https://doi.org/10.1093/oxford/9780198755609.013.46

CGAP. (2012). *Financial inclusion and stability: What does research show?* The Consultative Group to Assist the Poor. Retrieved May 23, 2018, from cgap@worldbank.org

Chibba, M. (2009). Financial inclusion, poverty reduction and the millennium development goals (M. F. Sinclair, Ed.). *European Journal of Development Research*, 213–230.

Choudhury, R., & Bagchi, D., (2016). Financial exclusion—A paradox in developing Country. *IOSR Journal of Economics & Finance, 7*(3), 40–45. Retrieved September Thursday, 2019, from http://www.iosrjournals.org/iosr-jef/papers/Vol7-Issue3/Version-1/G0703014045.pdf

Department for International Development. (2016). *Building jobs and prosperity in developing countries.* DFID. Retrieved July 2019, from file:///c:/users/user%20pc/downloads/growth_building_jobs_and_prosperity_in_d.pdf

EFInA & NBS. (2018). *Access to financial services in Nigeria 2018 survey.*

Fadun, S. (2015). Financial inclusion, tool for poverty alleviation and income redistribution in developing countries: Evidences from Nigeria. *Academic Research International, 5*(3).

Forgelli, A., & Rubino, C. (2016). Does mobile banking improve financial inclusion? Madrid: Universidad, Autonoma de Madrid. G20 Leaders Communique. http://www.g20.utoronto.ca/2012/2012-0619-loscabos.pdf (2012).

Hannig, A., Jansen, S. (2010). *Financial inclusion and financial stability: Current policy issues.* Asian Debelopment Bank Institute (ADBI).

Hick, R., & Lanau, A. (2018). Moving in and out of in-workpoverty in the UK: An analysis of transitions, trajectories and trigger events. *Journal of Social Policy*. https://doi.org/10.1017/S0047279418000028

Ibrahim, H. B., Manu, D., Adamu, I., Jediel, E. H., Kasima, W.,Hajara, B., & Yusrah, I. (2019). An examination of the impact of financial inclusion on poverty reduction: An empirical evidence from Sub-Saharan Africa. *International Journal of Scientific and Research Publications, 9*(1), 239 ISSN 2250–3153. https://doi.org/10.29322/IJSRP.9.01.2019.p8532; www.ijsrp.or

Isibor, A. A., Ojo, J. A. T., & Ikpefan, O. A. (2018). A study of financial deepening and capital accumulation in Nigeria. In *Peer-Reviewed Proceedings of the International Business Information Management Association Conference (31st IBIMA)* held on 25–26 April 2018. Italy: Milan.

Kabuya, F. I. (2015). Fundamental causes of poverty in sub-saharan africa. *IOSR Journal of Humanities and Social Science (IOSR-JHSS), 20*(6), 78–81.

Kima, D.-W., Yu, J.-S., & Kabir, H. (2018). Financial inclusion and economic growth in OIC countries. *Research in International Business and Finance, 43*, 1–14.

Koppensteiner, F., & Olukorede, A. (2016). *Financial inclusion, shocks and welfare: Evidence from the expansion of mobile money in Tanzania*. Research Gate.

McKinnon, R. I. (1973). *Money and capital in economic development*. Booking Instituion.

Ogunsakin, S., & Fawehinmi, F. (2017). Financial inclusion as an effective policy tool of poverty alleviation: A case of Ekiti state. *IOSR Journal of Economics and Finance (IOSR-JEF)* e-ISSN: 2321–5933, p-ISSN: 2321–5925. *8*(4) Ver. II (July–August 2017), 01–10. www.iosrjournals.org

Ratna, S., Martin, C., Diaye, P., Barajas, A., Mitra, S., Kyobe, A., & Mooi, Y. N. (2015). Financial inclusion: Can it meet multiple macroeconomic goals? International Monetary Fund (IMF) , Monetary and capital markets department with inputs from strategy and policy review department and other departments.

14

Adaptiveness of MSMEs During Times of Environmental Disruption: Exploratory Study of Capabilities-Based Insights from Nigeria

Ayodotun Stephen Ibidunni, Ayeni Adejuwon Ayobami Adebanji William, and Bisayo Otokiti

14.1 Introduction

Environmental disruptions are very often an essential change agent to the existence of firms. In one way they open opportunities for scaling firm operations, while in another sense they may pose a threat to business continuity and they redefine the operations of firms. A typical example is the wake of firms across the globe to the knowledge-driven economy that found its root in digitisation and technological advancements in the

A. S. Ibidunni (✉)
Department of Business Administration, Chrisland University, Abeokuta, Nigeria
e-mail: aibidunni@chrislanduniversity.edu.ng

International Centre for Policy Research and Industry Linkages (ICePRIL), Shaveh Consulting, Abeokuta, Nigeria

Centre for Economic Policy and Development Research (CEPDeR), Covenant University, Ota, Nigeria

A. S. Ibidunni et al. (eds.), *Innovation, Entrepreneurship and the Informal Economy in Sub–Saharan Africa*, Sustainable Development Goals Series,
https://doi.org/10.1007/978-3-031-46293-1_14

early 2000s. Despite that developed economies were yet awake to technological sophistication before this time, the millennial era starting from the year 2000 erupted in a global drive of businesses that could only survive with the digital advantage. During this period, whereas some firms were able to re-engineer to fit with digital transitioning, others had to go into extinction because they failed to procure, mobilise and utilise digital resources for the business continuity.

The years 2019 in 2020 experienced another significant environmental disruption in which the global business and human existence had to battle an unfamiliar strain of coronavirus disease, known as COVID-19. The disruptions caused to the global business existence are unique from existing forms of disruptions resulting from adjustments in economic policies and technological advancements. This is especially so because the COVID-19 pandemic resulted in a significant shut down of business activities in some cases. While in other cases, it slowed-down business activities across the nations of the earth. The impact of the pandemic resulted in large and small firms operating remotely, or not operating at all (Humphries et al., 2020). Not only were firms' operations disrupted, but human existence suffered from the threats of public health breakdown. In all these, the Micro, Small and Medium Enterprises (MSMEs) sector suffered a significant part of the impact of the pandemic because accounts from different parts of the world revealed that many businesses in the sector were negatively affected.

In Africa, the productivity of the MSMEs sector experienced a significant slowdown (Ighobor, 2020). Particularly given the informal context within which a large number of MSMEs in Africa operate, questions regarding what strategies are essential for these MSMEs operators to

A. A. A. A. William
Department of Business Administration, Landmark University, Omu-Aran, Nigeria
e-mail: ayeni.adebanji@lmu.edu.ng

B. Otokiti
Department of Business and Entrepreneurship, Kwara State University, Malete, Nigeria

adopt will arise. More so, there will be questions about what plans to establish to ensure a lasting future survival of the firms? Within Africa's fast-growing informal sector, the Nigerian MSMEs sector plays a very strategic role. Nigeria, being the most populous nation on the African continent, has an MSMEs sector that employs 65% of the country's population with over ninety per cent of businesses in Nigeria operating in the small and medium business sector (National Bureau of Statistics, 2019; Wale-Oshinowo et al., 2018). Therefore, the previously raised questions form the main focus of this study, given the challenges that MSMEs are confronted by in the present pandemic.

The present study has the objective of contributing to the strategic management literature by an explorative demonstration of MSMEs in the developing economies, particularly Nigeria, adaptiveness during periods of uncertain environmental disruptions caused by pandemics. Existing studies are limited to explaining firm capabilities and environmental disruptions within the context of industry competitiveness (Parker & Ameen, 2018), technological change (Colombo et al., 2020) and environmental dynamisms (Haarhaus & Liening, 2020). The earlier explained views have focused mainly on artificial, or human-made, dimensions of disruptions arising from policy fluctuations, economic conditions and innovations. Nevertheless, there is an existing gap about how firm capabilities can be adjusted and sustained during periods of uncertain health-related pandemics, with an overwhelming, disruptive effect on human and economic activities. This present study aims to fill this gap within the context of the developing African informal economy, precisely in Nigeria.

14.2 Literature Review

The Trajectory of Nigeria's MSME Sector During Disruptions

The peculiarity of every developing nation such as Nigeria is the challenge of finding well-suited policies that address the present needs of the nation. This was articulated by Oluranti et al. (2015) on the premise that sustainability of the enacted policy does not transcend time and thus becomes redundant. With the aid of KPMG (2020), it was asserted that there is a replication with the occurrence of COVID-19, a pandemic with a speedy means of transfer when an infected person sneezes or coughs and invariably transmits the virus in close contact with fewer than two metres (Centres for Disease Control and Prevention, 2019). Furthermore, from the desk of the Centres for Disease Control and Prevention (2019), touching infected objects within a stipulated timeframe was included as the possible cause of transfer. Hence, with all the discovered means of transfer for the pandemics, business activities are affected.

The peculiarity of Nigeria being a growing economy with a reverse growth of increasing unemployment has been the dangerous occurrence that was to be addressed (Olawoyin, 2020) and with the COVID-19 pandemic, an influx of unemployment surge should be expected. Undeniably, there are recovery plans in view and proposed by the executives of the Nation for the business activity on the coping strategies of the pandemic with the absence of the circumventing the economic strains businesses have been going through (McKie et al., 2020; Centres for Disease Control and Prevention, 2019).

The impending impact of collected debts over the years and recent times aid in positing the views stated with the position of KPMG Nigeria (2020) on the long-lasting impact of the already seeing COVID-19 disruptions. KPMG Nigeria (2020) ascertained these views with evidence of 94% of the fortune 1000 businesses with those in Nigeria, inclusive being imparted with the COVID-19 disruption. Evidence of this was the mass retrenchment in many big firms across the world, and in some cases, the government had to step in (Sahara Reporters, 2020).

In line with historical epidemics that succeeded in bringing the world economy to its knees, the same can applies to COVID-19. The main difference, however, is that MSMEs have developed adaptiveness over time. For a nation like Nigeria, where the MSMEs conduct business activities in a complex and policy porous environment (Ayeni, 2016). Hitherto, the use of electronics business apparatus redirects respective business engagement and ensures business survival in the ongoing and post-COVID-19 occurrence (Baldwin & Mauro, 2020).

The electronics system of business was fully adopted to soften the decline of business operation in Nigeria as ILO (2020) noted the depreciation of economic activity with the occurrence of constraints on peoples' movement for both manufacturing and services. This was attributable to the quarantine measure in restraining the spread of the virus but without the due consideration of necessitated economic activities. From the view of McKibbin and Fernando (2020), the shock magnitude was similar to the experienced growth as MSMEs forcefully thinking out of the regular business engagement with the requirement of essential commodities while complimentary products and services were ignored. Hence, the target of every business, mostly the MSMEs was to survive the pandemic and to do this in a developing nation such as Nigeria, persuasion and marketability of products/services must have engaged by the business owners.

Disruptive Business Environment and Performance of MSMEs

The business environment in Nigeria is a perfect place that distorts the expected planned process as it requires the presence and involvement of other parameters. This was noted by (Abiodun et al., 2015) in the case of MTN, Nigeria displayed the current trend of a successful invasion of the telecommunication business in the country (Aaron & Marlen, 2013; Afutu-Kotey & Gough, 2019; Neuwirth, 2011). The assertion was confirmed by the stance of Ibidunni et al. (2016) on the divergence of business owners in response to the societal strains experienced in line with survival.

With the help of COVID-19, it became apparent that the view of Ibidunni et al. (2016) was not a developing nation adjustment but rather Lee and Cho (2016) had reflected in their study the potentiality of such being the case for a developed society. Thus, becoming a new occurrence for the global reaction to the pandemic.

From the identified parameters that are linked to opportunity exploitative facilitators, Ayeni et al. (2018) noted avoidance and manipulative ability. Webb et al. (2009, 2013) were the first researchers to identify these parameters. In an unprepared situation such as a pandemic, it is of essence that the ability of a business owner must support the identification of opportunity, where chaos is situated. Such has always been the occurrence in most developing nations such as Nigeria, where the silent encouragement is given by the Government to be a personalised local government (Yulita et al., 2020).

These attributes, being empirically tested by Ayeni et al. (2018) led to the knowledge of the social dialogue that must be in existence between the consumers and business owners after a business transaction has taken place, leading to customer retainment. The beauty of this is best reflected when electronic adverts with mobile devices, among others promote goods and services to the retained customers (Shan et al., 2016). This constructive and persistent interaction by the MSMEs leads to an adaptiveness response. Thus, leading to the acceptance of the disruption in the business environment (Sulkowski et al., 2018). In this case, the transformation of an electronic application transcending to a marketing platform for existing customers, vis-a-vis, becoming the business markers at a little or no charge.

This occurrence makes up the excuse for eliminating existing middlemen, products and services that would have been engaged (Nikiforou et al., 2020). This becomes acceptable with the COVID-19 situation where the business survival is deemed necessary, alongside the recuperation after the pandemic. Thus, calling for the reduction of cost at the barn of innovativeness while detecting opportunities in chaos to aid business operations at break-even. The globally unplanned and adjusted template was made possible with the pandemic occurrence in an electronic age.

A Capabilities-based Perspective to Surviving Environmental Disruptions

The impact of various epidemics resulting in disruptions in firm operations has formed an essential discourse in business periodicals and literature in very recent times. Etherington (2020) recounted the 2009 H1N1 pandemic that caused the Mexican tourism sector to a standstill and the 2003 SARS outbreak in Southeast Asian nations. Similarly, the outbreak of the West African Ebola Virus disease in 2014, according to the Centers for Disease Control and Prevention (2019) slowed-down growth in the agricultural sector leading to threats of food insecurity, and largely curtailed cross-border travel as a result of restrictions of movement of people, goods and services. According to Smith-Bingham and Hariharan (2020), the COVID-19 pandemic has primarily disrupted the business economy of China and supply chain operators around its economy resulting in the massive loss of jobs due to the closure of factories. Additional hundreds of millions have been restricted from travelling, hence halting air travel activities.

Organisational concerns about environmental disruptions are well established in the strategy and organisational behaviour literature, especially in the context of investigating firms' responsiveness to disruptions that arise from natural disasters and human-made attacks (Essuman et al., 2020). The perspective about firms' adaptiveness amidst pandemic outbreaks and having widespread global effects on human and economic activities remains an emerging issue of discourse in the literature. According to Duchek (2020), the adaptiveness of firms during disruptive times helps them to develop capabilities that are necessary to support their survival and come out of the tough times stronger. Thus, adaptiveness is not merely a measure of firm survival. Instead, it reflects the capability that firms develop to grow during and after a disruption. To develop such capabilities, firms need to have a view of adaptation to the tough times (Fiksel et al., 2015). Parker and Ameen (2018) suggest that by adopting the dynamic capabilities theory, firms will usually identify and deploy their strategic combination of resources to survive environmental turbulence and volatility.

14.3 Methodology

The study adopted a qualitative method to investigate strategies that are relevant to ensuring the adaptiveness of MSMEs during and after the current COVID-19 pandemic (Jong & van der Voordt, 2002) as a way to contribute to existing knowledge in the field of strategic management.

The reason for adopting a qualitative approach bares on the fact that the majority of MSMEs in Nigeria are newly exposed to the experiences of the present pandemic. Also, the purpose of this study centred around understanding respondents' opinions, feelings and thoughts about strategies that are critical to MSMEs' adaptiveness during and after the COVID-19 pandemic.

In particular, semi-structured interviewing was conducted to collect data from the respondents about what they have started adopting or intend to begin taking as viable strategies for continuing in business during and after the COVID-19 pandemic (Tsoukas & Vladimirou, 2001). This pattern of enquiry guided this research into determining new areas of knowledge and developing new research hypotheses rather than testing existing theories. Data were analysed using thematic analysis. Thematic analysis is a flexible method of analysis that identifies patterns and forms themes from a qualitative survey and raises discussions that are relevant to the objective of the study (Clarke & Braun, 2013).

Measures

A pilot interview helped to clarify various questions being asked, especially concerning the research context and to ensure seamless administration of the main fieldwork stage (Hoinville & Jowell, 1978). In the final interview guide, seven open-ended questions covered issues related to the focus of the research. These questions were further supplemented with probing questions. The probing questions allowed for further examination of the research issues and for more information on any point that was not entirely clear. Where the responses provided were not apparent to the interviewer, the question was rephrased to ensure meaningful interpretation by the interviewee.

Sampling

The population for this study included MSME operators in Nigeria, especially those in Lagos State because Lagos State is the commercial nerve of Nigeria. The Nigerian MSME sector is predominantly informal, and it accounts for more than 90% of economic activities in Nigeria (Wale-Oshinowo et al., 2018). Consequently, a study of this nature that seeks to identify strategies for the adaptiveness of MSMEs during and after the present COVID-19 pandemic will shed light on the socio-economic implications of the pandemic on Nigeria, and similar developing economies of the world.

The sample used for this study were thirty-one MSME operators that were conveniently chosen across different sectoral groups of the MSME sector according to respondents' willingness to partake in the interview, yet having vast experience in their various fields of economics and business engagements. The adoption of a purposive sampling technique was beneficial for this research for its minimal cost, reduced time advantage, implementation logistics and easy accessibility of the research participants (Patton, 2015). Moreover, this sample size is considered to be sufficient to identify the strategies that guide MSMEs' sustenance at these times, mainly relying on Morse's (2000) recommendation that for a qualitative study, a sample size of eight to twelve participants is adequate to attain in-depth descriptions and deduce implications from patterns of responses. Nonetheless, a total of thirty-one (31) MSME operators responded favourably and participated in this study.

Interview Protocol

The semi-structured interview instrument consisted of short and straightforward questions presented in an open-ended format to MSMEs operators to have them extensively share their personal opinion about strategies that they are adopting or intend to utilise to ensure the adaptiveness of their businesses during and after the COVID-19 pandemic. All interviews were conducted and completed in May 2020. The semi-structured interview instrument was administered to each respondent, through their emails, and they had sufficient time ranging between Forty-five minutes and one hour to respond to the interview questions. From the interviews, the study generated themes that were commonly expressed by the respondents and were significant to the objective of this research.

Table 14.1 shows the background information of the interviewees. In total, 31 MSME operators were interviewed. The respondents' nature of business services to manufacturing lines of business. Also, according to the Small and Medium Enterprises Development Agency of Nigeria (SMEDAN) (2007) and the Bank of Industry (2020), Microenterprises have employees of less than 10, and small enterprises have an employee size of 10–49. Hence, the majority of participants for this study are within the circle of micro and small enterprises. The table also shows that the firm age of the companies spans from 20 years (created in the year 2000) to less than one year (established in 2020).

14.4 Results and Discussion

This study developed and discussed the following themes.

Theme One: Effects of COVID-19 on MSMEs

The general comments from respondents revealed that the pandemic had positive effects on some businesses (see Fig. 14.1). According to a respondent, *"It offers the possibilities of running the business at very minimal cost to stay alive and in business. For example, we are taking advantage of digital mediums to reach out to our customers, rather than having to spend heavily on phone calls" (Respondent 1).* Another respondent who shared their views on the positive effects of the pandemic disclosed that *"We had a lot of requests from organisations to supply computers for Staff that work from home, and people order more gadgets due to the digital direction of the economy" (Respondent 4).* Respondent 14 shared the following view *"What I do is poultry farming in Kwara State. During the first phase of the lockdown, in which Kwara State embarked, we found difficulties in selling our products (eggs and chicken) even getting feed ingredients was another issue entirely. Then the value and price of products were falling drastically"*.

Meanwhile, some other participants perceived opportunities that translated into positive effects of the pandemic on their businesses. For a very minute few respondents, their views reflected in a state of partial to complete lockdown of business. A respondent established that *"We could not get new businesses while even the existing contracts were stalled because of*

Table 14.1 Background information of interviewees

Respondents	Nature of business	Firm size	Firm age	Number of matching cases (%)
R1	Management consulting	5	2018	6.45
R2	Telecommunication Services	5	2020	6.45
R3	Management consulting	8	2012	3.23
R4	Telecommunication Services	4	2015	6.45
R5	Food Services	5	2016	3.23
R6	Fashion	4	2008	3.23
R7	Photography	4	2017	3.23
R8	Farming	7	2018	3.23
R9	General merchandise	1	2019	3.23
R10	Fashion designer	3	2012	3.23
R11	Retail Service	50	2002	3.23
R12	Electronics Business	1	2007	3.23
R13	Education	52	2002	3.23
R14	Retail Service	3	2017	3.23
R15	Hospitality	6	2014	3.23
R16	Financial Services	8	2017	3.23
R17	Shoemaking	1	2017	3.23
R18	Rental services	1	2000	3.23
R19	Baby & Child care	1	2011	3.23
R20	Web Application development and business advisory	8	2010	3.23
R21	Event planning and catering services	4	2016	3.23
R22	Publishing	3	2009	3.23
R23	Manufacturing	12	2005	3.23
R24	Waste recycling	6	2007	3.23
R25	Jersey Sales	10	2019	3.23
R26	Graphics and Publicity Solutions	3	2015	3.23
R27	Event Planning Services	6	2019	3.23
R28	Retail	4	2019	3.23
R29	Fashion	1	2020	
R30	Branding Services	2	2017	
R31	Consultancy	5	2017	

Fig. 14.1 Analysed response on effects of COVID-19 on MSMEs

lockdown" (Respondent 3). Respondent 10 simply replied that "*Due to the nature of my business, no one is ready to make dresses because all occasions have been cancelled*".

However, the largest number of these respondents identified the opportunities that abounded with the harmful surrounding disruptions and were able to redirect theirs and their firms' efforts to a more positive direction that ensured business continuity. For example, Respondent 21 opined that business has suffered "low sales—lack of access to the market. The high cost of the product" but on a positive note, the pandemic has "*opens my eyes to another method of doing business. Help me build and focus my business online*". Similarly, another respondent shared that the downside of the pandemic is that "*It has reduced the number of walk-in customers, and sewing cloth is not a priority for people now*", yet the positive side is that it has resulted in *an "Increase in demand for the hand-made facemask" (Respondent 29)*, hence diversifying the respondent's area of business.

The mixed findings from this study about how MSMEs operators perceive and develop capabilities around the impact of disruptions on the businesses are consistent with reports from the literature (for example, Dogbe et al., 2020; Mohamud & Sarpong, 2016). MSME operators generally have entrepreneurial traits and characteristics that help them convert difficulties into opportunities and hence ensure the adaptiveness of their businesses. Opportunity identification and strategic resources mobilisation to fulfil those opportunities is a strategic capability that entrepreneurs engage in ensuring that environmental turbulences are converted to firm-based advantages (Adegbuyi et al., 2018). The insertion of opinion of the effect of COVID-19 on MSMEs as displayed in the Fig. 14.1 shows the collated response of the respondents on utilising the online business with the perception of change coming with involving the financial institutions. This in some cases required training and where not possible, the need to request the personnel comes in. thereby increasing the tech jobs demands. We could therefore state that the pandemic has resulted into the adoption of an overhaul to partial change of MSMEs businesses. This comes without their permission as the urgency to survive thrives in.

Theme Two: Operational Strategies of MSMEs During Corona Virus Disease Pandemic

Respondents were asked about their operating strategies during the pandemic and a possible change of strategy in their operations. The answers revealed that MSMEs operators in Nigeria have opened up to virtual reality and digital platforms for ensuring business continuity as forms of maintaining adaptiveness during the period of disruptions caused by the pandemic (see Fig. 14.2). For example, Respondent 7 who claimed that before the pandemic the business operated by "*Customer relations, fast response time to projects*" further established that since the pandemic began, the business has had to settle for "*virtual communication*" as its principal operating strategy. Similarly, Respondent 13 which operates an education services firm opined that the business' primary operating strategy has been "*We provided high quality educational primary and secondary school services at an affordable rate*". Nevertheless, with the emergence of the environmental disruptions caused by the pandemic, the business operations have been through "*virtual*" means. Hence the focus of the business has not only resided in a cost advantage strategy or a low-cost strategy. However, there is now the inclusion of virtual means of reaching customers at the same lost cost and quality.

Also, the responses from several respondents revealed that part of the coping strategies for sustaining business operations during the pandemic

Fig. 14.2 Analysed response on operational strategies of MSMEs during Corona Virus Disease Pandemic

was the diversification strategy, either in the complete form or a horizontal diversification. For example, a respondent claimed that "*yes*" the business has had to diversify and that *"the new line of business is an essential service most especially at this time" (Respondent 15).* Another respondent also affirmed that during the pandemic the business has diversified into essential needs *"We focused on products that customers will need during this period, such as tripod stands for online training, tabs for children, and so on... did massive adverts and got great feedback" (Respondent 4).*

The findings from the present study reveal that the pandemic has forced MSME operators to become more innovative and adaptable to the current disruptions. The result from our study is consistent with the suggestions made by Fiksel et al. (2015) that disruptions propel firms to engage their capabilities in ensuring adaptability to the challenges posed by the environment rather than thinking of failure as an option. The current trends with the pandemic have opened MSMEs to new digital realisation and the possibilities of adjusting their firms' operations and supply chain modalities to virtual possibilities, while yet sustaining the firm's existence. The main adaptation was to be involved int eh online presence and this was shown in Fig. 14.2. Furthermore, the attachment of the services rendered with delivery strategies was needfully employed as stated by the business owners. We can postulate at this junction that marketability of the products/services entrails the customers to the businesses and as such during the pandemic volume was not the essence but the operational strategy was the quality of the product/services delivered periodically or rendered.

Theme Three: Directions for Future Operations and Possible Policy Frameworks

The opinion gathered from this theme provided insight into the futuristic thinking of the MSME operators. It reflects, also, their opinion about the role of government in supporting the continuity of MSMEs and policy directions to consider hereafter. The general opinion of respondents revolved around the need to become more digitally oriented in the operations of the firms (see Fig. 14.3). For example, a respondent established that the business would *"be more tech-savvy never undermining the importance of IT"* *(Respondent 7)*. Also, another respondent opined that *"We would continue to deploy our services remotely" (Respondent 16)*.

Fig. 14.3 Analysed response on future business operations and probable strategy contexts during corona virus disease pandemic

About the possible areas of support from the government, the insights supplied by the respondents will serve as eye-openers. A respondent established that *"the government is not doing anything to ensure business survival. The Covid-19 funds advertised come with highly unreachable requirements" (Respondent 20).* Hence, calling attention to the fact that funding must be available and accessible, based on the assurance that the requirements support the peculiarity of the informal MSMEs in Nigeria. Also, another respondent raised the challenge of power *"do we have a government? Our government are not helping businesses as far as am concerned, imagine in a country where you cannot operate fully well because of power holding and their high tariff" (Respondent 24).*

This research has answered the question of whether MSME operators in Nigeria have gathered sufficient experience from the present pandemic that will inform their preparedness for future unforeseen disruptions. Organisational adaptiveness encompasses the capabilities that firms have to survive pandemics and sustain existence and growth over time. The present findings from the study reveal that the MSME operators are having a strategic view towards the future sustenance of their firms. For business operators, technological adaptability and operational dynamism are critical resources for adaptiveness. Indeed, Yu et al. (2019) affirmed that supply chain dynamism supports firms' responses to the business environment. The engagement of the QSR Nvivo 12 on the gathered data furthered aided suggested theme of the future operations ad possible framework of the businesses in COVID-era and it was spatulated that the upshot of delivery businesses must be intwined with online services for sustainability. The reference to timeliness by the clients was much-added preference for retainment of their respective businesses in all sectors. Marketing was purely never undermined for a reference by clients. From the attached Fig. 14.3, it can be seen that the loyalty flows seemliness well with quality and type of services rendered irrespective of the tie and season.

14.5 Implications for Theory and Practice

The present study has made an original contribution to the field of strategy and organisational behaviour by establishing the adaptiveness of firms during periods of unexpected disruptions caused by health-related outbreaks. Whereas the strategy literature has widely established firms' responsiveness to human-made and natural disruptions, the event of the coronavirus disease with its widespread and global shut down of economies opened businesses to the need for more responsive strategies to organisational adaptiveness (see Fig. 14.4). The context of this current research, being MSMEs in an informal developing economy, presents new insights into how firms are reacting swiftly to ensure continuity and sustained economic performance. The key ideas from this research reflect the need for MSMEs operators to diversify their operational strategies into technology-induced business models, rather than the current over-reliance on in-person methods of operating business. The findings imply the need for practices such as virtual operations, consciousness in empowering technology-driven supply chains, and more concentration on fulfilling customer demands in the most minimal time possible. The findings from this study also suggest that governments of developing economies must now give more focus to technology-based investments that can support businesses to thrive. Indeed, this will imply the need to ensure a technology-driven society where supply chains and businesses can operate smoothly with minimal in-person contact.

Theoretically, this study has demonstrated the appropriateness of the dynamic competencies theory in supporting the growth of developing economies during times of unforeseen environmental disruptions. There is also, therefore, a call for more intense interrogations into the different peculiar roles and applicable methods that the dynamic competencies theory could take to support the growth of Africa's, and other developing economies during disruptions.

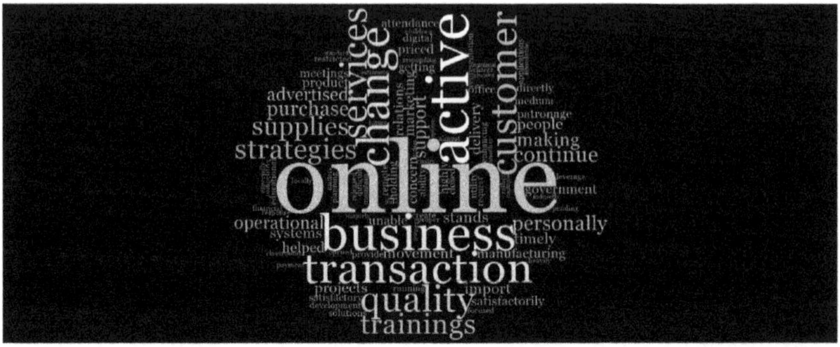

Fig. 14.4 Analysed response on implication of Corona virus disease pandemic on developing economies

14.6 Conclusion and Further Research

This study concludes that MSMEs in Nigeria demonstrate capabilities that help them to be adaptive during times of environmental disruptions. Respondents for this present study included MSMEs operators in Nigeria. The findings reflect the capability of entrepreneurs in Nigeria, and the importance that they place, on ensuring that their businesses continue to operate during health-induced global environmental disruptions and remain sustainable beyond the disruptions. This was shown in the evidence of firms responding with fast adopting digital methods and the possibilities of adjusting their firms' operations and supply chain modalities to virtual possibilities, while yet sustaining the firm's existence. Earlier in this study, the contributions were discussed. Nevertheless, this study recommends that further research extends investigations into the applicability of dynamic competencies theory within other developing competencies to identify specific strategies and characteristics of MSMEs during times of environmental disruptions.

References

Aaron, B., & Marlen, L. (2013, May 29). *Supporting people to legitimise their informal businesses*. JRF. https://www.jrf.org.uk/report/supporting-people-legitimise-their-informal-businesses

Abiodun, A. J., Ibidunni, A. S., & Kehinde, O. J. (2015). Demographic determinants of communication and information technology appreciation and usage among health care professionals. *International Journal of Health Economics, 5*, 5–19.

Adegbuyi, A. A., Oladele, O. P., Iyiola, O. O., Adegbuyi, O. A., Ogunnaike, O. O., Ibidunni, A. S., & Fadeyi, O. I. (2018). Assessing the influence of entrepreneurial orientation on small and medium enterprises' performance. *International Journal of Entrepreneurship, 22*(4), 1–7.

Afutu-Kotey, R. L., & Gough, K. V. (2019). Bricolage and informal businesses: Young entrepreneurs in the mobile telephony sector in Accra, Ghana. *Futures,* 102487. https://doi.org/10.1016/j.futures.2019.102487

Ayeni, A. W. (2016). *Assessing an electronic market in an informal economy*. LAP LAMBERT Academic Publishing.

Ayeni, A. W., Ogunnaike, O. O., Iyiola, O. O., Ezenwoke, O. A., & Ibidunni, S. (2018). Data article on institutional framework and business survivals of informal entrepreneurs in the electronics market, Southwest, Nigeria. *Data in Brief, 19*, 1297–1304. https://doi.org/10.1016/j.dib.2018.05.092

Baldwin, R., & Di Mauro, B. W. (2020). Economics in the time of COVID-19: A new eBook. *VOX CEPR Policy Portal*, *2*(3). Retrieved on 31st August 2023 from https://fondazionecerm.it/wp-content/uploads/2020/03/CEPREconomics-in-the-time-of-COVID-19_-A-new-eBook.pdf

Centres for Disease Control and Prevention. (2019). *Ebola (Ebola Virus Disease).* https://www.cdc.gov/vhf/ebola/history/2014-2016-outbreak/cost-of-ebola.html. Accessed on 31 August 2020.

Clarke, V., & Braun, V. (2013). Teaching thematic analysis: Overcoming challenges and developing strategies for effective learning. *The Psychologist, 26*(2), 120–123.

Colombo, M. G., Piva, E., Quas, A., & Rossi-Lamastra, C. (2020). Dynamic capabilities and high-tech entrepreneurial ventures' performance in the aftermath of an environmental jolt. *Long Range Planning*. https://doi.org/10.1016/j.lrp.2020.102026

COVID-19: *A Business Impact Series—KPMG Nigeria*. (2020, July 1). KPMG. https://home.kpmg/ng/en/home/insights/2020/04/covid-19--a-business-impact-series.html

De Jong, T. M., & van der Voordt, D. J. M. (2002). *Ways to study and research: Urban, architectural and technical design*. Delft University Press.

Dogbe, C. S. K., Tian, H., Pomegbe, W. W. K., Sarsah, S. A., & Otoo, C. O. A. (2020). Effect of network embeddedness on innovation performance of small and medium-sized enterprises: The moderating role of innovation openness. *Journal of Strategy and Management, 13*(2), 181–197. https://doi.org/10.1108/JSMA-07-2019-0126

Duchek, S. (2020). Organisational adaptiveness: A capability-based conceptualisation. *Business Research, 13*, 215–246. https://doi.org/10.1007/s40685-019-0085-7

Essuman, D., Boso, N., & Annan, J. (2020). Operational adaptiveness, disruption, and efficiency: Conceptual and empirical analyses. *International Journal of Production Economics, 229*, 107762. https://doi.org/10.1016/j.ijpe.2020.107762

Etherington, J. (2020). *The business effects of pandemics*. https://www.tenentrepreneurs.org/blog/6y5flr3m5556ke61aa19zxolyf3s07. Accessed on 31 August 2020.

Fiksel, J., Polyviou, M., Croxton, K. L., & Pettit, T. J. (2015, Winter). From risk to adaptiveness: Learning to deal with disruption. *MIT Sloan Management Review*, 1–18. https://sloanreview.mit.edu/article/from-risk-to-adaptiveness-learning-to-deal-with-disruption/

Haarhaus, T., & Liening, A. (2020). Building dynamic capabilities to cope with environmental uncertainty: The role of strategic foresight. *Technological Forecasting & Social Change, 155*, 120033. https://doi.org/10.1016/j.techfore.2020.120033

Hoinville, G., & Jowell, R. (1978). *Survey research practice*. Heinemann.

Humphries, J. E., Neilson, C., & Ulyssea, G. (2020). *The evolving impacts of Covid-19 on small businesses since the cares act* (Cowles Foundation Discussion Paper No. 2230). Retrieved on April 26, 2020, from http://cowles.yale.edu/

Ibidunni, S., Osibanjo, O., Adeniji, A., Salau, O. P., & Falola, H. (2016). Talent retention and organisational performance: A competitive positioning in Nigerian banking sector. *Periodica Polytechnica Social and Management Sciences, 24*(1), 1–13. https://doi.org/10.3311/PPso.7958

Ighobor, K. (2020). *Small businesses in Africa must innovate to survive COVID-19 impact*. https://www.un.org/africarenewal/magazine/july-2020/small-businesses-africa-must-innovate-survive-covid-19. Accessed 1 September 2020.

International Labour Organization (ILO) (2020). ILO Monitor: COVID-19 and the World of Work. Seventh Edition Updated Estimates and Analysis. https://www.ilo.org/wcmsp5/groups/public/%40dgreports/%40dcomm/documents/briefingnote/wcms_767028.pdf

Lee, A., & Cho, J. (2016). The impact of epidemics on labor market: identifying victims of the Middle East Respiratory Syndrome in the Korean labor market. *International Journal for Equity in Health, 15*(1), 1–15.

McKie, R., Helm, T., & Savage, M. (2020, April 18). Don't bet on vaccines to protect us from Covid-19, says world health expert. *The Observer*. https://www.theguardian.com/world/2020/apr/18/dont-bet-on-vaccine-to-protect-us-from-covid-19-says-world-health-expert

McKibbin, W., & Fernando, R. (2020). Economics in the Time of COVID-19. *London: Centre for Economic Policy Research*, 45–51.

Mohamud, M., & Sarpong, D. (2016). Dynamic capabilities: Towards an organising framework. *Journal of Strategy and Management, 9*(4), 511–526. https://doi.org/10.1108/JSMA-11-2015-0088

Morse, J. M. (2000). Determining sample size. *Qualitative Health Research, 10*(1), 3–5. https://doi.org/10.1177/104973200129118183

National Bureau of Statistics. (2019). *2019 poverty and inequality in Nigeria: Executive summary*. http://nigerianstat.gov.ng/elibrary?queries[search]=poverty

Neuwirth, R. (2011, December 6). How MTN is profiting from Nigeria's informal economy. *How We Made It In Africa*. http://www.howwemadeitinafrica.com/how-mtn-is-profiting-from-nigeria%e2%80%99s-informal-economy/13808/

Nikiforou, A. "Iro," Lioukas, S., & Voudouris, I. (2020). Network structure and firm-level entrepreneurial behaviour: The role of market and technological knowledge networks. *Journal of Business Research, 106*, 129–138. https://doi.org/10.1016/j.jbusres.2019.09.008

Olawoyin, O. (2020, August 14). *Update: Nigeria's unemployment rate rises to 27.1%—NBS*. https://www.premiumtimesng.com/news/top-news/408790-nigerias-unemployment-rate-rises-to-27-1-nbs.html

Oluranti, S., Odunaike, B. A., & Jawando, J. O. (2015). Informal economy operators and the challenges of growth in Oyo Kingdom, Nigeria. *International Journal of Social Sciences and Humanities Review, 5*(3), 162–167.

Parker, H., & Ameen, K. (2018). The role of adaptiveness capabilities in shaping how firms respond to disruptions. *Journal of Business Research, 88*, 535–541. https://doi.org/10.1016/j.jbusres.2017.12.022

Patton, M. Q. (2015). *Qualitative evaluation and research methods*. Sage.

Sahara Reporters. (2020, May 3). *COVID-19: Group condemns mass retrenchment of workers, deduction of salaries*. Sahara Reporters. http://saharareporters.com/2020/05/03/covid-19-group-condemns-mass-retrenchment-workers-deduction-salaries

Shan, L., Lin, L., Sun, C., & Wang, X. (2016). Predicting ad click-through rates via feature-based fully coupled interaction tensor factorization. *Electronic Commerce Research and Applications*, *16*, 30–42.

Smith-Bingham, R., & Hariharan, K. (2020). *This is the impact of the Coronavirus on business*. https://www.weforum.org/agenda/2020/02/why-is-coronavirus-a-global-business-risk/. Accessed on 31 August 2020.

Sulkowski, A. J., Edwards, M., & Freeman, R. E. (2018). Shake your stakeholder: Firms leading engagement to cocreate sustainable value. *Organization & Environment, 31*(3), 223–241.

Tsoukas, H., & Vladimirou, E. (2001). What is organisational knowledge? *Journal of Management Studies, 38*(7), 973–993.

Wale-Oshinowo, B. A., Lebura, S., Ibidunni, A. S., & Jevwegaga, H. (2018). Understanding survival strategies in micro and small enterprises in Nigeria: A brief review of the literature. *Covenant Journal of Entrepreneurship, 2*(1), 72–78.

Webb, J. W., Bruton, G. D., Tihanyi, L., & Ireland, R. D. (2013). Research on entrepreneurship in the informal economy: Framing a research agenda. *Journal of Business Venturing, 28*(5), 598–614. https://doi.org/10.1016/j.jbusvent.2012.05.003

Webb, J. W., Tihanyi, L., Ireland, R. D., & Sirmon, D. G. (2009). You say illegal, i say legitimate: Entrepreneurship in the informal economy. *Academy of Management Review, 34*(3), 492–510. https://doi.org/10.5465/amr.2009.40632826

Yu, W., Jacobs, M. A., Chavez, R., & Yang, J. (2019). Dynamism, disruption orientation, and adaptiveness in the supply chain and the impacts on financial performance: A dynamic capabilities perspective. *International Journal of Production Economics, 218*, 352–362. https://doi.org/10.1016/j.ijpe.2019.07.013

Yulita, M. S., Kulub Abdul Rashid, N., Hussain, N. E., Mohamad Akhir, N. H., & Ahmat, N. (2020). Resilience as a moderator of government and family support in explaining entrepreneurial interest and readiness among single mothers. *Journal of Business Venturing Insights, 13*, e00157. https://doi.org/10.1016/j.jbvi.2020.e00157

15

Entrepreneurship and Economic Development: A Leadership Framework

Abdullah Promise Opute, Bridget N. Irene, Caroline Jawad, and Patricia C. Agupusi

15.1 Introduction

Over the last decades, the importance of entrepreneurship activity as a core economic growth factor has been reiterated (e.g., GEM, 2017/2018; Opute et al., 2021; Schumpeter, 1911, 1934). Given that importance, entrepreneurship activity remains a critical global thematic for scholars as

A. P. Opute (✉) · C. Jawad
University of Wales Trinity Saint David, Lampeter, Wales, UK
e-mail: a.opute@uwtsd.ac.uk

C. Jawad
e-mail: c.jawad@uwtsd.ac.uk

B. N. Irene
Coventry University, Coventry, UK
e-mail: Ad3587@coventry.ac.uk

P. C. Agupusi
American University, Washington, DC, USA
e-mail: agupusi@american.edu

A. S. Ibidunni et al. (eds.), *Innovation, Entrepreneurship and the Informal Economy in Sub–Saharan Africa*, Sustainable Development Goals Series,
https://doi.org/10.1007/978-3-031-46293-1_15

well as governments and policy makers. Consequently, there is increasing advocacy for knowledge development in this domain (e.g., Nwankwo & Gbadamosi, 2020; Opute et al., 2021; Piñeiro-Chousa et al., 2020). Within the entrepreneurship discourse, a major contrast is found from the point of how entrepreneurship activity has enabled economic growth: while Western context insights document a significant economic growth impact (e.g., Audretsch et al., 2018; Colombo et al., 2014; OECD, 2019), insights from the SSA setting point to less productive outcome despite increasing entrepreneurship endeavours (e.g., GEM, 2017/2018; Iwu & Opute, 2019; Iwu et al., 2020c). As a matter of fact, in both latter cases, Iwu and his colleagues lament the typical survivalist nature of entrepreneurship in the SSA domain, and consequently the incapacity to contribute to economic growth.

Recent literature that supports the advocacy for more productive alignment of entrepreneurship activity in the SSA setting underlines the pertinence for rethinking the strategies to enable economic growth impacting entrepreneurship (e.g., Ibidunni et al., 2022; Opute et al., 2021). It is this rethinking logic that drives this chapter which aims to contribute to the increasing effort for more illumination of entrepreneurship activity, and economic growth impact, in the SSA context. Taking this rethinking approach is a critical way forward towards steering entrepreneurship activity for combating the ever-increasing unemployment and poverty levels in the SSA setting.

Economic development theorists have severally underlined the importance of entrepreneurship leadership towards driving economic growth impacting entrepreneurship (e.g., Fritsch, 2017; Schumpeter, 1911, 1934). In a recent Call for Chapters that lend a voice to the advocacy for further knowledge development of entrepreneurship in the SSA setting, Eniola et al. (2021) emphasise not only critical entrepreneurship bottlenecks in the SSA context but also the pertinence for strategic leadership initiatives. Succinctly captured, while domain literature flags numerous impediments to productive entrepreneurship outcome in the SSA setting, a common thread in the discourse relates to ineffective entrepreneurship ecosystem alignment (Eniola et al., 2021). In the contemporary global economic landscape where economies are facing massive challenge in containing increasing unemployment and poverty, the aforementioned advocacy could not be more valid. Organisations need to embrace strategic and pro-active leadership initiatives towards enabling them to effectively cope with the increasing challenge of competing effectively in the market (and satisfying the customers) (e.g., Hussain et al., 2017; Opute, 2020; Opute et al., 2020b). Furthermore, literature underlines the criticality for entrepreneurship to embrace effective leadership that enables them to adapt effectively to turbulent developments (e.g., Ibidunni et al., 2022; Opute et al., 2020b). This is a major research premise and this chapter aims to contribute to knowledge in this domain and offer a strategic guide for a more economic development enhancing entrepreneurship focus in the SSA setting where unemployment and poverty remain enormous challenges.

The chapter is organised thus: First, the theoretical framing is explained. In doing that, the theorising of entrepreneurship and underlying rationality are also explained. Following that, the leadership focus of this chapter is explained, emphasising the importance of this approach to achieving productive entrepreneurship towards boosting economic development and combating unemployment and poverty in the sensitised context. A dual leadership conceptualisation that combines entrepreneur and government aspects is forwarded in this chapter. To conclude, this chapter offers relevant recommendations and flags directions for further knowledge development in this domain.

15.2 Conceptual Framing of This Chapter

While literature has re-echoed the importance of entrepreneurship in steering sustainable economic growth and national well-being (e.g., GEM Report, 2017/2018; Opute et al., 2021, 2022b), entrepreneurship literature about sub-Saharan Africa (SSA) suggests that the economic growth impact of entrepreneurship remains relatively low (e.g., Iwu & Opute, 2019; Iwu et al., 2020; Zachary, 2020), and as a result the economic challenges of high levels of unemployment and poverty remain major concerns in that setting. As noted further by these scholars, entrepreneurship activity in the SSA contest is relatively survivalist natured. This chapter supports the thesis that productive entrepreneurship that would boost economic growth and combat unemployment and poverty can be achieved in SSA if entrepreneurship effort is strategically initiated and implemented. Next, the entrepreneurship viewpoint forwarded in this chapter is specified. Following that, key entrepreneurship statistics about the SSA context compared to other contexts are presented.

15.3 Entrepreneurship and Entrepreneurship Measures in This Chapter

In a perspective that recognises the importance of strategic orientation and marketing logic, Kraus et al. (2010) submit thus: "'entrepreneurship' is an adjective that describes an approach to marketing that embraces the opportunities of the marketplace in terms of an effective implementation of price, place, promotion, and product tactics (four Ps) by being risk-taking, innovative, and proactive" (p. 21). Emphasising the criticality of innovation in development discourse, Schumpeter—a pioneer in entrepreneurship discourse and once referred to as "prophet of innovation" (McCraw, 2007, cited in Croitoru, 2012, p. 137), describes the activity of entrepreneurs to include, amongst others, creating new investment, growth and employment opportunities (Schumpeter, 1911/2008). Recent literature has not only reinforced the new investment creating substance (e.g., Opute, 2020; Opute et al., 2021) but also underlined the importance of more strategic and entrepreneurial marketing focus towards driving productive entrepreneurship (e.g., Nwankwo, 2020; Nwankwo & Gbadamosi, 2020; Opute, 2020).

Grounded in the development viewpoint, this chapter takes into consideration the aforementioned (Opute, 2020; Opute et al., 2021; Schumpeter, 1911/2008) views. Therefore, we conceptualise an entrepreneurship viewpoint that leverages Schumpeter (1911)—Schumpeterian "theory of economic development" and Schumpeterian vision of the entrepreneur; bearing in mind however the importance for a strategic orientation for achieving productive entrepreneurship (e.g., Opute, 2020; Opute et al., 2021).

In the entrepreneurship contextualisation for this chapter, we invoke GEM's conceptual framework for steering development and enhancing entrepreneurship. GEM's framework recognises that "entrepreneurship is part of a complex feedback system and makes explicit the relationships among social values, personal attributes and various forms of entrepreneurial activity" (GEM Report, 2017/2018, p. 13). The framework underlines the interdependency between entrepreneurship and economic development to (GEM, 2017/2018, p. 12):

- identify conditioners (enablers or disablers) of entrepreneurial activity, particularly regarding societal values, personal attributes, and entrepreneurship ecosystem;
- offer a platform for gauging the association between entrepreneurial activity and economic growth in individual economies; and
- ascertain policy implications with regards to boosting entrepreneurial capacity in an economy.

GEM (2017/2018) describes a two-component framework (NFCs and EFCs—see Leadership Theory, Strategic Leadership and Entrepreneurial Effectiveness) of entrepreneurship indicators for economic development. Comparative to other regions, SSA is significantly underachieving in the majority of the entrepreneurship indicators (see Tables 15.1 and 15.2).

As documented in GEM (2017/2018), at 6.9 (see Table 15.3), Africa has a significantly higher discontinuation of business rate (percentage of population aged 18–64) compared to other regions—Asia and Oceania (5.5), Latin America and Caribbean (5.2), Europe (2.9) and North America (5.5). This is a major concern and as the statistics for South Africa show (see Table 3), business discontinuation rate has been on the increase except in 2016. Thus, African entrepreneurships have a shorter longevity, an outcome that no doubt is traceable to inadequate entrepreneurial ecosystem alignment. Based on statistical evidence (see Table 15.2), GEM (2017/2018) pinpoints a major contributing factor to the low economic development impact of entrepreneurship in the SSA context: despite the encouraging high level of opportunity-driven

Table 15.1 Ranking of Entrepreneurial Activity Types in Africa (GEM, 2017) Percentage of Population aged 18–64 years

Economy	Nascent Entrepreneurship rate		New business ownership rate		Early-Stage entrepreneurial activity (TEA)		EEA		Established business ownership rate		Discontinuation of businesses*	
	Score	Rate /54	Score	Rate /54	Score	Rate /54	Score	Rate /54	Score	Rate /54	Score	Rate /54
Egypt	6.5	25	7	11	13.3	19T	2.2	29	5.7	38	10.2	1
Madagascar	10.9	8	11.2	6	21.8	7	0.6	45T	29.4	2	6.7	10
Morocco	4.2	38	4.6	26T	8.8	37	0.5	48T	10.4	14T	4.5	23
South Africa	7.5	21	3.8	33T	11	27	0.5	48T	2.2	50	6	15T
Total	7.3		6.6		13.7		0.9		11.9		6.9	

* Business Discontinuation—percentage of nascent stage entrepreneurs or owner-manager of businesses (aged 18–64 years) who discontinued their business in the 12 months before the study

Table 15.2 Opportunity- and Necessity-drive TEA rates amongst the adult population of South Africa. Percentage of population aged 18–64 years

	2001	2005	2010	2013	2015	2016	2017	Africa Region 2017 (Average)
Necessity-driven (%of TEA)	N18.2*	39.5	36.0	30.3	33.2	23.6	24.9	27.9
Opportunity-driven (% of TEA)	64.7	57	60.7	68.6	65.7	74.4	75.1	70.9
Ratio (Necessity vs. Opportunity	0.3	0.7	0.6	0.4	0.5	0.3	0.3	0.4

* Read as 18.2% of TEA activity in 2001 was necessity-driven
Source Global Entrepreneurship Monitor (GEM) (2017/2018: 25)

Table 15.3 Prevalence Rates (%) of Adult Population Entrepreneurial Activity in South Africa, 2001–2017. Percentage of Population aged 18–64 years

	2001	2005	2009	2013	2015	2016	2017	Africa Region 2017 (Average)
Nascent Entrepreneurial Rate	5.3	3.6	3.6	6.6	5.5	3.9	7.5	7.3
New Business Ownership Rate	1.4	1.7	2.5	4.1	3.8	3.3	3.8	6.6
TEA	6.5	6.2	5.9	10.6	9.2	6.9	11.0	13.7
Established Business Ownership Rate		1.3	1.4	2.9	3.4	2.5	2.2	11.9
Business Discontinuation Rate		2.9	3.5	3.9	4.8	4.5	6.0	6.9

TEA, not enough is done in the area of necessity-driven TEA towards absorbing the unemployment and underemployment pressure arising from the ever-increasing population.

15.4 Leadership Theory, Strategic Leadership and Entrepreneurial Effectiveness

The importance of effective leadership to organisational well-being has been substantially documented (e.g., Hussain et al., 2017; Knies et al., 2016; Opute, 2014; Opute et al., 2020b), Responding to increasing advocacy for further illumination of this importance (see Introduction), this chapter forwards a leadership framework towards enhancing entrepreneurship impact on economic growth. Literature distils several leadership styles. It is not a central focus in this chapter to engage with the various leadership typologies, rather, the aim is to provide a leadership viewpoint that draws from the fit theory. Thus, the term leadership in this chapter draws from Schumpeter's (1911, 1934) connotation of entrepreneurship leadership and refers to a leader's method and how the leader strategises and implements the entrepreneurship activity.

Economic development theorists have emphasised the criticality for effective leadership in steering entrepreneurship for economic development (e.g., Fritsch, 2017; Schumpeter, 1911, 1934). Over 100 years after Schumpeter (1911) underlined the importance of entrepreneurship leadership, this significance is ever increasing as nations globally struggle to contain unemployment and poverty challenges. Scholars have categorised good leadership qualities to include being honest, forward looking, competent and inspiring, as well as flexibility and adaptability to operational environment (Kouzes & Posner, 2007). In a marketing perspective that recognises crisis response (Covid-19) pertinence, Opute et al. (2020b) underline forward looking, competence, flexibility and pro-activeness as critical attributes. Elaborating, Opute et al. (2020b) emphasise that leadership must be strategic, responsive and operationally aligned towards profitably satisfying customers who, as noted by Opute et al. (2022) are increasingly becoming powerful in their purchase decision making due to globalisation and technological evolution impact.

Sustainability perspective on leadership underscores the criticality for caring and inspiring others, bearing in mind the well-being of humanity and other aspects of life and nature (Avery & Bergsteiner, 2011). This chapter recognises these management, marketing and sustainability perspectives in forwarding knowledge on how entrepreneurship in the sub-Saharan Africa setting could be productively steered.

Having effective entrepreneurship leadership in place is fundamental to achieving entrepreneurship activity that would enable the entrepreneurship focus in this chapter and economic growth potency of entrepreneurship. Effective entrepreneurship leadership is essential to ensure that the entrepreneurial processes are strategically organised and core elements of marketing (product, price, place and promotion) are effectively implemented to satisfy the customers at a profit. Offering a comprehensive guide for optimising economic growth enhancing entrepreneurship, GEM (2017/2018) underlines the pertinence of two critical components (pp. 12–13): National Framework Conditions (NFCs) and Entrepreneurship Framework Conditions (EFCs). While the former considers societal advancement "through the three phases of economic development (factor-driven, efficiency-driven and innovation-driven)", the latter emphasises entrepreneurial ecosystem quality, such as "entrepreneurial financing, government policy, government entrepreneurship programmes, entrepreneurship education, research and development (R&D) transfer, commercial and legal infrastructure, internal market dynamics and entry regulations, physical infrastructure, and cultural and social norms". In conceptualising leadership in this chapter, a dual approach that leverages GEM's (2017/2018) NFCs and EFCs viewpoint, is taken. Specifically, the leadership focus in this chapter aligns to the importance for factor-driven, efficiency-driven and innovation pertinence in strategizing entrepreneurship for optimum economic development impact. Also, recognising the importance of the government to play an active role in facilitating entrepreneurship activity and economic development outcome, the leadership focus takes into consideration the EFCs of entrepreneurial financing, government policy, government entrepreneurship programmes, entrepreneurship education and physical infrastructure (specifically technological facilities). Within that focus, we forward a leadership lens that underscores the importance of entrepreneurial skills-set for steering productive entrepreneurship. Secondly, we forward a leadership aspect that recognises the critical facilitating role that governments play in steering economic growth impacting entrepreneurship.

15.5 Leadership Perspective One: Entrepreneurial Skills-Set

The need to effectively skill entrepreneurs has been re-echoed in entrepreneurship discourse. For example, much research effort has been invested into understanding entrepreneurship education (e.g., Iwu et al., 2020b; Opute et al., 2021, 2022b; Ratten & Jones, 2020) and other related entrepreneurship aspects. In this chapter, we focus on three elements of entrepreneurial skills-set (entrepreneurial marketing, innovative drive and technology and social media).

Entrepreneurial Marketing

Effectively achieving economic development requires a dynamic approach (e.g., Fritsch, 2017; Schumpeter, 1911, 1934). From the entrepreneurial point, insights that align to this dynamic approach foundation have re-echoed the need for entrepreneurial marketing approach (e.g., Nwankwo & Gbadamosi, 2020; Opute, 2020; Theodoraki et al., 2018). To thrive and fulfil its snowballing economic growth impact, entrepreneurial marketing tool must be leveraged to strategically steer entrepreneurial activity (Opute, 2020).

Entrepreneurs must possess leadership skills that enable them to understand the importance of entrepreneurial marketing and how to contextualise it for optimum entrepreneurial productivity. Entrepreneurs must embrace marketing logic that prioritises the target of creating value. Entrepreneurs' leadership initiatives should focus around strategic marketing orientation to identify market problems in the entrepreneurial space, finding novel solutions, leveraging opportunities, embracing flexibility and creativity and staying pro-active in the entrepreneurial activity focus.

Innovative Drive

According to economic development theorists (e.g., Fritsch, 2017), the German economist Schumpeter, in his book titled *Theorie der wirtschaftlichen Entwicklung* (1911), was the pioneer in underlining the importance of innovation to entrepreneurship and economic development. Fritsch (2013) notes that innovation spurs the growth process while (Piñeiro-Chousa et al., 2020) add that innovation is one of the bases of economic growth. Schumpeter notes that anyone seeking profit must innovate (Schumpeter, 1911, 1934). The critical importance in steering economic growth impacting entrepreneurship has been numerously underlined in the literature (e.g., McAdam et al., 2016; Opute, 2020; Opute et al., 2021). Indeed, literature notes that innovation is a core driver of competitiveness (e.g., Ibidunni et al., 2021; Opute, 2020) and economic dynamics (e.g., Opute et al., 2021). Schumpeter (1934) distilled five innovation strategies:

1. New product launch or enhancing already existing products with unique features (see also, Opute, 2020);
2. Application of innovative (new in the industry) strategies in production or product sales;
3. Penetrating a new market (see also Opute, 2020);
4. Exploring new supply channels for raw material or semi-finished goods;
5. Explore options for creating a new industry structure (leading to, or destruction of a monopoly position.

Unlike other regions, SSA is yet to recognise the criticality of innovation orientation in entrepreneurship (see Table 15.4) (GEM, 2017/2018). Recognising the importance of innovation and enforcing innovation orientation in entrepreneurship requires a leadership focus that galvanises innovation mindset. Entrepreneurship leadership would not only need to be conscious of these innovation options but must also make a committed effort to strategically and effectively initiate and implement such innovation effort.

Utilising Technology and Social Media

As technology constantly evolves, global dynamics are witnessing tremendous transformations as a consequence. For example, in marketing literature, technological evolution enabled marketing paradigm shift from physical place (marketing mix) to virtual place has been documented (e.g., Opute et al., 2020b, 2022a; Rachinger et al., 2019). Thus, selling is no longer physical domain based but rather transpires digitally. The challenges faced by organisations, as well as individuals, as a consequences of the Covid-19 induced movement restriction have reminded of the pertinence for alternatives to the physical place operational modus. Technology-enabled marketing is a critical alternative that entrepreneurs must utilise in their entrepreneurial marketing initiatives. Entrepreneurs must possess leadership skills that would enable them to understand the technology utility for marketing and also effectively organising their entrepreneurial marketing strategies to optimise that utility. With such leadership skills, entrepreneurs would also be able to effectively utilise social media to network with other entrepreneurs and engage closely with customers. Such leadership skills would also enable the entrepreneur to strategically organise the marketing practices to secure competitive capacity in both local and global markets (Opute, 2020; Rachinger et al., 2019) and also keep in mind inclusivity aspects for ensuring broad consumers coverage (Opute et al., 2022a).

15.6 Leadership Perspective Two: Government as Facilitator

The pertinence for the government to actively fulfil its facilitating role in driving economic growth impacting entrepreneurship has been lauded in entrepreneurship discourse (e.g., Iwu & Opute, 2019; Iwu et al., 2020c).

Table 15.4 GEM economies by geographical region & economic development level 2017

Country	Factor-driven Economies	Efficiency-driven Economies	Innovation-driven Economies
Africa	Madagascar	Egypt, Morocco, South Africa	
Asia and Oceania	India, Kazakhstan, Vietnam	China (PRC), Indonesia, Iran, Lebanon, Malaysia, Saudi Arabia, Thailand	Australia, Israel, Qatar, Republic of South Korea, Taiwan, United Arab Emirates, Japan
Latin America & Caribbean		Argentina, Brazil, Chile, Colombia, Ecuador, Guatemala, Mexico., Panama, Peru, Uruguay	Puerto Rico
Europe		Bulgaria, Bosnia & Herzegovina, Croatia, Latvia, Poland, Slovakia	Cyprus, Estonia, France, Germany, Greece, Ireland, Italy, Luxembourg, Netherlands, Slovenia, Spain, Sweden, Switzerland, United Kingdom
North America			Canada, United States

The government can fulfil this facilitating role in several ways that include supporting mechanisms and strategies for enabling new business start-ups and sustenance towards contributing to economic growth (Iwu & Opute, 2021). In this leadership aspect, this chapter considers three facilitating strategies that the government can exploit to boost productive entrepreneurship (government policies, financial facilitation and digital enablement).

Government Policies

As a primary institutional change agent in national economies, the government must understand and strive to fulfil its primary responsibility in enhancing regional economic competitiveness and igniting entrepreneurship spirit in the information economy era (Yoon et al., 2015). A critical element in that responsibility relates to ensuring appropriate policies GEM (2017/2018). As noted by Bjerke and Johansson (2015), knowledge exchange amongst innovation networks is the secret to the success of small and medium-sized businesses in entrepreneurship. The government must develop practical policies for key players in entrepreneurial innovations to enhance initiatives in order to absorb knowledge and its capacity to transform that knowledge (Huggins & Thompson, 2015).

The government can play a major facilitating role in promoting competition and overall economic efficiency by ensuring policies that enable entrepreneurships effectively navigate business environment constraints. A 2016 MENA survey of businesses found that large corporations are more productive, but they use capital inefficiently. Insights on SMEs in South Africa point to business environment's inefficiencies and lack of government policies that enable these businesses to effectively navigate through such challenges (Iwu & Opute, 2019; Iwu et al., 2020c). Government policies that would eliminate bottlenecks, ease restrictions and enable strategic entrepreneurship activity and generally improve competitiveness are critical for equitable economic growth (EBRD, 2016). The ability of businesses to thrive, invest, create jobs and innovate, which in turn boosts productivity and competitiveness, hinges critically on a supportive business environment.

As noted by EBRD (2016), policy makers continue to place a high focus on understanding the variables that might be limiting the expansion of private enterprises and on resolving these limitations through regulatory changes (EBRD, For instance, the Arab Spring and their aftermath, as well as unsolved social tensions and conflicts in the MENA region, are all reflected in the MENA ES findings, which identify political instability as the most frequently cited barrier to private sector development (EBRD, 2016). Strategic government policies would not only facilitate the ability of affected businesses to effectively navigate such challenges but also enable start-ups and sustenance of entrepreneurships. GEM has consistently emphasised that while it is not the government's job to launch new businesses, it is unquestionably their duty to create an environment that is conducive to doing so. This includes eliminating obstacles that hinder easy launch of new ventures, and ability to succeed, and potentially, create new jobs (GEM, 2017/2018).

Financial Facilitation

Another aspect that the government can play a facilitating leadership role relates to finance. According to Huang et al. (2022), fiscal and tax policies/strategy encourages innovation and productivity growth by enticing start-ups to enter the market, mostly in the form of financial subsidies and tax advantages (Aghion et al., 2015). Improving enterprise innovation performance is made possible by the relationship between tax incentives and business R&D spending (Dai & Chapman, 2022). A good fiscal and tax policy can encourage businesses to file for patents on their inventions and can provide a favourable climate for independent innovation. Enterprise finance policies would enable entrepreneurs (Qi et al., 2020), and the enterprise innovation index is a significant reflection of entrepreneurship and innovation, and in general, fiscal and tax policies can directly assist enterprise innovation activities (Fan et al., 2020).

According to the EBRD's, 2016 study of the MENA ES economies, the private sector remains largely unconnected to the financial system in the majority of the nations surveyed. The potential for private sector growth may be substantially hampered by this. As further noted by EBRD (2016), the loss of job growth is a cost of financial exclusion. These expenses are especially significant in communities where persistent underemployment is a problem. Even while demand and supply considerations may both contribute to such financial exclusion, it is obvious that this is a less-than-ideal result. The research also identifies possible avenues for re-establishing business relationships with the financial sector. Access to financing is projected to benefit from increased bank competition and decreased governmental funding requirements. The EBRD, 2016 study also demonstrates how the large level of credit extended to governments and state-owned businesses makes the MENA ES area unique. By formulating policies, governments can offer risk-adjusted returns that are more attractive than private sector borrowing, driving out the marginal private sector borrowers. Some governments have increased spending in the wake of the "Arab Springs" in an effort to maintain social harmony and economic activity. For instance, in Egypt, demands on the public sector rose from 27% of GDP in 2010 to more than 50% in 2015. There are few options to fiscal consolidation, which is expected to reverse some of the crowding-out seen in recent years, as a result of the expansionary policies' strain on the fiscal buffers. Programs to improve banks' ability to evaluate credit risk should go hand in hand with a regulatory shift in favour of more competition. The authors of the EBRD (2016) report argues that financial stability should not be sacrificed in order to increase financial access. To avoid competition-driven reckless lending practises, the institutional structure needs to be modified. Such initiatives may also lessen possible reform resistance from incumbents, who will be better equipped to handle the difficulties that come with increased competition (Campos et al., 2015; McKenzie & Woodruff, 2017).

Previous reports on the state of entrepreneurship such as GEM (2017/2018), OECD (2020/2021) have suggested that government policies can support initiatives to increase the capacity of banks and the supply of bankable businesses. Such initiatives, they argue, ought to be designed to decrease information asymmetries that hinder lending to SMEs by making them less opaque. In actuality, this can entail assisting business owners in creating a business plan or an organisational structure. However, such programmes are limited by the fact that they are inevitably tiny in comparison to the size of the economy (Yu et al., 2014). Increased competition might encourage banks to look for new market niches like SME financing. As long as the proper organisational structure is not in place, SME lending may not be appealing to banks focusing on corporates. However, competition might encourage organisational and procedural reform, which would make it easier for people to get financing. In light of this, government/bank regulators may want to consider the level of competition when assessing licence applications.

Digital/Technology Enablement

Societies globally are increasingly becoming digital and technology enabled (Opute, 2022). The pertinence therefore for businesses to recognise this technology era transition and ensure competition fit for the post-pandemic era has been repeatedly lauded in recent literature (e.g., Opute, 2022; Opute et al., 2022a, 2022b). For entrepreneurships, achieving the stakes in this dispensation requires government actively playing its leadership role by ensuring facilitating mechanisms. Economic transformation, which includes a digital transformation strategy, has an impact on how competitive innovation systems, particularly when it comes to changes in resource demand, network operations and communication channels in entrepreneurial activities (Satalkina & Steiner, 2020). Innovative small and medium-sized firms are now faced with multiple challenges in the form of heavy financial burden, technical challenges and a skills scarcity (Gamache et al., 2019). Through strategic policy and hands-on-deck mechanisms, the government can play a significant facilitating role in helping entrepreneurs effectively navigate these challenges. For example, the government can enforce digital transformation laws to aid businesses in navigating the complexity of change and to appreciate the value of sharing information, expertise, data and technology in order to encourage entrepreneurship (Hao & Zhang, 2021).

The government could also initiate ways to enhance management model and strengthen entrepreneurship (Oluwatobi et al., 2015). According to Urbano and Alvarez (2014), the likelihood of entrepreneurial success can be increased by reducing the number of entrepreneurial procedures and raising cultural knowledge. Government-sponsored e-government initiatives can streamline the procedures and steps needed for entrepreneurship, lower the time and money expenses for entrepreneurs, and foster enterprise innovation (Das & Das, 2021). Additionally, government exposure and entrepreneurial initiatives may help to build an entrepreneurial culture and inspire entrepreneurs. As part of its leadership strategies, government's facilitating initiative could also involve funding technology hubs (Opute et al., 2022a) that could be leveraged by entrepreneurships that may not have the capacity to own relevant technology and digital infrastructure.

15.7 Recommendations

Over the years, the fact that entrepreneurship impact on economic development remains significantly low in sub-Saharan Africa has been reiterated (e.g., Iwu & Opute, 2019; Opute et al., 2021). Recognising the pertinence for a committed effort to change the tide, entrepreneurship in Africa has featured significantly in academic discourse (e.g., Adeola et al., 2023; Ibidunni et al., 2022; Irene et al., 2022; Opute et al., 2021, 2022b), as well as gained much governmental attention in the last decade. According to Schumpeter (2008), entrepreneurial profit constitutes an "independent value phenomenon fundamentally connected with the role of leadership in the economic system" (p. 147). Responding to increasing advocacy for pro-active and futuristic entrepreneurship perspective (e.g., Ivanova & Rimanoczy, 2022; Opute et al., 2021, 2022b), this chapter concurs with Schumpeter's leadership role viewpoint and forwards a leadership framework (See Fig. 15.1).

Re-echoing critical guideline for economic development enhancing entrepreneurship (GEM, 2017/2018), the leadership framework

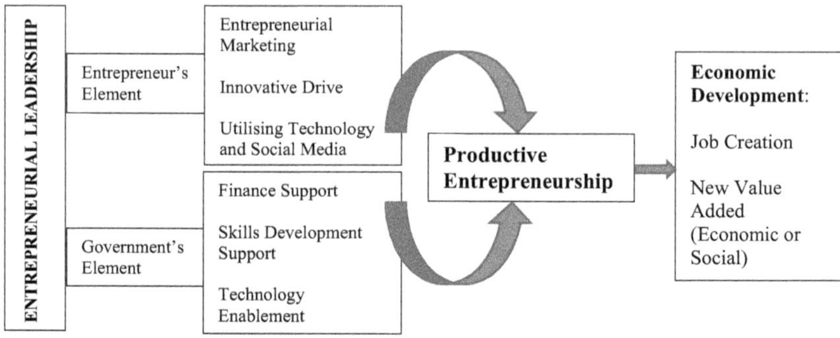

Fig. 15.1 A leadership framework for steering economic growth impacting entrepreneurship

forwarded in this chapter aligns with the foundation that entrepreneurship activity is the outcome of the tripartite interaction between an individual's perception of an opportunity, an entrepreneur's motivation and skills to act and the respective environmental conditions of the individual (entrepreneur).

GEM has consistently suggested a direct association of the level of education to an individual's business start-up and sustainability beyond the nascent stage of development (GEM Report, 2017/2018) By implication, people with higher level of education are highly likely to be entrepreneurial as they perceive themselves to be skilled enough to successfully run a business. Recent literature has not only reinforced that logic (e.g., Iwu et al., 2020a; Valencia-Arias et al., 2021) but also lauded the advocacy for more illumination of entrepreneurship education and entrepreneurship impact (e.g., Iwu & Opute, 2021; Iwu et al., 2020b; Opute et al., 2022b). Specifically, on the SSA setting, GEM (2017/2018) Global Competitive Index report notes that poor quality of the education system is a hindrance to improving entrepreneurial activity while Opute et al. (2022b) lament not only the inadequateness of the curriculum content but also failure to strategically structure entrepreneurship education to effectively galvanise entrepreneurial uptake and equip students with necessary problem-solving, entrepreneurial marketing and pro-active mindset. Genuine efforts must be made towards addressing these bottlenecks of entrepreneurial activity. To fully achieve that and meet the level for realising reasonable entrepreneurial indicators (social values, individual attributed and entrepreneurial activity) levels to secure the economic development indicators (see Fig. 15.1), the government must committedly play its supporting and facilitating role in analysing the ecosystem and ensuring mechanisms that would help entrepreneurs embraces steps in productively steering their entrepreneurial activities.

As shown earlier (see entrepreneurship and entrepreneurship measures in this chapter), the level of business discontinuation in Africa is high, which is worrying given the ever increasing population in this region. Poor alignment of the entrepreneurial ecosystem is associated to this discontinuation and overall entrepreneurial failure in this region and of multiple central issues in that regard relates to the fact that "entrepreneurs lack the necessary skills and experience to start and run a business" (GEM, 2017/2018, p. 25). Critical leadership effort relates to strategic government facilitating initiative towards providing entrepreneurship coaching (on innovation, problem-solving mindset), technical training (on entrepreneurial marketing, entrepreneurial networking, technology-enabled marketing) and mentorships. In its leadership role, the government can facilitate these targets by adequately funding entrepreneurial universities and working closely with all relevant stakeholders (universities, entrepreneurial consultants, coaches, research institutes and relevant government partners) in the drive to raise entrepreneurial awareness, galvanise necessity-driven entrepreneurial start-ups and also aid established businesses for sustainability. Innovation is a critical element in driving productive entrepreneurship (Schumpeter, 1911, 1934; GEM, 2017/2018). In its leadership and facilitating function, the government should not only ensure policies that underline that importance but also play an active role in realising and sustaining innovation-driven entrepreneurship.

Technology has become a constituent part of daily life (Opute, 2022), and as underlined by Opute et al. (2020b), the consequences of the Covid-19 induced movement restriction has intensified technological importance in societies and post-Covid organisations must not only have a futuristic mindset but also be technologically fit. Strategic government facilitating initiative should also recognise the pertinence for government to invest in public information and communication technology (hubs) that can easily be utilised by small entrepreneurships that may not afford own technology/digital infrastructure (Opute et al., 2022a). Government can fund ICT infrastructures that enable digital economy. Effort must also be made to ensure that entrepreneurship education curriculum is strategically structured to enhance the ICT skills of trainees to equip them with relevant Know-How for entrepreneurial activity. Such ICT skills are vital to enabling entrepreneurs to think outside the box and embrace a futuristic, innovative approach that meets digital marketing requirements for the post-pandemic era.

15.8 Future Research Directions

Innovation is a critical entrepreneurship element for driving economic growth (Opute, 2020; Schumpeter, 1911, 1934). Further literature has emphasised the need for government to fully play its supporting role in steering productive entrepreneurship (e.g., Huang et al., 2022; Opute et al., 2021, 2022b). Exploring Chinese context, Huang et al. (2022) forward that the extent of association to regional innovation capability (RIC) and extendedly entrepreneurial success would hinge on the nature of entrepreneurship policies. For the SSA setting, research is needed to understand the nature of entrepreneurship policies (entrepreneur's and government's aspects) and how these impact on innovation capability and overall economic development impact of entrepreneurship.

Further studies should also give more attention to start-up elements of entrepreneurship to illuminate the antecedents and success rate from the point of longevity and contribution to economic growth (including also job creation). Further on the point of entrepreneurship longevity, a significant level of business discontinuation has been documented in the SSA setting compared to other continents (see Table 15.3). For appropriate leadership intervention actions, future research should aim to shed more light on the factors that explain that trend.

Steering entrepreneurship activity in the SSA setting to a point where the economic growth snowballing impact can be achieved requires a comprehensive ecosystems approach. Within that approach is a committed research drive that is also steered towards understanding the different entrepreneurship forms (e.g., SMEs, family entrepreneurships, women entrepreneurships, informal entrepreneurships, amongst others) and the different entrepreneurship growth levels.

Though not considered in the conceptual framing of this chapter, the critical importance of entrepreneurial networking in the pursuit of active entrepreneurship for enhancing economic development has been reiterated in the literature (e.g., McAdam et al., 2018; Nwankwo & Gbadamosi, 2020; Opute, 2020; Opute et al., 2022c). Re-echoing Opute et al.'s (2022c) advocacy, we draw attention to the need for more effort (empirical and conceptual) towards enhancing the understanding of how entrepreneurship networks could be optimally leveraged for economic growth enhancing entrepreneurship. In that regard too, requisite leadership requirements should be illuminated.

References

Adeola, O., Opute, A. P., Chukwuka, B., Adisa, I., & Orekoya, I. (2023). *Entrepreneurship and COVID-19: A socio-psychological perspective*. Palgrave Macmillan.

Aghion, P., Cai, J., Dewatripont, M., Du, L., Harrison, A., & Legros, P. (2015). Industrial policy and competition. *American Economic Journal: Macroeconomics, 7*(4), 1–32. doi:10.1257/mac.20120103

Audretsch, D. B., Belitski, M., & Desai, S. (2018). National business regulations and city entrepreneurship in Europe: A multilevel nested analysis. *Entrepreneurship Theory and Practice, 4*, 6.

Avery, G. C., & Bergsteiner, H. (2011). *Sustainable leadership: Honeybee and locust approaches* (1st ed.). Routledge.

Bjerke, L., & Johansson, S. (2015). Patterns of innovation and collaboration in small and large firms. *The Annals of Regional Science, 55*, 221–247.

Campos, F., Goldstein, M., McKenzie, D. J., & Campos, F. M. L. (2015). *Short-term impacts of formalization assistance and a bank information session on business registration and access to finance in Malawi* (World Bank Policy Research Working Paper 7183).

Colombo, M. G., De Massis, A., Piva, E., Rossi-Lamastra, C., & Wright, M. (2014). Sales and employment changes in entrepreneurial ventures with

family ownership: Empirical evidence from high-tech industries. *Journal of Small Business Management, 52*(2), 226–245.
Croitoru, A. (2012). Schumpeter, J. A. (1934/2008). The theory of economic development: An inquiry into profits, capital, credit, interest and the business cycle (Translated from the German by Redvers Opie, New Brunswick [U.S.A] and London [U.K.]): Transaction Publishers. *Journal of Comparative Research in Anthropology and Sociology, 3*(2), 137–148.
Dai, X., & Chapman, G. (2022). R&D tax incentives and innovation: Examining the role of programme design in China. *Technovation, 113*, 102419. https://doi.org/10.1016/j.technovation.2021.102419
Das, A., & Das, S. S. (2021). E-Government and entrepreneurship: Online government services and the ease of starting business. *Information Systems Frontiers*, 1–13. doi:10.1007/s10796-021-10121-z
EBRD. (2016). *What is holding back the Private Sector in Mena? Lessons from the Enterprise Survey*. Report by the European Bank for Reconstruction and Development, the European Investment Bank, and the International Bank for Reconstruction and Development/The World Bank.
Eniola, A. A., Iwu, C. G., & Opute, A. P. (2021). *Call for chapters—The future of entrepreneurship in Africa, challenges and opportunities post-pandemic*. Palgrave Macmillan. Routledge, Taylor & Francis.
Fan, F., Lian, H., & Wang, S. (2020). Can regional collaborative innovation improve innovation efficiency? An empirical study of Chinese cities. *Growth and Change, 51*(1), 440–463. https://doi.org/10.1111/grow.12346
Fritsch, M. (2013). New business formation and regional development: A survey and assessment of the evidence. *Foundations and Trends in Entrepreneurship, 9*, 249–364. https://doi.org/10.1561/030000004
Fritsch, M. (2017). The theory of economic development—An inquiry into profits, capital, credit, interest, and the business cycle. *Regional Studies*. https://doi.org/10.1080/00343404.2017.1278975
Gamache, S., Abdul-Nour, G., & Baril, C. (2019). Development of a digital performance assessment model for Quebec manufacturing SMEs. *Procedia Manufacturing, 38*, 1085–1094.
Global Entrepreneurship Monitor (GEM). (2017/2018). *Is there a change in attitude towards the small and medium business sector in South Africa?* (M. Herrington & P. Kew, Eds.). https://www.gemconsortium.org/file/open?fileId=50411. Accessed on 29 November 2022.
Hao, W., & Zhang, J. (2021, May). *The reality, risk and governance of regional innovation ecosystems under digital transformation background*. IOP Conference Series: Earth and Environmental Science. IOP Publishing 022052.

Huang, Y., Li, S., Xiang, X., Bu, Y. & Guo, Y. (2022). How can the combination of entrepreneurship policies activate regional innovation capability? A comparative study of Chinese provinces based on fsQCA. *Jorúrnal of Innovation and Knowledge, 7.* https://doi.org/10.1016/j.jik.2022.100227

Huggins, R., & Thompson, P. (2015). Entrepreneurship, innovation, and regional growth: A network theory. *Small Business Economics, 45*, 103–128.

Hussain, S. T., Abbas, J., Lei, S., Jamal Haider, M., & Akram, T. (2017). Transactional leadership and organizational creativity: Examining the mediating role of knowledge sharing behavior. *Cogent Business & Management, 4*(1), 1361663.

Ibidunni, A. S., Ayeni, A. W., Ogundana, A. M., Otokiti, B., & Mohalajeng, L. (2022). Survival during times of disruptions: Rethinking strategies for enabling business viability in the developing economy. *Sustainability,* 14. https://doi.org/10.3390/su142013549

Ibidunni, A. S., Ufua, D. E., & Opute, A. P. (2021). Linking disruptive innovation to sustainable entrepreneurship within the context of small and medium firms: A focus on Nigeria. *African Journal of Science, Technology, Innovation and Development.* https://doi.org/10.1080/20421338.2021.1975355

Irene, B. N. O., Opute, A. P., & Murithi, W. (2022). *An empirical insight into the factors affecting the oscillation of women between self and paid employment in South Africa*. Palgrave Macmillan.

Ivanova, E., & Rimanoczy, I. (2022, Forthcoming). Revolutionising sustainability education: Stories and tools of mindset transformation. *The Principles for Responsible Management Series*. Routledge. ISBN 9781032135380

Iwu, C. G., Eze, I., Opute, A. P., Dongo, G., & Dongo, O. W. (2020a). Scavenging for survival and its health implications. The Nexus between unemployment and ill-health. *WSEAS Transactions on Environment and Development, 17*(1), 1–18.

Iwu, C. G., & Opute, A. P. (2019). Eradicating poverty and unemployment: Narratives of survivalist entrepreneurs. *Journal of Reviews on Global Economics,* 1438–1451. DOI:https://doi.org/10.6000/1929-7092.2019.08.127

Iwu, C. G, & Opute, A. P. (2021). Steering productive entrepreneurship activities in emerging markets: The Role of the University. In *The role of universities and their entrepreneurial ecosystems in advocating sustainability* Chapter 14 in *Universities, entrepreneurial ecosystems and sustainability* (C. Fernandes, M. Ramírez-Pasillas, & J. J. Ferreira). De Gruyter studies in knowledge management and entrepreneurial ecosystems. Walter De Gruyter GmbH, Berlin/Boston. ISBN 9783110670165.

Iwu, C. G., Opute, A. P., Nchu, R., Babatunde, A. A., Iwu, C. H., & Eze, I. F. (2020b). The antecedents of University students' entrepreneurship intention. The Theory of Planned Behaviour Viewpoint. *Harvard Deusto Business Research, IX*(2), 221–240.

Iwu, C. G., Opute, A. P., Nchu, R., Eresia-Eke, C., Tengeh, R. K., Jaiyeoba, O., & Aliyu, O. A. (2020c). Entrepreneurship education, curriculum and lecturer—Competency as antecedents of student entrepreneurial intention. *International Journal of Management Education.* https://doi.org/10.1016/j.ijme.2019.03.007

Knies, E., Jacobsen, C., & Tummers, L. (2016). Leadership and organizational performance. In J. Storey, J. Hartley, J.-L. Denis, P. 't Hart, & D. Ulrich (Eds.), *The Routledge companion to leadership* (pp. 404–418). Routledge.

Kouzes, J. M., & Posner, B. Z. (2007). *The leadership challenge* (5th ed.). Jossey-Boss.

Kraus, S., Harms, R., & Fink, M. (2010). Entrepreneurial marketing: Moving beyond marketing in new ventures. *International Journal of Entrepreneurship and Innovation Management, 11*(1), 19–34.

McAdam, M., Harrison, R. T., & Leitch, C. M. (2018). Stories from the field: Women's networking as gender capital in entrepreneurial ecosystems. *Small Business Economics, 53*, 459–474. https://doi.org/10.1007/s11187-018-9995-6

McAdam, M., McAdam, R., Dunn, A., & McCall, C. (2016). Regional horizontal networks within the SME agri-food sector: An innovation and social network perspective. *Regional Studies, 50*(8), 1316–1329.

McCraw, T. (2007). *Prophet of innovation: Joseph Schumpeter and creative destruction.* Belknap Press of Harvard University Press.

McKenzie, D., & Woodruff, C. (2017). Business practices in small firms in developing countries. *Management Science, 63*(9), 2967–2981.

Nwankwo, S. (2020). Contemporary issues in entrepreneurship marketing, sustainability, ethics and social responsibility. In S. Nwankwo & A. Gbadamosi (Eds.), *Entrepreneurship marketing: Principles and practice of SME Marketing*. Routledge.

Nwankwo, S., & Gbadamosi, A. (Eds.). (2020). *Entrepreneurship marketing: Principles and practice of SME marketing*. Routledge.

OECD. (2019). *OECD SME and entrepreneurship outlook 2019.*

Oluwatobi, S., Efobi, U. R., Olurinola, I. O., & Alege, P. O. (2015). Innovation in Africa: Why institutions matter. *South African Journal of Economics, 83*, 390–410. https://doi.org/10.1111/saje.12071

Opute, A. P. (2014). Cross-functional bridge in dyadic relationship: Conflict management and performance implications. *Team Performance Management, 20*(3/4), 121–147.

Opute, A. P. (2020). Small and medium enterprises marketing: Innovation and sustainable economic growth perspective (Chapter 2). In *Entrepreneurship marketing: Principles and practice of SME marketing*. Routledge.

Opute, A. P., Irene, B. N., & Iwu, C. G. (2020a). Tourism service and digital technologies: A value creation perspective. *African Journal of Hospitality, Tourism and Leisure, 9*(2). ISSN:223-814X.

Opute, A. P., Iwu, C. G., Adeola, O., Mugobo, V., Okeke-Uzodike, O. E., Fagbola, S., and Jaiyeoba, O. (2020b). The Covid-19 pandemic and implications for businesses: Innovative retail marketing viewpoint. *Retail Marketing Review, 16*, SE.

Opute, A. P. (2022). Virtual teams: The new work norm for the post Covid-19 era. In O. Adeola, J. N. Edeh, R. E. Hinson, & F. Netswera (Eds.), *Digital service delivery in Africa.* Palgrave Studies of Marketing in Emerging Economies. Palgrave Macmillan, Cham. https://doi.org/10.1007/978-3-030-83909-3_13

Opute, A. P., Chukwuma-Nwuba, E. O., Iwu, C. G., Eniola, A. A., Ojra, J., & Irene, J. (2022a). *Productive entrepreneurship: Entrepreneurial networking perspective and research agenda.* Palgrave Macmillan, Springer Publications.

Opute, A. P., Kalu, K. I., Adeola, O., & Iwu, C. G. (2021). Steering sustainable economic growth: Entrepreneurial ecosystem approach. *Journal of Entrepreneurship and Innovation in Emerging Economies, 7*(2), 1–30.

Opute, A. P., Kalu, I. K., Chukwuma-Nwuba, E. O., Ojra, J., & Iwu, C. G. (2022b). Technology and marketing: Understanding the interface and Post-Covid-19 implications (Chapter 12, pp. 208–220). In *Critical perspectives on diversity, equity and inclusion in marketing* (A. Gbadamosi, Ed.). IGI Global Publishers. DOI: https://doi.org/10.4018/978-1-6684-3590-8.ch012.

Opute, A. P., Kalu, I. K., Mezieobi, K. C., Iwu, C. G., Hagos, S. B., & Obor, D. O. (2022c). *Entrepreneurship education and productive entrepreneurship.* Palgrave Macmillan, Springer.

Piñeiro-Chousa, J., López-Cabarcos, M. A., Romero-Castro, N. M., & Pérez-Pico, A. M. (2020). Innovation, entrepreneurship and knowledge in the business scientific field: Mapping the research front. *Journal of Business Research, 115*, 475–485. https://doi.org/10.1016/j.jbusres.2019.11.045

Qi, Y., Peng, W., & Xiong, N. N. (2020). The effects of fiscal and tax incentives on regional innovation capability: Text extraction based on python. *Mathematics, 8*(7), 1193. https://doi.org/10.3390/math8071193

Rachinger, M., Rauter, R., Müller, C., Vorraber, W., & Schirgi, E. (2019). Digitalisation and its influence on business model innovation. *Journal of Manufacturing Technology Management, 30*(8), 1143–1160.
Ratten, V., & Jones, P. (2020). Entrepreneurship and management education: Exploring trends and gaps. *The International Journal of Management Education.* https://doi.org/10.1016/j.ijme.2020.100431
Satalkina, L., & Steiner, G. (2020). Digital entrepreneurship and its role in innovation systems: A systematic literature review as a basis for future research avenues for sustainable transitions. *Sustainability, 12*(7), 2764.
Schumpeter, J. A. (1934). *The theory of economic development: An inquiry into profits, capital, credit, interest and the business cycle* (Vol. 46). Harvard University Press.
Schumpeter, J. A. [1911] (2008). *The theory of economic development: An inquiry into profits, capital, credit, interest and the business cycle* (Translated from the German by Redvers Opie, New Brunswick [U.S.A] and London (U.K.)]. Transaction Publishers.
Theodoraki, C., Messeghem, K., & Rice, M. P. (2018). A social capital approach to the development of sustainable entrepreneurial ecosystems: An explorative study. *Small Business Economics, 51*(1), 153–170. https://doi.org/10.1007/s11187-017-9924-0
Urbano, D., & Alvarez, C. (2014). Institutional dimensions and entrepreneurial activity: An international study. *Small Business Economics, 42*, 703–716. https://doi.org/10.1007/s11187-013-9523-7
Valencia-Arias, A., Arango-Botero, D., & Sanchez-Torres, J. A. (2021). Promoting entrepreneurship based on university students' perceptions of entrepreneurial attitude, university environment, entrepreneurial culture and entrepreneurial training. *Higher Education, Skills and Work-based Learning*. DOI https://doi.org/10.1108/HESWBL-07-2020-0169.
Yoon, H., Yun, S., Lee, J., & Phillips, F. (2015). Entrepreneurship in East Asian regional innovation systems: Role of social capital. *Technological Forecasting and Social Change, 100*, 83–95. https://doi.org/10.1016/j.techfore.2015.06.028
Yu, B., Hao, S., Ahlstrom, D., Si, S., & Liang, D. (2014). Entrepreneurial firms' network competence, technological capability, and new product development performance. *Asia Pacific Journal of Management, 31*, 687–704.
Zachary, D. (2020). *What is the future of poverty in Africa?* Institute for Security Studies. https://issafrica.org/iss-today/what-is-the-future-of-poverty-in-africa

16

Conclusion: Informal Economy as a Springboard for Innovation and Entrepreneurship Development in Sub-Saharan Africa

Ayodotun Stephen Ibidunni, Oyedele Martins Ogundana, and Maxwell Ayodele Olokundun

16.1 Introduction

While there is generally no established description of the informal economy (IE) in the literature (Luque, 2022), phrases like the unreported economy, shadow economy, or black economy (Medina et al.,

A. S. Ibidunni (✉)
Department of Business Administration, Chrisland University, Abeokuta, Nigeria
e-mail: aibidunni@chrislanduniversity.edu.ng

International Centre for Policy Research and Industry Linkages (ICePRIL), Shaveh Consulting, Abeokuta, Nigeria

Centre for Economic Policy and Development Research (CEPDeR), Covenant University, Ota, Nigeria

O. M. Ogundana
Accounting and Finance Department, Nottingham Trent University, Nottingham, UK
e-mail: Oyedele.ogundana@ntu.ac.uk

A. S. Ibidunni et al. (eds.), *Innovation, Entrepreneurship and the Informal Economy in Sub–Saharan Africa*, Sustainable Development Goals Series,
https://doi.org/10.1007/978-3-031-46293-1_16

2017). Also, it is established that the informal economy exists as a global phenomenon; however, there are variations within and across countries, especially in terms of size, characteristics, motivations for participation, regulations and contribution to the national economy (Williams & Kedir, 2018).

The concept of informality was brought to light in the late 1960s when Hart coined the concept of the informal sector to describe economic activities that rural migrants in Accra, Ghana, engaged in to overcome external constraints and seek autonomous capacities for generating income (Hart, 1973). Hart (2009) established that the conceptualization of the informal sector emanated from "a sequence of events that took in America's losing war in Vietnam, the dollar's detachment from gold in 1971, and the subsequent dismantling of the Bretton Woods regime of fixed parity exchange rates". The concept was later developed into the informal economy to establish that informality is not limited to a sector but reflects economic activities (Luque, 2022). The International Labour Organization (ILO, 2002) clarified that the informal economy refers to all economic activities carried out by workers and economic units that—in law or practice—are not covered or are insufficiently covered in formal systems. Later, the International Labour Organization (ILO, 2015) further clarified that the term informal economy "does not cover illegal activities and that the expression "economic units" in the definition refers to units that a) employ labour, b) correspond to people who work on their account; c) they function as cooperatives and social and solidarity economy units". Williams and Horodnic (2016) corroborate that the informal economy consists of socially legitimate activities but remain undeclared to the authorities for tax, social security or labour law purposes.

Sub-Saharan Africa (SSA), in the year 2021, has an approximated population of 1.18 billion people (World Bank Group, 2023), and

---

M. A. Olokundun
Department of Business Administration, London Metropolitan University, London, UK
e-mail: maxwell.olokundun@covenantuniversity.edu.ng

it accounts for nearly 85% of employment in the region (International Labour Organization, 2023). The growing interest of sub-Saharan Africans in IE results from the challenges of tax burdens, the continued growth in unemployment, and the inequitable distribution of income (Makochekanwa, 2020). Much of the economic activities included in the informal economy of SSA are street trading and vending, sit-at-home services, workers on building sites, road works, kiosk operators, ship-droppers, independent business operators and temporary job workers.

The motivations for venturing into informal economy entrepreneurship in the SSA remain an emerging discussion in the literature (Ibidunni, 2022). Researchers have investigated the necessity-versus opportunity-driven thesis of entrepreneurial engagement in SSA's informal economy (Afreh et al., 2019). The necessity-driven entrepreneurs are motivated or forced into participating in entrepreneurship from economic and social challenges that affect their living conditions. Thus, venturing into self-employment is perceived as a bailout (Etim & Daramola, 2020). Meanwhile, opportunity-driven entrepreneurs are motivated by entrepreneurial participation from identified market gaps or innovations that solve well-defined problems of value (Ibidunni et al., 2020). However, there are arguments that many necessity-driven entrepreneurs only started in that form but have transited into identifying opportunities (opportunity-driven) which now establishes them as scaling businesses that contribute to the economic strength of SSA (Afutu-Kotey et al., 2017). Thus, there are calls for more robust investigations into the amalgamation of necessity-opportunity entrepreneurship and innovations in SSA, especially concerning identifying required competencies, institutional and policy environments and every other dynamics that support the growth of business in this category (Adom, 2014; Li et al., 2020).

Therefore, in this concluding chapter of the book "Innovation, Entrepreneurship and the Informal Economy in Sub–Saharan Africa: A Sustainable Development Agenda", our focus is to discuss the SSA informal economy as a springboard for entrepreneurship development and innovation in the region. We are responding to earlier calls to highlight competencies and frameworks that unravel SSA's entrepreneurship and innovation dynamics. Although the informal economy is recognized as a self-reliant economy (Lal, 2012), and it requires the support of its ecosystem to thrive (Opute et al., 2021), there is little emphasis in the existing literature on how the informal economy actors should adapt to the factors that account their success. Thus, this chapter fills this gap by elaborating on the informal economy as self-reliant and identifying the factors, actors, and mechanisms that enhance entrepreneurship development and innovation within its ecosystem.

16.2 Theoretical Foundation of the Informal Economy in Sub-Saharan Africa: Synthesizing the Institutional Logic and Self-reliance Theory

With the minimal support of the informal economy from the formal institutions, actors in the informal economy resort into constructing assumptions and values that will guide and determine their business sustenance. For example, in order to accomplish economic sustenance, business operators in the informal economy resort to augmenting the lapses from formal structures through self-reliance structures that define how they develop intra-industry networks for their continuity in business. According to Thornton and Ocasio (1999) institutional logic represents "the socially constructed, historical pattern of material practices, assumptions, values, beliefs, and rules by which individuals produce and reproduce their material subsistence, organize time and space, and provide meaning to their social reality" (p. 804).

The institutional logic theory of organizations, including large firms and SMEs, suggests that the firm's behavioural antecedents and outcomes are structured around formal, and sometimes informal, factors in the firm's environment (Martinez & Dacin, 1999). However, much of the evidence that supports the assertion of the institutional theory (for example, Larsen, 2008; Silva & Figueiredo, 2017) draws from the developed and highly stable economies. While there are scattered literature from the developing economies (Genin et al., 2021; Huang et al., 2017), there remains scantily demonstrated evidences for the adaptation of the institutional theory within informal economy SMEs in the developing contexts. Yet, understanding this adaptation is critical as firms in the informal economy must manoeuvre highly unpredictable economic conditions, and many of the firms' sustenance is tied to the individual economy of the business owner. Consequently, in the paper, we point out that it may be more useful to think of institutional theory and a self-reliance theory as a way of better understanding entrepreneurship and innovation of informal economy SMEs. The complementary nature of these two approaches is important because neither perspective in its own right has the capacity to fully explain the mechanisms that enhance entrepreneurship development and innovation by firms in SSA's informal economy. On the one hand, institutional logic is able to explain the structures that define entrepreneurial and innovation outcomes of the firms. On the other hand, the self-reliance theory is able to demystify the unstructured and spontaneous responses that firm operators must demonstrate in dealing with unexpected changes from the business environment.

The theorization of self-reliance, especially within the informal economy and development field, rests upon the notion that individuals depend on their sufficiency for survival. At the same time, communities take responsibility for their existence (Mhando, 2018). Conditioned upon the developmental politics in Tanzania and intertwined with the *ujamaa* (familyhood concept propounded by Tanzanian founding father—Julius Nyerere) national program (1967–1975), the self-reliance theorization establishes hard work and cooperation of individuals, families, cooperatives, villages, regions or the nation as the means to development (Lal, 2012).

de Beer and Tumaine (2020) opine that entrepreneurship and innovation are pathways to self-reliance among African informal economy entrepreneurs. In their view, African immigrants contribute to solving community-based challenges through innovative solutions that derive economic and social values to their settlement areas. Furthermore, different scholars have demonstrated the possibilities of informal economy business operators to adapt internal resources and entrepreneurial capabilities to achieve higher innovation performance and sustainable business outcomes (Ibidunni et al., 2020, 2021a, 2021b,

2022; Lu et al., 2010; Mamun et al., 2019; Setini et al., 2020). Hence, given external constraints in many business economies around SSA, the principal roles and conceptualization of constructs that pertain to the self-reliance of business in the informal sector remain a viable field for research.

16.3 Informal Economy in Sub-Saharan Africa: Its Occupancy in the Entrepreneurship and Innovation Ecosystem Across the SSA Region

The entrepreneurship and innovation ecosystem consists of interacting factors and actors and their operational mechanisms that foster the growth of businesses (Ibidunni et al., 2021b). While it is confirmed that different types and levels of entrepreneurs and innovation stages require specific and unique policy guidelines (Adu-Gyamfi et al., 2022), and the peculiarities of nations place a demand on the tailored entrepreneurship framework for businesses in that geographic space (Sheriff & Muffatto, 2015); it also holds that there are commonalities of interest among entrepreneurship and innovation ecosystems (Beugré, 2017).

The entrepreneurship ecosystem in SSA covers all significant factors that contribute to the region's entrepreneurship and innovation value chain. It consists of policy and regulatory frameworks, R&D drivers, institutions for building capacity and providing financial support and mechanisms for facilitating logistics, such as market and customer accessibility (Ibidunni et al., 2018). According to the study by Mushayavanhu and Chitumba (2022), micro and small enterprises in Harare opined that the critical factors to their businesses include financial support, physical infrastructure, access to domestic and export markets and support systems. Opute et al. (2021) opine that these factors of the entrepreneurship ecosystem must link together within a socially constructed and networked culture to optimize the contributions of informal firms in SSA. Meanwhile, David-West et al. (2019) opined that the role of regional governments and governance structures is critical to coordinating stronger partnerships among the ecosystem factors and for establishing innovation hubs and programs, and facilitating the environment for practical entrepreneurship and innovation ecosystem.

Discussing the self-reliance theorization within SMEs' entrepreneurship and innovation ecosystem in SSA's informal economy spotlights the fact that these SMEs must devise their means of business continuity and sustainable existence, regardless of external resources and network constraints. The literature describes the entrepreneurship ecosystem's ability to adapt to changes and shocks as characteristic of its resilience (Igwe & Ochinanwata, 2021). Entrepreneurial and innovation ecosystem resilience shapes informal sector SMEs' perspectives in identifying that the ecosystem is complex and heterogeneous (Roundy et al., 2017) and that early planning for resilience is critical to the sustainability of firms operating within the ecosystem (International Economic Development Council, 2015). According to Roundy (2017), the resiliency of ecosystems is influenced by the diversity of the ecosystem (in terms of the types, demographic characteristics and participants' motivations). It holds that highly diversified entrepreneurship and innovation ecosystems can survive shifts in market conditions and mitigate unforeseen risks.

16.4 Conclusion and Further Research

The concluding chapter of the "Innovation, Entrepreneurship and the Informal Economy in Sub–Saharan Africa: A Sustainable Development Agenda" book project has focused on discussing the SSA informal economy as a springboard for entrepreneurship development and innovation in the region, especially from a self-reliance theorization perspective. Informal economy SMEs in the SSA region represent a formidable force within the economic and social context of the region. However, these SMEs are constrained by the paucity of formal institutional responsiveness to implementing a practical entrepreneurship and innovation ecosystem. Therefore, we have explained the self-reliance theory as a workable option for the sustainability of the Informal economy SMEs' entrepreneurship and innovation ecosystem in SSA. We also supported the notion of ecosystem resilience as an adaptive pathway to ensure the success of both the entrepreneurship and innovation ecosystem and the firms operating in the informal economy of SSA.

Acknowledgements The editors of this book project appreciate Liz Barlow, Palgrave's Senior Commissioning Editor for Business and Management, for the careful guidance and support all through the developmental stages of this book project. The editors are equally very appreciative of the anonymous reviewers for their constructive comments and suggestions that have improved the quality of the chapters included in this book project. Also, all the authors who contributed to this book project are appreciated. In addition, the author remains grateful to the International Centre for Policy Research and Industry Linkages (ICePRIL) for setting the mentorship platforms that assisted in disseminating the call for contributions to the book project and other externally solicited papers that were submitted.

References

Adom, K. (2014). Beyond the marginalization thesis: An examination of the motivations of informal entrepreneurs in Sub-Saharan Africa: Insights from Ghana. *The International Journal of Entrepreneurship and Innovation, 15*(2), 113–125. https://doi.org/10.5367/ijei.2014.0144

Adu-Gyamfi, R., Kuada, J. E., & Asongu, S. (2022). *An integrative framework for formal and informal entrepreneurship research in Africa* (AGDI Working Paper, No. WP/22/015). African Governance and Development Institute (AGDI), Yaoundé.

Afreh, B., Rodgers, P., Vershinina, N., & Williams, C. C. (2019). Varieties of context and informal entrepreneurship: Entrepreneurial activities of migrant youths in rural Ghana. *International Journal of Entrepreneurial Behavior & Research, 25*(5), 996–1013. https://doi.org/10.1108/IJEBR-02-2018-0109

Afutu-Kotey, R. L., Gough, K. V., & Owusu, G. (2017). Young entrepreneurs in the mobile telephony sector in Ghana: From necessities to aspirations. *Journal of African Business, 18*(4), 476–491. https://doi.org/10.1080/15228916.2017.1339252

Beugré, C. D. (2017). The need for entrepreneurial ecosystems in Sub-Saharan Africa. In *Building entrepreneurial ecosystems in Sub-Saharan Africa*. Palgrave

Studies of Entrepreneurship in Africa. Palgrave Macmillan. https://doi.org/10.1057/978-1-137-56894-6_3

David-West, O., Muritala, O., & Umukoro, I. O. (2019). SME techno-entrepreneurship: Drivers and barriers in Sub-Saharan Africa. In *Handbook of research on techno-entrepreneurship* (3rd ed., pp. 277–298). Edward Elgar.

de Beer, J., & Tumaine, N. (2020). Innovation in refugee economies: Supporting intermediaries that embrace informality. In *Research handbook on development and the informal economy* (pp. 387–409). Edward Elgar. https://doi.org/10.4337/9781788972802.00027

Etim, E., & Daramola, O. (2020). The informal sector and economic growth of South Africa and Nigeria: A comparative systematic review. *Journal of Open Innovation: Technology, Market, and Complexity, 6*(4), 134. https://doi.org/10.3390/joitmc6040134

Genin, A. L., Tan, J., & Song, J. (2021). State governance and technological innovation in emerging economies: State-owned enterprise restructuration and institutional logic dissonance in China's high-speed train sector. *Journal of International Business Studies, 52*, 621–645.

Hart, K. (1973). Informal income opportunities and urban employment in Ghana. *The Journal of Modern African Studies, 11*(1), 61–89. http://www.jstor.org/stable/159873

Hart, K. (2009). *On the informal economy: The political history of an ethnographic concept* (CEB Working Paper, 9, 042).

Huang, Y., Xie, E., Li, Y., & Reddy, K. S. (2017). Does state ownership facilitate outward FDI of Chinese SOEs? Institutional development, market competition, and the logic of interdependence between governments and SOEs. *International Business Review, 26*(1), 176–188.

Ibidunni, A. S. (2022). Editorial: Sustainable business models for the growth of indigenous businesses in Africa. *World Review of Entrepreneurship, Management and Sustainable Development, 18*(5/6), 491–499. https://doi.org/10.1504/WREMSD.2022.126160

Ibidunni, A. S., Ayeni, A. A. W., Ogundana, O. M., Otokiti, B., & Mohalajeng, L. (2022). Survival during times of disruptions: Rethinking strategies for enabling business viability in the developing economy. *Sustainability, 14*, 13549. https://doi.org/10.3390/su142013549

Ibidunni, A. S., Kehinde, O. J., Ibidunni, O. M., Olokundun, M. A., Olubusayo, F. H., Salau, O. P., Borishade, T. T., & Peter, F. (2018). Data on the relationships between financing strategies, entrepreneurial competencies and business growth of technology-based SMEs in Nigeria. *Data in Brief, 18*, 988–991.

Ibidunni, A. S., Kolawole, A. I., Olokundun, M. A., & Ogbari, M. E. (2020). Knowledge transfer and innovation performance of small and medium enterprises: An informal economy analysis. *Heliyon, 6*(8), e04740. https://doi.org/10.1016/j.heliyon.2020.e04740

Ibidunni, A. S., Ogundana, O. M., & Okonkwo, A. (2021a). Entrepreneurial competencies and the performance of informal SMEs: The contingent role of business environment. *Journal of African Business, 22*(4), 468–490. https://doi.org/10.1080/15228916.2021.1874784

Ibidunni, A. S., Ufua, D. E., & Opute, P. A. (2021b). Linking disruptive innovation to sustainable entrepreneurship within the context of small and medium firms: A focus on Nigeria. *African Journal of Science, Technology, Innovation and Development.* https://doi.org/10.1080/20421338.2021.1975355

Igwe, P. A., & Ochinanwata, C. (2021). How to start African informal entrepreneurial revolution? *Journal of African Business, 22*(4), 514–531. https://doi.org/10.1080/15228916.2021.1954447

International Economic Development Council. (2015). *Developing an entrepreneurship ecosystem for resiliency*. Retrieved on 25 February 2023 from https://restoreyoureconomy.org/clientuploads/2015/08/IEDC_Webinar_080615.pdf

International Labour Organization. (2002). *Resolution and conclusions concerning decent work and the informal economy*. Retrieved on 23 February 2023, from https://www.ilo.org/global/topics/dw4sd/themes/informal-economy/WCMS_080105/lang--es/index.htm

International Labour Organization. (2015). *Recommendation No. 204 concerning the transition from the informal to the formal economy*. Retrieved on 23 February 2023, from https://www.ilo.org/ilc/ILCSessions/previous-sessions/104/texts-adopted/WCMS_377774/lang--es/index.htm

International Labour Organization. (2023). *Informal economy in Africa: Which way forward? Making policy responsive, inclusive and sustainable*. Retrieved on 17 February 2023 from https://www.ilo.org/africa/events-and-meetings/WCMS_842674/lang--en/index.htm

Lal, P. (2012). Self-Reliance and the state: The multiple meanings of development in early post-colonial Tanzania. *Africa: Journal of the International African Institute, 82*(2), 212–234. http://www.jstor.org/stable/41485040

Larsen, C. A. (2008). The institutional logic of welfare attitudes: How welfare regimes influence public support. *Comparative Political Studies, 41*(2), 145–168. https://doi.org/10.1177/0010414006295234

Li, Y., Huang, S., & Song, L. (2020). Opportunity and necessity entrepreneurship in the hospitality sector: Examining the institutional environment influences. *Tourism Management Perspectives, 34*, 100665. https://doi.org/10.1016/j.tmp.2020.100665

Lu, Y., Zhou, L., Bruton, G., & Li, W. (2010). Capabilities as a mediator linking resources and the international performance of entrepreneurial firms in an emerging economy. *Journal of International Business Studies, 41*, 419–436.

Luque, A. (2022). Analysis of the concept of informal economy through 102 definitions: Legality or necessity. *Open Research Europe, 1*, 134.

Makochekanwa, A. (2020). *Informal economy in SSA: Characteristics, size and tax potential*. Retrieved on 17 February 2023 from https://mpra.ub.uni-muenchen.de/98644/1/MPRA_paper_98644.pdf

Mamun, A. A., Fazal, S. A., & Zainol, N. R. (2019). Economic vulnerability, entrepreneurial competencies, and performance of informal microenterprises. *Journal of Poverty, 23*(5), 415–436.

Martinez, R. J., & Dacin, M. T. (1999). Efficiency motives and normative forces: Combining transactions costs and institutional logic. *Journal of Management, 25*(1), 75–96. https://doi.org/10.1177/014920639902500104

Medina, L., Jonelis, A. W., & Cangul, M. (2017). *The informal economy in Sub-Saharan Africa* (IMF Working Papers, 156), A001. Retrieved February 17, 2023, from https://www.elibrary.imf.org/view/journals/001/2017/156/article-A001-en.xml

Mhando, P. C. (2018). Managing in the informal economy: The informal financial sector in Tanzania. *Africa Journal of Management, 4*(3), 282–305.

Mushayavanhu, T. P., & Chitumba, C. (2022). Enabling entrepreneurial ecosystem framework as a panacea to formalisation of manufacturing MSEs in Harare, Zimbabwe. *Journal of Research and Innovation for Sustainable Society (JRISS), 4*(2), 55–75. https://doi.org/10.33727/JRISS.2022.2.7:55-75

Opute, A. P., Kalu, K. I., Adeola, O., & Iwu, C. G. (2021). Steering sustainable economic growth: Entrepreneurial ecosystem approach. *Journal of Entrepreneurship and Innovation in Emerging Economies, 7*(2), 216–245. https://doi.org/10.1177/23939575211024384

Roundy, P. T. (2017). Social entrepreneurship and entrepreneurial ecosystems: Complementary or disjoint phenomena? *International Journal of Social Economics, 44*(9), 1252–1267. https://doi.org/10.1108/IJSE-02-2016-0045

Roundy, P. T., Brockman, B. K., & Bradshaw, M. (2017). The resilience of entrepreneurial ecosystems. *Journal of Business Venturing Insights, 8*, 99–104.
Setini, M., Yasa, N. N. K., Supartha, I. W. G., Giantari, I. G. A. K., & Rajiani, I. (2020). The passway of women entrepreneurship: Starting from social capital with open innovation, through to knowledge sharing and innovative performance. *Journal of Open Innovation: Technology, Market, and Complexity, 6*(2), 25.
Sheriff, M., & Muffatto, M. (2015). The present state of entrepreneurship ecosystems in selected countries in Africa. *African Journal of Economic and Management Studies, 6*(1), 17–54. https://doi.org/10.1108/AJEMS-10-2012-0064
Silva, M. E., & Figueiredo, M. D. (2017). Sustainability as practice: Reflections on the creation of an institutional logic. *Sustainability, 9*(10), 1839.
Thornton, P. H., & Ocasio, W. (1999). Institutional logics and the historical contingency of power in organizations: Executive succession in the higher education publishing industry, 1958–1990. *American Journal of Sociology, 105*(3), 801–843. https://doi.org/10.1086/210361
Williams, C. C., & Horodnic, I. A. (2016). An institutional theory of the informal economy: Some lessons from the United Kingdom. *International Journal of Social Economics, 43*(7), 722–738. https://doi.org/10.1108/IJSE-12-2014-0256
Williams, C. C., & Kedir, A. (2018). Explaining cross-national variations in the prevalence of informal sector entrepreneurship: Lessons from a survey of 142 countries. *Journal of Developmental Entrepreneurship, 23*(01), 1850005.
World Bank Group. (2023). *Population, total—Sub-Saharan Africa*. Retrieved on 17 February 2023 from https://data.worldbank.org/indicator/SP.POP.TOTL?locations=ZG

Index

A

Adoption 7–9, 77, 82, 134, 137, 201, 203, 218–220, 224, 228, 229, 240, 241, 284, 361, 365

Africa 1–5, 9, 27, 31, 52, 54, 55, 94, 122, 123, 126, 127, 133, 134, 181, 182, 189, 218, 250, 255, 258, 259, 263, 264, 333, 354, 355, 369, 390, 391, 395, 397

B

Banks 23, 25, 68, 72, 77, 172, 186, 269, 272, 276, 310, 312–314, 316, 327, 334, 335, 341, 344–347, 393, 394

Business discontinuation 12, 381, 397, 398

Business environment 54, 56, 69, 77, 84, 151, 156, 218, 286, 357, 358, 368, 391, 392, 409

D

Developing country 98, 99, 111, 175, 189, 190

Digital technology 43, 82, 210

Digital/Technology Enablement 391, 394

Disruptions 4, 12, 71, 147, 211, 263, 354–356, 358, 359, 364–366, 368–370

- environmental disruptions 12, 81, 353, 355, 359, 369, 370
- pandemics 12, 354–356, 364–366, 368

Dynamic capabilities 29, 33, 86, 220, 224, 359

A. S. Ibidunni et al. (eds.), *Innovation, Entrepreneurship and the Informal Economy in Sub–Saharan Africa*, Sustainable Development Goals Series,
https://doi.org/10.1007/978-3-031-46293-1

E

Eco-innovation 8, 9, 218–226, 228, 229, 231, 233, 234, 237, 240, 241
Economic growth 7, 10, 20, 56, 100, 121–123, 127, 130, 137, 172, 190, 191, 198, 200–203, 217, 249, 274, 285, 313, 314, 328, 335–339, 377–381, 385–389, 391, 398, 399
Economy 2, 4, 5, 10, 11, 22, 35, 40, 48, 57, 67, 69, 72, 77, 85, 93–95, 100, 107, 109–111, 122, 124, 130, 133, 136, 137, 199, 200, 203, 212, 219, 223, 240, 249, 270, 279–281, 283, 285, 287, 291, 293, 313, 314, 328, 335–337, 353, 356, 359, 369, 381, 391, 394, 398, 405, 406, 408, 409
Entrepreneurial activities 4, 5, 9, 10, 13, 44, 94, 100, 149, 163, 172, 279–281, 283, 286, 287, 289–291, 296, 299, 394, 397
Entrepreneurial ecosystem (EE) 4–6, 20, 27, 30–35, 38–45, 52, 54–56, 171–177, 184, 186, 188–191, 381, 386, 397
Entrepreneurial marketing 380, 387, 389, 396, 397
Entrepreneurship education (EE) 7, 143–145, 148, 150, 152, 154, 156–163, 386, 387, 396, 398

F

Financial facilitation 391, 392
Financial inclusion 11, 198, 310, 325, 334–347

G

Gender equality 10, 11, 311, 316–318, 325, 328, 329
Government policies 71, 298, 391–393

I

Income 4, 8, 10, 11, 68, 69, 72–75, 77, 80, 81, 124, 132, 133, 205–208, 271, 274, 309, 311–313, 315, 335–341, 344, 345, 406, 407
Informal economy (IE) 1, 3, 4, 7, 12, 122, 124, 126, 127, 130, 132–134, 315, 355, 405–409, 411, 412
  informality 7, 134, 406
Innovation value chain 9, 250, 251, 255, 256, 259, 261–265, 267–269, 271–274, 276, 410
Innovative entrepreneurship 7, 143–157, 160, 162, 280–282, 284, 285, 290, 291, 293, 295–299
Institutional sustainability 7, 155–157, 160, 162
Institutional theory 29, 45, 282, 408, 409

L

Leadership 12, 30, 47, 150, 153, 222, 298, 378, 379, 385–389, 391, 392, 394, 395, 397–399

M

Manufacturing sector 8, 132, 218–220, 228, 229, 240, 326

Microfinance 10, 11, 309–317, 319, 320, 323–325, 328, 329, 334
Models 2, 5, 7–10, 29, 33, 40, 48, 124, 145–147, 149, 154–160, 162, 163, 172, 173, 184, 190, 191, 201–203, 212, 213, 225, 227, 234, 237, 250, 256–259, 262, 265, 269, 276, 288, 291, 295–297, 316, 317, 340, 344, 369, 395
Motivating factors 101, 110
Multinational Enterprises (MNEs) 5, 6, 172–177, 184–191

O

Open Innovation 9, 250, 255, 258, 259, 262–266, 273, 274, 276
Organisational adaptiveness 368, 369

P

Poverty 7, 8, 10–12, 56, 93, 94, 96, 110, 121, 124, 127, 133, 172, 198, 212, 310–317, 320, 323, 328, 329, 334–346, 378–380, 385
Productive entrepreneurship 20, 23, 30, 31, 36, 45, 47, 56, 378–380, 387, 391, 397, 398
Profitability 4, 69, 73–75, 77, 80, 81, 175, 273, 297, 298

S

Sales 4, 69, 72–75, 77, 80, 81, 99, 124, 146, 223, 268, 388
Scaleups 20, 55
Self-reliance theory 409, 411
Skills Development Support 377
Small and Medium Enterprises (SMEs) 3–5, 54, 68, 69, 71–78, 80, 81, 83–86, 100, 146, 189, 190, 255, 259, 263, 335, 391, 394, 399, 408, 409, 411
  small and medium business 355
Start-ups 5, 94, 152, 154, 161, 162, 171, 176, 183, 185–187, 189, 190, 212, 262, 273, 315, 326, 391, 392, 396–398
Sub-Saharan Africa (SSA) 1–6, 10, 12, 13, 46, 48, 94, 110, 124, 126, 127, 174, 290, 297, 299, 335, 336, 338, 339, 341, 342, 344–346, 378–381, 386, 388, 395, 396, 398, 406, 407, 409–412
Sustainable development 2, 3, 5, 110, 190, 217, 337
  sustainability 3
  sustainable development goals (SDGs) 5, 7, 77, 190, 191
Sustainable industrialization 121

T

Transportation systems 197–199, 201, 209, 212

U

Unemployment 8, 12, 73, 94, 96, 110, 212, 337, 339, 356, 378–380, 385, 407

GPSR Compliance
The European Union's (EU) General Product Safety Regulation (GPSR) is a set of rules that requires consumer products to be safe and our obligations to ensure this.

If you have any concerns about our products, you can contact us on

ProductSafety@springernature.com

In case Publisher is established outside the EU, the EU authorized representative is:

Springer Nature Customer Service Center GmbH
Europaplatz 3
69115 Heidelberg, Germany

www.ingramcontent.com/pod-product-compliance
Ingram Content Group UK Ltd.
Pitfield, Milton Keynes, MK11 3LW, UK
UKHW021420091026
15624UKWH00010B/261
9783031462924